Laura Borchert
Suspect Subjects

American Culture Studies | Volume 42

This open access publication was enabled by the support of POLLUX – Informationsdienst Politikwissenschaft

and a network of academic libraries for the promotion of the open-access-transformation in the Social Sciences and Humanities (transcript Open Library Community Politik 2024).

Vollsponsoren: Technische Universität Braunschweig | Carl von Ossietzky-Universität Oldenburg | Eberhard-Karls Universität Tübingen | Freie Universität Berlin – Universitätsbibliothek | Niedersächsische Staats- und Universitätsbibliothek Göttingen | Goethe-Universität Frankfurt am Main | Gottfried Wilhelm Leibniz Bibliothek – Niedersächsische Landesbibliothek | TIB – Leibniz-Informationszentrum Technik und Naturwissenschaften und Universitätsbibliothek | Humboldt-Universität zu Berlin | Justus-Liebig-Universität Gießen | Universitätsbibliothek Eichstätt-Ingolstadt | Ludwig-Maximilians-Universität München | Max Planck Digital Library (MPDL) | Rheinische Friedrich-Wilhelms-Universität Bonn | Ruhr-Universität Bochum | Staats- und Universitätsbibliothek Carl von Ossietzky, Hamburg | SLUB Dresden | Staatsbibliothek zu Berlin | Bibliothek der Technischen Universität Chemnitz | Universitäts- und Landesbibliothek Darmstadt | Universitätsbibliothek „Georgius Agricola" der TU Bergakademie Freiberg | Universitätsbibliothek Kiel (CAU) | Universitätsbibliothek Leipzig | Universitäts- und Landesbibliothek Düsseldorf | Universitäts- und Landesbibliothek Münster | Universitäts- und Stadtbibliothek Köln | Universitätsbibliothek Bielefeld | Universitätsbibliothek Erfurt | Universitätsbibliothek der FernUniversität in Hagen | Universitätsbibliothek Kaiserslautern-Landau | Universitätsbibliothek Kassel | Universitätsbibliothek Osnabrück | Universität Potsdam | Universitätsbibliothek St. Gallen | Universitätsbibliothek Vechta | Zentralbibliothek Zürich

Sponsoring Light: Bundesministerium der Verteidigung | Bibliothek der Hochschule für Technik und Wirtschaft Dresden | Bibliothek der Hochschule für Technik, Wirtschaft und Kultur Leipzig | Bibliothek der Westsächsischen Hochschule Zwickau | Bibliothek der Hochschule Zittau/Görlitz, Hochschulbibliothek | Hochschulbibliothek der Hochschule Mittweida | Institut für Auslandsbeziehungen (IfA) | Landesbibliothek Oldenburg | Österreichische Parlamentsbibliothek

Mikrosponsoring: Bibliothek der Berufsakademie Sachsen | Bibliothek der Evangelische Hochschule Dresden | Bibliothek der Hochschule für Musik und Theater „Felix Mendelssohn Bartholdy" Leipzig | Bibliothek der Hochschule für Bildende Künste Dresden | Bibliothek der Hochschule für Musik „Carl Maria von Weber" Dresden | Bibliothek der Hochschule für Grafik und Buchkunst Leipzig | Bibliothek der Palucca-Hochschule für Tanz Dresden | Leibniz-Institut für Europäische Geschichte | Stiftung Wissenschaft und Politik (SWP) – Deutsches Institut für Internationale Politik und Sicherheit

Laura Borchert

Suspect Subjects

Queer Legal Futures in the US after Bostock

[transcript]

Justus-Liebig-Universität Gießen, FB 05 Sprache, Literatur, Kultur

Bibliographic information published by the Deutsche Nationalbibliothek
The Deutsche Nationalbibliothek lists this publication in the Deutsche Nationalbibliografie; detailed bibliographic data are available in the Internet

First published in 2024 by transcript Verlag, Bielefeld

transcript Verlag | Hermannstraße 26 | D-33602 Bielefeld | live@transcript-verlag.de

Cover layout: Kordula Röckenhaus, Bielefeld
Printed by: Elanders Waiblingen GmbH, Waiblingen
Print-ISBN: 978-3-8376-7272-5
PDF-ISBN: 978-3-8394-7272-9
EPUB-ISBN: 978-3-7328-7272-5
ISSN of series: 2747-4372
eISSN of series: 2747-4380

For Missy, Jenso, and my mother.

Contents

Abstract

Queer rights are equally dependent on progressive legal decisions as they are on cultural developments. In the U.S., the Supreme Court's pro-LGBTQ+ landmark cases *Obergefell v. Hodges* (2015) and *Bostock v. Clayton County* (2020) have introduced the fundamental right to marry, and employment discrimination protection for sexual minorities. On a state level, however, the proposal and introduction of various forms of anti-queer legislation has been growing with record numbers of anti-LGBTQ+ laws introduced since 2020. This seemingly mismatch corresponds to an increasing politization and polarization of minority rights in cultural and constitutional discourses.

The U.S. Supreme Court has the power to address discriminatory regulations concerning sexual orientation with a constitutional tool, derived from the Fourteenth Amendment's Equal Protection Clause: suspect classification. Classifying sexual orientation as a legal category against which any kind of discrimination is suspect would effectively render anti-queer legislation unconstitutional, and signal the Court's willingness to challenge existing legal hierarchies. This, in turn, would influence sociocultural orders acting analogous to legal ones as I argue in this book.

Cultural narratives such as the guarantee of legal equality for everyone, and constitutional imaginaries that marriage equality is indicative of a tantamount status for queer couples contribute to a marred perspective on LGBTQ+ rights claims. Post-*Obergefell* and -*Bostock* demands for equal rights are thus met with a lack of understanding by the general public: Why would the LGBTQ+ community need *more* equality if there already are these fundamental legal victories? This view mistakenly equates *de jure* equality gains with *de facto* legal, social, and cultural equality, leading to an affectively felt lifted responsibility to stand in for more rights.

This book analyzes how cultural narratives and constitutional imaginaries work together by examining some of the twenty-first century's most important

U.S. Supreme Court decisions for LGBTQ+ individuals. I argue for a heightened constitutional protection for sexual orientation in the U.S. ('suspect classification') by deconstructing legal categories, processes of categorization, and cultural inkings of law in connection to sexual orientation. In this analysis, law and culture are mutually dependent on each other.

Shedding light on the entanglements of law and culture, this book also advocates for a more prominent place of queer cultural analyses of law. The affective power of cultural-constitutional imaginaries supports the hypothesis that constitutional protections for LGBTQ+ people have a higher cultural-legal authority than legislative acts. Calling for a strengthening of sensibilities for cultural-legal entanglements, I conduct a cultural analysis of law and establish what I call a queer hermeneutics of law.

Introduction

Over the course of the last years, this book has taken on a more political character than originally intended. What started off as a book with the aim to analyze the constitutional and sociocultural implications of legal protections for LGBTQ+[1] in the United States has now become a larger argument for law's role in and for queer emancipation. This shift is influenced by many political and legal factors. The 2020s saw an unusually volatile development of legal protections for LGBTQ+ people as well as a politically charged struggle over the personal set-up of the Supreme Court, the highest court in the United States. The process of appointing two of the Trump-nominated justices to the Supreme Court, Brett M. Kavanaugh replacing Antonin Scalia in 2018 and Amy Coney-Barrett replacing Ruth Bader Ginsburg in 2020, has become a highly medialized event. The announced retirement of Stephan G. Breyer in the summer 2022 enabled then-president Joseph Biden to put Ketanji Brown Jackson on the bench.[2] The decision to nominate a Black female justice, the first of her kind, adds to the Court's diversity and picks up on the development of U.S. presidents aiming to get justices on the Supreme Court who are in line with the sitting government's political beliefs.

1 LGBTQ+ refers to anyone who identifies as lesbian, gay, bisexual, trans, queer. Varying gender identities and/or sexual orientations, including those considering themselves as questioning, inter, asexual, pansexual and/or something other, are implicitly included by the use of the plus; their omission does not reflect exclusion. While this acronym is in constant development and negotiation, the use of LGBTQ+ has been chosen for this book to provide more readability. This footnote hopefully brings across that sexual and gender identities are, similar to the ways of referring to them, in constant flux and evolution.

2 While the president gets to nominate a candidate, it is the senate's task to confirm them – an equally politicized, and by now also medialized, event.

The development of queer rights discourse follows this highly polarized pattern of fighting over political power. This is most visible in the discrepancies between federal and state-level decision-making: With 2020's *Bostock v. Clayton County* being the most current one, the U.S. Supreme Court issued several landmark decisions in favor of LGBTQ+ rights in the past decades. This contrasts the individual states' processes of re-negotiating sociocultural and political hegemonies by targeting sexual minorities, particularly trans, queer, and non-binary youth with ever rising numbers of hostile laws since 2020. So, what happened?

2015's legalization of same-sex marriage in the Supreme Court's *Obergefell v. Hodges* was considered to be a queer victory – at least from a heteronormative point of view. At this time, several states had already recognized same-sex marriage but only since the Supreme Court's decision are all states required to do so. The discourse about marriage equality became synonymous with progressive judicial decision-making and legislative policies. *Obergefell* has come to be seen as an indicator of a tolerant and inclusive U.S. society over which a non-biased Supreme Court watches. To some, the legal possibility of same-sex marriage even heralded a new era, one that was post-homophobia.

This view, however desirable it may seem, neglects the sociocultural and legal diversity of the U.S.'s federal system – or, in other words, the powerful fragmentation of state laws. For instance, while in 2003 the City of New York had already introduced the *Sexual Orientation Non-Discrimination Act (SONDA)* which "prohibits discrimination on the basis of actual or perceived sexual orientation in employment, housing, public accommodation, education, credit, and the exercise of civil rights" (Schneiderman), recently introduced anti-queer legislation such as Florida's House Bill 1557 'Parental Rights in Education,' also being referred to as a 'Don't Say Gay' bill, "prohibit[s] classroom discussion about sexual orientation or gender identity in certain grade levels or in a specified manner" (1). These stark contrasts show that U.S. American law is a heterogenous and ambiguous system in which LGBTQ+ individuals have to face an almost non-navigable patchwork.[3]

Despite its revolutionary outlook, marriage equality has not bettered this situation. In fact, the high number of nationwide legal discrimination cases[4] and the current political backlash concerning pro-LGBTQ+ measures[5] rather indicate that the general sociocultural acceptance of sexual minorities is not improving. To put it more bluntly: *Obergefell*, being considered a fundamental victory for those fighting for sexual minorities' rights, appears to be anesthetizing rather than curing the symptoms of discrimination.

This development could have been prevented by the Supreme Court's reasoning. Instead of only resolving the question of whether same-sex partners are legally allowed to marry,[6] the justices should have included the question of whether discrimination based upon sexual orientation[7] is constitutional. Yet, with their focus on the right to marry, the justices in *Obergefell* have failed to add much needed anti-discrimination protections to LGBTQ+ individuals in areas other than the private institution of marriage.

---

3 As the Movement Advancement Project succinctly puts it in their 2010–2020 report, "[a]s of January 1, 2020, the overall LGBTQ policy landscape across the country varies greatly from state to state and region to region. What's more, there are significant differences in the landscape for laws related to sexual orientation and the landscape for laws related to gender identity. These findings … illustrate how an LGBTQ person's legal rights and protections can change dramatically across state lines and depending on where they call home, even in 2020" ("Mapping" 4).

4 Discrimination cases which, among others, see same-sex partners being declined a wedding cake at a bakery (see *Masterpiece Cakeshop v. Colorado*) and employers being fired for mentioning their husband (see *Altitude Express, Inc. v. Zarda*) indicate that the right to same-sex marriage does not equal the sociocultural acceptance of such.

5 For instances of the Trump's administration's efforts to roll back LGBTQ+ rights see, e.g., *Karnoski v. Trump*.

6 Technically, *Obergefell* did not even this. The Court ruled in its decision that the right to marry is a fundamental right, not that same-sex marriages are constitutional; the latter only follows out of the former and makes the decision a decidedly liberal-rights-based instead of "group-based equality jurisprudence" (Yoshino 754).

7 Sexual orientation here refers to non-normative, i.e., non-heterosexual, sexual orientations if not indicated otherwise. As heterosexuality is the sociocultural norm in U.S. America as in most Western societies, discrimination cannot occur against the majority. Heterosexual orientation refers to sexual attraction towards the 'opposite' sex following a dualistic understanding of biological sex, i.e., biologically, there only exist men and women. The rather clinical term sexual orientation follows legal nomenclature.

Obergefell may thus serve as a gateway for further considerations about sexual orientation's legal protection in general; yet it left sexual orientation still highly susceptible to laws and practices which limit or reverse LGBTQ+ rights. These challenges to a holistic anti-discrimination policy, meaning one that would protect queer persons[8] unequivocally across state borders and make them immune to volatile mood shifts of state legislatures and the judiciary, mirror the U.S.'s legal patchwork, and underline the need for a coherent federal regulation.

This need is also backed when looking at *Bostock v. Clayton County*: In 2020, the Court ruled that Title VII of the Civil Rights Act of 1964 extends to sexual orientation, making discrimination against gays, lesbians, bisexuals or anyone else because of their sexual orientation in employment unconstitutional. *Bostock* filled a significant legal lag *Obergefell* left wide open: the newly heightened visibility and thus vulnerability of queers who were allowed to marry but who were still subjected to discrimination in other areas of their everyday lives. Stating that "an LGBT person could get married on Saturday, post photos of their wedding on Sunday, and get fired from their job or thrown out of their apartment on Monday" ("Cicilline"), the Democratic politician David N. Cicilline captures the gist of post-*Obergefell* discrimination. Being allowed to marry without protection in all other areas of life such as housing or workplace discrimination effectively makes married queers more susceptible to unequal treatment.[9]

Both landmark cases were depicted as highly progressive, even revolutionary rulings by a growingly conservative Supreme Court, decided amidst a conservative, right-wing government.[10] What is often not part of the public consciousness is that *Obergefell* did not decide on the equality of same-sex mar-

---

8 The term queer is used synonymously with LGBTQ+. While I acknowledge that queer may serve as a distinct identity category for many, and that not all who identify as part of the LGBTQ+ community may identify as queer, its usage has been chosen because of readability.

9 As of July 2021, 26 states and the District of Columbia prohibited employment discrimination based on one's sexual orientation (Hentze and Tyus). This includes firing, hiring, and discrimination in the workplace. Further, only twenty-two states and the District of Columbia had anti-discrimination laws for housing, including eviction and the owners' refusal to rent or, based on one's sexual orientation as of February 2016 (Mallory and Sears 1).

10 The political implications of these decisions and the philosophies of those on the Court's bench are subject to closer analysis in Chapter III.

riage, and that *Bostock* did not explicitly decide that sexual orientation should be protected in employment contexts. Although both cases' outcomes do impact queer lives, arguably for the better, they were neither framed nor understood as *a priori* pro-LGBTQ+ decisions from a constitutional perspective.

Obergefell aimed at the recognition of the fundamental right to marry, thereby implicitly involving same-sex couples but explicitly avoiding to make concessions to the queer community. The fundamental right to marry, as a universalizing rights claim, thus works to continue discrimination and to foster invisibilization of the demands of sexual minorities while appearing progressive. *Obergefell* can therefore be regarded as not only a legal decision but also an important political positioning of the Supreme Court.

Similarly, the justices interpreted Title VII in *Bostock* as extending to sexual orientation based on their specific constitutional reading: They argued that sexual orientation is connected to one's sex, and while sex is protected under Title VII and sexual orientation and sex are connected, sexual orientation should also be protected, under sex's legal umbrella. The justices' modes of constitutional interpretation have been the deciding factors in this ruling, particularly textualism, a mode which is typically associated with political conservatism.[11] Further, connecting matters of sexual orientation to biological sex, the Court's reasoning employs the heterosexual matrix of equating (binary) sex with gender and desire.

Bostock's argumentation sounds appealing on first sight, and while this strategy was presumably the best way to argue for an expanded understanding of Title VII, the implications of this decision irritate. If sex and sexual orientation are two sides of the same coin in the sense that a (cis) man would not have been fired for being in a relationship with a (cis) woman but a (cis) woman would have been fired for this, how does *Bostock* account for, for instance, intersex individuals or those in relationships with someone non-binary? *Bostock* has solved this issue by covering gender identity as well, yet it gave away the opportunity to comment on these identity categories' place in the U.S.'s legal-cultural hierarchy. By applying an informed, non-binary, non-biologistic understanding of sexual orientation and sex, the Court would have been able to move away from a medical-biological emphasis on sex, sex's sociocultural over-emphasis, and its legal over-regulation.

---

11 The various modes of constitutional interpretation are introduced in detail in Chapter III.

This omission seems even more unfortunate as public discourse about sexuality, gender, sexual orientation, and sexual practices becomes blurrier and more politicized. Sex still polarizes and attracts forces wishing to police, contain, and punish it in all its forms. The legal backlash on state levels following out of the *Bostock* decision speaks to this claim, as does the sociocultural response to past pro-LGBTQ+ rulings by the Supreme Court. On the federal level, claims to further sexual orientation's legal protection and the rights of the LGBTQ+ community are perceived as insatiable, and even unnecessary demands post-*Obergefell*. The very reference to same-sex couples' now legalized access to marriage licenses as 'equality' perpetuates the belief in the Court's establishment of a morally and politically tantamount status quo for non-heterosexual couples. According to associate law professor Leonore F. Carpenter, these "formal equality gains can actually encourage a false belief that a previously unfair system is now fair, which can mask the reality of discrimination" (259). Even more than covering discriminatory realities, believing in marriage equality as a measurement of a reformed legal system for LGBTQ+ individuals creates a lack of understanding, confusion, and lifted responsibilities for those confronted with post-*Obergefell* and -*Bostock* demands of the queer community.[12] Even more, the subsequent legal lag, i.e., the U.S. legislation's and judiciary's failure to adjust anti-discrimination laws to the new sociocultural environments and visibilities created by Supreme Court decisions, allows for a variety of cases involving discriminatory behavior on the basis of a person's known or suspected sexual orientation.

Thus, *Obergefell* has contributed to silencing sexual orientation on the legal landscape while not adding anti-discrimination protection in areas other than marriage until 2020. While *Bostock* was able to fill this gap for employment contexts, there is still no federal nondiscrimination law for, among oth-

---

12 The decision to refer to a homogenous queer community in terms of legal-political participation is elaborated in Chapter I.

ers, housing,[13] public accommodation,[14] or credit regulations.[15] Additionally, there are major differences between states when it comes to anti-discrimination regulations for criminal law,[16] religious exemption laws,[17] and laws targeting LGBTQ+ youth such as conversion 'therapies.'[18]

The constant and growing backlash on state levels, increasingly taking on moral, religious and biologistic lines of argumentation,[19] illustrates that formal equality gains do neither automatically result in sociocultural equity nor resolve the issue of discrimination for all areas of life. In order to analyze legal measures' impact on sociocultural processes of anti-discrimination, the legal measures would need to tackle discrimination as complex issue(s), emerging out of and reflecting back on sociocultural conditions and sentiments. This would involve deconstructing the essentializing modes of producing legal

---

13 As of June 2024, 18 states have no housing anti-discrimination laws based on sexual orientation or gender identity. These laws would "protect LGBTQ people from being unfairly evicted, denied housing, or refused ability to rent or buy housing based on their sexual orientation or gender identity" ("Equality Maps Housing").

14 As of June 2024, 21 states have no public accommodation anti-discrimination laws based on sexual orientation or gender identity. These laws would "protect LGBTQ people from being unfairly refused service, denied entry to, or otherwise discriminated against in public places based on their sexual orientation or gender identity" ("Equality Maps Accommodation").

15 As of June 2024, 31 states have no credit anti-discrimination laws based on sexual orientation or gender identity. These laws would "protect people from being unfairly denied credit and lending services, such as opening a bank account, taking out a loan, and more" ("Equality Maps Credit").

16 As of June 2024, 31 states have no bans on so-called gay or trans panic defenses (see "Equality Maps Bans"). In a criminal court, these defenses "seek to partially or completely excuse crimes such as murder and assault on the grounds that the victim's sexual orientation or gender identity" (American Bar Association 1).

17 As of June 2024, 14 states have for instance religious exemption laws for adoptions. This means that these states allow "state-licensed child welfare agencies to refuse to place and provide services to children and families, including LGBTQ people and same-sex couples, if doing so conflicts with their religious beliefs" ("Equality Maps Religious").

18 As of June 2024, 19 states have not banned so-called conversion therapies which aim at changing LGBTQIAP* youth's sexual orientation and/or gender identity ("Equality Maps Conversion").

19 These aspects are expanded on in Chapters IV and V; prominent examples of biologistic argumentations involve the fight over trans rights in the context of school sports (see Esseks; ACLU "Coordinated"); examples for religious argumentations involve religious exemption laws.

norms, especially by working with legal categories, and addressing the actors who construct and interpret them, such as the Supreme Court. Additionally, one has to take into account sociocultural conditions which may challenge the application of legal norms, such as anti-queer sentiment which results in the proposal and introduction of anti-queer state laws in response to pro-queer federal decisions.

Being aware that the legal arena of marriage rights may not be the most important one for all members of the queer community, and that employment discrimination protection is a victory but the backlash coming from the state level is fierce, this book wants to raise awareness for the diverse social, cultural, political, and legal entanglements of constitutional protection and stress their importance for queer rights discourses. Going beyond an argument that sees sexual orientation's heightened constitutional protection as the ultimate solution against discrimination and lack of acceptance, *Suspect Subjects* aims to:

a) advocate for a more prominent place of a queer theoretical, cultural study of law in research and activism, and calls for further examination of this discipline's ability to contribute to anti-discrimination projects by
b) arguing for a class-based equal protection of sexual orientation, and offering a blueprint for doing so; and
c) deconstructing legal categories, the process(es) of categorization, and cultural inkings of law in connection to sexual orientation.

These aims are bold, and the ways of getting there, including risking misrepresentation and omitting many non-normative ways of living and loving, may appear to many as not worth it. After all, law should adopt to those it governs and not the other way around. Strategic essentialism, in Gayatri Chakravorty Spivak's understanding, meaning the political strategic practice of embracing essentialism temporally as a community/group to strengthen one's position,[20] may yet be useful for gaining support from those who grant law its authority and power – our neighbors, class mates, colleagues, elected officials.

To approach these aims, it is necessary to look at the current narratives and imaginaries that are connected to constitutional processes, which is one of this book's main foci. This aspect is covered in Chapter II by conducting a

20 For Gayatri Chakravorty Spivak's understanding of the term, see her interview statements on this concept in Harasym 51, 109. For a definition of the term see Spivak 205–6.

wide reading of the Constitution's Fourteenth Amendment. Here, I put emphasis on the Equal Protection Clause and link constitutional rights to what has been labeled 'legal affects' or *Rechtsgefühle* in Rudolf von Jhering's and Greta Olson's understanding.

In this context, the constitutional principle of suspect classification sheds light on the cultural self-understanding of the U.S. While the Constitution lays down that everyone is to be treated equally under the law, suspect classification steps in whenever there are social groups which are more likely to be discriminated against than the majority. However, even if groups are more prone to suffer from unequal treatment, they need to fulfill other criteria to be granted more protections – and what these criteria involve is up to the Court to decide. The Constitution's cherished U.S. American ideal of equality is being circumvented by the legal idea of specific requirements for suspect classification. *Suspect Subjects* claims that these criteria are meant to make the application of equal protection more demanding and thus shield this right against culturally "unwanted" contenders for equal rights. Although members of these social groups may be members of American society, suspect classification's criteria serve as constitutional policing of culture and shall prevent these social groups' entering into cultural narratives and imaginaries. They remain suspect outsiders as I argue.

Taking these legal dynamics into account, this book is also interested in why a class-based equal protection is culturally relevant for sexual orientation. The assumption is that sexual orientation fulfills the criteria for suspect classification, yet the Supreme Court, which increasingly acts as a political player in U.S. American cultural-legal discourse, hesitates to make a commitment to LGBTQ+ rights. While the legal arguments against considering sexual orientation a suspect classification are void as this book shows, the Court's reluctance to do so reveals itself to be a political strategy in struggles over cultural hegemonies. Arguments against sexual orientation's suspect classification therefore appear not as constitutional hurdles but as cultural limitations of the law.

Looking at these entanglements between law, culture, and LGBTQ+ realities, I am interested in making a cultural study of law relevant for a queer (rights) project from an academic perspective. Variations of 'Law and X' projects (re-)emerge and collapse, with Law and Literature, Law and Narrative, Law and the Humanities only being a small fraction of the academic sub-disciplines law touches upon. As these research areas show, in all its expressions and iterations, is dependently situated in a cultural framework.[21] To make sense of the connections within this framework, law has to be approached and understood as a culturally contingent practice, being shaped by the narratives, norms, and groups it negotiates with. In order to access these entanglements, three analytical foci will be of particular importance for this book, 1) how the Supreme Court's functions as both a judiciary branch, a political player, and a mediator of cultural and normative values, 2) how law, sexuality, and culture are mutually constitutive of each other as reflected by legal norms aiming to protect (or police) sexual minorities, necessitating a queer cultural analysis of law, and 3) how the constitutional principle of suspect classification holds the power to grant both legal and cultural legitimacy to queer rights claims.

Supreme Court Decisions as Cultural Texts

The examples of anti-queer rights responses underline that talking about sexual minorities' rights needs to include analyses of sociocultural realities. *Obergefell* illustrates that rulings, especially by the highest court in the U.S., are not merely legal documents[22] but that they have the potential to act as catalysts for cultural developments and norms, to uncover discrepancies between an ideal the law wants to achieve and the sociocultural obstacles it does not (yet) cover. For instance, *Brown v. Board of Education*, the 1954 Supreme Court ruling that formally ended school segregation, illustrates that decisions by the highest U.S. court have the power to initiate sociocultural changes through legislative means instead of merely responding legislatively to sociocultural transformations the majority calls for. Regarding *Brown*, this contrast became obvious in the fierce backlash Black students faced when trying to enter formerly segregated high schools.

However, if one only reads the decision and the procedural points of the ruling, they cannot deduct much about its embeddedness in a society and culture.[23] A case's transcript as such gives the reader only limited information

---

21 See also the work by Rosemary Coombe, Robert Cover, Lawrence Rosen, Paul Kahn, Robert Weisberg, Austin Sarat, Greta Olson, and Robin West to name some of the most seminal scholars in the field.

22 Since the Supreme Court decides on constitutional matters but also on matters of statues or laws, the term legal documents, as understood here, serves as umbrella for each of these different cases unless indicated otherwise.

23 See on this aspect also Susanne Baer "Speaking Law" 275: "In particular, an interdisciplinary analysis might be interested in discovering how the ruling was arrived at. There is the wish to understand how the decision was made, which matters were con-

about why there was a need to decide it, and the text does not include observations about its reception, for instance whether it was a landmark decision or not noticed by the general public, about the groups of people affected and the reasons why they have been affected. Thus, legal cases, particularly Supreme Court cases, shape and are being shaped by the (legal) culture they are negotiating with. Only by including a discourse analysis, by looking at the contexts these texts are emerging in, can an analysis begin to understand the reasons why certain legal texts influence a collective's processes of (cultural) meaning-making. This is shown by the high degree of responsiveness certain legal cases possess. Sometimes even the name of a case, such as *Brown*, evokes associations about its sociocultural significance, and signals its importance for processes of collective cultural memory formation. Cases like *Brown* live on in the cultural consciousness due to their high sociocultural impact. They become part of the U.S.'s severely questioned cultural narrative of equality and liberty, and evoke affective responses to granting liberal rights to particular social groups. The function(s) of these legal-cultural texts stretch far beyond the legal realm and also yield affective power over those they address (or fail to address). Both in cultural and legal texts, meaning is constructed discursively and not text-inherent, stressing the need for cultural analyses of law.

What's Law Got to Do with It? Towards a Queer Cultural Analysis of Law

Legal topics are still marginalized within Cultural Studies while law evolves around seemingly naturalized cultural concepts, including sexuality in all its iterations. Siding with queer theorists such as Gayle Rubin and Michel Foucault, the misunderstanding that sex is "a natural force that exists prior to social life and shapes institutions" (Rubin 146) is at the core of the Western cultural belief in sexual essentialism. Sex, in this view, is "eternally unchanging, asocial, and transhistorical," (146) meaning it is equally important in every society, every culture, and to every individual. With such essentialized and essentializing notions of a socioculturally constructed concept like sex, Rubin's 1982 assertion that "in Western culture, sex is taken all too seriously" (181) still seems valid today. What is more, cultural preoccupations with sex have come to encompass not just sex as a bodily activity but sexuality as a complex, which

sidered significant, and which not. Yet the text of the decision offers limited information about these matters, and this represents a methodological challenge. The type and amount of information given in a decision is also not only limited, it also differs in relation to the legal culture in which it is written."

includes biological sex, gender, gender identities, sexual orientation, sexual practices, and desires. This complex shapes and is being shaped by legal attempts of containing, controlling, and policing what Rubin identifies as "the sexual value system," which establishes a hierarchy of those sexualities that are "'good,' 'normal,' and 'natural'" and those that are "'bad,' 'abnormal,' or 'unnatural'" (151).

As concepts of sexuality become more differentiated, their distinctions and respective boundaries are becoming more difficult to distinguish in the sociocultural imagination and consciousness. Equating, for instance, gender identities with sexual orientations, sexual orientations with sexual practices, and gender identity with sexual desires not only blurs what each of these categories refers to, but it also loads these concepts with sociocultural meaning. This way, trans identities are becoming falsely associated with sexually abusive behaviors,[24] gays are stigmatized as sexual perpetrators who prey on those too young to give consent,[25] and those differing from the cisgender norm have to explain their ways of experiencing attraction to those already incapable of grasping the implications of not identifying with the gender having been assigned to their biological sex.

All of these connections between law, culture, and sexuality need to be deconstructed in order to fully understand how to arrive at a more equal antidiscrimination law. Queer Theory serves as useful tool in this endeavor. Its disruptive and disrupting force of questioning the normative and troubling those who normativize can be made fruitful for academic and activist purposes.

---

24 For a detailed overview of anti-trans stereotypes and how they have been picked up and perpetuated in popular culture, see Sam Feder's *Disclosure*. For an overview of how anti-trans and anti-non-binary stereotypes come to shape legal decisions and influence legal discourse, see Alex Sharpe, "Criminalising Sexual Intimacy", and Sharpe's *Sexual Intimacy and Gender Identity 'Fraud;'* also Florence Ashley as well as Talia Mae Bettcher.

25 For a historic contextualization of connecting gay men with child molesters, see Rubin 140. For more on the vicious stereotypes of homosexuality as threatening to children, see also Kite and Whitley 464: "Vestiges of the idea that gay men and lesbians are deviant remain in common stereotypes, however, such as the belief that gays and lesbians are cross-dressers and are child molesters." See Kosofsky Sedgwick on the plot of Oscar Wilde's *Dorian Gray*, which "seems to replicate the discursive eclipse in this period of the Classically based, pederastic assumption that male-male bonds of any duration must be structured around some diacritical difference – old/young, for example, or active/passive – whose binarizing cultural power would be at least comparable to that of gender" (160).

It is thus with a queer theoretical lens that I propose a heightened legal protection for LGBTQ+ individuals through judicial decision-making rather than legislative changes. The power of constitutional decisions, as compared to legislative action, is analyzed in Chapter II, which offers an argument for the affective and imaginative force of the Constitution, what I call 'constitutional imaginaries.' Qualitative analyses of the most important U.S. Supreme Court decisions concerning sexual orientation in the twenty-first century in Chapter III strengthen this claim of the affective primacy of judicial decision-making. Wide reading the cases affecting sexual minorities is then supplemented by an analysis of cultural narratives found in the U.S. Constitution.

It is important to note that this book advocates for taking law seriously without venerating it. Law is already a rather serious discipline, given its dogmatic rules and how it may affect its subjects' lives. Yet law's seriousness is often misinterpreted as having to blindly stand in awe before it. This reverence does a disservice to taking law seriously in all its capabilities and possibilities of affecting queer realities positively by making one shy away from engaging in its critique.

Taking a stroll through the most important research on queer legal theory, Law and the Humanities, and Law and Culture, I clearly agree with, among others, Rosemary Coombe, William Eskridge, H.L.A Hart, Lawrence Rosen, Tamsin Wilton, and Chase Strangio that legal and (socio)cultural phenomena are closely related and that (queer) rights are equally dependent on progressive legal decisions as they are on cultural developments. In other words, how we narrate, regulate, and imagine queer identities and realities is connected to how law protects or fails to protect these spheres.

New Queer Rights with Old-Established Tools

The United States Supreme Court has the power to address discriminatory regulations concerning sexual orientation with a constitutional tool, derived from the Fourteenth Amendment's Equal Protection Clause: the so-called suspect classification. Classifying sexual orientation as a legal category against which any kind of discrimination is suspect would effectively render anti-queer legislation unconstitutional. Although there have been progressive legislative and judicative developments such as in *Obergefell* and *Bostock*, the Court has been reluctant to even tackle the question whether sexual orientation as a legal category should receive this form of constitutional protection.

The political reasons for not commenting on sexual orientation's distinctive constitutional status in the twenty-first century by such a powerful institution as the Supreme Court are at the core of this book. However, it is equally important to grasp the procedural and constitutional implications of not deciding on this question, which to legal lay persons may appear as a seemingly rather dry, specialized issue.

Affirming that sexual orientation is indeed a category which warrants a special form of constitutional protection would signal the Court's willingness to challenge existing legal hierarchies and thus influence sociocultural orders. Such orders meander into legal discourse and manifest as legal norms (further) discriminating those who are socioculturally already stigmatized. Sociocultural orders therefore have the power of acting analogous to legal ones – this insight is central to *Suspect Subject*'s claim that overcoming discriminatory legal systems must involve challenging socioculturally naturalized perceptions.

Cultural narratives such as the guarantee of legal equality for everyone as well as constitutional imaginaries about marriage equality being indicative of a tantamount status for non-heterosexual couples contribute to a marred understanding of LGBTQ+ right claims today. Post-*Obergefell* and *-Bostock* demands for equal rights are thus met by the general public[26] with a lack of understanding and felt lifted responsibilities by mistakenly equating *de jure* equality gains with *de facto* legal, social, and cultural equality.

The interplay between cultural narratives and constitutional imaginaries becomes most obvious when it comes to sexual orientation's status in twenty-first century U.S. America. Queer rights and analyses of law and culture thus belong together and should be granted more attention in academic discourse. Taking legal norms and those who interpret them as case studies, I look at the relation between legal and cultural-legal norms and power, and thereby establish a queer hermeneutics within law. Doing so, I argue for a heightened constitutional protection for sexual orientation in the U.S. ('suspect classification') as means to challenge both legal and cultural anti-queer sentiments. Using an intersectional, feminist, and queer theoretical approach, I believe in the compatibility and entanglements of law and culture, and advocate for its expanded

26 This rather simplistic umbrella mostly includes those unaccustomed and unaffected by queer rights discourses, namely those who identify and are read as cis, heterosexual, White, monied/propertied, able-bodied persons. However, choosing not to engage in struggles for equal rights is based on individual layers of privilege, which may or may not coincide with socioculturally accepted forms of sexuality, gender, dis/ability, race, and class.

use in academic and activist contexts. Whenever possible, I try to offer alternatives to established forms of law, culture, and sexuality. Academic work on sociocultural conditions profits from activistic approaches that seek to queer, challenge, develop, abolish, and/or deconstruct the what *is* in order to arrive at a what *should be*.

However, as imagined queer legal futures are as diverse as the LGBTQ+ community, making normative claims about any ideal-typical scenario would only feed into a static prescriptiveness I want to avoid. Instead, it is my wish to sensibilize my readers for the importance of legal-cultural educational work in academia and activism, and to argue for a strengthening of democratic, anti-discriminatory structures via doing pluralistic queer legal analysis. This view is controversial. Especially queer activists, who have been subjected to institutionalized forms of violence, reject the legal system as a heteropatriarchal, sexist, classed, racist, ableist, transphobic, inherent discriminatory instrument. To some, this system was meant to disadvantage, oppress, abuse, violate, and murder those bodies who are not read as White, cis gendered, educated, wealthy, male, heterosexual, able-bodied, or those who refuse to comply with those governing over this system. And they are right to do so. As legal scholar William Eskridge Jr. notes about the double-edged character of legal norms for queers:

> The law was a chief mechanism for the 1950s *Kulturkampf*, or state-sponsored culture war, against homosexuals and other gender-benders, yet simultaneously became the hunted's chief refuge from that assault. Since 1969 the law's hostility to gay people has relented, and today the law sometimes protects gay people against private violence and discrimination. (*Gaylaw* 1)

These two sides of law are even more prevalent today. While LGBTQ+ activists advocate for legal reforms such as the *Equality Act*, conservative state Congressmembers push for ever more anti-trans and anti-queer legislation, with each year since 2021 becoming record-breaking (ACLU "Mapping;" Krishnakumar). This struggle shows how law's protective character is closely linked to those who have the power of granting or gatekeeping rights.

Those skeptical of the reformability of law may reject calls for thinking about sexual orientation's constitutional protection as undesired – because the system was not designed to emancipate queers, queers should not try (or can only fail) to re-/transform it. I share this view to some degree, yet argue that such abolitionist thought and law-inherent solutions to queer emancipation are not mutually exclusive. Using existing modes of the law to improve the lives of LGBTQ+ may seem contradictory given its long history as a tool for queer oppression. Taking law as *a priori* discriminatory, however, means misjudging its transformative power. This is why I understand law and its oppressive, discriminatory force not as separate, as Marxist critique of law's power do, but as separable, agreeing with Hart's understanding of law (xvi).

So, what *is* abolitionist about arguing for suspect classification from a queer cultural-legal perspective? First, both abolitionism and queer cultural-legal studies in this book's understanding call for holistic analyses of entangled, oppressive systems in order to arrive at legal norms which respond to queer realities in an equitable way. In this sense, abolitionist studies' aims of naming, acknowledging and seeking to dismantle oppressive structures within the U.S. are highly instructive for considerations about queer rights. Second, both abolitionism and this book's analyses draw on the importance of personal experience and emphasize positionality. Acknowledging the need for admitting non-academic and/or activist forms of knowledge production into academia, most importantly knowledge of experience, I believe that queer forms of critiquing law need to recognize their own positionality, lack of neutrality, and need to make themselves accessible to a larger, meaning non-academic, audience. Minimizing academic codes is meant to abolish gatekeeping and thus contributes to a queering of academic practice.[27]

Overview

What can be gained from a cultural studies approach to law is a deeper understanding of how the culture(s) we are surrounded by permeate and dictate legal categories, subjects, and norms. For doing so, Chapter I will introduce the methodology and theoretical framework I am working with, and survey the development of the cultural study of law. Chapter II looks at the constitutional and cultural framework of the Equal Protection Clause and its principle of suspect classification. By analyzing equal protection's legal objectives and linking them to cultural narratives, this chapter draws on Peter Häberle's research on the connection between constitutions and culture, and stresses that

27 This will not always be successful and is still conducted within rather inflexible academic structures. These structures necessitate adhering to some fixed formal requirements of 'proper' academic work in order for this book to become part of academic discourse in the first place.

both the U.S. Constitution and U.S. culture are subject to ongoing transformations and act as mirrors of a people's normative self-understanding and their shared moral concepts.

Taking the culturally transformative role of the Constitution as starting point, Chapter III looks at the Supreme Court as the institution which constantly (re-)interprets and thus shapes this cultural and legal document. The chapter offers a dogmatic historization of the Supreme Court's rulings regarding sexual orientation in the twenty-first century, thereby analyzing the justices' different forms of judicial interpretations and political affiliations over the years. The aim of this chapter is to establish whether and if, to what degree, the Supreme Court functions as political player in the discourse about sexual orientation's constitutional protection, and to determine its role in constituting and maintaining sociocultural imaginaries.

Chapters IV and V deal with the way(s) law constitutes queer subjects, and attempt to establish a queer hermeneutics of law. These chapters give insights into the cultural concept of sexual orientation in the twenty-first century, and shed light on the social norms and hierarchies associated with it. Drawing on social constructionism, queer theory, and critical legal theory, Chapter IV discusses the conceptualization of sexual orientation in constitutional discourses. In law, sexual orientation holds a specific meaning, which is shaped by cultural understandings, yet which is also distinctly legal. My claim here is that this conceptualization works to (re-)produce an essentialist matrix of sexuality which facilitates legal attempts at gaining formal equality but fails to establish substantive equality.

Chapter V analyses the Supreme Court's criteria for suspect classification from a queer theoretical standpoint, and introduces queer alternatives to legal futures. The chapter examines whether sexual orientation fulfills the classification's four criteria (history of discrimination, status as a politically powerless minority, immutability, moral neutrality) from a cultural studies of law perspective. The aim of Chapter V is to provide concrete legal guidelines for arguing sexual orientation's suspect classification while calling for a revision of the Court's criteria. Acknowledging the flaws and inconsistencies of the law, this chapter introduces potential (queer) alternatives to the current legal system. It looks at arguments for and visions of a legal system that is beyond law as we know it, something 'post' the current legal system, a more inclusive, less heteronormative, and possibly more just queer legal future.

I. A Few Notes on Concepts
A Note on Definitions

In addition to the most prominent terms presented in this chapter, further terms are being clarified with the use of footnotes, following the legal tradition of referencing. I try to avoid attributing terminology at any cost because they often imply and generate derogatory associations. These terms are often catalysts for stereotypical thinking; they foster the impression that a certain characteristic of a person, sexual orientation or gender identity in this case, is an indicator of other aspects of an individual such as their intelligence, character, or morality. However, what one may perceive as rather neutral (if there is such a thing), another may find harmful. Identifying these terms is particularly difficult in the context of sexual orientation and gender identity as many attributing terms such as *gay*, *queer*, and *faggot* have already been reclaimed and appropriated by the LGBTQ+ community. Any exclusionary and discriminatory terms and concepts are not willingly used, and those who feel misrepresented by them are invited to approach me for finding a more fitting term, concept, or way of framing.

I.1. Mapping Our Language

Sexuality is messy. Talking about it makes matters worse in some cases. This may even be more prevalent in the twenty-first century. The contemporary focus on the policing of language is undoubtedly connected to the sensibility of an audience's ears in terms of identity politics. One's pervasive medial training in paying attention to words, phrases, and symbols has not only heightened one's awareness of what is being communicated by whom, but it has also strengthened one's mistrust in who is communicating what or to which ends. As this kind of systemic questioning targets any speaker, it seems all the more important to develop a precise terminology for academic and public discourse(s) about non-normative sexual orientations, gender (identity), sexual practices, and their legal recognition in order to prevent any misunderstandings on the level of rhetoric whenever a mutual teleological perspective is given.

Trying to avoid exclusion by using an exclusively academic code, I wish to circumvent the discourse about queer rights' inaccessibility for those outside the respective discipline so, to use Michael Warner's words, not to "allow people to speak in code and forget questions that might be posed from the outside" (116). This chapter clarifies my understanding and usage of the most important terms and concepts connected to sexuality and law, and explains why certain terms and concepts are chosen in favor of others. Drawing on Donna Haraway's concept of "situated knowledge," (581) such an endeavor can only be conducted from a subjective, necessarily limited perspective. Only by acknowledging this limitation and by locating this book within the feminist strand of deconstructing the notion of the default masculinist, cis, heterosexual, White, able-bodied academic and knowledgeable subject, *Suspect Subjects* takes on a feminist objectivity and refuses to make itself "[i]rresponsible [which] means unable to be called into account" (583).

Drawing attention to the power and relevance of specific wordings and ways of framing is all the more important for those interested in legal thought. As emphasized by justices' modes of constitutional interpretation (Chapter III), and as held by legal scholars (Hart vi; Baer *Rechtssoziologie* 18), language matters when navigating law's realm because words carry meaning, associations, and also ideological freight. Words are even more important in law because, to use Robert Cover's much quoted insight, "[l]egal interpretation takes place in a field of pain and death" ("Violence" 1601), making judicial approaches to words essential to questions of labor regulations, housing, civil rights, citizenship, and also survival.[1]

---

1 One may think of the Supreme Court's interpretation of the Constitution's Eighth Amendment, which prohibits "cruel or unusual punishments," as not applying to capital punishment. See for instance *Bucklew v. Precythe*, majority opinion by Justice Gorsuch: "The Constitution allows capital punishment. ... In fact, death was 'the standard penalty for all serious crimes' at the time of the founding. ... Nor did the later addition of the Eighth Amendment outlaw the practice. On the contrary—the Fifth Amendment, added to the Constitution at the same time as the Eighth, expressly contemplates that a defendant may be tried for a 'capital' crime and 'deprived of life' as a penalty, so long as proper procedures are followed."

Sex, Gender, Identity

Throughout this book, I use 'sex' as referring to one's genital anatomy or chromosomal set-up as indicative of biological group membership constructed along the binary categories of female and male (one's sex assigned at birth), or the act(s) considered as sexual activity. Although 'biological' is closely connected to sex in this context, it is acknowledged that even this seemingly clear-cut category has undergone a process of sociocultural construction (Laqueur 8; Fausto-Sterling 5–7).

'Gender' refers to the socially, and culturally, constructed notions of being and doing, in the sense of performing, a certain sex, generally also conceived of in binary terms of male and female. The pre-fixes 'cis' and 'trans' refer to whether one identifies with the gender, i.e., their socioculturally constructed sex, assigned at birth (cis), or whether one does not identify with the gender assigned at birth but a different one (trans). While these two 'gender identities' are currently the most prominent ones and often depicted as antagonist and binary, this book acknowledges the existence of multiple forms of gender identity subsumed or beyond those cis and trans. 'Sexual orientation,' as explained in more detail below, refers to the sexual and/or romantic preference(s) one has. In this context, 'queer' is used as an umbrella term for non-heterosexual, non-cis identities and practices which "mean different things to different people, at different moments, in different contexts" (Stychin 140). The fluidity and un-grasp-ability of queerness is elaborated on later in this chapter as will the subversive force of queering as both identity term and way of thinking. Although it is often used in legal and sociocultural contexts as an identity category, this meaning is considered but also questioned here.

Approaching sexuality may best start with posing some questions: Is a cis gendered woman who is in a sexual relationship with a cis man but falls in love with another cis or trans woman a lesbian or heterosexual? Are trans men who have sexual intercourse with women 'allowed' to call themselves lesbians? Is a gender-queer person, whose birth certificate considers them male and who engages in sexual activity with men, gay, bisexual, or something else entirely?[2] As these examples show, language influences and determines the way one is thinking about and perceiving of sexuality, and linguistic precision enables one to reflect upon one's own inclusionary or exclusionary cognitive patterns. However, the current, unreliable, yet dominant nomenclature with regard to sexual

---

2 See also Jagose 8 on similar questions which trouble static conceptualizations of sexuality and gender.

orientation and gender creates tensions both outside of and within the community of members and allies of non-normative sexual orientations.[3] Further, these (in-)abilities to speak of and thus gasp sexuality in all its messiness result in issues for those making, interpreting, and aiming to abide by laws. As put by legal scholar Peter Nicolas,

> when a law says that a "homosexual" cannot adopt children or serve in a particular kind of job, or that marriages between persons of the same "sex" are prohibited, what do those terms mean? Stated somewhat differently, what does it mean for someone to be a "homosexual," or a "man," or a "woman"? In almost all cases, laws of the sort described above do not define such terms, leaving it to those applying the laws (and, to the extent that litigation ensues, the courts) to determine their meaning. Thus, a necessary prelude to addressing the constitutionality of such laws is statutory interpretation. (Sexual Orientation 3–4, emphasis in original)

Working with a clear and transparent vocabulary when it comes to concepts of sexuality thus makes discourses accessible, and may contribute to educating others who (have to) work with them. Similarly, spelling out laws' understanding of sexuality and gender may contribute to a deeper insight on the (mis)use of legal norms in policing these spheres. A recent example is Florida's HB 1557, which was introduced in January 2022 to target LGBTQ+ youth. By stating that the bill "prohibit[s] classroom discussion about sexual orientation or gender identity in certain grade levels or in a specified manner" (1) without explicitly mentioning queer, lesbian, gay, or trans issues, Florida's law could be interpreted to effectively ban any kind of discussion about gender and sexuality. This view was sported in a letter gone viral a Florida teacher wrote:

> Dear Florida parent/caretaker: … To be in accordance with this policy, I will no longer be referring to your student with gendered pronouns. All students will be referred to as "they" or "them." … Furthermore, I will be removing all books or instruction which refer to a person being a "mother," "father," "husband" or "wife" as these are gender identities that also may allude to sexual orientation. (Bernstein)

---

3 Probably the most prominent example is the discourse about who to include in the abbreviation for the queer community. For instance, while some argue for the use of LGBT+, others do not feel represented being merely a '+'. The same applies to other forms of writing such as LGBTQ*, LGBT, LGBTQIAP*, and others.

While this letter has merely been a satirical attempt at criticizing the law and showing its hypocrisy (Isger), this example illustrates how contested the field of legal interpretation is and how much the cis gendered, heterosexual norm becomes invisibilized by and in legal and cultural discourse. In legal discourses, it is also pivotal to stress that constitutionality of laws may be directly linked to the sociocultural meaning of concepts and terms (Nicolas *Sexual Orientation* 4). A recent instance would be the legal understanding of 'sex' as encompassing biological sex, sexual orientation, and gender identity as decided in *Bostock v. Clayton County* (2020).[4] Before 2020, the meaning of 'sex' has not included these aspects of identity and thus, Title VII of the Civil Rights Act of 1964 did not cover LGBTQ+, making firing them because of their sexual orientation or gender identity constitutional. While the use of sex in this case was decided in a legal context, the decision to expand sex to refer to more than biological make-up has arguably been influenced by sociocultural developments, and an updated understanding of how sexual orientation, gender, and sex are entangled and (co-)constructed.

Sociocultural Constructions

The need to dissect the constructedness of concepts and terms is important for (re-)negotiations of their power as especially sexual terminology always comes with ideological freight. For instance, today's Western understanding of homosexuality, which was only 'invented' in the nineteenth century, comes with the historical baggage of pathologizing and criminalizing same-sex desires.[5] As queer theorists have noted, the term 'homosexual' was firstly used in 1868 (Havelock Ellis 19; Katz *Invention* 10), and picked up alongside the term 'heterosexual' in the U.S. American context firstly in 1892 in Dr. James D. Kiernan's article "Responsibility in Sexual Perversion" (Katz *Invention* 10, 19).

4 The Supreme Court decided in *Bostock* that Title VII of the Civil Rights Act of 1964 extends to sexual orientation and gender identity, making discrimination against gays, lesbians, bisexuals, trans persons, or anyone else because of their sexual orientation and/or gender identity in employment unconstitutional.

5 See McIntosh 183–4: "The creation of a specialized, despised, and punished role of homosexual keeps the bulk of society pure in rather the same way that the similar treatment of some kinds of criminals helps keep the rest of society law-abiding. … The way in which people become labeled as homosexual can now be seen as an important social process connected with mechanisms of social control. … [A]s we have seen, psychologists and psychiatrists on the whole have not retained their objectivity but become involved as diagnostic agents in the process of social labeling."

Back then, both concepts had an entirely different meaning than they do today, with heterosexuality signifying a sexual perversion, namely unreproductive sex (Katz "Questioning" 44). Understanding the history of concepts of sexuality helps contextualizing and deconstructing their implications. As Jacques Derrida points out, deconstruction "means not 'destroying' but 'undoing', while analysing the different layers of a structure to know how it has been built" (2). Deconstruction, in this sense, is a tool which needs to "emphasiz[e] the history of the construction" (2) to understand each role's part.

While one perceives them as 'natural' in the twenty-first century, these categories of human differentiation are in fact historically changing in their meaning. In the context of sexual orientation, the current perception is only a rather new interpretation. There simply were no 'homosexuals' or 'heterosexuals' in today's understanding in other historic periods such as Ancient Greece (Foucault *History* 42–44, 188, 192) although, from today's standpoint, we might label them as such. The most important distinction between concepts of sexual orientation back then and today is their essenzializing notion. Back then, sexual orientation was something defined with regard to what somebody *did*, comparable to today's meaning of sexual practices or sexual behavior, while today, this notion rather evolves around the question of what somebody *is*, allowing for an essentialization, pathologization, and criminalization (Foucault *History* 192; Jagose 11; Katz "Questioning" 45). As Michel Foucault states, starting in the nineteenth-century, "the homosexual became a personage, a past, a case history, and a childhood, in addition to being a type of life, a life form, and a morphology, with an indiscreet anatomy and possibly a mysterious physiology" (*History* 43). These historical developments show that today's terminology of sexuality is influenced by the specific time, culture, and geographic position one lives in and is not a static, universal, objective ordering category.

Such concepts are thus not 'naturally' given but socially and culturally constructed, necessitating that the sociocultural conditions in which these concepts emerge are being questioned and deconstructed. This understanding supposes that cultures are different from each other and that what may be of importance for one culture may be irrelevant to another. This view rejects cultural universalism and calls for a culture-specific investigation of legal and sexual norms while evading cultural essentialisms. Questioning cultural frameworks means also questioning the concept of sexuality as such because of culture's and sexuality's interconnectedness. This anti-foundational perspective ('questioning everything') follows queer theorists who deconstruct seemingly 'natural' basic assumptions such as the relevance of sexual object-choice for categorizing people.

Following this approach, I view social group membership on basis of one's sexual orientation as becoming only meaningful in terms of its discursively established meaning. The gender and sex of the person(s) one loves, is in relationships with, and/or has sex with only becomes meaningful for analysis when met by cultural or legal norms. This information then gives much insight into legal cultures and what they perceive as important to police.

Sexual Orientation(s)

The decision to use the term 'sexual orientation' is a conscious one and meant to signal the political project of this book. Sexual orientation follows the legal nomenclature, which uses this clinical term to indicate any (legal) form of sexual preference. But, more importantly, using the term sexual orientation means reclaiming and politicizing it. Following lesbian activist and human sexuality scholar Tamsin Wilton's approach of "dis/orientating," I take Wilton's work as role model for queering theories about legal-cultural conceptions of sexual orientations (11). Dis/orientating then refers to questioning, deconstructing and transforming seemingly naturalized notions of sexual orientation in the sense of disturbing the fixedness of this concept. This approach situates the discourse on sexual orientation and the law not within one's individual (private) sexual desire(s) but in a public sphere, making sexuality (again) political.

Speaking of 'orientation' instead of sexual 'identity' also mirrors recent human rights scholarship's favoring of the former term to signal the contextuality of its importance. While for some, their sexual orientation may be an important part of their identity, others might prefer to see it as less integral to their being (Waites 144).

The term 'sexual minorities' is used to refer to the sociocultural perception of LGBTQ+ groups as deviant[6] from the norm. While some may not feel represented under the umbrella of being 'queer,' and one can also consider

6 In this book, the term deviant is defined as describing any kind of behavior "that violates the standards of conduct or expectations of a group or society" (Schaefer 159) unless indicated otherwise. It is used to indicate behaviors, appearances, or orientations which differ from the social norm, i.e., the predominant status quo in a society. The situational description of these hegemonic conditions does not imply approval or disproval as such. The term non-normative is preferred here.

themselves as queer in relation to the LGBTQ+ community,[7] I perceive the term queerness as the state of being regarded, regarding oneself, and acting in opposition to the heterosexual, cis gendered sociocultural norm. In this sense, non- or anti-normative behavior within the realm of sexuality is regarded as queer. 'Queer' is thus understood as more than a form of sexual or gender identity, it is perceived as a political stance which seeks to trouble those normative settings one is surrounded by. Although this term may be rather specific to the Anglo-American and European context,[8] the implications of queer as an identity term, meaning non-normative, troubling, defying and refusing attempts of categorization, is also mirrored in using it as a verb. To queer then means to question, to disrupt and to dismantle something in order to look at all its parts before re-assembling it again in a different manner.

Admittingly, this approach is already flawed. In current discourses about 'gay rights' or 'queer rights,' claiming one's gay, lesbian, queer or other identity is vital for the emancipatory project of gaining more visibility, legal protection(s), and recognition. Depending on one's socioeconomic situation, national origin, ethnicity, dis/ability, sociocultural norms, or religion, it may not be possible for people to proudly claim their sexual orientation without risking stigmatization, criminalization, and/or punishment and exclusion. For those people, 'queer rights' are not only emancipatory, they are the foundation for economic, social, or physical survival. However, others may feel that these rights and connected fights are not theirs. For instance, same-sex marriage has not been a demand of a unified LGBTQ+ community but rather something only parts of the community argued for while others opposed it as a continuation of the patriarchal instrument of oppression and means of swarming over to heteronormatively controlled forms of living, often referred to as homonormativity.

7 As LGBTQ+ and queer are not fixed identity categories but discursively constructed terms, feelings of not belonging to or being underrepresented in discourses about these social groups applies especially to those genders, sexual orientations, and intersections which are marginalized and invisibilized. Examples include asexuality, bisexuality, trans, queer people of color, and queer people with disabilities. However, feeling queer within the queer community may differ individually based on location, personal sentiment, and time.

8 I thank Edith Frankzelia Otero Quezada for alerting me to the different ways people of the queer/LGBTQ+ community refer to their identities, and the Western-centric assumption of using 'queer' as a more general term.

The most prominent concepts of gender identity used in this book are cis and trans as explained above. One's gender identity is based on whether their biological sex fits their socioculturally constructed sex (gender). The plus (+) used in the abbreviation LGBTQ+ indicates that there is more to the concept than explained here. It functions as a *Leerstelle* ('placeholder') which can be filled with meaning and which offers people an opportunity to connect. It also underlines that categories of sexual orientation and gender identity refuse to give into a binary and exclusionary logic, i.e., trans does not equal transgender or transsexual but "it can be understood as the most inclusive umbrella term to describe various communities and individuals with nonconforming gender identities and/or expressions en masse" (Jones qtd. in Garvin). Originally, my preferred way of writing trans would also include an asterisk (trans*). However, over the course of writing, transness has taken on more political meaning. So, in order to distinguish itself from other struggles such as those of non-binary or intersex folk, it is necessary to address trans singularly and without an inclusionary asterisk.

During the writing of this book, I have received numerous questions on why I include trans (or non-binary or agender or else) folx in a book about sexual orientation. While I acknowledge that issues of gender identity are distinct from issues of sexual orientation, I do not understand them as separate, at least not in the legal sphere. The decision to include them is thus not only a linguistic one but also, again, political. This kind of allyship is vital for the queer community and for discourses about queer rights and sexual politics, and I wish to avoid reproducing trans-exclusive feminist perspectives. However, equating transness with non-normative sexual orientations would strengthen the illusory correlation that trans individuals are necessarily non-heterosexual, and that transness is not only an expression of gender identity but also of sexual orientation.

Legality, Illegality, Discrimination

A reoccurring reaction to this book has been, "but don't we already have (enough) legal protections for everyone?," which has alternatively been put as "who still cares about this? Everyone should love who they want!" As academics and activists know, engaging with these questions, and those posing them, is equally important as it is exhausting. Anyone who has experienced instances of discrimination because of their actual or perceived sexual orientation can attest to the fact that being treated differently, and, even more, oftentimes hostilely, is at any time worth talking about. Discourses and questions as stated above seem to equal legality or illegality of certain conducts as indicative of their existence in everyday life – what cannot be there legally, is not there socially. This perception is both over-emphasizing law's power and denying one's own's responsibilities. It is also conspicuous that such affective responses to minority rights are often voiced by people who are not identifying as non-normative in terms of their gender identity and/or sexual orientation. To those, these issues seem non-existent because they perceive these issues to be too troubling, and too disturbing. Or, in a more benevolent reading, people asking such questions follow a humanitarian understanding of equality and feel everyone should be treated the same.

Discrimination, as understood here, is any instance of unequal treatment someone suffers due to their actual or perceived sexual orientation. This discrimination is always a form of violence, – either physically, mentally, economically, legally, socially, culturally, or sexually, – because it restricts and polices behaviors and thus has an impact on how one allows oneself or is allowed to live. According to social psychologist Gordon W. Allport, discrimination takes place whenever a "prejudiced person makes detrimental distinctions of an active sort" (15), with segregation being "an institutionalized form of discrimination, enforced legally or by common custom" (15). While Allport explicitly mentions only those acts actively conducted to distinguish between groups or individuals, he considers hostile ways of speaking about groups or individuals one dislikes (antilocution), avoiding them, physically attacking them, and exterminating them as different stages of a "fateful progression" (15) of acting out prejudice, with discrimination being in the middle of this spectrum. To Allport, "activity in one level makes transition to a more intense level easier" (15), which is why for the purpose of this book, discrimination is understood to cover even those less active contributions to discriminating groups such as antilocution and hate speech as well as avoidance.

As legal scholar Robert Wintemute[9] argued in 1995, scholars have focused more on instances of direct discrimination in the U.S. legal context as "the gay, lesbian, and bisexual minority still faces a tremendous amount of legislation that discriminates directly on the basis of sexual orientation ..., and many litigated cases of sexual orientation discrimination involve direct discrimination" (10–11). Direct discrimination refers to laws that explicitly target, or fail to protect people of a particular sexual orientation. By 2024, this situation has

9 I quote Wintemute as expert on the rights same-sex couples, also in human rights discourse, yet strongly disagree with his stances on gender identity.

changed. Today, direct discrimination is still relevant as many areas of social life are not covered by existing anti-discrimination laws, and many states are constantly pushing against pro-queer legislation by issuing discriminatory bills, but the U.S. is arguably in an intermediate situation in which instances of direct and indirect discrimination intersect (see Chapter IV).

It is especially these indirect instances of discrimination that illustrate how concepts of legality or illegality may clash with realities. Indirect discrimination occurs when there is "a neutral requirement (other than being of a particular sexual orientation) with which a disproportionate number of persons of the other person's sexual orientation are unable to comply, and which cannot be justified" (Wintemute 10). This difference and disparity between *de jure* and *de facto* conditions, not only in connection to discrimination, has a strong affective component. While one may know about the legality of a certain conduct, for example that same-sex marriage is constitutional (*de jure* condition), they may still exercise their power to not issue marriage licenses to same-sex couples (*de facto* condition). Likewise, one may know that a certain conduct is illegal, such as having oral and anal sex before its de-criminalization in *Lawrence v. Texas* in 2003 (*de jure*), yet they decide to ignore the legal conditions to do what they *feel* is right (*de facto*). As Carpenter states by offering anecdotal evidence to post-*Obergefell* realities for same-sex couples wanting to get married,

> nonjudicial staff often perform critical gatekeeping functions that are virtually unregulated, and that take place outside of the courtroom and off the record. Where court administrators and other bureaucrats are hostile to LGBT people, or do not comprehend their legal position, that gatekeeping function can actually act as a practically impermeable barrier to access to the announced right. (273)

These instances of *de facto* discrimination where *de jure* rights are given illustrate that "rights do not self-enforce" (271), strengthening the argument for a thorough legal-cultural education and a simultaneous tackling of discriminatory legal and cultural notions.

Affective Orders: Rechtsgefühl, Legal Consciousness, Legal Subjectivities, Legal Mentalité

As both instances show, one's affective relation to legal norms, i.e., how one feels about their rightness or wrongness, influences whether one challenges, questions, ignores, or acts in accordance to them. This affective dimension of law is being referred to by some scholars working on the frictions between law and culture as one's *Rechtsgefühl* ('legal affect'),[10] borrowing from German legal scholar Rudolf von Jhering, or legal consciousness (Merry; Ewick and Silbey; Silbey "Studying"), legal subjectivities (Olson *Legality*), or legal mentalité (Legrand "Comparative," "Converging").[11]

The notion of *Rechtsgefühl* has another equally important aspect to it. While one may know about the legality of a certain conduct, they may still *feel* like they are doing something illegal and vice versa, depending on the environment the conduct is happening in. This feeling, whose causes at times remain unconscious to its feeler, is connected to extra-legal norms that are equally and sometimes even more powerful than legal ones. Imagine an apartment building with alternating schedules for cleaning the stairway – a rather typical scenario in German cities. Forgetting that you are due for cleaning the stairs may not be sufficient reason to terminate your tenancy but it certainly makes you feel uneasy when meeting your neighbors. Social and cultural norms, social pressure and social control all feed into the establishment and maintenance of legal orders or those acting analogous to them.

In this sense, legal-cultural orders are understood as orders that do legal work, i.e., police and maintain conducts – be it social norms that police behaviors, cultural norms that hierarchically value some conducts over others, or intra-community norms which obligate one to act in accordance with them and threaten those with exclusion who do not.

Narratives, Imaginaries, Constitutional Processes

Instances of felt, imagined, and narrated legal realities play a prominent role in this book. In the fields of law and culture, the former is often associated with rational, fact-based, and ordered inquiries whereas the latter represents

---

10 The specifics of the German language allow for a hybrid concept that is difficult to grasp in English: *Rechtsgefühl* does not only imply the affective relation to law but also the affective relation to justice.

11 See Legrand "Comparative" 265–6: "The law, in its many manifestations, is an incorporative cultural form. Just as culture is a source of identity, legal practices are a source of identity. They encode experiences. To my mind, legal practices are very much a reflection of a given culture and of a given legal mentalité (in the sense of the interiorised culture). They reveal an implicit structure of attitude and reference, or a way of experiencing legal order."

a more irrational, associative, and muddy area.[12] For instance, many people seem to have a clearer understanding about the tasks of a lawyer than they do about a scholar in cultural studies. This dualism is approached here via narratives and imaginaries in order to uncover and analyze the affectively experienced truths which bind together both realms. Cultural narratives, in my understanding, are stories which add and carry meaning to sociocultural processes, and "by and through which a group of people legitimizes their claims to a given national identity" (Olson "Futures" 56). In this sense, they can serve as explanatory models, which help people make sense of their world, they can be politically instrumentalized for establishing or maintaining sociocultural hierarchies, they can offer spaces of identification, or they can add legitimacy to a group's actions. An example would be the U.S. (grand) cultural narrative of one's ability to overcome class lines and socioeconomic hierarchies simply by hard work and dedication, stressing that the U.S. is built on the promise of equal opportunity.

What such narratives have in common is their focus on affect. Cultural narratives not only carry meaning but they also appeal to people's emotional reaction to a certain event. Thus, they do not necessarily rest on historical or scientific facts to become true; they find their way into a collective truth by being subjectively *felt* as true. Expanding on the forms and functions of cultural narratives, Chapter II gives examples of this process with regard to the Constitution and the ideals inscribed in it.

Legal-cultural imaginaries are introduced in this book as supplements to cultural narratives, which share characteristics of the latter, yet differ from cultural narratives in that they are less established, i.e., they are not as prominently anchored in people's minds, less identifiable, and they are less static. However, imaginaries are considerably more fueled by affect than cultural narratives. Imaginaries strongly focus on phantasmatic configurations of realities while narratives' already claim a quasi-factual, narrativized truth to them. Imaginaries thus work towards changing existing sociocultural conditions while narratives rather legitimize and add meaning to them. The concept of cultural-legal imaginaries picks up on the notion that Cultural Studies, Critical Legal Studies and other disciplines notice a "turn to affect" (Fischer-Lascano; Krasmann; Shaw).

12 For a detailed analysis of the gendered relationship between law and the humanities, see Olson *Legality* 26–30.

Cultural narratives and imaginaries could also be distinguished along their spatial capacity of questioning or maintaining existing power structures. Narratives serve as rather conservative tools, aiming to maintain existing structures and legitimizing past events in a people's history, while imaginaries serve as progressive catalysts, aiming for change. However, this distinction seems to become blurrier when analyzing current constitutional processes. Current perceptions of how the Constitution works and how laws in general (ought to) operate have significantly been transformed during the twenty-first century due to the ongoing politization and polarization of the U.S. legal system. Among others, I claim that a general trust in the legal system, i.e., the narrative that the system is able to fix itself without interference, has been supplemented by a strong belief in one's entitlement to absolution, i.e., the imaginary that one has the right to have their particular *Rechtsgefühl* represented and accounted for in legal norms and the subsequent right to enforce this *Rechtsgefühl* via violence if legal norms fail to acknowledge that right.

Analyses of legal and cultural orders thus have to involve a multitude of constitutional processes, which refer to any operation (or imagined operation) of actors and actresses as well as to any ideals that are linked to or are invoking the Constitution, including but not limited to Supreme Court justices, those claiming their fundamental rights, and the rights themselves. Just as one might perceive of 'constitutional processes' as a muddy term, the affective relation to it is equally blurry because of imagined realities, narratives of individual and institutional legitimization, and felt 'truths.'

Normativity

Suspect Subjects emphasizes non-normativity and deviance over normativity and conformity. From a legal perspective, this focus becomes clear when revisiting the Equal Protection Clause's historical and thus original meaning. Although the first section of the Fourteenth Amendment refers to "any person under the law," the phrase was originally directed at any discriminatory behavior towards formerly enslaved people, of whom most were forcefully migrated from Africa. The Equal Protection Clause's claim to protect anybody was then primarily directed at people of a certain race, i.e., Africans and African-Americans who have been serving as slaves. Consequently, the Equal Protection Clause's legal recognition and protection aims at what is differing from the norm, i.e., what – in the sense of characteristics –, and who – in the sense of members of social groups – is likely to be discriminated against.

It is important to note that the discourses about LGBTQ+ rights evolve around the notion that those outside the normative heterosexual, cisgendered matrix face distinct forms of discrimination and challenges based on their respective identity. This is why they need special forms of protection. However, this view neglects the diversity, multiplicity, and fluidity of personal identities and experiences of discrimination. Even special forms of protection cannot account to this highly individual need, at least not thoroughly. Legal protection for LGBTQ+ individuals may thus need to take a detour through assimilationist perspectives on and legal categorizations of sexual orientations. Yet, for gaining social equity, it is important to bear in mind that rigid identity categories are merely legal fictions which serve the interests of justice and do not represent an objective, historical truth or reality.

I.2. State of Research: Mapping the Field

Culturalist approaches to legal studies have arguably only recently found their way into the study of law. While feminist studies, anthropology, history and critical legal studies have already been analyzing law's mechanisms and implications for decades (Branco and Izzo 48; Olson "Mapping" 245), the so-called 'cultural turn' of critical legal studies only started in the 1980s (Knox and Davies 3–6; Silbey "Legal Culture" 470). Since then, Law and Culture scholarship has come to be known as one of many Law and X projects[13] that continue to shape humanistic interrogations of legal studies.

Approaching law from a cultural studies perspective means acknowledging law's function as upholding and establishing forms of social control and normative orders (Silbey "Legal Culture" 473; Olson and Schillings 2), yet simultaneously de-constructing the underlying cultural assumptions of what and who needs being socially controlled and normatively ordered (Olson and Schillings 2). Researchers in the field have embraced cultural legal studies as an interdisciplinary and transdisciplinary endeavor[14] which goes beyond the strict dis-

13 These projects include, but are not limited to, Law and Literature, Law and Narrative, Law and Economics, Law and Visual Culture, Law and Media Studies.

14 See also Kahn "Freedom" 145–46: "The claims of the doctrinal science of law, however, were thoroughly discredited by the legal realists, who left the law professor looking like a snake oil salesman who had illegitimately worked his way into the university. Legal decisions and legal rules, the legal realists taught us, have to be understood in a social/political context that is not captured by the categories and descriptions of law.

ciplinary confinement of legal studies.[15] Analyzing law as "pluralistic" (Olson "Mapping" 234), i.e., diverse in its forms and functions, means understanding legal processes "to be cultural-political phenomena that need to be comprehended with methods extending beyond those developed in more traditional forms of legal scholarship" (Olson "Mapping" 235).

Scholars such as Rosemary Coombe and Lawrence Rosen call for de-juxtaposing legal studies with cultural studies by questioning the dualistic perception of law and culture and thereby advocating for an understanding of law *as* culture as well as a distinct academic home for the discipline. Claiming that "a cultural studies of law will only emerge as a distinctive field of academic inquiry when scholars stop reifying law and start analyzing it as culture" ("Cultural Studies" 36), Coombe promotes an interdisciplinary endeavor that expands textualist approaches to include analyses of "the social power of forms of legality or their meaning in forms of life that exist anywhere outside of the legal trial or the reported case" ("Cultural Studies" 55). Rosen also stresses these entanglements of law and culture and calls for an understanding of both realms' impact on each other:

> [L]aw is so inextricably entwined in culture that, for all its specialized capabilities, it may, indeed, best be seen not simply as a mechanism for attending to disputes or enforcing decisions, not solely as articulated rules or as evidence of differential power, and not even as the reification of personal values or superordinate beliefs, but as a framework for ordered relationships, and orderliness that is itself dependent on its attachment to all the other realms of its adherents' lives. ... nowhere is law (in this sense of ordered relationships) without its place within a system that gives meaning to its people's lives. (Rosen 6–7)

Law satisfies none of the normative criteria of autonomy: it is not objective, neutral or coherent."

15 See also Kahn "Freedom" 142–43: "Traditionally, the autonomy of the discipline of legal study was located within the doctrinal rules, which were thought to be capable of generating solutions to every actual controversy. The expert – a position claimed by both the judge and the law professor – could remain wholly within the domain of law in order to resolve social conflicts. To reach outside was to commit either the sin of 'result-oriented' jurisprudence or that of 'usurping the legislative role.' Legal practice and legal study formed a seamless whole."

Rosen approaches law as a vital part of culture and influenced by culture's overarching function as meaning-making faculty of ordering human relationships. The concept of culture Rosen follows is reminiscent of the one by Clifford Geertz, who understands culture as "webs of significance he [man; lb] himself has spun" (*Interpretation* 5). Analyzing culture is thus to Geertz "not an experimental science in search of law but an interpretive one in search of meaning" (*Interpretation* 5). By treating the meaning of cultural texts as dependent on the culture they are settled in, Geertz claims that

> the cultural patterns involved are not general but specific-not just "marriage" but a particular set of notions about what men and women are like, how spouses should treat one another, or who should properly marry whom; not just "religion" but belief in the wheel of karma, the observance of a month of fasting, or the practice of cattle sacrifice. (*Interpretation* 52)

The Geertzian cultural relativism is at the heart of Law and Culture scholarship. "[T]his field [cultural legal studies; lb] embraces a social-constructionist framework where the law is seen not simply as applying to a preexisting social world but as actively creating the social world as we experience it" (Coombe "Cultural Studies" 36). The postmodern skepticism towards universal beliefs and the de-construction of essentialism links cultural approaches towards legal studies to other critical inquiries which equally perceive of law as contextual and geographically and temporally specific (Olson and Schillings 4; Kahn "Freedom" 150).

In this sense, law is not merely understood as a constitutive force which shapes culture but as equally constitutive of culture as culture is for law. The most important perspective of Law and Culture scholarship is to perceive of law and culture as entangled, interrelated fields which feed on and influence each other; academic analyses within each field need to look beyond disciplinary boundaries in order to arrive at holistic insights, as many cultural-legal scholars assert to (Legrand "Converging;" Eskridge *Gaylaw*; Rosen; Stone *Constitution*). Indeed, law is not only part of a cultural frame but also simultaneously constituting it. Law itself may be considered "a system of meaning rather than an imposition of force" (Cover "Nomos" 12).

Gender, Identity, and Sexual Orientation in Legal Scholarship

In U.S. American society, the sociocultural sensibilization for conceptualizations of normativity and non-normativity in terms of gender, gender identity, and sexual orientation seems to develop more rapidly than the legal assessment of these categories despite the overregulation of sexuality in U.S. American law.[16] A prominent instance of this claim can be found in the struggle for woman suffrage. While organized forms of women rights struggles can be traced back to as early as 1848's Seneca Falls Convention, it was not until the 18th August 1920 that the Constitution was amended to include "the right of citizens of the United States to vote" (amend. XVIIII, sec. 1) regardless of one's sex.

Similarly, differentiations between sexual orientations have only been introduced as socioculturally meaningful concepts in the late nineteenth century (Katz *Invention* 10; 13) and then emerged into "new regulatory categories [which] affected the evolution of law between 1880 and 1946" (Eskridge *Gaylaw* 18). Another watershed moment is the only recently gained visibility and public awareness during the 1960s and 1970s when the AIDS epidemic forcefully pulled gay men out of the closet (Stone *Constitution* 448). Social movements have thus increased cultural sensibilities before legal recognition (in the form of control or protections) was established.[17]

Given these concepts' respective histories, it is not surprising that the Supreme Court of the United States (SCOTUS) has already classified gender as a quasi-suspect classification,[18] while sexual orientation has largely and, as I argue, strategically been ignored by the Court. Although there have been rulings on discrimination based on sexual orientation,[19] it was not until the beginning of the twenty-first century that the Court adopted a decidedly pro-LGBTQ+ stance; its decisions in *Lawrence v. Texas* (2003) and *United States v. Windsor* (2013) are regarded as leading the way for recognizing same-sex marriages in *Obergefell v. Hodges* (2015), which then facilitated *Bostock v. Clayton County* (2020).

---

16 See Olson "Futures" 52–53 for an analysis of the influence of popular cultural outlets on socio-legal processes and these fictional platforms' ability to convey and negotiate issues in an accessible way.

17 It is equally correct that legal recognition of certain issues has influenced social and cultural developments. This claim is important for understanding why today's progressive legal developments are met with increasing anti-queer backlash, see also Chapter V. For more on this claim in a historical perspective, see Eskridge *Gaylaw* 18.

18 See *Mississippi Univ. v. Hogan* 724–26 (1982); *Craig v. Boren* 197–200 (1976).

19 On the constitutionality of sexual acts between consensual adults of the same sex see *Bowers v. Hardwick*; on the question if a state's constitutional amendment may explicitly bar sexual orientation from legal protection see *Romer v. Evans*.

The academic discourse about sexual orientation's equal protection has mostly been focusing on the case of homosexuality as potential suspect classification (Green; "Constitutional Status"), on intradisciplinary elaborations on the Supreme Court's opinions and the Constitution as such (Yoshino), and on the structural relationship between the Due Process Clause and the Equal Protection Clause (Miller; Sunstein; Rush). These analyses have provided insights into the character of the Equal Protection Clause and the argumentative trends of the Supreme Court justices, yet they have largely ignored sexual orientation's potential suspect classification. Another weakness of this approach is the laser-focus on homosexuality. Only analyzing homosexuality's potential suspect class status (over-)stresses notions of fragility and Otherness of this particular sexual orientation and thereby fixates stereotypes and categorizations (Baer "Chancen und Risiken" 13–15).

Further, these elaborations have not established analytical connections between legal and cultural processes. James Boyd White's seminal work on the discipline of Law and Literature, as well as Peter Häberle's work on constitutions and culture, have shaped and re-vitalized the discourse about the entanglements of jurisprudence and the humanities. Their interdisciplinary approaches were considered rather progressive, even though such considerations have a long academic tradition of thinking about law from a humanities perspective.[20] While jurists have historically proven to be more open to interdisciplinary endeavors (Gephart *Recht* 9; Gephart "Erforschung" 20–22),[21] legal scholarship on suspect classification and equal protection has not yet examined this discourse's cultural and social scope.

Evan Gerstmann's third edition of *Same-Sex Marriage and the Constitution* (2017) opens up the discourse about marriage equality by including social psychological, political, and cultural considerations. However, when touching on sexual orientation's suspect classification, Gerstmann's analysis shies aways

---

20 See, for instance, Jacob Grimm's essays on poetry and law, *Von der Poesie im Recht* (1957 [1816]).

21 Acknowledging that this statement is controversial, I draw from my own experience in the areas of American Studies, Cultural Studies, and Law. Further, legal scholars are more dependent on investigating those realms law touches upon while cultural studies scholars tend to refer to laws less often. Also, Supreme Court opinions and dissents usually pick up on historical, cultural, and social developments and sentiments while Cultural Studies scholars tend to treat law as distinct from other scientific disciplines, particularly their own, see also Steel 88.

from assigning responsibility to the Court and defending its lack of intersectional analysis as simply too complex (65–69).[22] By referring to his prior work in *The Constitutional Underclass* (1999), Gerstmann reiterates his point that suspect classification is "a dead letter" (*Same-Sex* 75) because of the Court's incoherent application of its criteria and the reluctance to include more suspect classifications since the 1970s. Gerstmann advocates for a different approach, one that does not "exacerbate[] the public perception that they are seeking *special* rights rather than equal rights" (*Same-Sex* 75; emphasis in original) and which "show[s] that they were just seeking the same rights that heterosexual couples already had and that they were not seeking any sort of privileged status" (*Same-Sex* 75). This way, he uncritically reiterates his lacking queer theoretical perspective and fails to engage with the heteronormative implications of this suggestions and its consequences for the cultural narratives and imaginaries surrounding LGBTQ+ people. While Gerstmann's analyses can also be read as simply laying out the most successful route to more protections for queers, his views do not seem to question the very legal-cultural foundation on which these analyses stand.

Peter Nicolas' research is arguably the most seminal work currently being done on sexual orientation's suspect classification. Nicolas argues that "a clear, class-based equal protection decision declaring sexual orientation a suspect or quasi-suspect classification" ("Squandered" 138) would circumvent future voting stalemates at the Supreme Court when it comes to cases involving sexual minorities. His analyses provide a historical and procedural overview of the challenges sexual orientation's suspect classification has to face, and clearly outline the judicial consequences its non-recognition has for the LGBTQ+ community. Although Nicolas does not comment on the sociocultural entanglements of sexual minorities' constitutional protection, his work succeeds in framing the issue as not primarily a legal one but most of all an epistemological and conceptual one, which combines questions of social constructionism versus essentialism, and pits biologistic arguments against sociocultural ones (Nicolas *Sexual Orientation*).

22 See also, for instance, Gerstmann *Underclass* 66: "So the difficulty with linking homophobia to sexism is not that the link is false. The problem is that so many other such links exist. ... Is it really stronger than, for example, the link between racism and sexism? Are the courts in any position to make such a judgment? ... Such an approach would turn the Supreme Court into our sociologist-in-chief."

One of the main obstacles of the discourse about sexual orientation's potential suspect classification is not the application of the criteria for suspect classification nor is it the Supreme Court's reluctance to argue the matter, which, again is informed by the illusory claim sexual orientation would not fulfill the criteria. Sexual orientation's suspect classification's biggest issue is that "even the most liberalizing legislation will – inevitably – continue to replicate the orientationist discourses of sexuality which attempt to contain desire within restrictive parameters in the interests of reproducing heteronormativity," as Tamsin Wilton lays out (178).

Wilson's work ties into current research on Queer Legal Theory (QLT). Building on important queer theorists such as Eve Kosofsky Sedgwick's and Michel Foucault's understanding of sex, gender, and sexual orientation, QLT applies these de-constructionist perspectives to the legal realm. Legal Gender Studies, as a teaching and research field which has gained more attention in the German-speaking contexts with the help of scholars like Elisabeth Holzleithner and Susanne Baer, is interested in how gender relations are manifested in and perpetuated by legal systems. Feminist Jurisprudence, which is often used synonymously for Legal Gender Studies, is associated with Legal Gender Studies as both fields aim at reforming legal norms to reach a more equal treatment of all genders, and to draw attention to specific struggles of individuals based on their respective gender, gender or sexual identities, or sex.

While all three disciplines share this goal, QLT differs from its related disciplines in its basic premises and arguably also radicalness. Queer Legal Theory not only examines how existing gender and legal systems legitimate themselves, it also radically questions the foundations upon which our concepts of sexuality and law are built. Queering legal, cultural, and sexual concepts thus means conceiving of them as unstable, fluid, discursively established, and human-made. Disrupting the assumption that these concepts are ahistorical, natural and universal is part of QLT's aim. Just as Queer Theory problematizes heterosexuality as much as it does homosexuality (Wilton 12; Jagose 16), Queer Legal Theory includes questioning both non-normative and normative categories of sexuality, and examining approaches towards the legal system. This emphasis on questioning assumptions, critically deconstructing conditions, and asking about motivations of those who established a certain status quo makes QLT, together with Critical Race Theory or Critical Legal Theory, a significant tool for navigating jurisprudence and for questioning legal norms and those establishing them (Baer *Rechtssoziologie* 12).

Following a postmodern, anti-essentialist approach, QLT uses Queer Theory's key aspects, i.e., "its skepticism toward universalist theory, foundationalism, and stability; its emphasis on embedded cultural ideas and local narratives; and its recognition of the legitimacy of multiple identities" (Kepros 282), to analyze the connections between social, legal, and cultural biases which are reflected in and reproduced by legal norms.

Law professor Francisco Valdes problematizes the muddied application of distinct concepts relating to sexuality. This imprecise understanding feeds into processes of knowledge production and socio-legal treatment, and vice versa. Conflation, "the historic and contemporary confusion and distortion of sex, gender, and sexual orientation as social and legal constructs" (qtd. in Kepros 3) is for Valdes the key issue in societal treatment of sexuality, which typically manifests in three "legs:"

> The first leg conflates sex and gender such that every person's sex is also his or her gender. The second leg conflates gender and sexual orientation so notions of masculinity and femininity become coalesced into models of sexual orientation (e.g., society recognizes "sissies" and "tomboys" as evolving into "fags" and "dykes"). The third leg conflates sex and sexual orientation such that society concludes an individual's participation in a same-sex couple means he or she has a "homosexual" orientation. (qtd. in Kepros 294)

To Valdes, QLT can and should be used as a tool to acknowledge and address these conflations because it is able to "introduce[] Queer cultural consciousness into jurisprudence—which has not yet recognized meaningful legal identities for sexual minorities" (294). Stressing the contextuality and doubting the universality of cultural notions of sexuality and legal norms relating to it, queer legal theorists problematize the processes of legal categorization and how meaning is already inscribed in or prior to this process.

In addition to Valdes, social psychologist Gregory M. Herek's research emphasizes that sexual orientation is perceived differently than gender, race, or sex. To Herek, bias against non-heterosexual persons should be referred to as "sexual prejudice," reminding of the importance of linguistic precision for conceptual differentiation:

> The term homophobia has gained widespread usage since 1972, even as its limitations have become increasingly apparent. Chief among these is its construction of prejudice as an individual pathology. … [T]his clinically de-

> rived perspective limits our ability to understand hostility toward sexual minorities, both among individuals and in society at large. I have argued instead for the value of framing heterosexuals' negative responses to sexual minorities in terms of *sexual prejudice* and of conceptualizing sexual prejudice as the internalization of societal stigma … . (65; emphasis in original)

Herek claims that structural inequalities bear societal stigma which then affects the individual and their prejudice. The pervasive visibility and normativization of heterosexuality in cultural realms such as law and medicine "embedd[s] sexual stigma in society's institutions … [to] ensure that sexual minority individuals have less power than heterosexuals" (67). This is why reducing sexual prejudice also needs to involve cultural transformations and changes in structural stigma (88), emphasizing the need to include cultural considerations in the study and analysis of law.

Herek's work provides a social psychological foundation for arguing that sexual orientation discrimination differs from sex discrimination because of the particular ways cultural and societal stigma intersect with individual prejudices. Sexual minority individuals face specific forms of discrimination, which are influenced by gender norms (Herek and McLemore 321), which are not identical to gender prejudice. This view is important for deconstructing legal arguments which conflate sex and sexual orientation. As seen in the decision *Bostock v. Clayton County* (2020), arguments that sex discrimination is sexual orientation discrimination-on-route have gained momentum in recent legal scholarship and judicial decision-making.

Acting as custodian of the Constitution and thus as one pillar of U.S. American moral authority, the Supreme Court interprets and translates the intention(s) of its framers for twenty-first century U.S. American society.[23] This adaptation to contemporary conditions enables the Court's justices to use their own understanding of the Constitution's words, public opinion, and morality to shape the legal and sociocultural landscape. This power is also mirrored in the increasing politicization of the Court's personnel decisions. By blocking or enabling nominations of justices, both the Republican Party and the Democratic Party aim to affect legislation and politics for decades, thereby (trans-)forming the United States' national self-image and social hierarchies according to their ideological principles.

23 For the distinction between textualism, intentionalism, and the degree of interpretation of the Constitution by textualists, see Hiebaum 156–59 and Chapter III.

The relationship between law's authority and cultural identity, especially with regard to a national self-understanding, stresses the importance of an inter- and transdisciplinary analysis of law's pluralistic character.[24] Examining law's role as enforcer of social norms, its ability to (de-)establish forms of social inclusion and cultural acceptance is not only linked to rational considerations but also to feelings of justice (or lack thereof). Thus, an interdisciplinary and intersectional analysis of sexual orientation as one marker of social group membership needs to evolve around questions of political, moral, cultural, and societal hegemonies which serve as gatekeepers for this group's suspect classification and sociocultural acceptance.

The Equal Protection Clause's practice of considering individuals only in terms of their social group membership approaches identity as a unidimensional construct and complicates the case for sexual orientation. The conceptual and terminological closeness of gender, gender identity, sex, sexual conduct, sexual preference, and sexual identity complicates sexual orientation's legal situation, and may be cited as one of the reasons why the Court is reluctant to regard it as a suspect classification.[25] However, as the very idea behind suspect classification involves the application of strict scrutiny in cases where discrimination against a suspect class is given, laws which serve a compelling governmental interest can still be enacted. Consequently, claims that sexual orientation's suspect class status might serve as gateway for preferences including non-consent or otherwise legally questionable behaviors, or as the beginning of softening the Equal Protection Clause's impact by including too many groups, appear to be merely politically motivated instead of legally valid.

Simultaneously, suspect classification functions as site where ideologies of (in)equalities are being negotiated and cultural identities are being constituted or maintained. This connection between the Constitution and culture stresses the notion of the Constitution as culture. By analyzing how and why the Equal

24 See Olson's definition of the term: "The term pluralities keys into the call for a transdisciplinary approach to law, legal processes, and legality that understands them to be cultural-political phenomena that need to be comprehended with methods extending beyond those developed in more traditional forms of legal scholarship" ("Mapping" 235–7).

25 There are political reasons for not including all of these categories: Fearing a disruption of the Constitution's impact and reputation, the Court's reluctance to include more suspect classes corresponds to a "pluralism anxiety" (Yoshino 747), reflecting U.S. America's struggle to maintain a coherent national identity while remaining socially and ethnically diverse.

Protection Clause protects minorities, and how and why the four criteria of suspect classification have been established by the Court, one is able to draw conclusions about the cultural self-understanding of the U.S. and how this self-understanding has been manifested in the Clause and is constantly being adjusted in the judiciary's decisions. Moreover, these analytical connections are modes of critique of the way the Supreme Court has approached the possible bond between suspect classification and sexual orientation so far, and the way the Court upholds sociocultural hierarchies by continuing to do so.

I.3. From Cultural Studies of Law to a Queer Legal Hermeneutics

As a conceptual frame, I work with an interpretive concept of culture as developed by Clifford Geertz, yet acknowledge the Eurocentric and colonial legacy of modern conceptualizations of 'culture.'[26] This concept of culture self-identifies as sociological in that it follows Schaefer's understanding that the term 'culture' "does not refer solely to the fine arts and refined intellectual taste" (53) but involves "the totality of learned, socially transmitted customs, knowledge, material objects, and behavior," including "the ideas, values, and artifacts ... of groups of people" (53).

However, the underlying implications of what a 'culture' constitutes, already visible in Schaefer's distinction towards 'fine arts' and 'intellectual,' still permeate Western colonial and racist understandings of what is "cultured" or "primitive." Thus, acknowledging and actively writing against notions of culture that devalue and silence non-Western, non-normative, and non-White people, customs, ideas, and values is important for critical inquiries into law. This is even more true when considering that even allegedly scientifically neutral conceptualizations of terms such as culture may lead to hierarchizing distinctions based on class, race, gender, sexuality, or other.

My concept of culture, based on and expressed through signs, is not meant to be a normative one but rather self-referential, taking into account those cultural imaginaries and narratives found in official cultural-legal documents

26 Rosemary J. Coombe succinctly traces the genealogies of Western understandings and constructions of law and culture: "Culture derives its modern meaning in processes of colonization, even in its meaning as the tilling of soil, which emphasizes the physicality of territory to be occupied, cultivated, and possessed to the exclusion of tribal others" ("Cultural Studies" 23).

such as the Constitution, the Declaration of Independence, and court opinions. The primary sources used here are the U.S. Constitution, especially the Fourteenth Amendment, and, since the American legal system is based on case law, Supreme Court decisions which have interpreted and thus shaped the Equal Protection Clause of the Fourteenth Amendment. These decisions are being understood as legal documents and cultural texts in the Geertzian tradition.

Additionally, other cultural texts such as popular cultural depictions of the workings of law, and culture as a text in itself, reinforce, challenge and (trans)form these imaginaries and narratives. These imaginaries and narratives continue to be used as umbrellas for affectively experienced forms of belonging to the U.S. This approach to culture, being "in search of meaning" (Geertz *Interpretation* 5), does thus not aim at excluding pluralist considerations nor negate the existence of various cultures of legality within a society (Olson "Mapping" 247–8); it rather claims that there is an overarching, discursively dominant culture within the U.S. based on historically valid cultural narratives. On a codified, formal level, this constant negotiation of cultural values and legal regulations manifests itself in judicial opinions, state law, and constitutional amendments, which shape the cultural narratives and imaginaries they are situated in. One has to understand these legal-cultural frameworks in order to bring about social, cultural, and legal change.

This book employs queering, wide reading, and critical legal reading as its poststructuralist, qualitative-analytical methodology. Following Wolfgang Hallet's understanding of wide reading (294), I take the legal texts this book engages with as only analyz-able in connection with cultural discourses about equality and LGBTQ+ issues as well as political developments concerning U.S. party politics and the Supreme Court.

By conducting a qualitative analysis of the most relevant Supreme Court cases dealing with sexual orientation in the twenty-first century, I examine how sexual minorities are constituted by the Court. This method of analyzing cultural texts which deal with the legal protection of queers serves to uncover, question, and deconstruct cultural conceptualizations of sexuality and its legal treatment, and aims to establish a queer hermeneutics of the law.

A discipline-specific form of close reading, critical legal reading constitutes in "itself a form of legal reasoning," which "is a constituent and fundamental aspect of critical legal thinking" (Steel et al. 190). To understand the reading of law as closely connected to its interpretation mirrors the hermeneutic similarities between this discipline and literary studies. Close reading and critical legal reading therefore both evolve out of different strands of critical theory, New Criticism and New Legal Criticism (West 144). While close reading is perceived rather as a tool, critical legal reading also encompasses specific understandings of law and its critique, making it more of an approach. Fajans and Falk add to this interpretation by stating that "to read judicial opinions closely and critically is to talk back to power" (165), reinforcing Robert Cover's notion that "[l]egal interpretation takes place in a field of pain and death" ("Violence" 1601).

Critical legal reading and reasoning, in the tradition of the Critical Legal Studies movement, is fueled by critiques of power rather than morality (West 148),[27] whereas New Legal Criticism considers moral principles drawn from law itself (West 147). I wish to pick up on these notions from the Critical Legal Studies movement and New Legal Criticism and add a queer theoretical perspective. Considering that "law could and should be unmasked, deconstructed, and criticized, not because it falls short of a moral ideal, but rather because it embodies, legitimates, renders invisible, or promotes various forms of social, economic, or legal power" (West 148), Queer Theory provides the necessary tools for this endeavor.

Drawing on José Esteban Muñoz' concept of disidentification, queer theoretical analyses of law are "meant to be descriptive of the survival strategies the minority subject practices in order to negotiate a phobic majoritarian public sphere that continuously elides or punishes the existence of subjects who do not conform to the phantasm of normative citizenship" (4). While Muñoz is explicitly interested in forms of belonging, the analyses here emphasize queer survivalist notions of legal personhood. Following Fatima El-Tayeb's work on queering ethnicity in her seminal book *European Others*,[28] I consider queer-

27 This perspective excludes of course considerations of morality as a tool for maintaining or establishing power relations such as in the form of Christian or generally religious forms of exercising force via moral or religious norms (see Foucault "Subject" 782).

28 See El-Tayeb on the survival strategies of European minority communities: "Circumventing the structures that exclude them, these preliminary collectives use new media and popular culture in order to radically rewrite European history through a queer practice, a revised definition of political agency as well as national identification, and a reassessment of the relationship between community, space, and identity in a post-ethnic and translocal context. This process of alternative community building might best be defined as the queering of ethnicity, that is, as a movement in which '[i]dentity, too, becomes a noun of process' (Gilroy 2000, 252)" (xxx).

ing as a positioning beyond, apart, contrary to, or in opposition of the dominant norm, both with regard to identity categories of sexuality and sociocultural, legal, and political practices. Queering then indicates a dynamic process of resisting one's unchallenged normative surroundings and a reassessment of law's structurally heterosexist configurations of the queer subject. Carl F. Stychin also acknowledges the entanglements of Queer Theory and legal analyses when he states that "[i]n providing a critique of categorical thinking in general, and by denaturalizing the meaning which has been discursively invested in categories, queer theory has obvious applications to law" (148). It is especially Chapter IV which will pick up on Stychin's claim and offer a queer perspective to contemporary legal categories and meaning-making.

The methodological access to critically reflecting on the concepts of both sexual orientation and suspect classification is transdisciplinary, interdisciplinary, intersectional, and, in the legal realm of constitutional interpretation, intradisciplinary. By adding an inter- and transdisciplinary perspective to the issue of sexual orientation's constitutional protection, it becomes possible to link the logic of constitutional anti-discrimination laws to the shifting sociocultural imaginaries and those who are constructing them.

Against a Disciplinary Confinement

The connection between Queer Theory and cultural studies of law shows how the discourse about equal protection of sexual minorities needs to be situated at the intersection of Cultural Studies, American Studies, abolitionist studies and Queer Theory and (Critical) Legal Studies in the form of Queer Legal Theory. The interdisciplinary bond of American Studies' methodological unorthodoxy, Queer Legal Theory's disrupting qualities, and Legal Studies' rather dogmatic theoretical frame may be off-setting to the purely culturalist, queer theoretical or jurist reader. Yet, these disciplines enrich each other by providing analytical sharpness with sociocultural contextualization and denaturalizing, critical inquiries.

The focus on Queer Studies and Theory instead of Gender Studies is linked to the need of constantly questioning the normative and thus aiming to circumvent categorizations both on a legal level and in terms of sexuality. As employed here, Queer Theory is committed to resisting categorizing, and especially binarizing, people according to their sexual and/or gender identity, sexual preferences, or gender performance. This approach wants to address the realities of lesbian, gay, trans, inter, women, men, agender people but also speak to those in-between, everyone queer, everyone*. In this sense, binary conceptualizations are rejected in favor of a pluralized and fluid understanding of sexuality following queer critics such as Eve Kosofsky Sedgwick, Annamaria Jagose, or Tamsin Wilton.

Further, this inquiry into sexual orientation from a cultural-legal perspective examines normative sexual orientations and gender identities by arguing for a protection of non-normative ones. Queer Theory is about queering processes of knowledge production, categories, and ways of thinking, making it highly relevant for legal analysis. It is a way of engaging with the material rather than a disciplinary container or place of discourse. Eluding a definite description in this context corresponds to Kepros's assessment: "'Queer' escapes definition because its meaning expands with every individual assertion of Queerness" (282). Even more, "[t]o attempt an overview of queer theory and to identify it as a significant school of thought, which those in pursuit of general knowledge should be familiar with, is to risk domesticating it, and fixing it in ways that queer theory resists fixing itself" (Jagose 2). This post-structural, deconstructionist approach corresponds to Coombe' understanding that "[d]econstruction is a means of making visible those others who are invisible in legal discourse and the dominant narratives it reproduces" ("Cultural Studies" 52).

Cultural Studies of Law

Research on the frictions of law and culture has various names and even more varieties of methodological access. While some refer to the 'Cultural Studies of Law'/'Cultural Study of Law' (Coombe; Knox and Davies), 'Law as Culture' (Rosen) or 'Cultural Legal Studies' (Sharp and Leiboff), others prefer to speak of 'Law and Culture,' mirroring this scholarship's embeddedness in a web of manifold 'Law and Xs.'[29] The methodological access to each of these fields is connected to its main analytical concerns. Popular cultural approaches to law are more likely to use Media Studies' tools and methods and to analyze television shows or films (Olson *Legality*), while anthropologists would rather use methods such as ethnographies (Sharp and Leiboff), or employ comparative methods to analyze different 'legal cultures' (Häberle *Verfassungsstaat*; Häberle *Feiertagsgarantien*; Häberle *Verfassungslehre*; Blankenburg).

The understanding of law and culture here follows a Geertzian, Hartian approach which considers law to be a social construction (Hart xvii) and a cultural

29 Other dominant fields of research in this area are, among others, Law and Literature, Law and the Humanities, Law and Visual Culture, and Law and Society.

sign (Geertz *Interpretation* 21; 118). Law in this understanding may constitute a distinct system with specific dogmatic rules, symbols, and methods, yet it is a cultural product which can be read, interpreted, analyzed, deconstructed and possibly abolished just as literary texts, historic monuments, musical compositions, or religious rituals. Law then constitutes a certain perspective on society and culture while also influencing the society and culture it is embedded in. This ambiguity of cultural-legal entanglements makes the connection(s) between law and culture arguably harder to grasp, but it also illustrates how both realms lend authority and thus validity to each other.

Following Hermann Kantorowicz that the personality of judges matters when interpreting legal norms (Chapter III), the analytical approach here positions itself among the theories of the German Free Law School and Critical Legal Studies which consider law's indeterminacy connected to social, political, and, as I argue, cultural conditions. This is in line with a legal positivism of Eugen Ehrlich and H.L.A. Hart in that law is considered to be everything that is posited by people (Hart xix) and influenced as well as influencing sociocultural realities.[30]

Toward a Queer Legal Hermeneutics

As the concept of suspect classification is highly complex, accessing its implications, and understanding them may at times challenge the general reader, who is not familiar with legal language and thinking. The same is true for sexual orientation, whose conceptualization may differ depending on the discipline it is employed in. These heightened difficulties in engaging in the discourse about sexual orientation's potential suspect classification, however, are not considered liabilities but assets. They enable the reader to connect law, here mostly in the form of the judiciary and the Constitution, to their respective areas of expertise, however unrelated to jurisprudence they may seem. This invitation to a transdisciplinary engagement in the material may at times be difficult due to discipline-specific terms, ways of thinking, or knowledge. I try to consider and work with these obstacles.

This approach is in line with James Boyd White's way of accessing the legal landscape by "establish[ing] a way of looking at the law from the outside, a way of comparing it with other forms of literary and intellectual activity, a way of

30 Note, however, that this legal positivism is not corresponding to Hans Kelsen's Pure Theory of Law, which is considered normative legal positivism, see also on this Baer *Rechtssoziologie* 29–31.

defining the legal imagination by comparing it with others" (*Imagination* xx). The Whitean approach of opening up the discourse's access to a legal and non-legal audience also holds true for the non-culturalist readership as it attempts to translate cultural concepts for the non-culturalist reader. The reader's background may therefore influence their access to the legal and sociocultural issues described here, yet it is not meant to exclude them from, but rather to enable an enrichment of, the discourse. White, referring to the generic masculine readership of his own law students, voiced this idea by stating that the reader shall "[feel] free to bring into play anything that he knows or is" (*Imagination* xxi). Opening up the discourse about sexual orientation's constitutional protection not only transdisciplinarily to a wider audience, including legal and non-legal readers, but also to a more liberal, interdisciplinary approach, which is not restricting readers to their knowledge within a discipline, circumvents traditional knowledge hierarchies which value professional training more utilitarian than personal experience.

This hybrid of contributing what one 'knows and is' to a book is also mirrored in the author's access. My way of writing and thinking is decisively academic, and some argue it may even be too law-y at times, yet this book's aim and my personal beliefs are also activistic. Thus, *Suspect Subjects*, which is written in an activist academic tradition, hopes to resonate in those who perceive themselves as academic activists and who are willing and able to use my work for their own academic and/or activist purposes to get in conversation with other queer legal theorists, and to approach me to discuss what I omitted. Growing up and being educated in a German-European environment, I acknowledge and actively attempt to counteract racist, sexist, and otherwise discriminatory ways of thinking this privileged perspective brings with it. As identifying one's own sexism, culturalism, and racism is not always successful, feedback on these parts is highly welcome.

However, as this disclaimer only touches upon a small fraction of where I am coming from as a person, it is not indicative to what I, as the author, am or know. Acknowledging my own socialization in predominantly cis, heterosexual, White, propertied, non-migrant, able-bodied, rather religious contexts, this information is necessarily incomplete without my situatedness in these contexts as a queer person who cannot but refuse a clear-cut cis identity. This attempt at a disclaimer already foreshadows some of the inherent tensions in situating oneself, and the necessarily gap-y and incomplete approaches towards identity discourses while trying to evade inflexible categorizations. Queer theoretical academic activism, in my understanding, may make use of disclaimers like these to enable being held accountable and position oneself, yet it ultimately has to question, refuse, deconstruct or challenge processes of categorization. Since categorizations are key factors for approaching sexual orientation and its eligibility as suspect classification, yet their processes of formation and their meanings are contextual, disciplinary, and not historical, their usefulness and applicability are critically questioned in the upcoming chapters – and for now impossible to engage with without generating stereotypical associations with categories which have not been defined yet.

These social-psychological mechanisms of categorization have been taken up by Feminist Legal Theory and constitute one important issue of anti-discrimination laws. Using a feminist anti-essentialist, intersectional approach, one analytical focus is the interplay between legal protection against discrimination and what Susanne Baer and Ute Sacksofsky call "perpetuated stigmatization"[31] (*Autonomie* 15). According to Baer and Sacksofsky, this aspect of the "ambivalence of legal regulation"[32] (15) examines law's dualistic balancing of protecting minorities while not contributing to the sociocultural transfer of knowledge about their inferiority. In other words, whenever a legal regulation aims to protect someone, it runs the risk of weakening this person by stressing, and drawing attention to, their historically, economically, and/or politically inferior status in a society's hierarchy.

To Baer, Sacksofsky and to other scholars of Legal Gender Studies, Queer Studies, and Gender Studies, the route to legal and sociocultural equality needs to cross the intersections of different people's living conditions and experiences without using the White, able-bodied, heterosexual, cis gendered dominant group's perspective as its basis. Thus, arguing for anti-discrimination protections needs to take into account that the umbrella of non-normative sexual orientations does not cover a homogenous group of people. However, one can observe how a particular queer subject is constituted through law, and how sexual orientation continues to be meaningful as identity, legal, and sociocultural category. As Chapter IV analyzes in more depth, non-normative sexual orientations are constantly constructed against and in opposition to the dominant heterosexual norm.

The categories of race, gender, and class serve as equally important axes of social stratification following Kimberlée Crenshaw's originally legal understanding of intersectionality. To Crenshaw, intersectional analysis is

31 The German original reads: "perpetuierte Stigmatisierung." My translation.

32 The German original reads: "Ambivalenz rechtlicher Regulierung." My translation.

understood as a concept that opposes "a way of thinking about discrimination which structures politics so that struggles are categorized as singular issues" (167). While the origin of intersectionality has been attributed to Crenshaw, who made this theory applicable for academia, the idea of multi-dimensional oppression can already be found in the Combahee River Collective's manifesto from 1977. The radical Black feminist group declared that:

> We believe that sexual politics under patriarchy is as pervasive in Black women's lives as are the politics of class and race. We also often find it difficult to separate race from class from sex oppression because in our lives they are most often experienced simultaneously. We know that there is such a thing as racial-sexual oppression which is neither solely racial nor solely sexual, e.g., the history of rape of Black women by white men as a weapon of political repression. (19)

It is central to acknowledge this development of intersectionality to de-academize the concept and stress its origins in activists' work. Intersectionality is a concept critical of categories that enable and maintain patriarchal, capitalist, male, cis, White, able-bodied, monied, heterosexual hegemonies, pivotal for legal thinking, and evolving out of both activist and academic discourses. Consequently, using an intersectional queer feminist approach towards analyzing sexual orientation means being aware of how activist and academic work is connected and fuels each other.

Sexual orientation is understood as one factor of social stratification, resulting from and reflecting on different axes of inequalities. For instance, a Black, lesbian woman may experience forms of exclusion and discrimination different from those of a White, gay men although they share a non-normative sexual orientation. Perceiving of inequalities as multifactorial corresponds to the Equal Protection Clause's maxim of treating those individuals similarly who share the same characteristics, i.e., those in similar conditions and circumstances (Tussmann and tenBroek 345). In order to establish these similarities, the multi-level entanglements of social group membership(s), e.g., sexual orientation, class, race, gender, dis/ability, and education, have to be examined interdisciplinary.

Theories and concepts in terms of sexual orientation from sociology, Critical Legal Studies, social psychology, Literary Studies, Cultural Studies, Gender Studies, and American Studies are not merely overlapping; they complement each other. This interdisciplinary and intersectional queer feminist approach to sexual orientation's relation to legal recognition aims at making visible and understanding underlying sociocultural hierarchies and the simultaneities of power relations on different levels in twenty-first century U.S. American society by taking sexual orientation's legal situation as a starting point for re-negotiating its potential for sociocultural change.

Since intersectionality aims at making visible and understanding underlying social hierarchies, the simultaneities of power relations on a social, political, and legal level in the context of sexual orientation require the examination of the following questions: In what instances does U.S. American society need to police sexuality, and what are the benefits and respective limitations for this intervention in the citizen's private sphere? How does legally regulating sexual behaviors socially influence the individual and their preferences? What are the objectives and political motives of denying or respectively granting sexual orientation suspect class status? The following chapters approach these questions and move from a cultural studies of law towards establishing a queer hermeneutics of law, a distinct way of looking at law using a queer, cultural-legal perspective.

II. Narrativized, Constituted, Imagined

II.1 The Constitution's Equal Protection Clause, Suspect Classification, and Cultural Narratives

As a sub-discipline of the larger project of Law and the Humanities, Law and Culture constitutes a both underrepresented and contested research area. While legal scholars such as Peter Häberle have had a significant influence on the field, their work is rarely picked up by cultural scholars, leaving Law and Culture dominated, and admittedly more appreciated, by jurists. Their research acknowledges a connection between legal and cultural developments and phenomena cultural scholars are yet to admit.[1] Häberle's work on constitutional culture(s) highlights how collective legal identities are formed through cultural heritage ("Verfassungskultur" 3) and stresses the need for a culture-specific constitutional interpretation (4). Such analyses remain incomplete without acknowledging the force of cultural narratives fundamental to constitutional story-telling.

At a time that is marked by an increasing importance of interdisciplinary research and a simultaneous need for scholars to demarcate their distinct research fields, Law and Culture appears to threaten those who feel intimidated by the quasi-imperialistic implications of law's masculinist force.[2] This academic neglect of Law and Culture's influence and significance for both Legal and Cultural Studies thus seems to implicitly respond to the gendering of this

1 With a few important exceptions as indicated by the work of, for instance, Clifford Geertz, Rosemary Coombe, Werner Gephart, or Robert Weisberg as laid out in Chapter I.

2 Note in this context also how legal scholar Susannah W. Pollvogt addresses equal protection jurisprudence as an "aging patriarch, exerting a level of control that far exceeds its actual efficacy" (739).

interdiscipline's parties. Law, being perceived as the more rational, clear, instrumental, objective and thus masculine part, leads the field's direction while culture, being perceived as the more emotional, fluid, erratic, subjective and thus female part, is the one that is dominated. This gendering of academic disciplines has been widely commented on (MacKinnon "Feminism;" Siegrist and Sugarman; MacKinnon *Women's Lives*; Olson "Turgid;" Olson "Futures").[3]

Analogous to false and essentializing assumptions about inherent gender differences, this framing does not do justice to lived reality's diversity in which law is also an emotional, affective endeavor far from being always rational and clear (Olson "Futures;" Gephart *Recht*; Olson *Legality*). As legal philosopher Leslie Green puts it, "[l]aw pretends to an objectivity it does not have" (Hart xv). Interestingly, this perception of law's masculine force is also mirrored in Marxist critiques which assign law the role of a repressive device in conservatives' toolbox, too unfeeling and violent to treat culture right (MacKinnon "Feminism"). These tensions result in Law and Culture's need to address the following questions: How can an academic field which consists of such seemingly antagonistic systems work? Why is the connection, if there is any at all, between legal and cultural phenomena relevant?

This highly problematic understanding of a presumed antagonism, based on an implicit gendering of academic fields, picks up on oversimplifying and sexist notions of inherent and binary (gender) characteristics while leaving cultural analyses of law in a position which needs legitimation and explanation. The following chapter offers alternatives to this view by illustrating how the U.S. Constitution and culture have been transforming and evolving in connection with each other. The following subchapters comment on and incorporate these two realms by seeing them as equally constitutive of each other, and thus serve to deconstruct the static matrix of opposing academic fields – again in a queer theoretical tradition of challenging binaries.

This chapter's starting point is that the Constitution is not only a legal document but also, maybe even more so, a cultural artefact. Reading the Constitution as such, it is possible to grasp the contemporary dividedness of the United States. At the time of this writing, political parties and their supporters are said

3 One may argue that this hierarchical imbalance in power is also unconsciously mirrored by the academic world's choice to refer to this field and related ones predominantly as Law and Culture, Law and Literature, Law and X, instead of Culture and Law, Literature and Law, X and Law.

to be more divided than ever over domestic issues, identity politics, and matters of racism, sexism and other forms of discrimination based on social group membership. The entanglements of law, culture, and legal affect are particularly salient when it comes to the Constitution and the rights it confers (or fails to confer) to its citizens. It is therefore necessary to unmask exactly those cultural mechanisms and imaginaries at work in twenty-first century U.S. American society which add meaning to Supreme Court decisions. Only by reading these legal texts next to culture, culture as text in this sense, are those who are affected by legal decisions fully able to grasp these cases' implications for an individual's everyday life, their fundamental rights, and their ability to speak back to the document which grants those rights – the Constitution –, and to those in charge of interpreting it – the Supreme Court's justices.

Culture and law, here in the form of spoken, or judiciary, law, are thus mutually constitutive and intertextually connected.[4] They reflect on each other and initiate changes via the individual who is willing and able to test their cultural realities against legal imaginaries, and their legal realities against cultural imaginaries.

The Fundamentality of Rights

Turning to the Constitution and the rights it provides can be observed regardless of one's party affiliation. This pervasive demand of rights, which are inscribed in the Constitution as a legal document, meets an understanding of a cultural-specific taken-for-granted-ness of access to these, which mirrors the cultural dimension of the Constitution. The idea of 'unalienable' rights can be traced back to the early constitutional beginnings of the United States and is

4 The concept of intertextuality in this context refers to idea that culture and law cannot exist without each other, i.e., that each legal decision is informed by, and reflects on, cultural transformations and vice versa. Intertextuality in law also includes referring back to precedents for decision-making and for adding legitimacy to decisions; see Steel 88; Holzleithner and Mayer-Schönberger. However, legal practices of commenting on, quoting, and using both literary and academic texts to clothe or legitimatize arguments mirrors another aspect of intertextuality in legal discourse; see Gadbin-George; see also WWU Münster's Collaborative Research Centre 1385's work, and particularly the project by Petersen, Korten, Steigler, Wittmann, on why courts quote. See also any given Supreme Court opinion for further instances of overlaps of the literary and the legal, for example *US v. Virginia* 556, in which Justice Ginsburg quotes from *The Dialogues of Plato*.

found in the works by James Madison,[5] John Locke,[6] George Bancroft,[7] and the Constitution itself. Regarding "these truths to be self-evident, that all men are created equal, that they are endowed by their Creator with certain unalienable Rights, that among these are Life, Liberty and the pursuit of Happiness" (preamble), the Constitution codifies the notion that there are rights which are so fundamental to being human, independent of the society one lives in, that they cannot justly be taken away from someone. Just as much as equality is part of the U.S. American cultural narrative, the notion of access to justice is also mirrored in this concept of 'unalienability,' dominant founding myths and constitutional history.

By conceiving of this document as something that protects individuals regardless of their race, class, gender, sex, or other social markers of identity, the Constitution becomes larger than politics or the law; it evolves into a representation of a collective identity based solely on an affectively experienced belonging to U.S. America and thus a manifestation of the cultural narratives, which are most dominantly established in the Constitution's preamble.

These cultural narratives and the imaginaries surrounding the U.S. legal system, as this chapter argues, are attempts at establishing a collective self-understanding. They act as a cultural glue, which aims to unite the states over political and federal borders, rendering the U.S. Constitution as an important part *of* U.S. American culture instead of a merely singled out instance of self-expression found *within* this culture. This understanding of the realms of law and culture is vital for any further investigation as it undermines the idea that both spheres are in competition or opposition to each other. If, for instance, one perceives of law as a corrective of culture, or of culture as giving directions to law, one cannot but fail to grasp the multidirectional entanglements between these two as stated by Lawrence Rosen:

> When we hear a court speak "the conscience of the community," "the reasonable man," or "the clear meaning of the statute," when we watch judges grapple with parenthood as a natural or functional phenomenon, or listen

5 See on this James Madison's 1835 *Essay on Sovereignty*, in which he reiterates John Locke's argument that there are 'unalienable' rights.

6 See John Locke's *Two Treaties*.

7 See George Bancroft's 1834 *History of the United States*. Interestingly, Bancroft's 10-volume set can also itself be seen as an instance of Law and Literature as Bancroft, a historian and poet, traces back his rather subjective account of the United States' history by comparison with literary tradition of Goethe and Schiller, among others.

> to counsel debate whether surrogate motherhood or a frozen embryo should be thought of in terms of "ownership," we know that the meaning of these concepts will come not just from the experience of legal officials or some inner propulsion of the law but from those broader assumptions, reinforced across numerous domains, that characterize the culture of which law is a part. And when we seek law outside of specialized institutions – when a kinsman mediates a dispute or members of a settlement use gossip or an informal gathering to articulate their vision of society – the terms by which they grasp their relationships and order them will necessarily be suffused by their implications in many interconnected domains. (6–7)

To understand law as linked to other cultural domains, and culture as informed by a variety of domains of which law is one means also to question whether it is useful to approach each domain's impact on the other in a monodirectional manner. For instance, asking "How did the Supreme Court decision X influence people's perception of Y?" presupposes a constitutive power of an institution which appears to stand above sociocultural forces, with the ability to change sociocultural perceptions. In other words, the Court cannot decide something its justices cannot think as the perspectives of each legal cultures' members, including judges and justices, on equal legal treatments are informed by what their surrounding cultural contexts deem worthy of protection or punishment. This view acknowledges the sociocultural situatedness of members of the judicial branch and their necessarily limited positionality.

The justices who make up 'the Court' are socialized in the culture in which they decide legal cases that are feeding back into this culture. Consequently, to think of law as a-cultural would ignore the human role in establishing it, and contributing to a reification of 'the Law,' thus rendering it more powerful and morally superior than other human-made cultural achievements or domains. One therefore needs to acknowledge that Supreme Court decisions are influenced by other, non-legal demands for social and cultural change such as civil rights movements, popular cultural depictions, and (dominant) sociocultural discourses in general as well as justices' (affective) relationship to them in particular.

Only by cracking open these invisibilized connections between law and culture are we able to see that the "inevitable dialectic" (Wodak et al. 3) of equal protection and discrimination/punishment is intertwined with negotiations of normative and non-normative behaviors on a sociocultural level.[8] To approach these aims and to conduct a queer, cultural analysis of law, Supreme Court decisions and justices' stance on constitutional interpretation need to be analyzed with regard to their ability to impact cultural narratives and by extension collective legal-cultural identities ("How does Supreme Court decision X challenge or substantiate cultural narratives of X? How does decision X influence current collective legal-cultural identities?").

Narrated Identities

Work on constitutions and their cultural impact has evolved around the idea that national identities are constructed and transmitted through narrative elements which stress the unique position of a people at a given historical moment.[9] By referring to Paul Ricoeur's work on 'narrative identity,' Wodak et al. describe how "the narrative configuration [of a nation's and individual's identity; lb] has to mediate between concordance and discordance in such a way that the story can be understood as a whole by its recipients" (14). Being in search of meaning, this process of mediation makes it "possible to arrange and interpret, to rearrange and to reinterpret past events" (14).

National identities are therefore constructed discursively (Wodak et al. 7–10), i.e., via a reciprocal relationship between social practice and the discourse(s) about national identity – what people do and implement with regard to their national identity/ies is interacting with what people discuss and express about their national identity/ies. Narrative elements in the form of stories and myths assist in the process of constructing meaning about nationalities and cultures because these narratives act as cultural glue which sticks historic events, people, and the latter's affective responses to the former together over time. In many post-Enlightenment, Western nations, constitutions pick up or establish these most fundamental cultural narratives, often

8 This understanding of culture's influence on (non-)normativity corresponds to Wodak et al.'s view which "understand[s] 'culture' as a system of rules and principles for 'proper' behaviour, analogous to the grammar of a language, which sets the standards for 'proper' speaking" (20–21). Following this understanding, culture is not approached as an overarching authority which defines what is normative, non-normative or deviant behavior but rather as a system which maintains the "plans, recipes, rules, instructions (what computer engineers call 'programs') for the governing of behaviour" (Geertz qtd. Wodak et al. 21).

9 See on this particularly Peter Häberle, Hans Vorländer and Gert Melville, Benedict Anderson, and Ruth Wodak.

in the form of proclaimed ideals or moral maxims, and combine them with a nation's most fundamental legal principles.

Apart from constitutions' original aim, i.e., to organize and regulate the state they are settled in, the narrative elements, or narremes, found in these documents add an identity-establishing function for the collectives they belong to. Such foundational legal texts thus constitute a common national identity, feelings of belonging in the form of nationalism, and basic legal ground rules for organizing the state. Benedict Anderson traces back nationalism's cultural roots partly to religious communities:

> All the great classical communities conceived of themselves as cosmically central, through the medium of a sacred language linked to a superterrestrial order of power. Accordingly, the stretch of written Latin, Pali, Arabic, or Chinese was, in theory, unlimited. (In fact, the deader the written language – the farther it was from speech – the better: in principle everyone has access to a pure world of signs.) (Anderson 13)

Strongly evocative of American Exceptionalism in the idea of cosmical centrality, Anderson's analysis can be applied analogously to today's U.S. The community of U.S. Americans may today not be imagined qua a homogenous religion, but adhering to the quasi-divine character of American 'civil religion' (Bellah 1967) certainly establishes what Anderson calls "*unselfconscious coherence*" (16; emphasis in original): an affectively experienced belonging to the U.S. and, by extension, to those who are sharing this feeling of belonging. Similar to what Anderson describes with regard to languages as carries of affective belonging, the Constitution also constitutes a system of both legal and cultural signs. Thus, associations with and evocations of the Constitution are highly individual, making its impact and reach temporally and spatially limitless as this sign can be added with (affective) meaning by anyone at any time, regardless of 'actual' knowledge of, for instance, the Bill of Rights, or other legal doctrines established in this document.

In this sense, constitutions act as 'carriers' for the discourse on national identity, and combine both the idea of nations as "imagined political communities" (Anderson 6) and "systems of representations" (Hall 17). Scholars such as Richard Posner, James Boyd White, and Hans Vorländer and Gert Melville have predominantly focused on preambles as texts which introduce constitutions and provide an ideological framework for a collective's shared identity. As these textual frames are set apart from the legal-political technicalities they introduce, its authors are more likely to give explanations about why they believe that what follows is in line with a larger ideological and cultural belief system. This way, constitutions do not only establish a legal order but they also construct a cultural authority which affectively and ideologically binds a collective to the established legal norms. This authority adds validity to what constitutions say across time.

Constitutions' Geltung

As constitutions need to be negotiated against what has been, the old system, and what is going to be, the new system, Hans Vorländer identifies *Geltung* (validity) as a distinct element which serves as legitimization for the quasi-eternal character of constitutional systems (Melville and Vorländer xv).[10] *Geltung* adds meaning to a people's (supposedly uniform and uncontested version of) history and processes of self-governing, links contradicting belief systems, and is thus able to claim absolute authority over a historical moment of state-formation. *Geltung* is in part being established through narratives which aim at conserving and constituting meaning, yet it is not exclusively bound to preambles as the U.S. American case shows. The Constitution's preamble reads:

> We the People of the United States, in Order to form a more perfect Union, establish Justice, insure domestic Tranquility, provide for the common defense, promote the general Welfare, and secure the Blessings of Liberty to ourselves and our Posterity, do ordain and establish this Constitution for the United States of America.

Although the Constitution's preamble comments on the aim of the document, "to form a more perfect Union" and following, and the speaker, i.e., "we the People of the United States," the legal and cultural significance of the document can only be derived by reading it in connection with the claims made in the Declaration of Independence. The Declaration, which is "in fact not an intellectual

---

10 See also Benedict Anderson's assessment of the origin of nations: "If nation-states are widely conceded to be 'new' and 'historical,' the nations to which they give political expression always loom out of an immemorial past, and still more important, glide into a limitless future" (11–12). This connection between adding meaning to what has been and generating meaning for what is going to be is a reoccurring theme in discourses about both nationalism and constitutionalism.

but an inspirational text" (White *Words* 239),[11] strongly relies on the narrative that there is a 'natural' and God-given entitlement to self-government for the U.S. American people,[12] thus legitimizing the need to establish a new constitutional system and "a more perfect Union" as voiced in the Constitution.

In his fascinating analysis of the Declaration of Independence and the U.S. Constitution as agents of establishing collective identities, James Boyd White finds that

> It [the Declaration of Independence; lb] creates in its ideal reader a resolve based on a sense of common identity, on the justice of the cause, and on necessity, and it does this enormously well. ... Its effects are repetitive and cumulative; the reader is moved not once and for all but again and again into the state of feeling it defines. (*Words* 239)

White illustrates that the Declaration's references to ideals such as equality serve to "work a change of feeling in the reader," (239) namely to strengthen the affective belonging to the newly established nation. This affective framing of an aspired history, one that is based on equal opportunity for everyone, aims to build a common identity. This collective 'we' is then constituted through the U.S. Constitution, which "does purport to speak in a single voice for the people as a whole" (240).

White's analysis shows the importance of affects for the development of legal and cultural entities and stresses how these foundational texts are "lifeless and inert unless ... put to work in the world by the citizens who live under [them]" (247). This invocation of the Constitution and re-assessment of its intentions are the basis for constitutional interpretation. The Supreme Court is

---

11 Although it may be argued that the Declaration *de ipso* also had a semi-legal character based on declaring political independence and thus establishing a new political and legal order, the *de facto* legal significance of this document is not given. One may regard the Declaration rather as political document which necessitated legal consequences.

12 See the Declaration of Independence: "When in the Course of human events, it becomes necessary for one people to dissolve the political bands which have connected them with another, and to assume among the powers of the earth, the separate and equal station to which the Laws of Nature and of Nature's God entitle them, a decent respect to the opinions of mankind requires that they should declare the causes which impel them to the separation."

tasked with evaluating what the Constitution says about legal questions presented to the justices, and it needs to take into account the cultural narratives inherent to this document.

The Declaration of Independence provides the narrative framework for establishing a common identity based on an affectively felt legitimacy to become politically independent. By referring to the "destructive"[13] and abusive character of the old system, namely being governed under England's rule, the struggle for political independence is legitimized as a just cause, rendering those fighting for it heroic. Their struggles are informed by a common goal, which unites them in their pursuit of achieving those "truths [found; lb] to be self-evident." In this sense, the Declaration of Independence defines those ideals the newly formed union seeks to achieve, and establishes the need for setting up the legal instruments to do so.

Geltung is thus not only established through *narratio* but also through *consuetudo*, i.e., actions (praxes) that follow out of these narratives and thus seem to strengthen these narratives' cultural-legal significance (Melville and Vorländer x-xv). James Boyd White refers to this concept of *consuetudo* by stating that "the [U.S. American; lb] Constitution has no force except to the extent that it is invoked and used by individual Americans pursuing actual goals" (*Words* 244). These "actual goals" refer back to the historical need to set up legal rules and procedures for the newly formed United States and can today be found in any constitutional claims made before the Supreme Court. Essentially, Boyd White states that the Constitution is without force if not added with meaning by those turning to it.

Boyd White's understanding of the Constitution as "inert" (*Words* 244), i.e., without force on its own but only becoming dynamic and powerful through its discursively established meaning, corresponds to Clifford Geertz's concept of culture as being "in search of meaning" (*Interpretation* 5), thereby linking legal and cultural spheres. Perceiving of the Constitution as an almost empty sign, which needs to be filled with meaning by the collective it seeks to establish, forces the individual to implicitly, via accepting the narrative framework, and explicitly, via actions, to adhere to the binding force of this cultural-legal document. Over time, constitutional narratives' use may change; the actions speak for themselves and continue to maintain valid, as stated by Vorländer

13 See the Declaration of Independence: "That whenever any Form of Government becomes destructive of these ends, it is the Right of the People to alter or to abolish it, and to institute new Government."

and Melville: "It then may happen that there is no further need for a narrative, and that the validity story ultimately triumphs when being kind of encapsulated in institutional practice" (xv).[14]

The cultural and legal significance of the U.S. American Constitution is therefore established through narrative elements, what Vorländer and Melville termed *narratio*, and also through the praxes of interpreting, invoking, and turning to the Constitution, *consuetudo*. Over time, however, these distinct elements seem to merge together and create a binding force of the document itself. Although not everyone invokes their constitutional rights in a court of law, and although not everyone explicitly knows about the specific narratives anchored in the Constitution, the cultural meaning of this document is discursively established, maintained, and reproduced by representations in popular culture. In this sense, television series, movies, but also newspaper reports and other cultural texts contribute to how one imagines the Constitution and its force – without ever having dealt with it in a legal context. As anthropologist Lawrence Rosen states, "we create our experience, knit together disparate ideas and actions, and in the process fabricate a world of meaning that appears to us as real" (4–5).

Constitutional Narratives

As posited by legal narrative research, constitutions not only operate on a legal level by setting up rules for governing people's behavior (Rosen; Cotterrell), but they also establish communities and coalesce group identities (Anderson; Wodak et al.; Olson "Narration and Narrative"). The way these functions are achieved is through a specific form, namely by using storytelling elements (Olson "Narration and Narrative"; Olson and Copland).

The cultural narratives which inform constitutional documents cannot only be found in preambles. As each part of a constitution refers back to the idea(l) of a common collective identity, its ideological work cannot be separated from and delegated back to a constitution's introductory remarks. The U.S. American Constitution's history of being amended and constantly being (re-)assessed by the Supreme Court illustrates how cultural considerations continue to inform constitutional interpretations and how each Amendment

14 The German original reads: "Dabei kann es vorkommen, dass es gar nicht mehr der Erzählung bedarf und die Geltungsgeschichte ihren ultimativen Triumph erfährt, wenn sie in einer institutionellen Praktik quasi 'eingekapselt' ist." My translation.

discursively comments and picks up on those cultural narratives it grew out of.

The Supreme Court's practice of interpreting the Constitution and mediating between conflicting normative orders of groups corresponds to what Paul Schiff Berman succinctly labels as "jurisgenerative constitutionalism," drawing on Robert Cover's concept of "jurisgenesis" ("Nomos" 11), yet also subverting it. When Berman conceives of law as a negotiator between diverging normative communities, his call for allowing for diverse, even contrasting legal and quasi-legal spheres next to each other (667; 695) adds to Roger Cotterrell's insight that "[l]aw's interpretive communities now reflect the patterned differentiation of the social" (100). Understanding law to be "potentially jurisgenerative and creative" (695), Berman makes a compelling case for legal pluralism, for "seek[ing] dialogue across difference," (695) and for "accept[ing] unassimilated otherness" in order to "have some hope of navigating the hybrid legal spaces that are all around us" (695). However, this view is already a highly privileged one as Berman advocates for enabling "spaces for productive interaction among multiple, overlapping legal systems ... that aim to manage, without eliminating, the legal pluralism we see around us" (669). The legally pluralistic patchwork one observes in the U.S., in which states' regulations of anti-discrimination laws clash harshly with other states' and in some cases also with federal regulations, comes close to Berman's vision of "legal hybridity" (669) but fails to take into account the systemic violence legally pluralistic systems may yield on those social groups which have yet to have their voices and legal claims acknowledged.

In this sense, Berman's jurisgenerative constitutionalism has to be approached from an intersectional perspective, which takes into account the various entanglements of legal, cultural, and social hierarchies and normative orders, mirroring Cover's view that "the creation of legal meaning – 'jurisgenesis' – takes place always through an essentially cultural medium. Although the state is not necessarily the creator of legal meaning, the creative process is collective or social" ("Nomos" 11). Cover, who introduced the idea of jurisgenesis in his seminal "Nomos and Narrative," recognizes the dependence of legal systems and actors on their cultural framework when he states that "[n]o set of legal institutions or prescriptions exists apart from the narratives that locate it and give it meaning" (4).[15] Referring to "narratives," Cover supplies

15 This stance becomes even clearer in Cover's equally seminal "Violence and the Word," in which he clarifies this connection: "In 'Nomos and Narrative,' I also emphasized the

his readers only with a rudimentary definition, namely that narratives are prescriptively moral ("Nomos" 5), established through imposing "normative force upon a state of affairs" ("Nomos" 10), and they can be historic, fictional, tragic, or comedic ("Nomos" 10). It is especially Cover's view on the creation of new texts that is important here:

> Prescriptive texts change their meaning with each new epic we choose to make relevant to them. Every version of the framing of the Constitution creates "new" text in this sense. When the text proves unable to assimilate the meanings of new narratives that are nonetheless of constitutive significance, people do create new texts – they amend the Constitution. Thus, the adoption of the 13th, 14th and 15th amendments may be seen as the creation of new texts to fit new constitutive epics. ("Nomos" 4–5, fn. 4).

I pick up on Cover's understanding of narratives and argue for what he calls "new texts" by advocating for suspect classification instead of an amended Constitution, new laws, or other solutions law offers. This call is reinforced by the Constitution's, and particularly the Fourteenth Amendment's, failed promise of equality (see Chapter II.4). New texts of minority protections are all the more important at a time in which "new constitutive epics" in the U.S. are met with a growingly politicized judicial and adversial political landscape, making the creation of new texts through the political process increasingly difficult. The legal affects and cultural imaginaries surrounding the Constitution supplement and at times substitute "new constitutive epics."

The Fourteenth Amendment's Equal Protection Clause and its embedded suspect classification are thus being approached as sites where this ideological work continues. Although the Amendment's voice differs from the preamble's, the cultural narratives which inform the preamble influence the impact of the Amendment up to this day. Even more, as William N. Eskridge Jr. argues, the Fourteenth Amendment's Equal Protection is based on a similar cultural narrative as the Constitution itself:

> The idea that minorities need protection from tyrannical majorities has been part of America's constitutional tradition from the beginning. Among the general goals of the Constitution of 1789, as immediately amended

world-building character of interpretive commitments in law. However, the thrust of 'Nomos' was that the creation of legal meaning is an essentially cultural activity which takes place (or best takes place) among smallish groups" (1602, fn. 205).

> by the Bill of Rights, was protection of property-owning and religious minorities against oppressive measures sponsored by temporary "factions." ("Political" 2)

Eskridge places the concept of protection from stronger, unjust forces within the set of traditionally U.S. American values. Referencing James Madison, who advertised "break[ing] and control[ing] the violence of faction" ("The Federalist No. 10" 50) as early as 1787,[16] Eskridge's contextualization insinuates that while equality and liberty are probably the American values most readily associated with the Founding Fathers, protection of minority groups has been part of the founding processes as well.[17] Following this argumentation, the question whether to include more minority groups within the list of suspect classifications exceeds the legal realm and continues to be a pivotal consideration with both constitutional and cultural weight.

The aim of this second chapter is to introduce the readership to the constitutional tool of suspect classification, – what it is, how it works, and why any of that matters, – to the intersections of law and culture within this part of the Constitution, – what is at stake here and for whom, – and to the relationship between the Constitution and U.S. American culture, – how these two respond to each other and (have) develop(ed) in relation to each other. In other words, this chapter provides its readers with the necessary legal and cultural terminology and concepts to understand how suspect classification, equal protection, cultural narratives, and constitutional imaginaries interlock.

Suspect Classification as a "New Text"

With the Equal Protection Clause's suspect classification, the Supreme Court has the power to address all of the discriminatory regulations concerning sexual minorities with a single decision based on constitutional law. As Chuck Stewart succinctly points out, "[i]f sexual orientation ever achieves suspect class status with the U.S. Supreme Court, a host of discriminatory laws against lesbians and gay men should fall" (186). Suspect classification is a principle

16 Madison understands a faction to be "a number of citizens, whether amounting to a majority or minority of the whole, who are united and actuated by some common impulse of passion, or interest, adverse to the rights of other citizens, or to the permanent and aggregate interests of the community" ("The Federalist No. 10" 51).

17 From today's standpoint, we also need to acknowledge that the propertied, able-bodied White men responsible for drafting the Constitution were the ones who perceived themselves to be the minorities they wanted to protect from English rule.

derived from the Equal Protection Clause of the Fourteenth Amendment and conferred to those groups which share a trait against which governmental discrimination is perceived as being inherently suspect. This status is determined by looking at generally four criteria (see Chapter II.3). These criteria have been developed through judicial decision-making, which means that they are not codified principles written down in a code of law or to be found in the Constitution itself. Only by looking at a variety of Supreme Court decisions from 1868, the year the Fourteenth Amendment and the Equal Protection Clause were established, until today, can one trace how suspect classification developed and has been interpreted by different courts at different times. What is codified, however, is the Fourteenth Amendment's first section, which is where the Equal Protection Clause is to be found:

> All persons born or naturalized in the United States, and subject to the jurisdiction thereof, are citizens of the United States and of the State wherein they reside. No State shall make or enforce any law which shall abridge the privileges or immunities of citizens of the United States; nor shall any State deprive any person of life, liberty, or property, without due process of law; *nor deny to any person within its jurisdiction the equal protection of the laws.* (U.S. Const. XIV Amendment, sec. 1; emphasis added)

This very last sentence, "nor deny to any person within its jurisdiction the equal protection of the laws," is what is called the Equal Protection Clause, the clause which lays down the constitutional principle that everyone in the U.S. shall, in principle, be equally protected by the law – this applies to both citizens and non-citizens. However, the Constitution, with its exclusionary understanding of the concept of equality, failed from the beginning to fulfill this promise – both culturally and legally. As social recognition of the discrepancies and gaps of the Constitution grew, another differentiation for a higher form of protection was needed for minorities, which was at first the Fourteenth Amendment and, as this was also not sufficient to protect certain social groups, suspect classification.[18] In this sense, suspect classification has always been a "new text" in Robert Cover's sense in that the Fourteenth Amendment proved unable to respond to the new notions of equality after the abolition of slavery. I argue that

18 This development is indicative of the evolution of the U.S. Constitution in general. After having ratified it in 1788, it soon became clear that there were issues not thought of at the time of ratification, leading to amending it in 1791.

it could also be used to fit the new constitutive epic of sexual minority protection.

This principle's wide and forceful impact has been compared to the "constitutional equivalent of the atomic bomb" (Gerstmann *Same-Sex* 75–76) as it leads to the most searching, and thus most severe, judicial review for cases involving these suspect classes and is therefore "'strict' in theory and fatal in fact" (Gunther 8). In effect, suspect classification hands the burden of proof of discriminatory legislation to the states, which must prove that the discrimination serves a compelling state interest, the law is narrowly tailored to serve this interest, and that the law is the least restrictive means for achieving this interest. This means that "the Court presumes the law to be unconstitutional, and the law must be 'legitimated' by the State" (Culverhouse and Lewis 240). Because of these strict requirements, which are elaborated on in more detail in the following subchapters, cases involving suspect classes are most likely to be ruled unconstitutional. Further, once the Supreme Court has established a category's suspect classification, this category's formal protection covers a wide range of areas and its factual protection may be enforced by the president.[19]

Although the Equal Protection Clause's suspect classification primarily applies to federal legislation and not to private businesses, its impact and scope of legal norms in general, and the Equal Protection Clause's suspect classification in particular, reaches beyond the statutory or even legal level, influencing sociocultural developments – with statutory law and sociocultural imaginaries being mutually constitutive of the clause. By establishing sexual orientation's suspect classification, the Court would signal its willingness to support the LGBTQ+ community, and to prevent sexual orientation-related stereotypes, prejudice, and discrimination from further manifesting in society and culture. Thus, suspect classification is not only approached as a constitutional tool but also as a potential catalyst for shifting sociocultural value systems, which then again may manifest in how private businesses treat LGBTQ+ individuals.

19 Probably the most famous instance of enforcement of an equal protection decision has been President Dwight Eisenhower's order to have the U.S. Army oversee the process of desegregation at Little Rock Central High School in 1957 following the Supreme Court's landmark decision *Brown v. Board of Education*.

II.2. The Inequalities of Equal Protection

The first section of the Fourteenth Amendment to the U.S. Constitution was the result of unequal times. Following the American Civil War (1861–1865), which was fought over the moral, economic and political question of slavery,[20] the Thirteenth Amendment, ratified in 1865, abolished slavery on a federal level. However, many Southern states were dissatisfied with this Amendment and began to enact specific legal regulations, so-called Black codes, a development which *Harper's Weekly* editor George William Curtis described back then as proof that "the *spirit* of slavery does [still] exist" (355; emphasis in original). In 1865, Mississippi and South Carolina were the first states which effectively re-introduced slavery and slavery-like conditions for Black people and formerly enslaved persons through such codes. Equality, or at least notions of it, was undermined by state-level backlash to cultural-legal developments.

By ratifying the Fourteenth Amendment as a consequence of these developments, and by putting political pressure on the South via limiting representation in Congress as well as adding military pressure by having the Union Army being deployed in these states, formerly enslaved persons were now granted the same civil and legal rights as free persons. The Amendment guarantees that any person, domestic or foreign, shall enjoy the same legal protections as others in that same jurisdiction. Adopted during the Reconstruction era in 1868, this part of the Constitution, the so-called Equal Protection Clause, was meant to prevent freedmen from being discriminated against and to protect their rights, making race the first category in U.S. American legal history to have warranted special protection.[21] Given the legal and sociocultural history of race in the U.S., the constitutional treatment of this category is vital for the legal discourse about sexual orientation's equal protection and the ambiguity of anti-discrimination politics.

Over the years, the Supreme Court of the United States has interpreted the clause, originally referring to the protection of the formerly enslaved, accord-

20 This view, however, is contested and today there only seems to be agreement among scholars "that slavery was 'somehow' the cause of the war, [but] they argue over just how slavery did so, why the Confederacy lost and slavery ended, and what kind of freedom arose from the ruins" (Rothman 76).

21 See *Slaughter-House Cases* at 38 (1872): "The clause ... was clearly intended to prevent the hostile discrimination against the ... [Black] race so familiar in the States where he had been a slave, and, for this purpose, the clause confers ample power in Congress to secure his rights and his equality before the law."

ing to its wording, namely that "any person" shall be treated equally under the law, which resulted in making equality before the law a fundamental right.[22]

Despite this idealistic constitutional premise, historic instances of discrimination and racial segregation, most notably the so-called 'Jim Crow' laws, complicate today's assessment of what equal protection means and what it wants to achieve both on a legal and a sociocultural level. As the introduction of the Fourteenth Amendment has been followed by laws enforcing racial segregation from the 1870s up until approximately the 1960s, claims about the 'equal' protection of 'any' person apparently do not operate beyond historical, cultural, social, and/or political contexts. Contemporary prejudice factors into any interpretation of the Constitution as does the public, individual and state-level backlash towards such interpretations.

It thus becomes clear that even universalizing human rights claims and generalizing statements such as the Fourteenth Amendment's guarantee of equal protection under the law for any person operate from a specific image of being human and from a specific image of those who appear worthy of rights. The Constitution, but even more so its interpretation by the Supreme Court, both imagine a specific, default rights-holding subject while also actively constituting such a subject by forcing one to submit to the regulations the law prescribes.[23] Historically, this "rights-ability" has excluded, for instance, Black people, people of color, women, indigenous people, people without citizenship, and trans people (Evans; Fredrickson; Fitzgerald; Richardson; Olson and Borchert).

Whenever the Supreme Court deals with a case in which an individual claims a violation of their civil rights by a state or federal government, the main question is: Is the legal text in violation of the Equal Protection Clause ("Equal")? Or, in other words, does the legal text deny to any person within its jurisdiction the enjoyment of a right others are free to exercise? This also means that in order to equally protect someone, the person needs to have a

22 The understanding that equal protection applies to "any person" dates back to the Supreme Court decision *Yick Wo v. Hopkins* in 1886, in which Justice Stanley Matthews stated that "these provisions are universal in their application to all persons within the territorial jurisdiction, without regard to any differences of race, of color, or of nationality, and the equal protection of the laws is a pledge of the protection of equal laws" (369, majority opinion).

23 This claim becomes clearer in Chapter III and IV and their analyses of legal sexual orientationism and the ways the Supreme Court constitutes queer subjects along a heterosexual default.

comparable group which enjoys the rights this person is denied. Otherwise, there would be no unequal treatment because nobody enjoys the right.

For deciding on this, it is important which group of people is affected because different groups enjoy different levels of constitutional protection. So firstly, the Court needs to determine the classification this group shares, e.g., their race, gender, sex or similar ("Equal;" "Equal Protection Violation"). Secondly, depending on the classification, the Court applies different levels of scrutiny, which is the fierceness of reviewing a case. Thirdly, the Court proves whether the legal text passes this review and is thus in line with the constitutional requirements of equal protection ("Equal Protection Violation").

1896: *Plessy v. Ferguson*

The idea behind this differentiation and complex process is that the concept of equality has been applied unequally throughout the U.S.'s cultural-legal history. Among the most unequal Supreme Court decisions by today's standards, and paradoxically the starting point for suspect classification, is undoubtably *Plessy v. Ferguson*, which dealt with the constitutionality of racial segregation in public facilities: In 1896, the Supreme Court had to decide on a Louisiana statute of 1890 which required "railway companies carrying passengers in their coaches in that State, to provide equal, but separate, accommodations for the white and colored races" (163 U.S. 537). The Court found the statute to be constitutional since it treated all races identically and consequently discriminated neither. While the Declaration of Independence states that "all men are created equal," such discriminatory Jim Crow laws were based on an unequal understanding of equality, in this case that separated public facilities for Whites and non-Whites are constitutional as long as they were equal.

Decisions like *Plessy* have historically been used to undermine the very idea of equality by establishing equal conditions only on the surface while simultaneously enabling covert forms of discrimination. This perspective on what 'equality' means in the U.S. context stands in stark contrast to what cultural narratives about the U.S. want one to readily associate, namely a free, democratic, and equal society protective of all its members (and those wanting to become ones). The U.S. cultural narrative of exceptionalism, not only in terms of a God-given nation but also in terms of the equality of the laws, thus meanders into constructions of (superior) morality, enabling pluralism and fostering minority participation.

1944: *Korematsu v. United States*

Soon, this view on equality proved to be socioculturally untenable. In the early 1940s, the Court began discussing the implications of equal protection for minorities in its 1944 *Korematsu v. United States*. Again, *Korematsu* was a case dealing with racial prejudice, namely the constitutionality of forcefully deporting people of Japanese ancestry into camps ("Facts and Case Summary"). So, while texts such as the Fourteenth Amendment, the Equal Protection doctrine, and *Plessy* had already tackled racial discrimination, it was far from extinct by 1944. The *Korematsu* decision, which upheld the constitutionality of these internments, was the first one which laid out the idea of what was later perceived as 'suspect classification:'

> It should be noted, to begin with, that all legal restrictions which curtail the civil rights of a single racial group are immediately suspect. That is not to say that all such restrictions are unconstitutional. It is to say that courts must subject them to the most rigid scrutiny. Pressing public necessity may sometimes justify the existence of such restrictions; racial antagonism never can. (Justice Hugo Black, *Korematsu* at 216)

Although *Korematsu* acknowledged the racial motivation for discriminating against Japanese Americans, it took the Supreme Court another 10 years before race was officially treated as a classification against which unequal treatment is suspect. This was also possible by looking back and retrospectively considering *Korematsu* as treating race with a higher level of judicial review. With the 1960s civil rights movement and the landmark decision *Brown v. Board of Education* in 1954, understandings of equality which favored a White, male majority became publicly more and more contested. Calls for (legal) emancipation by people of color, Blacks, and women then warranted the need to establish even higher forms of protection, post-equal, in the want of a 'more' equal protection of the laws. The constitutional tool of suspect classification was born.

Soon, other suspect classifications would follow suit or were retrospectively regarded as such. In *Graham v. Richardson* (1971), the Court treated alienage as suspect classification; *McLaughlin v. Florida* (1964) declared race suspect by referring to *Bolling v. Sharpe* (1954) and to *Korematsu*'s suggestion for a "most rigid scrutiny" in cases involving racial minorities. Nationality was considered a suspect classification in 1973 (*San Antonio Independent School Dist. v. Rodriguez* 61) and religion's special status derives from its important anchoring in the Constitution; both the First and Fourteenth Amendment make sure religious groups are not treated differently than others in similar conditions (Legrand "Suspect").

The legal practice of grouping people into classifications before applying the Equal Protection Clause illustrates that the Constitution's 'equality' has a certain meaning, which differs from what common use of the concept would typically entail. Equality, in the clause's understanding and in its legal application, also does not refer to the Declaration of Independence's ideal that "all men are created equal." It is rather the notion that only those shall be treated equally who are indeed equally situated based on characteristics such as social group membership, socioeconomic background, and parameters like age, which are constructed using medical-biologistic categories. The Declaration of Independence's sociocultural concept of equality has thus to be separated from the Constitution's legal concept of equality. While the ur-U.S. American ideal of (universal) equality has served as foundation for the new Union, as stated in the Declaration of Independence, it is also one of the main pillars upon which the cultural narrative of American Exceptionalism is based. The Constitution's equality, on the other hand, is conceptualized as equity, which aims to accommodate the specific needs of a specific social group at a specific time.

Legal and Cultural Notions of Equality

While the legal tools equal protection offers seem promising for those trying to achieve formal equity, the ways the Equal Protection Clause has been interpreted shed light on the discriminatory and exclusionary politics of this part of the Constitution. Formal equality gains are rendered unable to translate into lived equality because sociocultural realities prevent them from doing so. The Supreme Court's landmark decisions in *Plessy v. Ferguson* and *Obergefell v. Hodges* serve as prominent examples.

Plessy is better known as the landmark decision which established the "separate but equal" doctrine. Here, the Court ruled that racial segregation in public facilities is constitutional as long as the facilities are equal to those of the White population, paving the way for States to uphold a variety of discriminatory segregation laws known as the Jim Crow system. The Court's reasoning shows how the legal idea of equal protection can be interpreted in a way that reifies sociocultural hierarchies and thus becomes complicit in upholding institutional discrimination. This way, equal protection can serve as a legal tool of minority oppression on a sociocultural level while continuing to appear exceptional just on its legal face.

These dynamics can still be observed in the twenty-first century. In 2015, *Obergefell* legalized marriages between two individuals of the same sex. While the Supreme Court ruling forces all federal courts in all states to adhere to this decision, the sociocultural reality does not always reflect this as Leonore F. Carpenter states:

> Given the spate of court clerks refusing to issue same-sex marriage licenses, or even resigning rather than having to comply with the requirements of Obergefell, the issue of rogue court administrators refusing to allow LGBT people to access their rights is, if anything, more pressing than ever. (273)

The discrimination manifested here is different from the one described above regarding *Plessy*. Carpenter's assessment of *Obergefell* evolves around how individuals intentionally or unintentionally fail to act according to the laws. In *Plessy*, the Court failed to acknowledge the inherent racism and inequality its decision enabled to continue. Despite their differences, both cases shed light on the intersections of law and culture. *Obergefell* and *Plessy* illustrate how sociocultural realities surround and (co-)determine legal decisions, even by the highest court in the U.S., and how these realities may foster discriminatory applications of formally equal protection issues. In *Obergefell*, the sociocultural realities of administrators and bureaucrats Carpenter mentions accompany legal decisions and codetermine their factual effectiveness regardless of their formal premises. In *Plessy*, prevalent racial prejudice following the Reconstruction era fed into the Court's reasoning, making an unbiased decision solely based on law impossible.[24]

The way legal decisions feed back into sociocultural realities, how they are regarded, affectively felt, and implemented, is therefore both grounded in and constitutive of cultural narratives and sociocultural imaginaries. Consequently, the legal significance of the Equal Protection Clause cannot be separated from its cultural impact since the decisions it is based on inform people's lives and the overarching cultural narratives these lives are embedded in.

---

24 This reading is not meant to take away the justices' responsibility for *Plessy* but rather stress their embeddedness in a cultural framework, which influences their opinion.

Understanding Equal Protection from a Legal Point of View

In order to assess the equal protection doctrine's cultural impact, it is necessary to understand how the doctrine works on a legal level. As pointed out in the previous section, the concept of equality is vital to this part of the Constitution, yet the legal understanding of it differs from a purely moralistic one. Equality is not meant to be translated into an equal treatment of all individuals but conceptualized as an equal assessment of each individual's living conditions for the sake of governing different social group's needs. The way the Equal Protection Clause works is thus by focusing on equity, i.e., "proportional fairness" ("Usage") instead of equality, "sameness of treatment."[25] But what does this mean in practice?

Equal protection claims may be brought forward when a governmental action interferes with a fundamental right, and when a certain (suspect) classification is addressed (e.g., 1976's *Massachusetts Board of Retirement* v. *Murgia* at 312). This means the Equal Protection Clause is invoked when someone claims to have been treated unequally compared to others which share their respective characteristic. For instance, a famous equal protection decision focused on whether sex differences are constitutional in tax deductions for care work of a family member (*Charles E. Moritz v. Commissioner of Internal Revenue*). In *Moritz*, caregiver deductions were explicitly provided for "a woman or widower, or ... a husband whose wife is incapacitated or is institutionalized" (26 U.S.C.A. Sec. 214a), which did not apply to the plaintiff Charles Moritz, who cared for his mother but had never been married. Here, the deciding characteristic was (biological) sex – a woman could have deduced her taxes while a man could not, only if he had been married and his wife was unable to provide care. This decision contributed to the Supreme Court landmark decision *Reed v. Reed* (1971), which enshrined the unconstitutionality of sex-based classifications into law. After *Reed*, sex could no longer be explicitly used as distinguishing factor in legal regulations – at least not without a compelling governmental interest.

The idea to use classifications within the law to protect everyone equally goes back to 1896. Justice John Marshall Harlan's famous dissent from *Plessy* constitutes a turning point of the equal protection doctrine. *Plessy* established that the basis of equal protection lies in the principles of antisubordination and anticlassification. By arguing that "[t]he white race deems itself to be the

25 Also note that while both words share their linguistic origin in the Latin root *aequus*, equity is mostly used in legal contexts with its French derivative *equité* translating into justice or rightness ("Usage").

dominant race in this country ... [b]ut in view of the Constitution, in the eye of the law, there is in this country no superior, dominant, ruling class of citizens" (559), Harlan asserts that the Constitution is "color-blind, and neither knows nor tolerates classes among citizens" (559).

Following Harlan, the equal protection doctrine has to follow the principle of antisubordination, meaning particularly vulnerable groups of individuals are not allowed to be treated subordinately by the law, and the principle of anticlassification, meaning that law is not allowed to differentiate between groups of people, so that "irrational classifications are purged from the law and individuals are no longer treated differently across irrelevant criteria" (Copeland 283). Anticlassification, however, does not mean that there is no classification. Quite the contrary, as law evolves around classifications, equal protection merely aims at preventing 'irrational,' 'arbitrary' ones.

This legal constellation strikes as a paradox. On the one hand, equal protection claims to be anticlassificatory in nature, aiming to disregard and to resolve 'irrational' or 'irrelevant' classifications. On the other hand, it establishes classifications in order to arrive at more just, or more equal, legal decisions. This is because the very idea behind the Equal Protection Clause is that law *has* to classify in order to be able to protect its citizens equally.[26] To do so, "the measure of the reasonableness of a classification is the degree of its success in treating similarly those similarly situated" (Tussman and tenBroek 344). In other words, the rationale behind legally distinguishing between social groups is constitutional if those are treated equally who are indeed equal before the law according to their common category, e.g., age with regard to drinking alcohol or income with regard to paying taxes.

While these exemplary categorizations seem rational and relevant from a Western hemispheric standpoint, – the protection of minors[27] and the social (re-)distribution of financial means are arguably important cultural pillars of

---

26 This seemingly paradox has been commented on in Supreme Court cases involving sexual orientation; see *Romer v. Evans* at 631: "The Fourteenth Amendment's promise that no person shall be denied the equal protection of the laws must coexist with the practical necessity that most legislation classifies for one purpose or another, with resulting disadvantage to various groups or persons;" see *Perry v. Schwarzenegger* at 995: "The guarantee of equal protection coexists, of course, with the reality that most legislation must classify for some purpose or another."

27 For a critical assessment of how this aspect is weaponized in current queer rights discourses, see Chapters III and IV.

a Western democracy –, they are nonetheless arbitrary, socioculturally constructed distinctions between individuals. As these examples show, legislation always has to "impose special burdens upon or grant special benefits to special groups or classes of individuals" (Tussman and tenBroek 343) if it is to apply its principle of anticlassification. The Equal Protection Clause's concept of equality is therefore better understood as equity, aiming at protecting individuals not in the same way but in a way which fits their respective social group's needs – according to a state's assessment of what these needs are. This practice of categorizing people already foreshadows some of the problematic tendencies of the law and of those interpreting it. Having the decisive power over which categories are meaningful and who falls into which category lies with those who are already privileged members of society, e.g., politicians, judges, justices, and lobbyists.

Equal Protection's Cultural-Legal Entanglements

The Fourteenth Amendment's first section dictates that "the laws of a state must treat an individual in the same manner as others in similar conditions and circumstances" ("Equal Protection"). Legal equality is thus negotiated against already existing social categories, which are considered as a seemingly 'natural' given for the legal discourse. The (ir-)relevance of criteria for grouping individuals in the first place is not addressed. Consequently, the Equal Protection Clause does not guarantee that everybody is treated the same but that treatment under the law is reasonable and not arbitrary. This is why certain groups of people enjoy rights others do not, e.g., it is not allowed to consume or purchase alcohol under the legal drinking age of twenty-one. Consequently, in cases in which the laws of a state serve a justified objective, e.g., protecting minors from drinking alcohol, the legal distinction between groups of individuals is constitutional.

Deconstructing the implicit sociocultural notions attached to law, in this case that people are (better) equipped to make informed choices about their behavior at a certain age, is only rarely part of legal considerations. When it is, this openness is likely to indicate an already changing sociocultural climate, which visibilizes these concerns that formerly were unthinkable or possible to ignore for the people deciding on them. For instance, while the Court retrospectively claimed that "we think Plessy was wrong the day it was decided" (*Planned Parenthood of Southeastern Pa. v. Casey* at 863), and legal scholars agree in that it was "one of the two most egregious decisions in Supreme Court history (along with Dred Scott)" (Klarman 25),[28] the decision was not as harmfully or controversially perceived by a majority of people back then (Klarman 25–8; Siegel 1112–15).

Supporting the view that legal assessments, similar to cultural ones, are dependent on the specific time, place, and context they are situated in, one has to be cautious not to justify them on these grounds or to shy away from critically questioning them. Relegating responsibility to correct mistakes to a future society or judging the actions of a past court results in legitimizing present inequalities as follies of the time without acknowledging their severity or one's duty to address them. Another instance is Justice Antonio Scalia's dissent in the Court's 1996 *U.S. v. Virginia*:

> Much of the Court's opinion is devoted to deprecating the closed-mindedness of our forebears with regard to women's education, and even with regard to the treatment of women in areas that have nothing to do with education. Closed-minded they were—as every age is, including our own, with regard to matters it cannot guess, because it simply does not consider them debatable. The virtue of a democratic system with a First Amendment is that it readily enables the people, over time, to be persuaded that what they took for granted is not so, and to change their laws accordingly. That system is destroyed if the smug assurances of each age are removed from the democratic process and written into the Constitution. (at 566)

Scalia dissented in *U.S. v. Virginia* to the 7–1 majority opinion that the Virginia Military Institute's policy of only admitting (cis) men violated the Equal Protection Clause and is thus unconstitutional. To Scalia, this gender-biased policy is equal because it acknowledges the biological "facts" of "developmental differences" (at 566) between men and women. As another argument, he stresses that the institute's admission policy is "essential to that institution's character" (at 566). Scalia's view supports the idea that tradition should take precedence over changing sociocultural sentiments, scientific developments, and evolving legal norms – a conviction which will be important again when discussing justices' modes of constitutional interpretation in Chapter III. Framing women's access to education as a matter the people of the time did not conceive of as an issue ignores and explicitly rejects the realities of millions who were part of

28 Klarman further states that legal scholar Michael Perry, Judith Baer, Paul Oberst, Robert Harris, and Ronald Dworkin have been equally appalled by this landmark decision (25–6).

and witnessed women's struggle for their equal rights prior and after the Virginia Military Institute was founded in 1839, most notably 1848's Seneca Falls Convention.[29]

While Scalia acknowledges that legal systems are malleable and subject to sociocultural changes over time, he perceives this to be a task needing to be accomplished by the political process and not by the Supreme Court. Interestingly, Scalia seems to base his reasoning on the assumption that the drafting of the Constitution as well as the political process in the 1990s, when he issued his dissent, mirror an inherently democratic process which represents all of the people the legal system governs. If not for the apparent disregard of the historic context of slavery, this argument is perplexing for its use in a case that deals with equal access to education. If the democratic process were as equal (and in fact democratic) as Scalia assumes, it would not bear and maintain those mechanisms of educational hierarchization and gatekeeping *U.S. v. Virginia* deals with. Scalia's view thus both relieves past and present courts from their responsibility to ensure the equal protection of the laws.

Additionally, the underlying biologistic logic of Scalia's argument, one that is found in similar reiterations in current anti-trans and anti-non-binary state level legislation, is void of any engagement with the usefulness of negotiating legal categories based on one's genitalia. Biological sex is taken as a hard fact for establishing legal norms around those who are read as male or female, or around those having to comply with this binary system. The practice of categorizing people according to either one or the other sex in educational contexts seems reminiscent of *Plessy*'s separate-but-equal logic. Regardless whether one agrees or disagrees with Scalia on the democratic process and the Court's role in it, it becomes obvious how equal protection decisions are socioculturally embedded and part of ongoing transformations.

Levels of Review and The Three-Tiered Approach to Equal Protection Analysis

In order to better access equal protection claims, the Court uses a three-tiered approach for its analysis. Deciding on the criteria for distinguishing between social groups, i.e., their similarity, is the trickiest part of equal protection

29 This convention was the U.S.'s first women's rights convention and resulted in the *Declaration of Sentiments and Resolutions*, which mirrored the Declaration of Independence in speech, yet explicitly addressed women's needs and those equal rights they have been neglected. The document explicitly mentions unequal access to education (2; 4).

and arguably the onset for imposing sociocultural notions onto the law. The legal practice of distinguishing between people based on characteristics such as their skin color, class status, gender, able-bodiedness, age, or place of residence underwent certain changes over time and is tied to sociocultural negotiations of social group membership (and what counts as such) as already outlined.

Whenever such a differentiation between social groups within a legal statute is perceived as irrational or arbitrary, the U.S. Supreme Court employs a three-tiered approach to test the statute in question (e.g., differentiating between men and women in *Moritz*). This approach is used to prove whether a statute indeed violates a plaintiff's constitutionally protected interests by employing different levels of scrutiny depending on the respective group of people affected: the basic, the intermediate, and the heightened level of judicial review. As seen in the Supreme Court's *Plessy* decision, a class's degree of perceived irrationality and arbitrariness can change over time as it is embedded in and subject to sociocultural transformations. Race had not been considered an irrational and arbitrary criterion for differentiation in 1896 and only been tested using the basic level of judicial review. This perception changed over the years, and the Supreme Court responded to this development by ruling it indeed irrational and arbitrary in its *Brown* decision in 1954, using the heightened level of judicial review. As the category of race is since then considered a suspect classification, i.e., a category against which discrimination is inherently suspect and thus prone to a more searching judicial review, legal texts which draw distinctions between, e.g., white and Black people, are very likely to be ruled unconstitutional after being reviewed by the Supreme Court.

The basic level of judicial review is the so-called Lindsley test or rational basis review, which every classification must pass in order to be legitimated. This test tries to determine whether the classification drawn by the law is not "without reasonable basis"[30] and not "purely arbitrary",[31] plus it has to be "fairly related to the object of regulation."[32] Consequently, the Supreme Court may consider discriminatory federal laws constitutional as long as they are "reasonable, not arbitrary, and ... rest upon some ground of difference having a fair and

30 *Lindsley v. Natural Carbonic Gas Co.* at 78 (1911).

31 *Lindsley* at 78.

32 *Railway Express Agency, Inc. v. New York.* at 112 (1949).

substantial relation to the object of the legislation, so that all persons similarly circumstanced shall be treated alike."[33]

States' enactments of laws that classify individuals are constitutional as long as these laws are "based upon some reasonable ground – - something which bears a just and proper relation to the attempted classification, and is not a mere arbitrary selection."[34] For cases involving the Lindsley test, the burden of proof lies in the sphere of the assailant, which means that the party who perceives a law's classification to be unreasonable and arbitrary must hand in evidence for their claim. The difficulty of proving this results in most of these cases failing to prove a lack of legitimate governmental interest.

Equal Protection's Suspect Classifications

In cases which involve certain groups of individuals, the Court has to apply either intermediate or heightened review, depending on whether the Court is dealing with 'quasi-suspect' or 'suspect' classes. While social groups are referred to as quasi-suspect or suspect *classes*, e.g., African-American, immigrants, Catholics, the legal category under which they are subsumed is referred to as quasi-suspect or suspect *classification*, e.g., race, national origin, religion. In its legal meaning, the term 'suspect' does not refer to the suspiciousness of the classes or classifications themselves but to the unlawfulness of any discrimination against them. These classifications then appear suspect to the legal reader when appearing in legal norms while the suspectness of these classifications' existence, e.g., why people are categorized according to a socially constructed category such as race, is not part of the discourse.

33 Royster Guano Co. v. Virginia at 415 (1920).

34 *Gulf, Colorado & Santa Fe Ry. Co. v. Ellis* at 151 (1891).

Up to this point, suspect classifications include race,[35] national origin,[36] religious affiliation, illegitimacy of birth,[37] and alienage.[38] The Court argues that governmental discrimination against these classifications is inherently suspect and thus the statutes in question have to be reviewed with strict scrutiny, also known as heightened review. In this process, the Supreme Court has to analyze if a) the discrimination serves a compelling governmental interest, b) the law is narrowly tailored to serve this interest, and c) the law is the least restrictive means for achieving this interest. This means that "the Court presumes the law to be unconstitutional, and the law must be 'legitimated' by the State" (Culverhouse and Lewis 240), i.e., the burden of proof lies in the sphere of the state. Consequently, statutes which discriminate against an individual's race, national origin, religious affiliation, illegitimacy of birth, or alienage are less likely to become enacted than those discriminating against non-suspect classifications such as sexual orientation, gender, or age.

Since cases of heightened review are most likely to result in ruling that the statute in question is unconstitutional, the Supreme Court has been reluctant to consider too many classifications as suspect. This privilege to decide (or not to decide) which classifications are 'worthy' of more protections illustrates how much power the Court has in protecting minorities, and how much these decisions comment on sociocultural hierarchies. Considering distinction based on religious affiliation suspect but denying this stricter scrutiny to, for instance,

---

35 See *Loving v. Virginia* at 11 (1967), quoting *Hirabayashi v. U.S.* at 100 (1943), and *Korematsu v. U.S.* at 216 (1944).

36 See *Korematsu v. U.S.* at 216 (1944): "It should be noted, to begin with, that all legal restrictions which curtail the civil rights of a single racial group are immediately suspect. That is not to say that all such restrictions are unconstitutional. It is to say that courts must subject them to the most rigid scrutiny. Pressing public necessity may sometimes justify the existence of such restrictions; racial antagonism never can" (majority opinion by Blackmun).

37 According to Marcy Strauss, "illegitimacy is entitled to heightened—though not strict—scrutiny" because the Court did not find that "strict scrutiny was justified in this case because the history of discrimination of illegitimate children was not as severe as discrimination based on race" (140, fn. 24). See also *Mathews v. Lucas* at 518 (1976).

38 See *Graham v. Richardson* at 371–2 (1971): "It has long been settled, and it is not disputed here, that the term 'person' in this context encompasses lawfully admitted resident aliens, as well as citizens of the United States, and entitles both citizens and aliens to the equal protection of the laws of the State in which they reside" (majority opinion by Blackmun).

distinction based on dis/ability mirrors an ableist understanding of what constitutes a legal subject worthy of support.

Instead of granting more, and also more vulnerable, groups such a privilege, and thereby not commenting on these groups' position in the constitutional and sociocultural hierarchy, the Court constructed a middle-way: the intermediate approach, which applies to quasi-suspect classifications. As of today, gender,[39] status as minor children of illegal aliens,[40] and status as aliens are considered quasi-suspect classifications. The Supreme Court has not established a consistent handling of these 'in-between' classifications, which makes them more relevant politically than legally. Cases involving these classifications can be reviewed with heightened scrutiny, but the Court is likely to use an intermediate approach, i.e., "a heightened level of scrutiny falling between strict scrutiny and rational basis testing" (Widin 414). Since sexual orientation is neither regarded as a suspect or quasi-suspect classification, cases involving discrimination based on sexual orientation are likely to be reviewed with the most lenient judicial review, the Lindsley test. Political scientist Evan Gerstmann explains this hierarchy of equal protection, and sexual minorities's place in it as follows:

> Since the 1970s the United States Supreme Court has held that the equal protection clause protects different groups differently – an approach that has denied many citizens the equal protection of the laws. Some groups are "suspect classes" that receive strong judicial protection against discriminatory laws. Other groups are "quasi-suspect classes" that receive an intermediate level of protection. Courts rarely tolerate laws that discriminate against these classes. Still other groups, such as gays, lesbians, the elderly, and the poor, constitute neither suspect nor quasi-suspect classes and therefore receive very little protection under the equal protection clause; laws that discriminate against them will be tolerated so long as there is any "rational basis" for those measures. (*Underclass* 3)

---

39 See *Mississippi Univ. for Women v. Hogan* at 718 (1982); see also *Craig v. Boren* at 190 (1976): Responding to the growing number of cases in which sex classifications were perceived as unconstitutional, but yet unwilling to apply the same level of judicial review as for race, the Supreme Court decided to use a heightened, intermediate level of scrutiny when criteria of gender are involved.

40 See *Plyler v. Doe* at 224–5 (1982).

Gerstmann picks up on the Equal Protection Clause's idea of having to classify between social groups in order to treat them equally, and goes on to criticize that "the Supreme Court cannot adequately explain why [certain; lb] groups are frozen in this hierarchy" (3). However, while this logic may be convincing when thinking about social groups' distinctive needs, the reasoning behind protecting some vulnerable social groups more thoroughly while denying this degree of protection to others is not. Examples of these logical inconsistencies may be the different treatment of women and the elderly, or "illegitimate children and their parents [who are] protected more than gays and lesbians" (Gerstmann *Underclass* 3). [41] Ill-picking his examples, Gerstmann may have traced back the reasons for protecting the groups mentioned to the exploitation and utilization logic inherent in neoliberal capitalist societies: (Cis) Women's ability and expectation to reproduce offspring to guarantee national survival make them more worthy of legal protection, and children have an *a priori* higher need as they are socioculturally and legally troped and narrativized as innocent and vulnerable victims.[42] Static constellations within the Court's suspect classification decisions speak for an equally static understanding of sociocultural orders. Having arrived at a fixed set of groups which receive greater protection, paired with an uneasiness or unwillingness about adding more groups to this selected circle, the Court insinuates that the current legal order mirrors sociocultural and naturalized realities which need no altering.

II.3. The Cultural and Legal Significance of Suspect Classification

According to legal scholar Kenji Yoshino, the Court's decision to establish the in-between form of intermediate scrutiny for quasi-suspect classifications, and its reluctance to include more 'real' suspect classifications is connected to what he calls "pluralism anxiety" (747), which "flows from at least two sources – 'new' kinds of people and 'newly visible' kinds of people" (747). Yoshino considers this anxiety as the reason for the Court's changed approach to civil

---

41 Perceiving of the elderly, queers, and the poor as more vulnerable social groups in this legal context is not meant to essentialize or victimize these groups but refers to the lack and contestations of protections for them.

42 For more on the child and women as preferred victimized figures in human rights discourses, see Olson *Legaliy*; Hesford; Baxi.

rights legislation and its unwillingness to include sexual orientation in its canon of suspect classifications:

> For instance, the percentage of the population that has experienced same-sex desire has presumably not changed dramatically over time. However, the political visibility of gays, lesbians, and bisexuals has grown dramatically over recent decades. Even if a group is not comprised of "new" kinds of individuals, it can still trigger pluralism anxiety if it becomes newly visible. Because of "new" and "newly visible" groups, the nation has developed an increasing sense of its own pluralism. That sense has engendered significant anxiety across the political spectrum. For some time now, conservative commentators have expressed impatience with the seemingly endless proliferation of identities and identity politics. But the concern transcends political creed. Even liberal lion Professor Arthur Schlesinger Jr. cautioned as early as 1991 against the "disuniting of America," calling for a recommitment to the ideals of assimilation and integration. (751–52)

Yoshino constructs law and culture as spheres which monodirectionally influence each other in the sense that law responds to politico-cultural developments and not the other way around. To him, the political visibility of queers has increased, which resulted in an anxiety and impatience by conservatives, who oppose granting sexual minorities more rights. The reasons for this increased visibility, which has been a gradual process on a political, but also cultural, social, and legal level, are left undiscussed.

According to this understanding, the constructive element of law becomes a reactive one, and the idea of law being merely a device to correct or respond to current issues reinforces the notion of law and culture as juxtaposed realms. Although Yoshino explicitly mentions cultural factors by referring to Schlesinger, his focus on talking about either law or culture prevents him from seeing the politico-cultural ways of social stratification as legal orders in themselves. Those who assess this particular constitutional situation (legal scholars such as Yoshino himself) as well as those who sit on the bench of the Supreme Court are able to do so because of their respective opportunities – a very good educational background, which equals high socio-economic standing in most U.S. American cases, and no or only little institutional obstacles based on sex, race, national origin, gender, gender identity, sexual orientation, or ability. Referring to "new" or "newly visible" groups of people thus only appears plausible for those who are unquestioningly sustaining the very structures which invisibilize these groups.

Being granted or denied access to societal institutions, being able to integrate oneself, is oftentimes inhibited by sociocultural factors and contemporary forms of prejudice. In fact, the very requirements of what is perceived a 'successful' integration may themselves be part of a dominant cultural order.[43] These factors may be addressed through legal means as well as by strengthening sensibilities for cultural-legal entanglements.

Further, this rudimental characterization of how identity and social group membership work leaves out any intersectional entanglements. Someone might be legally protected for their status as a White woman, yet not for their sexual identity as lesbian. People have more than one social group they belong (or feel belonging) to, but some classifications seem generally more desirable than others and therefore appear more socioculturally acceptable than the others. For instance, Yoshino's privilege of being an Ivy-League educated professor of law seems more prominent here than his identity as a gay man which leaves the notion of agreement with such pluralism anxiety mentioned.

One's assessment of the constitutional situation in the U.S. is consequently influenced by one's worldview, which is influenced by one's socialization, which is likely to be (predominantly) influenced by one's privileged position. Deciding on who constitutes a "new" or "newly visible" class, and which of these classes need or deserve more protection is therefore already marred by one's own social positioning. This positioning implicitly presupposes that at least one position in society's hierarchy is taken – one's own.

Taking a human rights stance, Yoshino argues that moving from a group-based civil rights approach to protecting fundamental rights of all humans will not only be easier to achieve politically but will also help reducing distinctions between social groups (792–94). This argument reminds of calls to treat discrimination based on sexual orientation akin to discrimination based on sex.[44] Such approaches attempt to establish an effective anti-discrimination protection for LGBTQ+ individuals by finding a common, seemingly unproblematic category worthy of protection. Such ideas may seem promising with regard to

---

43 One may for instance think of Friedrich Merz' instrumentalization of the term *Leitkultur* to exclude ethnic Others in German integration discourses, see also Olson *Legality* 134.

44 The logic here is that if, for example, a lesbian (cis) woman is fired because she is in a relationship with another (cis) woman, she would not have been fired if she were a (cis) man who was in a relationship with a (cis) woman. Thus, discrimination based on sexual orientation is in effect discrimination based on sex according to this argument.

its outcome, yet they are far more dangerous than they seem.[45] For instance, the decision to consider marriage a fundamental right in *Obergefell* was benefitting same-sex couples the most, yet it was not a right directly granted to queers. *Obergefell* was a concession to the institution of marriage as such, and a decision for granting broader access to such a culturally, religiously, and legally important right. The right to get married served as seemingly common category many groups of people now had access to. However, a specific queer right would have signaled the Court's acknowledgement of queer realities and elevated sexual minorities in existing cultural-legal orders.

Moreover, Yoshino ignores the cultural implications of what he calls "new" and "newly visible" groups. Visibilities, or the lack thereof, are not *a priori* biological occurrences but socioculturally constructed phenomena based on threats to one's life, socioeconomic position, or political silencing. The "newness" of a social group is consequently only linked to how visible its members are in the public discourse – in other words, a "new" group is also a "newly visible" group because it has existed before but only now becomes visible, and a "newly visible" group is better conceived of as a "more visible" group than it was in the past.

The decision to become or make visible is closely linked to how law and culture develop in connection with each other. Claiming formal equity (or lived equality) for one's sexual orientation, race, or other social identity marker would be a too dangerous, or at least desperate, demand when there are no laws protecting an individual's Otherness. This is even more the case when there is no cultural openness for non-normativity and unassimilation. Similarly, fighting for one's visibility and recognition of one's rights, for instance in the form of activism, is ultimately only as effective as (lived) cultural responses to its (formal) legal results: County clerks' refusal to issue marriage licenses to same-sex couples post-*Obergefell* renders the (formal) right to marry ineffective for those facing (lived) discrimination and backlash. Post-*Brown*, president Eisenhower's deployment of 1,200 U.S. Army soldiers at Little Rock Central High School enforced the (formal) legal decision to desegregate public education facilities despite (lived) hostile resistance by a white mob. Whenever cultural and legal orders clash, the need to approach both simultaneously becomes evident.

45 Chapter III picks up on the implications of anti-discrimination laws and analyzes why the 'sex discrimination argument' to sexual orientation's legal protection has a narcotizing effect and is not the one LGBTQ+ persons should be arguing for.

Pluralism anxiety does not transcend political beliefs, as argued by Yoshino: When there are too many 'new' groups claiming their rights, even liberal commentators fear a disruption of the legal order. This view reifies the political notion that there is a unified majority – (presumably) White, cis, male, able-bodied, heterosexual –, which demands primacy. The angst of including more groups beside this unmentioned majority marks the Supreme Court's reluctance to consider more social groups as suspect classes a political decision with the establishment of quasi-suspect classifications as concessions to those calling for group-based protections.

Beyond these cultural-political considerations, the normative power of constitutional precedents lays the, arguably also not a-political, foundation for legal assessments of suspect classifications. In order for a classification to become suspect, it has to pass certain criteria which have been developed over time by Supreme Court justices. Although the American case law system does not adhere to codified laws, and different legal scholars identify different criteria,[46] the majority of legal commentaries considers four factors as crucial in determining a classification's need for heightened judicial review.

Criteria to Determine the Need for Heightened Judicial Review

In 1938's Supreme Court decision *U.S. v. Carolene Products Co.*, Justice Harlan Fiske Stone stated in his now famous Footnote Four[47] that "prejudice against discrete and insular minorities may be a special condition, which tends seriously to curtail the operation of those political processes ordinarily to be relied upon to protect minorities, and which may call for a correspondingly more

46 Scholars are divided upon the number of criteria determining suspect classification, with some identifying up to seven criteria (Wintemute 61–4). The four criteria mentioned here are generally considered the most important and controversial ones.

47 *U.S. v. Carolene Products Co.* at 144, footnote 4 (1938) reads: "There may be narrower scope for operation of the presumption of constitutionality when legislation appears on its face to be within a specific prohibition of the Constitution, such as those of the first ten amendments. ... It is unnecessary to consider now whether legislation which restricts those political processes which can ordinarily be expected to bring about repeal of undesirable legislation, is to be subjected to more exacting judicial scrutiny under the general prohibitions of the Fourteenth Amendment. ... Nor need we enquire ... whether prejudice against discrete and insular minorities may be a special condition, which tends seriously to curtail the operation of those political processes ordinarily to be relied upon to protect minorities, and which may call for a correspondingly more searching judicial inquiry."

searching judicial inquiry" (footnote 4). This footnote laid the foundation for the Supreme Court's differentiation of standards of judicial review by introducing the notion of strict scrutiny for cases which involve underrepresented, thus particularly vulnerable, social groups. The core idea of this definition is that a social group's status as politically powerless minority who is subjected to discrimination based on stereotypes is the most crucial factor which warrants an intervention by the Supreme Court in the form of declaring a category a suspect classification or a group a suspect class. Gerstmann explains what he refers to as 'political process theory' as follows: "In Stone's view, majority prejudice against unpopular and powerless minorities poisons the political process, and the Court must intervene to protect these groups" (*Underclass* 4).

Constitutional law scholar Bruce Ackerman attests to the impact of "the *Carolene* idea" (716, footnote 5), which is the "concern with the political powerlessness of 'discrete and insular' minorities" (716), by stating that "even when it is not cited explicitly, ... [it] plays a role in standard judicial justifications for strict judicial scrutiny of legislation burdening 'suspect' classes" (716). According to Ackerman, this is why in numerous cases social groups use the criteria laid out in *Carolene Products* to justify extraordinary protection. Based on the decision's Footnote Four, the Supreme Court generally identifies four criteria[48] of a suspect classification:

> (1) whether the classification is based on immutable traits or characteristics over which the individual has no control; (2) whether the classification reflects historic and incorrect stereotypes with no basis in fact; (3) whether the classification represents a politically powerless minority; and (4) whether there is a history of discrimination of unequal treatment towards the class. (Culverhouse and Lewis 240)

The first criterion refers to characteristics which are determined "solely by the accident of birth,"[49] making them innate rather than consciously chosen traits. Although it is not quite clear if these characteristics are biological or genetic conditions or if they are merely impossible to escape (as has been argued with regard to religious affiliations), the individual cannot be held responsible for the trait in question; it is part of their essence.

48 Please note that the number of requirements changes among legal scholar and courts, see also *Sail'er Inn, Inc. v. Kirby*, which recognizes three criteria. However, immutability is always cited and problematized.

49 *Frontiero v. Richardson* at 686 (1973).

The second criterion deals with historic and incorrect stereotypes, i.e., prejudices which contribute to a social group's discrimination. An example for such incorrect stereotypes would be the enduring prejudice of gay men molesting children. According to Culverhouse and Lewis, "such misconceptions and stereotypes have been used to justify sodomy statutes, employment discrimination and housing discrimination" (243). Stereotypes can be used to justify institutional discrimination, especially when they come with a notion of immoral or downright despicable behavior. This is why the second criterion also operates under the label 'moral neutrality.' This means that the trait in question has to be in accordance with religious and sociocultural principles which constitute a society's value system. Proving that a characteristic is not immoral and warrants extraordinary legal protection is a difficult endeavor: It involves convincing the highest court of the society that discriminates exactly against this trait that existing biases have to be reversed. The difficulty of this task is reinforced by the political powerlessness of the minorities involved, which makes up the third criterion.[50]

The legal understanding of a politically powerless minority refers to "a group's inability to rely on the legislative process to protect its interests" (Strauss 153): If a social group is left out of the majoritarian political process, it cannot represent its own interests by, for example, proposing statutes. In return, this requires that this otherwise powerless minority is extraordinarily protected. Measuring political powerlessness includes analyzing a group's ability to vote, looking at the amount of people belonging to this group, checking if there are statutes which might add political power to the group and examining if any members of the group hold positions of political power (see also Strauss 154).

The last criterion deals with a group's history of discrimination. Ackerman defines this criterion as follows:

> [A]lthough each of us cannot always expect to convince our legislators, we can at least insist that they treat our claims with respect. At the very least, they should thoughtfully consider our moral and empirical arguments, rejecting them only after conscientiously deciding that they are inconsistent

50 In *San Antonio Independent School District v. Rodriguez* at 28 (1973), the Court in the form of Justice Powell first used the term "political powerlessness" to consider whether a classification qualifies as suspect which was then picked up and quoted in *Massachusetts Board of Retirement v. Murgia* at 313 (1976).

> with the public interest. If a group fails to receive this treatment, it suffers a special wrong, one quite distinct from its substantive treatment on the merits. (738)

Ackerman considers the political silencing, or non-consideration, of a group's concerns as important for measuring the degree of discrimination. If over a long period of time in a democratic society a social group has been denied the same treatment as other groups, one can speak of a history of discrimination, which "is connected to the group's political power and indicates whether the legislative process has failed to protect it, warranting judicial intervention" (Strauss 150). Consequently, the aspect of unequal treatment is always connected to the lack of a group's representation in the majoritarian political process, requiring legislation to intervene.

It is unclear whether these four criteria, influenced by the Court's *Frontiero v. Richardson* decision in 1973, must all be fulfilled in order for a classification to be regarded as suspect. The Supreme Court has not supplied a coherent approach to its rulings on suspect classification, leaving "each writer seeking to apply [the criteria; lb] to a new classification ... to supply his or her own framework" (Wintemute 63).

The Significance of the Four Criteria

Proving that a group of individuals has been politically disadvantaged and treated unequally over a long period of time may be relatively easy with regard to existing statutes and lack of representatives in positions of power. The criteria of immutability and incorrect stereotypes are, however, more difficult to overcome for a minority seeking suspect class status. This is due to the lack of coherent definitions for these criteria and the difficulties in finding biological and ethical evidence for what is immutable and moral.

Another question is whether a politically disadvantaged group will be regarded as such: Although the perception of a social group may have changed over time, the group in question has to appeal to the courts of the society which established its status in the first place. This means a group seeking suspect class status has to prove its case before a court which is, consciously or unconsciously, governed by the political, sociocultural and religious processes making up a society's value system. Constitutional law scholar Paul A. Freund famously explained this thin line as "the Court should never be affected by the weather of the day but inevitably they will be influenced by the climate of the era" (qtd. in Coyle), a quote often used by Justice Ruth Bader Ginsburg.

In addition to the problems attached to the burden of proof for these criteria, the vague definition of factors that determine a suspect class make them difficult to apply. Although *Frontiero* and *Carolene Products* serve as foundation for the Court's decision-making, "the test for distinguishing between the three types of classes has [not; lb] been carefully crafted and precisely defined" (138) according to Marcy Strauss. By referring to Harvie Wilkinson, she states that "beyond the basic truism" (138) that a suspect classification should involve "politically powerless minorities that have historically been discriminated against" (138), the Court's determination of a suspect class status lacks consistency and clarity. This is shown in the fact that "different courts emphasize different factors without any real explanation why some are more important than others" (Strauss 138–9). While being a typical feature of the U.S. American juridical case law system, the lack of any coherently codified definition for the factors determining a suspect classification enables courts to interpret these criteria rather freely. This does not only lead to different interpretations of class categorizations, but it also complicates the case for social groups who are trying to achieve suspect class status.

The Court's incoherent line of argumentation becomes clear when looking at religion's status as suspect classification. Although there are groups that have been persecuted, politically disadvantaged and discriminated against,[51] characterizing religion as an immutable trait seems at least problematic from a secular perspective. If religious affiliations were innate, converting to another religion or being an atheist would certainly not be possible since it contradicts one's essential character. Despite these apparent inconsistencies regarding the practice of constitutional interpretation and the flaws in reviewing cases involving religion with strict scrutiny while cases involving sexual orientation, dis/ability, or gender are not, sexual minorities are still imagined as wanting too much and the Constitution is imagined to be an impeccable tool of establishing equality. These affectively felt truths about legal-cultural connections make arguing for a transformation of constitutional protections even more difficult. The next subchapter sheds light on such legal-cultural imaginaries and their relevance for queer legal discourses.

51 An example for such a group would be the Puritans who immigrated to New England in the seventeenth century because they had been persecuted in England, see Davis "America's".

II.4. What Constitutes a Culture? – Constitutional Transformations and Changing Cultural Imaginaries

The previous subchapters have commented on the Constitution and the cultural narratives inscribed in it, on the Fourteenth Amendment with its Equal Protection Clause and suspect classification, and on the relationship between law and culture. As has been argued throughout this chapter, the Constitution codifies the cultural narrative of equality as well as the notion that there is a guaranteed access to justice for U.S. citizens. The concept of equality has been an important ingredient of cultural narratives surrounding and establishing what is now the United States of America. The faultiness in assuming that there is or ever has been something close to equal rights or a general sociocultural equality between U.S. Americans has already been laid out. What remains is to look more closely at cultural-constitutional imaginaries and the functions they serve.

The following observations illustrate that a) cultural-constitutional imaginaries in the U.S. are not static but rather constantly changing, b) they have been powerfully weaponized in current anti-queer laws, and c) they are not new phenomena but rather reemerging as indicated by former Court decisions about racial segregation. What is central here is the insight that law and rights discourses are not negotiated from neutral and objective positions but rather that subjective and affective positions are constitutive of law-making, judicial decisions, and individual responses to law. Thus, power and affect play an important role in how legal cultures imagine themselves and their subjects.

The first part of this subchapter introduces the concept of cultural *imaginaries* as contrasted to cultural *narratives* before defining it in more detail by drawing on Kathleen Lennon's work on imaginaries, Jacques Lacan's imaginary order, and Clifford Geertz's, Baruch Spinoza's, and Benedict Anderson's seminal works on law and culture, affect, and collective identity. After doing so, I go on to discuss what I identify as the most prominent, contemporary cultural-constitutional imaginaries in the U.S. This chapter explicitly focusses on cultural *imaginaries* concerning constitutional rights, and shows how the narrative of access to justice has been perverted in recent political developments to the extent of curtailing other envisaged cultural-constitutional pillars such as equality and liberty.

Following Kathleen Lennon's understanding of the imaginary, cultural-constitutional imaginaries are understood here as specific kinds of legal affects that function as "encounters with alternative imagined configurations which can be recognized as making both cognitive *and* affective sense" (107; emphasis in original). While *imagination*, in the sense of a cognitive faculty, tends to be more interested in a distinction between the 'real' and the imagined object (Lennon 107; Iser 136), *imaginary* is closer to what psychoanalysts would consider "unconscious phantasy" (Whitford 53 qtd. in Lennon 109):

> Freud believes that phantasy provided us with a mode of representation of ourselves, our biological processes, our relationship to the world and others which was not governed by truth and falsity, but by the demands of affect and emotion. What is important to recognize here is that the content of such phantasmatic representations, the images and patterns that make them up, are the *vehicles* whereby these emotions become constituted. The relation between the affect and the phantasy is not simply one of causality but one of constitution. ... For Freud these phantasmatic representations of the world remain unconscious. They do, however, have effects in our life, underpinning and often disrupting the judgments of the conscious and apparently rational ego: "[T]hese unconscious (mis)representations can coexist in the mind with the knowledge acquired at a later stage, providing an affective substratum which determines a person's feelings (often unconscious) towards that later knowledge" (Whitford, 64). (Lennon 109; emphasis in original)

The 'real' in this understanding is not an objectively true, neutral condition but an affectively experienced and cognitively accepted one in the sense of "there being a real for us" (Lennon 111).[52] Following Wolfgang Iser's conceptualization, the imaginary is to be separated from processes which are more precise or aim to add precision. The imaginary is marked by its in-grasp-ability, its fluidity, and affectiveness:

> In our ordinary experience, the imaginary tends to manifest itself in a somewhat diffuse manner, in fleeting impressions that defy our attempts to pin it down in a concrete stabilized form. The imaginary may suddenly flash before our mind's eye, almost as an arbitrary apparition, only to disappear

52 The 'real' has different meanings in the various conceptualizations of what is imagined, real, and social. For instance, Lacan would consider the 'real' as connected to a pre-language state of need (see Lacan 93–100 for a thorough introduction of 'The Mirror Stage;' see also Lennon 110–11) while Iser labels the connection between the 'real,' the fictive, and the imaginary as a "triadic relationship" (3).

> again or to dissolve into quite another form. "The peculiar quality of fantasy," says Husserl, "is its self-will. And so ideally it distinguishes itself by its absolute arbitrariness." (3)

The imaginary functions to guide the affective responses to the sociocultural conditions one encounters via an unconscious process of meaning-making and knowledge production. Lennon builds on the work by Jacques Lacan and Luce Irigaray to critique the former's concept of imaginary as tied to "phantasy and illusion" (111) and to point out the latter's understanding of imaginary as "structured by the symbolic as well as constituting its affective dimension" (113). For Lennon, Lacan, and Irigaray, the social world, or symbolic order, informs the imaginary and is influenced by it.

Making these perspectives fruitful for the concept of cultural-legal imaginaries, I take imaginaries to be responses to external circumstances which happen on an affective level before they cognitively evolve. This process happens in a pre-narrativized stage (mirroring Lacan's pre-language stage of the imaginary order), which is only put into form by drawing on already available sociocultural scripts, tropes, and templates. I argue that before one cognitively accepts these imaginaries, – with cognitive acceptance being one of the important characteristics of Lennon's imaginaries, – they have to go through a process of being checked against and compared with available cultural (and legal) narratives. Agreeing with Lacan's conceptualization of the imaginary and the social order (54–57), what distinguishes the concept of cultural-legal imaginaries I outline from cultural narratives is the former's lacking intersubjectivity. In this understanding, imaginaries possess a high degree of narrativity, i.e., "qualities that elicit thinking structures that help to explain [them] as ... narrative[s]" (Olson "Futures" 44), yet they have not been explained cognitively, have not been thoroughly narrativized, thus are not (yet) narratives. Imaginaries' unconscious functioning is undoubtably influenced by the cultural narratives and norms individuals encounter in their sociocultural environment as well as the normativized structures and the constructions of reality which are formed by dominant views. Yet, narratives and imaginaries are not identical.

Imaginaries are less structured and narrativized since they are something the individual affectively experiences instead of cognitively tells oneself. The process of putting these affectively felt imaginaries into a tell-able and shareable form then happens via comparing them to already available cultural narratives and narrative structures. Only then, through this process of sociocultural and linguistic legitimation, can imaginaries become cognitively accepted. Thus, cultural-legal imaginaries and cultural narratives are entwined and draw on each other. Yet imaginaries are more intuitively taken for granted as 'objectively right' without engaging with their origins, implications, and concrete meanings. I argue that the identified imaginaries in this subchapter work even more effectively on a political level because they are already unconsciously accepted before being cognitively processed.

The imaginaries analyzed here are ones that are affectively experienced and, in Lennon's sense, establish something which is 'real for us' without needing to be based on observable realities. These 'imagined configurations' of the status quo may involve alternatives to established norms but also stereotypical, categorizable notions of 'the' legal subject. They differ from cultural narratives in that the former create something that does not (yet) exist in reality but is conceptualized or configured, – a template, – while the latter add meaning to something that may or may not have happened. Imaginaries have a more affective component and power than do narratives while their storytelling elements are missing. As Mazukatow and Binder observe with reference to Marcel Stoetzler and Nira Yuval-Davis, "the process of imagining does not only contribute to the stabilization of knowledge about society but it also belongs to the repertoire of critical practices aiming for change" (460).[53] Imaginaries then pick up and (re-)figure existing notions about sociocultural conditions. They function as modes of critique of established orders or to perpetuate fossilized notions of how something (or someone) should be. Imaginaries or the act of imagining can be seen as a specific form of knowledge production; they are not synonymous or related to legal fictions as used here.[54] Both cultural imaginaries and cultural narratives are culture-specific as Greta Olson points out with regard to cultural narratives of law ("Futures" 57).

Cultural narratives involve an aspect of intention and retrospect, of actively setting up a story to make sense of what has happened. Cultural imaginaries, on the other hand, are experienced more subconsciously and less rational as

---

53 The German original reads: "Somit trägt das Imaginieren nicht nur zur Stabilisierung eines Wissens um Gesellschaft bei, sondern gehört auch zum Repertoire kritischer, auf Veränderung zielender Praktiken." My translation. See also Stoetzler and Yuval-Davis, "Standpoint Theory" 316: "on the one hand, imagination constructs its meanings while, on the other hand, it stretches and transcends them," quoted in Mazukatow and Binder 460.

54 For more on legal fictions, see Hans Vaihinger, *Philosophie*. For a different understanding of the relation between legal imaginaries and legal fictions which draws on Wolfgang Iser's theory of the real, the fictional, and the imaginary, see Künzel.

they allow for more *Leerstellen*, i.e., blank spaces which can be filled by the recipient's own associations, fears, hopes, and actions. Cultural narratives, in this sense, are semi-fictional accounts of how an event took place, and are meant to add causality and legitimacy to this event. Cultural imaginaries, likewise imagined facts about a culture and working as efficient cultural glue, are yet more fluid, less obvious. Both, however, are successfully used for political purposes, most prominently by right conservative politicians as this subchapter shows.[55]

Drawing on Clifford Geertz's understanding of legal complexes, the cultural-constitutional imaginaries discussed here rather adhere to "the Western notion of 'right' *(Recht, droit)* than they [do] to that of 'law' *(Gesetz, loi)*" (*Knowledge* 187):

> They center, that is, less around some sort of conception of "rule," "regulation," "injunction," or "decree" than around one, cloudier yet, of an inner connection, primal and unbreakable, between the "proper," "fitting," "appropriate," or "suitable" and the "real," "true," "genuine," or "veritable": between the "correct" of "correct behavior" and that of "correct understanding." (Geertz *Knowledge* 187)

'Right' and 'law' in Geertz' understanding differ in their affectively experienced intensity and their relation to norms. The notion of a 'primal and unbreakable' inner connection between what is perceived as right and what is real resembles Baruch Spinoza's affect as laid out in his seminal 1677 *The Ethics*. Spinoza rejects the dualism of affect and rationality, of body and mind and instead argues for an understanding which sees these spheres as interconnected. Aiming to understand affects, Spinoza's theory considers affect as a specific form of knowledge production, similar to the imaginaries discussed here.

Benedict Anderson's understanding of imaginaries takes into account how they function as identity-building devices among collectives, adding yet another affective layer. Referring to medieval sacred communities, Anderson states in his *Imagined Communities* that "[w]e are faced with a world in which the figuring of imagined reality was overwhelmingly visual and aural" (22–23). In today's U.S., figures of speech and image iconography have arguably replaced church windows and sermons, yet their approach to aim at the masses in a way that is "always personal and particular" (Anderson 23) still holds true

---

55 The use of imaginaries as emancipatory tool is discussed in more detail in Chapter V, which looks at ways of imagining and creating a queer legal future.

– maybe even more so in times of algorithmic personalization on the internet. Anderson's imaginaries thus function as sociocultural glue and hold political power, thereby almost becoming cultural symbols themselves as indicated by the cultural-constitutional imaginaries surrounding the Supreme Court.

Imaginary 1: The Congruence of the U.S. Supreme Court and the Constitution

The quasi-sacred notion of cultural symbols, what Robert Bellah described in 1967 as America's civil religion, can also be found with regard to the Supreme Court. While the U.S. Constitution is already considered a semi-sacred text in the American cultural imagination, the Supreme Court's task to guard its implementation becomes a holy endeavor itself, making the Court equally venerable. This close connection between the Court, an increasingly political institution as laid out in Chapter III, and the Constitution translates into a unity in the cultural imagination, which elevates the Court's authority from a legal to a cultural one. The closeness of the Court and the Constitution, and the corresponding imagined superiority of the judiciary has already been identified in the very beginnings of the United States. In 1788, Alexander Hamilton observed "[s]ome perplexity respecting the right of the courts to pronounce legislative acts void, because contrary to the constitution, has arisen from the imagination that the doctrine would imply a superiority of the judiciary to the legislative power" (474). However, refusing a critique of the Court because of this imagined unity is as misleading as it is dangerous for democratic structures:

> Because traditional scholarship has tended to confuse the Constitution with judicial decisionmaking, it has imagined resistance to courts as a threat to the Constitution itself. This is a mistake. To criticize a judicial decision as betraying the Constitution is to speak from a normative identification *with* the Constitution. Citizens who invoke the Constitution to criticize courts associate the Constitution with understandings they find normatively compelling and believe to be binding on others. When citizens speak about their most passionately held commitments in the language of a shared constitutional tradition, they invigorate that tradition. In this way, even resistance to judicial interpretation can enhance the Constitution's democratic legitimacy. (Post and Siegel 375; emphasis in original)

Legal scholars Robert Post and Reva Siegel, who refute the imaginary that the Court and the Constitution are a quasi-sacred unity, frame critique of the judiciary as strengthening the Constitution. This founding document and courts' decisions are separate sources of law, and a legal culture which fosters a critical engagement with the Court and its decisions is vital for maintaining its democratic structure.

Imaginary 2: Racialized Minorities Get Special and Unjust Treatment

While the Supreme Court and its relation to the Constitution are imagined as a unity, some imaginaries have only developed with the help of constitutional interpretation. Among the most significant cases which de-established racial segregation and dismissed discrimination based on one's race as unconstitutional, the Supreme Court landmark cases *Brown v. Board of Education* (1954), *Loving v. Virginia* (1967), and *Batson v. Kentucky* (1986) fueled the popular narrative that racial discrimination has been overcome, both culturally and legally. This narrative of a 'post-racial' or 'color-blind' society finds further 'proof' in the election of Barack Obama as the first Black president in 2008 and instances of heightened racialized minoritarian visibility in the media. These misconceptions of constitutional history add legitimacy to the cultural narrative of equality.

As U.S. American legal culture narrates itself as 'post-racist' and as having overcome distinctions based on skin color, race, and ethnicity, legal means to establish racial equality are perceived as unnecessary and unjust. Minority quotas such as in Affirmative Action programs are thus subject to imaginaries which frame historically oppressed minorities as receiving preferential treatment. This perverted understanding of race relations and equality goes on to imagine the White majority as the one that is oppressed and treated unfairly. In this understanding, minorities get, for instance, placements at universities based solely on their racial or ethnic background and not due to their achievements or skills.

The history of systematic racism illustrates the faultiness of this imaginary, as does the very idea behind minority protection. The abolition of slavery after the Civil War led to the amendment of the Constitution, namely to the passing of Amendments XIII, XIV, and XV, which promised the formerly enslaved more civil rights. Abolishing slavery, already contested by many states and not a uniform decision, was met with other forms of structural racism and attempts to uphold racial hierarchies, most notably with the Supreme Court decision *Plessy v. Ferguson* (1896). As discussed earlier, *Plessy* not only established the so-called 'separate-but-equal' doctrine and enforced racial segregation, it also circumvented the legal promise of gaining more equality by subsequently establishing more laws which curtailed equal rights. Endeavors to tackle the constant backlash against minority rights are means to level out existing inequalities, which are far from being close to extinct. Using past Supreme Court decisions as light buoys in a sea of racial inequality overshadows the mass of contemporary discriminatory state bills, lower court decisions, and *de facto* practices of unfair treatment.

Imaginary 3: The Supreme Court Is Beyond Prejudice, as Is Contemporary Law

The decisions *Brown*, *Loving*, and *Batson* are considered all the more progressive and just because former legal and judicial attempts to establish racial equality have so obviously failed. While these decisions have undoubtably been important in ending *de jure* segregation, conceiving of them as the cases which solved *de facto* racial tensions in the U.S. or even establishing a race blind society would be window dressing. Still, they serve as credentials for imagining the contemporary Supreme Court as beyond prejudice and impartially objective. This imaginary serves to narrate the U.S. as 'post-racial,' morally enlightened and an exceptional nation. Siegel describes this invisibilization of contemporary prejudice as follows:

> We have demonized subordinating practices of the past to such a degree that condemning such practices may instead function to exonerate practices contested in the present, none of which looks so unremittingly "evil" by contrast. That which we retrospectively judge evil was once justified as reasonable. If we reconstruct the ground on which our predecessors justified subordinating practices of the past, we may be in a better position to evaluate contested practices in the present. (1113)

Siegel's view that focusing on past decisions instead of addressing current inequalities supports the claim that legal considerations should incorporate deconstructing cultural concepts. Taking as an example bills which regulate trans youth access to school sports, which are increasingly popping up in states throughout the U.S., legal and activist responses to these attacks on LGBTQ+ youth should focus on questioning the cultural emphasis on gender identity in and outside the law. Following Siegel, reconstructing the grounds on which past courts have justified their anti-LGBTQ+ decisions may initiate processes of deconstructing and rethinking legal (over)regulation of sexuality, sexual orientation, and gender identity. This may be done by, for instance, questioning why the state has an interest in assigning its citizens gender identities, and by extension examining whether this practice is a legitimate intrusion in one's private sphere. Engaging in this analysis and critique of legal decisions also necessitates scrutinizing the cultural framework which attributes meaning to sexual categories in the first place. Without this cultural-legal work, anti-trans and anti-queer narratives will feed into cultural imaginaries about LGBTQ+ and reify stereotypical misconceptualizations.

In the context of sex and gender equality, one observes similar dynamics of taking constitutional rights gains as equivalent to accomplished emancipatory efforts. *Frontiero v. Richardson* (1973) resulted in considering sex a quasi-suspect classification although the Court could have also opted to consider it a suspect classification and thus could have made discrimination based on sex unconstitutional in all areas of life. *Craig v. Boren* (1976) resulted in considering gender a quasi-suspect classification, making discrimination based on gender less likely to be considered constitutional, and *Roe v. Wade* (1973) de-criminalized abortion.

These decisions serve as moral credentials used to assert an exceptional sexual order and to imagine an already emancipated and equal society in terms of sex and gender, a 'post-sexist' society in no need for heightened legal or constitutional protections for sexual minorities and women. *Frontiero*, *Craig* and *Roe* thus fuel the constitutional-legal imaginary that sex and gender equality has been accomplished while truly progressive and more emancipatory constitutional solutions have not been considered. Declaring sex a suspect classification in *Frontiero*, gender a suspect classification in *Craig*, and emphasizing women's rights as grounds on which to base de-criminalizing abortion[56] would have also been emancipatory for a cultural order which still evolves around sexual hierarchies.

In her essay "Sexueller Exzeptionalismus" (sexual exceptionalism), Gabriele Dietze convincingly characterizes progressive legal decisions as important tools in immigration discourses and in maintaining sexual hierarchies by claiming to have overcome supposedly outdated and backwards

56 Although *Roe* was concerned with the fundamental right to privacy (at 152), including women's right to bodily autonomy with regard to abortions (at 153), feminist scholars including Supreme Court Justice Ruth Bader Ginsburg have criticized the opinion as using paternalistic language and being focused on "the doctor's freedom to practice" (Ginsburg qtd. in Heagney), claiming "it wasn't woman-centered, it was physician-centered" (Ginsburg qtd. in Heagney).

conceptualizations of sex and gender binary systems. "Sexually exceptional" refers to the societies' self-understanding with regard to sexual norms. To Dietze, sexually exceptional societies, typically within the global Northern hemisphere, understand their sexual order as outstandingly "progressive, privileged, and the best of all possible orders."[57] This imagined superiority necessitates an imagined sexist, patriarchal, queerphobic, and thus inferior counterpart, mostly found in immigrant communities, Muslim, non-Western or ethnically Otherized countries.

In immigration discourses, ethnosexist narratives serve to shield one's borders against supposedly less 'civilized' groups of people, who would bring with them their misogynistic, anti-LGBTQ+, and un-enlightened ideologies.[58] Examples of using images of Otherized bodies bringing with them something undesired in anti-migration discourses can be observed throughout history,[59] from framing immigrants as carriers of disease (Allman 6; Latour 123) to recent instances of Donald Trump's racist remarks about people who are immigrating to the U.S.[60] Relocating potential sexual and gendered violence to other countries serves to stress that one's own sexual orders and hierarchies are better, in the sense of more civilized, mirroring a colonial logic of alleged superiority.

The imaginary of a system without prejudice also involves the notion of an exceptionally fair and anti-hierarchical legal system. In this context, the U.S.'s cultural narrative of equality serves as proof of a superior legal system which guarantees everyone the equal protection of the laws. One could argue that the constitutional principle of suspect classification undermines this narrative as

---

57 Dietze speaks of "die am meisten 'fortgeschrittene', 'privilegierte' und 'beste' aller denkbaren Sexualordnungen" (27). My translation.

58 For a more detailed examination of images and imaginaries of migration, see Dietze 41–45.

59 See in this context also the concept of homonationalism in the work of Jasbir Puar, most notably *Terrorist Assemblages.*

60 See Reilly quoting Trump: "When Mexico sends its people, they're not sending their best. ... They're not sending you. They're sending people that have lots of problems, and they're bringing those problems with us [sic]. They're bringing drugs. They're bringing crime. They're rapists. And some, I assume, are good people." By labeling people from Mexico as rapists, Trump works to construct an image of immigrants not as merely foreign and thus *potentially* dangerous but as hostile and thus *definitely* dangerous. Interestingly, Trump chose to use several images of crime climaxing in the worst imaginable one, *sexual* violence.

well as the idea of an apolitical and neutral Supreme Court by offering minorities a more thorough protection. In this reading, the discrepancy between an assumed equal treatment for everyone and systemic inequalities for many becomes visible.

Claims for legal reforms, constitutional interventions in the form of reviewing laws that are perceived to be sexist, and the acceptance of social movements fighting for these issues are therefore doubly burdened. For one, they have to legitimize themselves in a sociocultural environment which *narrates* itself as post-sexist, equally protecting, and superiorly civilized. Further, these efforts meet an environment which wants to *imagine* itself this way because such an imaginary functions as a political, ideological, and economic tool to justify isolationist and unequal(izing) politics. In this constellation, different cultural-constitutional imaginaries reinforce and beget one another. An imagined exceptional legal system, which guarantees equal protection of the law for everyone in society, and an imagined exceptional cultural order, which accepts and tolerates sexual minorities, render granting more rights, deconstructing sociocultural norms, and cultural-legal education superfluous for the legal system already protects everyone in the best possible way.

Imaginary 4: A Sense of Justice Is a Value Inherent to True Americans

Increasingly, the U.S. American legal system is becoming increasingly defined via its justices and judges. Taking former U.S. president Donald Trump as reference point, his rhetoric not only influenced cultural narratives by stabilizing sexual orders, it is also directly connected to cultural-constitutional imaginaries. Using the trope of Mexicans as dangerous and criminal during his election campaign in 2015, Trump's questioned the impartiality of federal judge Gonzalo P. Curiel, who presided over two lawsuits against Trump University (*Tarla Makaeff v. Trump University*; *Cohen v. Trump*). He insinuated that Curiel would not judge cases involving Trump fairly because as a Mexican, Curiel disapproves of Trump's plans to build a boarder to Mexico. By combining xenophobic assumptions and name discrimination (Curiel is not Mexican) with anger over being prosecuted, Trump used the prominent right-wing narrative of an imminent loss of entitlement to draw on the cultural narrative of inalienable rights, which has constantly been (re-)formed and applied.

This evolving Trumpian sense of law and justice, which affects not only the judiciary but the legal system in general, has also spread into other cultural realms. It takes its starting points in neoliberal notions of freedom and heteropatriarchal power structures and merges them with cultural anxieties about imminent deprivation of economic, social, and power resources. The neoliberal notion of freedom as unchecked, unalienable fundamental right violently refuses any interference by the law (and those making or applying it), especially when minorities are granted more rights. In this logic, if the judiciary finds someone guilty, it is the judges' lack of partiality or knowledge, but never in line with existing law. One's legal affect, the *feeling* of being right, leads to the imaginary that the law is on one's side, and outweighs any actual legal provisions.

How this imaginary manifests becomes obvious by looking at Trump's speeches. In a December 2020 post-election rally, he talked about alleged voting fraud and called out to the courts by stating that "our legislatures [sic] and the United States Supreme Court will step forward and save our country" (Trump). The emphasis on the U.S. legal system mirrors notions of American Exceptionalism: Trump believes in its justice-yielding ability and its exceptional fairness based on his own feeling. Dragging legislators and the Court's justices into the political spotlight, Trump puts pressure on the democratic process. He supposes the *a priori* culpability of the enemy, i.e., the Democratic Party, without adhering to other legal principles such as due process, and he frames (in)justice as a matter of individual opinion (of the legislators and justices).

By calling on the legislative and the judiciary whenever a societal transformation is unwanted and expecting these branches to step in to correct this transformation, Trump transforms the narrative of unalienable rights into an imagined guaranteed legal protection for anyone who is American. Ironically, this understanding of 'anyone' is again as fragile as the Fourteenth Amendment's original meaning of 'any person:' It only addresses those who correspond to the Trumpian in-group and their preferred normative standards of being American, i.e., White, cis, able-bodied, heterosexual, non-immigrants. Despite these apparent exclusionary implications, the cultural-constitutional imaginary of guaranteed legal protection stresses the moral superiority of the Republican Party and the political far-right – and thereby forces others to respond to this affectively felt injustice done to others' voices and bodies.

What follows is an imagined entitlement of having one's own position represented in law. While cultural discourses become more politicized, which is apparent in contemporary notions of 'culture wars,' more emphasis is placed on courts, judicial decision-making processes, and legislators. Individualism, as an important American cultural value, and the emphasis of freedom of speech and personal liberty merge to bear a new fundamental belief: being entitled to have one's feelings about justice legally represented. This neoliberal understanding of demarcating one's space is not implemented in the form of private property but in the form of legal feelings or feelings of justice. Using the concept of German legal scholar Rudolf von Jhering, one's own and valid *Rechtsgefühle* (28) pose a threat to legal and cultural pluralisms whenever these are situated in illiberal democracies or are not able to endure diversity and discrepancies.

Highly controversial events such as Justice Brett Kavanaugh's confirmation hearing, the unsuccessfulness of both the impeachment process of Trump and investigations about Russia's involvement in the 2016 elections have constantly shifted the confines of what is possible without being charged or prosecuted. Yet these events have not only diluted democratic structures, they have also inflated cultural understandings of justice and law.

The implicit promise for those in power, namely that there is someone, from 2016–2020 in the person of Donald Trump, who will protect one's interests and help one to get away with ever more violent demands for 'freedom' has shaped the imaginary that the U.S. American citizen's (as imagined by Republicans and right conservative actors) inherent legal affect of justice is more in line with the Constitution and fundamental values than are democratic institutions. Thus, these larger-than-law Americans are entitled to favor their *Rechtsgefühle* over existing, supposedly unjust legal orders. In order to survive and remain powerful, this entitlement proves insatiable. It has to be fed by continuous territorial gains, be it in the form of surprisingly audacious public statements or by pushing back on those who challenge this view. This development culminated in the pro-Trump mob attacking and vandalizing the U.S. Capitol in January 2021 after more formal attempts[61] to secure this by now internalized entitlement had failed.

When challenged, now internalized demands to have one's *Rechtsgefühle* represented and accounted for step in and legitimize means, even violent ones, of self-empowerment and vigilantism. An important observation in this context of violent protests and attacks is that the governing law is not perceived as void, i.e., that one is indifferent to which laws are possibly broken, but that

61 Arguably, only the multiple law suits trying to demand a recount of the voting ballots after the 2020 election were formal. Other attempts were rather informal and illegal such as Trump's call to Georgia's Secretary of State, Brad Raffensperger, urging him to "find" votes in favor of the Republican Party.

breaking governing law is affective fuel which motivates those with hurt entitlements. Only by overstepping these boundaries, one has the feeling of redemption and making their conceptions of justice seen or heard.

Another instance is Florida Governor Ron DeSantis' reaction to Disney's critique of HB 1557, informally known as 'Don't Say Gay' bill. After initial refusal to comment on DeSantis' anti-LGBTQ+ bill, Disney, following protests by its workers, issued a statement on 28 March 2022 in which the company called "for this law to be repealed by the legislature or struck down in the courts" (@WaltDisneyCo). DeSantis condemned such an intervention and retaliated against Disney by revoking their special status in Florida.[62] The bill, which DeSantis signed into law in April 2022, took away Disney's ability to self-govern its theme park, which Disney had held for 55 years. DeSantis' decision to tackle a company like Disney, one of the biggest employers in the state and arguably a proponent of traditional gender roles and heteronormative structures, illustrates how contested and affectively charged any kind of critique is.

Imaginary 5: American Life, Born and Unborn, Is in Severe Need of Being Saved

This imagined right to entitlement and vigilantism has by now found its way into codified law. State bills such as Texas' Senate Bill 8/House Bill 1515 ("Texas Heartbeat Act") as well as Texas Governor Gregg Abbott's February 2022 order which charges trans children's supportive parents with child abuse explicitly call on citizens to report those not abiding to existing law. Arguably the most vigilante U.S. state in the cultural imaginary, Texas is currently constructing these laws to target both the culturally undesired Other and those supporting them. The Texas Heartbeat Act states that "a physician may not knowingly perform or induce an abortion on a pregnant woman if the physician detected a fetal heartbeat for the unborn child" (sec. 171.204), which typically develops six weeks into pregnancy. This regulation "does not apply if a physician believes a medical emergency exists" (sec. 171.205 a) or if the pregnancy resulted from rape or incest. However, Texas' law goes even further than this. The Heartbeat

62 DeSantis already warned against such an involvement by 'woke' companies in June 2021: "If you are in one of these corporations, if you're a woke CEO, you want to get involved in our legislative business, look, it's a free country … But understand, if you do that, I'm fighting back against you. And I'm going to make sure that people understand your business practices, and anything I don't like about what you're doing" (qtd. in Contorno).

Act awards "any person, other than an officer or employee of a state or local governmental entity in this state" (sec. 171.208 a) who spies and reports those breaking the law with $10,000. This incentive to enforce legal norms caters to the cultural imaginary of having the right to yield legislative and executive power and to the constitutional imaginary that one's own legal affects need to be mirrored in law. As legal scholar Josh Blackman puts it, "[e]very citizen is now a private attorney general" (qtd. in Goodkind):

> Politically, this move is particularly divisive because it undermines the democratic workings of the three governmental branches and strengthens the position of those in opposition to abortion. By enabling citizens to sue abortion clinics through reporting, governmental agencies are no longer the ones which initiate judicial persecution, which makes abortion providers unable to defend the constitutionality of their actions in court (Goodkind).

In a similar vein, Texas Governor Gregg Abbott issued an order in February 2022 which "imposes a duty on DFPS [Department of Family and Protective Services] to investigate the parents of a child who is subjected to [...] abusive gender-transitioning procedures, and other state agencies to investigate licensed facilities where such procedures may occur" ("February"). While the re-definition of what constitutes child abuse is part of the anti-LGBTQ+ agenda, Abbott's order adds yet another layer of violence to the struggle for cultural and constitutional hegemonies. Quoting the "fundamental right to procreation" ("February" 6), the Attorney General of Texas, Ken Paxton, issued an opinion which fills the gap legislative attempts such as Texas SB 1646 have failed at: Paxton adds gender-reassignment surgeries as well as "administering, prescribing or dispensing" puberty blockers and hormones to children to chapter 261 of the Texas Family Code (2), which defines child abuse.

Issuing an order and an opinion, Abbott and Paxton bypass the democratic process of the legislative to avoid that their measures do not find a majority[63], and to invoke a constitutional foundation for their arguments. Again, the cultural imaginary of having a rxfight to entitlement factors into the constitutional imaginary of bending the Constitution to match one's legal affects. Abbott's order to have state agencies investigate those not complying with the law, which, as of April 2022, is being challenged in court and temporarily

63 For instance, SB 1646 has died in the senate.

blocked, resembles the Heartbeat Act's deputizing of Texans for policing abortion providers and receivers. In both instances, one witnesses a coupling of social control with institutional violence, entitled by the imaginary of having the right to have one's legal affects represented and enforced.

From a historical perspective, stressing the ideals of liberty, individualism, and self-determination amplifies when confronted with cultural anxieties about heteronomy. Fearing a return to an oppressing, centralized form of government, Reconstruction Era constitutional cases negotiated the role of former slaves within U.S. American society and the relationship between federal and state governments. Legal scholars and politicians utilized anxieties about lack of representation by merging them with anxieties about Otherness.[64] Pending deprival of formerly enjoyed rights or feeling deprived of rights one feels entitled to has thus a history of being connected to anti-minority bias and politico-legal endeavors to challenge emancipatory reforms.[65]

This cultural imaginary about justice and its connected idea about what law should do for whom also affects those on other sides of the political spectrum. Violently dismissing others' demands for justice while defending one's own entitlement to absolution leads to a disenchantment with politics and bears the risk of establishing violence as *modus operandi* and suspends democratic institutions from their authority.

Consequently, the imaginary of the omnipresence of enemies within, and entitlement to individual absolution stretch into legislative and judicial terrains and create a network of distrust and new entitlements. However, there seems to exist an overarching belief in an American Exceptionalism of justice, which makes one rely on and trust in the system's self-regulating forces. The Supreme Court functions as a main ingredient in this imaginary.

Trump worked to form the image of the Supreme Court as most important instance of authority. First, especially for younger generations, associations with the Court will evolve around Kavanaugh and Barrett, whom Trump both nominated. Even after his presidential term, these justices are thought of

64 See Millhiser "Troubled:" Former Supreme Court Justice and then lawyer John Archibald Campbell asked the Court whether "there [can] be any centralization more complete or any despotism less responsible than that of a State legislature concerning itself with dominating the avocations, pursuits and modes of labor of the population." While Campbell legally challenged the *Slaughterhouse Act*, his personal motivation to do so has been traced back to anger about "black participation in government."

65 Support for this analysis can be found in social psychology's deprivation theory, see Kite and Whitley 312–4.

as place holders for Trumpian politics and representatives of the Republican party's political impact. Should these justices fail to adhere to Trump's political beliefs, they will nonetheless be remembered as 'Trump justices' and thus may even be considered as proof of his political skill.

Additionally, both Kavanaugh's and Barrett's nominations show how the Supreme Court is being used as a site for negotiating the ability to exercise political power, an aspect which will be dealt with in more detail in Chapter III, and of shaping cultural imaginaries. Having a majority of justices on the bench who were nominated by Republicans makes a conservative Court very likely. This way, overturning liberal decisions (and fears of having those decisions overturned) become powerful and dangerous tools in shaping sociocultural realities and deepening bipartisan distrust. The constant antagonization of Republicans vs. Democrats has a real foundation because Court decisions have real-life consequences for U.S. Americans. Hence the over-politization of justices as either conservative or liberal denies them the opportunity to act as mediators between party politics in the U.S. American people's imaginary. Justices are depicted and imagined as static political actors and actresses, thereby reinforcing binary thinking about politics and imagining an identity politics which disregards ambiguity and decision-based judicial impartiality.

Thus, the Court is transformed into a gatekeeper for cultural identity and into a political arena. The subsequent pressure to satisfy every political demand of every side poses the danger of creating distrust in the judiciary and the entire legal system when demands are not met. As a consequence, cultural imaginaries about the Court pose the danger of working to de-legitimize the Court.

As seen by looking at cultural imaginaries in the context of racial politics, changing cultural imaginaries factor into constitutional transformations only when there are equally important political, ideological, and economic goals to achieve. On the other hand, constitutional transformations factor into changing cultural imaginaries quite differently. Landmark decisions that have shaped and altered existing notions of equality illustrate that constitutional transformations have a direct impact on American society's and culture's setup and on how one perceives them. The power to form these imaginaries, and thereby potentially shed light on or mask sociocultural issues results in a morally, socially, and also politically heightened responsibility. In this understanding, one cannot but perceive of those holding this power as political actors. The next chapter sheds light on the polarization and politization of the Supreme Court as an institution and on the role the individual justices take on.

III. Neither Force nor Will?
The Supreme Court's Politics

III.1. Seeing the Supreme Court Through a Cultural-Legal Lens

Any interest in the highest court in the U.S., the Supreme Court, necessitates a readiness to engage with the United States' legal, cultural, and political history. The Supreme Court as we know it today would not have been possible, nor thinkable, without the British king George III.'s tax system. The feeling of being unfairly taxed was one of the reasons for the American Revolution, which in turn led Americans to draft and ratify the Declaration of Independence and the U.S. Constitution. The latter then signed into law the system of federalism with the three governmental branches of the judiciary, legislative and executive. Admittingly rather rudimental, this historic causation illustrates that the Supreme Court's existence has been constructed along the lines of a legal institution with limited power but high authority, balanced and checked on by the two other branches.

The Supreme Court was an institution designed as counterpart to what Americans experienced under British rule; a system perceived to be unjust and not accessible to the average citizen. A high court in the Americans' understanding would be all that British law was not to them: impartial, representative, and regularly checked on by the other governmental branches (see Madison "The Federalist No. 49"). By necessity, the Supreme Court is tied to the very political and legal beginnings of the United States as well as to their cultural foundations.

By wide reading Supreme Court landmark cases of the twenty-first century which deal with sexual minorities and scrutinizing the justices' modes of constitutional interpretation, this chapter stresses that suspect classification is the most promising option for securing queer rights. For doing so, the first part contextualizes the discussion about the Supreme Court's role for queer rights discourses by tracing back its historical origins, and commenting on its political dimensions. This subchapter argues that the Supreme Court is functioning as a political player in the discourse about sexual orientation's constitutional protection, and continues to become more politicized, publicly contested, and abusive in wielding its power. Part two (Chapter III.1) rudimentarily explains the differences between dominant modes of constitutional interpretation. It analyzes the ways allegedly neutral, or "*neutralizing*" (Lemos 851; emphasis in original), modes of interpretation do indeed carry political implications, and how covert ideological beliefs pave their way into these supposedly apolitical methodological divides.[1]

The case studies in part three then apply these findings to an analysis of the cultural and legal implications of the Court's most important decisions concerning sexual minorities in the twenty-first century. The Supreme Court cases these subchapters look at are those carrying the most weight with regard to sexual orientation's constitutional protection, i.e., only those which deal with sexual minorities and sexual politics (*Lawrence v. Texas* [2003]; *U.S. v. Windsor* [2013]; *Obergefell v. Hodges* [2015]; *Masterpiece Cakeshop v. Colorado Civil Rights Commission* [2018]; *Bostock v. Clayton County* [2020]). The case studies also illustrate how these decisions work to constitute and maintain sociocultural imaginaries, and establish that the Supreme Court functions as a political player.

The Supreme Court: Now and Then

The 2020s have already shaped U.S. America sustainably. Be it the Covid-19 pandemic, backlash against governmental measures trying to respond to the pandemic, protests for racial justice following the murder of George Floyd, the death of Supreme Court Justice Ruth Bader Ginsburg, – and the subsequent nomination of Justice Amy Coney Barrett, – and the U.S. American elections – they all share their emphasis on the judiciary. Most notably the Supreme Court but also lower courts serve as vital players in deciding whose voices prevail. This becomes obvious in matters of re-counting electoral ballots, preserving individual freedom vs. protecting the collective, and allowing questions about the (il)legitimacy of police action. Also, the Supreme Court was itself reviewed with strict scrutiny as in the question of who follows in Justice Bader Ginsburg's footsteps.

---

1 See Lemos for more on the connection between textualism and statutory interpretation.

This development has gained more momentum in the summer of 2022 when the U.S. American politics magazine *Politico* leaked draft opinion for a pending case, *Dobbs v. Jackson Women's Health Organization*, to the public. This incident was extraordinary because of the strict rules the justices and their law clerks are to follow,[2] and because of its content: The opinion argued for the overturning of *Roe v. Wade* (1973), which would make abortion a state matter again and resolve its de-criminalization on a federal level. As a result of this highly controversial opinion, the Court's justices faced increased media attention and needed more protection. The security measures for the Supreme Court building and the nine justices were increased, including 24/7 surveillance of their private homes (Breuninger "U.S. Marshals"), fencing off the Supreme Court building (Breuninger "AG Garland"), and proposed bills to fund higher security measures (Diaz). Even more, in trying to find out who leaked the draft, the Supreme Court initiated an "unprecedented probe to uncover who leaked the decision" which included that "authorities have demanded phone records, signed affidavits, and law clerks' devices" (Cahn). Foreshadowing the demise of abortion rights, the exploitation of digital and privacy rights, and ever more forceful demonstrations of power, these developments indicate the beginning of a new era in which the Supreme Court's politization, ongoing for several decades, now becomes publicly more visible and contested.

All of these matters share an inherently political character in how the public relates and responds to social hierarchies of power. As this chapter argues, the Supreme Court is not only an arena for (re-)negotiating power but also an institution which gatekeeps, accumulates, (re-)distributes, and longs for political power. As such, the Court is evidently political.

Ironically, the Supreme Court of the United States is apolitical qua definition and history. The highest part of the judiciary (Latin *iudicare* means to administer justice; to judge) is responsible for deciding legal cases according to the Separation of Powers doctrine. Together with the legislative, which establishes laws, and the executive, which executes laws, the judiciary is part of the

---

2 Constitutional policy analyst Ian Millhiser states that "There may be no modern precedent for a leak of this magnitude. The Court normally operates under a strict code of silence until the moment a decision is released. Supreme Court law clerks even have a special dining room in the Court's cafeteria, where they can discuss cases over lunch without risking anyone overhearing those conversations. … I'm aware of no precedent for an entire draft opinion being published before the decision is final" ("4 Things").

so-called *trias politica* that ensures that power within governments is equally distributed and that each branch checks and balances the other two. This system goes back to antiquity and has influenced Western law traditions and cultural conceptions of democracy. The Separation of Powers doctrine and the system of checks and balances is meant to prevent accumulation of political power in one institution or person. In the beginnings of the United States, this way of separating responsibilities and duties between different branches of government was perceived as particularly well-organized.[3]

Both official documents and statements by justices invoke and try to manifest this apolitical character. Chief Justice Roberts made several public statements over the last years in which he stresses that the Supreme Court is no political entity.[4] Likewise, the government informs visitors on their website that

> [j]udges and Justices serve no fixed term — they serve until their death, retirement, or conviction by the Senate. By design, this insulates them from the temporary passions of the public, and allows them to apply the law with only justice in mind, and not electoral or political concerns. ... Since Justices do not have to run or campaign for re-election, they are thought to be insulated from political pressure when deciding cases. ("Judicial Branch")

These instances of officials re-assuring the U.S. American public about the impartiality of the Court as well as the historical origin of the judiciary illustrate that the Supreme Court ought to be apolitical. Consequently, the idea that there exist political implications of how to interpret legal cases, so-called modes of interpretation, may appear as a paradox for the non-legal reader: How can the institution of the Supreme Court which is based on the very idea of impartiality, claimed objectivity, and unpolitical character be political at all? This chapter establishes that the paradoxical part about the Court's

---

3 In 1835, French philosopher Alexis de Tocqueville already praised the U.S. American system of decentralized power in his seminal *Democracy in America* (107–10).

4 In 2019, Roberts said during an interview at Temple Emanu-El: "When you live in a politically polarized environment, people tend to see everything in those terms. ... That's not how we at the court function and the results in our cases do not suggest otherwise." (Bump). In 2020, Roberts responded to a statement by Democrat Chuck Schumer by stating that "Justices know that criticism comes with the territory. ... But threatening statements of this sort from the highest levels of government are not only inappropriate, they are dangerous." (Millhiser "Controversy").

entanglements is not their political character but the general idea that this politization should not and thus does not exist.

The Politics of the Supreme Court

I argue that the Supreme Court is political in three major ways. In the process of nominating justices, in the justices themselves, both with regard to how they are being positioned by the media and to how they position themselves, and in methodological approaches to constitutional interpretation.[5] As legal scholars have noted,[6] the ongoing polarization of U.S. American politics has impacted the Court, too. In the election year of 2020, legal commentators have praised SCOTUS for deciding cases in a rather progressive manner, most notably in *Bostock v. Clayton County* (2020). With a conservative majority on the bench, commentators expected the Court to rule that discrimination based on one's sexual orientation is not covered by Title VII of the Civil Rights Act of 1964. The fact that the Court decided in favor of such a discrimination and that Chief Justice Roberts, a conservative centrist, joined the majority opinion, was considered as proof for an apolitical Court that decides based on facts and not sentiments, and which is able to generate trust in governmental institutions in highly politicized times. Acting as an impartial institution, the Court stands out as unbiased mediator between different political agendas in these times. Ironically, it is exactly this maneuvering of the Court that makes it inherently political as pointed out by jurists Dahlia Lithwick and Mark Joseph Stern:

> The irony of Roberts' endless maneuvering is that preventing the court from appearing political requires him to act politically. Brokering compromises behind the scenes, manipulating the docket to keep hot-button cases far away from the court, forecasting the impact of each decision on

---

5 Geoffrey R. Stone identifies "1) the politicization of the confirmation process; 2) the polarization and apparent politicization of the justices; and 3) the Court's current approach to constitutional interpretation" as three "possible reasons for the decline in public respect for the Supreme Court" ("The Supreme Court" 37). While agreeing that these three factors play a major role in the assessment of the Court's political character, I disagree with Stone's view that these aspects are the reasons for a negative shift in the Court's public perception. Rather, I would argue that a changing sociocultural climate of holding those in positions of power responsible influences how the public approaches the Court's legitimacy in recent years and how such power abuses are visibilized, perceived, and responded to.

6 See, among others, Stone "The Supreme Court" 38.

> the election—these are inherently political acts undertaken to convince public that the court is apolitical. They are not the traditional duties of a jurist. But Roberts is the exceedingly rare judge who understands politics, not just party politics, but also how to behave politically. And he recognizes that, as Americans lose faith in the other two branches of government, he has the power, and perhaps the responsibility, to cultivate more trust in the court.

Roberts is considered an 'institutionalist,' someone who is trying to preserve the legitimacy of the institution, the Court, by appealing to the public. For doing so, deciding cases in a rather progressive manner during an election year evokes the impression that governmental pressure does not impact the Court's decisions and that it is thus impartial and unbiased. Consequently, the Court aims to remain in a position of power and respect within the public so as not to risk potential criticism in highly politicized times. Achieving higher public ratings for the Court is a strategic way to maintain power and a political act in itself. This is all the more relevant at a time when only 40% of the U.S. American public approves of the Supreme Court, marking a historical low in the twenty-first century (Jones). These numbers affirm the pressure the Court is under to legitimate its actions.

Apart from these political tactics to preserve the institutional legitimacy of the Court, other recent examples of the politization of the Court are the nomination processes of Justice Brett M. Kavanaugh in 2018, and Justice Amy Coney Barrett in 2020. Kavanaugh was confirmed by the Senate with a vote of 50–48 with 49 Republicans voting in favor of and 46 Democrats against him.[7] In addition to the political salience of this nomination process, the public reaction to Kavanaugh's hearing included protests in front of the U.S. Capitol,[8] extensive (social) media coverage, and a revival of questioning the impartiality of the judiciary, which is feared to become unbalanced and conservative. The strong focus on this particular nomination was influenced by the fact that Kavanaugh had to respond to allegations of sexual assault voiced by psychology professor Christine Blasey Ford and several other women as part of his confirmation hearing. While these allegations may not have had a consequence

7 The Senate Judiciary Committee forwarded the nomination to the full Senate with a vote of 11–10 along party-lines with all Republicans voting in favor of Kavanaugh, all Democrats voting against his nomination ("Nomination").

8 See, for instance, Rosenblatt, and "In Photos." On the 6th of October 2018, the day Kavanaugh was sworn in as justice, more than 300 protestors were arrested.

for Kavanaugh's confirmation, their implications for what it means to have the U.S. Senate let an accused sex offender serve on the highest court in the nation influences discourses about sexual politics, so-called 'culture wars,' and imagined entitlements as discussed in Chapter II.

Concerns about an ideologically unified Court became also apparent in the process of nominating conservative judge Amy Coney Barrett. Barrett replaced the liberal and bipartisan respected Justice Ruth Bader Ginsburg, who passed away in 2020. Barrett's nomination became the arena of a political scramble for Supreme Court hegemony. With Barrett on the bench, conservative justices now make up six of the nine seats, with the two other Trump-nominated justices Neil Gorsuch and Brett Kavanaugh in addition to Bush-nominated justices Clarence Thomas, Samuel Alito and John Roberts. Arguably, the political salience of Barrett's nomination was even stronger than Kavanaugh's. Firstly, it happened in an election year and thus Democrats felt Republicans would not only take unfair advantage of their majority in Senate, but also betray what was once considered the 'Biden rule.'[9] Secondly, social tensions and 'culture wars' were fueled by dissatisfaction and outright anger about governmental measures to counteract the Covid-19 pandemic, the still prevalent issue of police brutality, and three years of presidential Trumpism. For those who did not support Trumpian politics, the nomination of Amy Coney Barrett invoked fears about a continuation of Trump's influence on U.S. politics and the lives of Americans regardless of the outcome of the elections. More specifically, her nomination triggered fears about using a conservative majority to review and potentially overturn the *Patient Protection and Affordable Care Act* ('Obamacare')[10] and Supreme Court cases which provided civil rights to minorities, legalized

---

9 Named after Joseph R. Biden, then chairman of the Senate Judiciary Committee and thus responsible for considering judicial nominations and passing them on for confirmation to the Senate. Biden gave a speech in 1992 in which he stated that, given a Supreme Court vacancy should arise during an election year, the sitting president should not "name a nominee until after the November election is completed" (Sherman). Republicans quoted this unofficial rule when they refused to consider Democratic nominee Merrick Garland's nomination by then President Barrack Obama in 2016.

10 It is important to note that curling back the *Affordable Care Act* (*ACA*) would also be a backlash for the LGBTQ+ community. Members of the community are statistically more prone to substance abuse and psychological distress while simultaneously being economically disadvantaged and thus in need of low-income health care. Further, before *ACA*, health care providers were allowed to discriminate against trans people by refusing to insure them and, as a non-cis gender identity was considered 'a pre-ex-

abortion (*Roe v. Wade*) and ruled same-sex marriage (*Obergefell v. Hodges*) constitutional. From today's perspective, these fears were justified as can be seen in the overturn of *Roe* in 2022's *Dobbs v. Jackson Women's Health Organization*.

From a European perspective, interest in the personal set-up of the highest court in the country may seem irritating as most justices in EU countries are not appointed for life[11] and thus, their powers to shape laws, society, and culture are temporally limited. Arguably, the limited time of service makes non-U.S. constitutional courts less political in that questions of who serves on the bench are not as person-centered and not as politically charged as in the U.S. However, decisions of constitutional courts are as politically loaded in Europe as they are in the United States, which is shown in, e.g., the case of stricter abortion laws, decided by the Polish supreme court *Trybunał Konstytucyjny* in 2021, or the amendment of the Hungarian constitution to redefine family as "based on marriage and the parent-child relation. The mother is a woman, the father a man" (Dunai and Komuves).[12] One may argue that the set-up of the court is equally important there, yet it is not so much focused on individual justices but on the judiciary's general affinity to the ruling government's politics and ideology.

In the U.S., this relevance of personnel decisions offers not only a different legal landscape but also one that is culturally distinct. Since constitutional courts arguably deal with a country's most controversial legal cases, and deciding these cases falls in the responsibility of only a selected few, interest in these few, including their respective moral and political beliefs feeds more into a society's consciousness than in other Western countries such as in Germany, France, or Spain. Consequently, cultural imaginaries about 'the' legal system, including the imagined entitlement and necessity of having one's *Rechtsgefühle*

---

isting condition,' providers were not required to cover any medical treatment related to being trans, including hormone therapy and gender reassignment surgeries.

11 For instance, justices at the highest court in Germany, the *Bundesverfassungsgericht*, are appointed for 12-year-tenures with no possibility of re-election, and they are to retire after the age of 68; the French *Conseil constitutionnel* and the Spanish *Tribunal Constitucional* appoint its justices for a regular term of 9 years with no possibility of re-election.

12 While this amendment was initiated by Hungarian prime minister Viktor Orbán and his party, the Hungarian constitutional court has been transformed to fit the political agenda of Orbán, with the election of Zsolt András Varga as chief justice in 2021 securing future pro-nationalist and anti-LGBTQ+ decisions by the court; see Kazai and Kovács.

represented and accounted for in laws, legal decisions, and the legislative and judiciary, are more closely connected to concrete people than to a nation's highest court as an opaque legal block.[13]

This U.S. focus on individual people in the legal system mirrors and reinforces the American ideal of individualism. While having some people decide on matters for an entire collective may seem to contradict individualism's core "vision of free individuals directing their own lives according to their own judgment" (Daniels 70), the cultural praxis of de-reifying the Court evokes the impression that 'the law' is dependent on individuals instead of having a life of its own. This emphasis on the people on the Court makes this institution more relatable and allegedly more transparent. Unlike at times impenetrable bureaucratic and political processes of decision-making, putting faces, names, and opinions to justices evokes the impression that one knows who is in charge. This alleged transparency, in addition to the constant re-assurance that SCOTUS is apolitical, contributes to the invisibilization of political processes within the Court.

The structure of the Court thus moves beyond merely providing organizational information or offering a politico-legal framework for decision-making to shaping cultural notions about legal personhood. Zooming in on the Court's nine individual justices with their individual moral and political beliefs, – for instance by reporting on individual justice's lines of argumentation, their religious beliefs, or the practice of lifetime appointments, – emphasizes the legal agency of the individual, personal responsibility for one's actions, and, by extension, a cultural self-efficiency which feeds on the idea of individual moral sovereignty and exceptionalism. The nine justices represent 'the' U.S. American as such, including legal citizens and those who feel belonging to the U.S., and act as guardians of the collective's constitution. The fact that of all nine justices, all are cis, four are women, only two are Black, one is Hispanic, and none are not heterosexual further complicates the Supreme Court's function as political representation of American citizens as such, and its implicit commentary on who is legally agentic.

13 I would argue that in Germany, associations with 'the' legal system are more closely related to governmental actors, including parties, than to courts or justices and judges. This perception became most obvious in discussions about the appropriateness of measures to counteract the spreading of Covid-19 in 2020 when debates in the *Bundestag* were often depicted as divided between the ruling governmental parties and the opposition.

III.2. A Dogmatic Historization of the Supreme Court's Modes of Interpretation in the Twenty-First Century

Although European constitutional courts are organized differently, the historic roots of constitutional courts' competencies to declare statutes unconstitutional goes back to the U.S. landmark decision *Marbury v. Madison*. This 1803 case established the U.S. Constitution's legal importance and the Supreme Court's authority to apply it. More specifically, *Marbury* laid down the Court's power to judicially review whether federal governmental actions are in line with what the Constitution says. This newly established task of judicial review was then also instructive for European constitutional courts.

Judicial review includes interpretation of the Constitution, a highly controversial endeavor. For the most parts, the Constitution uses a language which is not unambiguously clear to its readers,[14] and the last 220 years have created constellations which the Constitution's ratifiers could not have included simply because they were unforeseeable at the time. For instance, technological developments such as the invention of VCRs were most probably not part of the imagination of the Constitution's ratifiers, yet in the 1984's *Sony of America v. Universal City Studios* case, the Supreme Court had to decide on whether these devices violate copyright claims (Grossman).

The question that arises in these cases is then "What does the Constitution say?", or, for matters on which the Constitution is silent or not explicit, "Is there any hint what the Constitution might say about this?". For these gaps of meaning or ambiguous parts which require some clarity, justices have adopted different modes of how to read and interpret the words of the Constitution. While attorney Brandon Murrill has identified eight modes of constitutional interpretation for the Congressional Research Service (CRS),[15] other legal scholars consider different numbers of modes as dominant.[16]

Although there is no coherent canon and some modes are similar to others, constitutional interpretation can be observed along some rather clear lines,

14 Notable exceptions of straightforward constitutional language are the specific age requirements for public office, e.g., Art. II sec. 1 clause 5, which states that only those U.S. citizens are eligible for becoming president who are older than 35.

15 This enumeration does not represent an exhaustive taxonomy but merely refers to the most prominent styles of interpretation as defined by Murrill. Among them are textualism, originalism, strict constructionalism, judicial precedent, pragmatism, moral reasoning, national identity/ethos, structuralism, and historical practices.

16 For instance, legal scholar R. Randall Kelso identifies four main modes (126).

both legally and politically. In each case, the way a justice construes the text of a statue, law, or the Constitution is based on a philosophical and legal understanding rather than on a case-to-case basis.[17] Beyond these "politics of methodology" (Lemos 855), i.e., the discipline-specific considerations on the design of legal theories, the different methodologies of judicial interpretation are political themselves – or have at least been associated with specific political affiliations.

Understanding the process of reviewing the words of a legal document as more than a simply preference of one's legal approach, namely a question of how to understand the functions of the judiciary in general, makes the modes of judicial interpretation evidently political. Depending on what a justice believes to be the 'correct' approach, they would argue for an understanding which focusses on what has been written or intended by the framers of the legal text in question (*originalism* and *textualism*), or for an organic understanding which takes into account historical, political, and sociocultural developments since the respective legal passage's passing (*living constitution/organic/evolutionist*).[18] This distinction seems rather simplistic given the amount of theories some scholars identify, yet it is at the core of the theoretical divides among scholars.[19]

Distinguishing between originalist and evolutionist approaches is important for determining the scope of a justice's interpretation, a matter of whether their decisions scratch on legislative terrain or whether they remain in judicial territory. Deciding on a certain mode of interpretation is thus connected to one's understanding of the scope of the separation of powers, and therefore also to one's understanding of one of the U.S.'s cultural-legal pillars. Those who perceive law's meaning as text-inherent, meaning as able to fill gaps of meaning by itself, via examining the wording of legal norms and the legal norms in themselves, advocate for a jurisprudence which relies on what is written instead of referring to those interpreting it (Dregger 38;

---

17 While some legal scholars and justices believe that judicial interpretation is based on a philosophical mindset, others prefer to "remain agnostic on methodology, as most judges do" (Lemos 854).

18 My use of the term 'organic' is influenced by Ritchie's, who understands organic "in a more metaphorical sense" in that it is "inextricably linked to the social context in which it is situated" (2).

19 The overlappings of textualism, strict constructionalism, original meaning, as well as the entanglements of structuralism, judicial restraint and judicial activism speak in favor of such a simplified characterization for the purpose of this book.

Baer *Rechtssoziologie* 29).[20] This understanding emphasizes the power of the legislative while de-emphasizing the judiciary's power. Contrary to that, understanding law's gap-yness as in need of judges' and justices' interpretation, including taking into account non-textual, social, political, cultural realities, emphasizes the judiciary's influence and power. Textualism is thus connected to judicial restraint, while living constitutionalism is connected to judicial activism, which is a rather pejorative term in jurisprudence as it goes against the idea of an impartial judiciary which is staying in its lane and not acting legislatively.

Whenever the Supreme Court reviews a case, the questions whether justices are 'legislating from the bench,' or sticking to a formalist understanding of a legal text becomes of legal, political, and sociocultural importance, especially for cases involving minority groups. Since these groups are historically underrepresented, and thus often disadvantaged in contributing to public discourses, endeavors to prove their constitutional protection are tricky. The historical invisibility of these underrepresented groups and their sociocultural stigmatization, already in reciprocity to each other, create a legal situation which sees discriminatory laws against these groups (e.g., laws criminalizing homosexual activity) in correlation to precedents that confirm the constitutionality of these laws (e.g., 'sodomy'[21] laws and decisions affirming these laws such as *Bowers v. Hardwick*). Consequently, contemporary prejudice which has found its way into legal precedent continues to meander into subsequent cultural discourses. Cultural narratives and imaginaries about the protect-ability and -worthiness of these stigmatized groups then fed on legal norms, and legal norms contribute to the genesis of such narratives and imaginaries. In order to grasp the full extent of this claim, the followings paragraphs introduce the arguably most important modes of constitutional interpretation.[22]

---

20 See also Haferkamp for more on Georg Friedrich Puchta's "Begriffsjurisprudenz," which influenced this law-inherent approach.

21 'Sodomy' is put in quotation marks because it is an outdated, derogatory, and harmful term. It is only used to refer to the language used at that time and to situate this chapter's discussion in the respective legal discourse.

22 Analyses and definitions of these modes compile a research field on their own. The definitions offered here are meant to serve as an introduction into this field and to equip the reader with sufficient knowledge to follow this chapter's line of argumentation; they are by no means exhaustive nor are they meant to be.

Textualism and Originalism

Textualism refers to a mode which zooms in on the formal meaning of a legal text, i.e., the specific wording of a law without taking into account historical context or the intentions of the people ratifying it. Similar to New Criticism's textual analysis in literary studies, legal textualism searches for meaning within a text in the form of a close reading which is largely concerned with itself and leaves social context aside. Legal textualism, unlike a poststructuralist literary textual analysis, believes in the dominance and objective certainty of one textual interpretation over a multitude of equally possible and subjective ones.[23]

Closely related to textualism, originalism construes of a legal text by referring back to what its ratifiers originally had in mind (*original intent*; an interpretivist approach) or, a view most originalist Supreme Court justices hold, to what ordinary people living at the time of ratification would have understood (*original meaning*; a formalist approach). Both of these originalism theories trace a legal document's meaning back to the time of its ratification. Textualists and originalists agree that turning to the framers and ratifiers of the Constitution reduces the chance of the application of a justice's subjective legal opinions; their understanding of the Separation of Powers doctrine places the judiciary in a non-activist, restraint position.

Conservative politicians tend to prefer originalist legal philosophies because they draw on sociocultural narratives and fuel sociocultural imaginaries as exemplified by former President Donald Trump: "Both Justice Kennedy and Justice Scalia were appointed by a President [sic] who understood that the best defense of our liberty and a judicial branch immune from political prejudice where [sic] judges that apply the Constitution as written. That President [sic] happened to be Ronald Reagan" ("Remarks"). In this understanding, the exceptionally just legal system in the U.S. and its equally superior sociocultural orders (see Chapter II.4) do not need adjustments but rather objective jurists who simply read the Constitution as it was intended by its framers. This view both shields the legal system and its judges and justices from the suspicion of bias and imagines a legal and sociocultural order which is already equally

23 This perspective on texts follows a strictly pre-poststructuralist understanding, eschewing a close reading in Roland Barthes' and other poststructuralists' understanding which takes into account external information. Interestingly, Justice Antonin Scalia's father, a Romance languages professor, was strongly affected by New Criticism, see also "Textualism's Mistake."

protecting (all of) individuals. Any further calls for minority protection or expansion of civil rights to marginalized groups appear as never sated demands. Thus, justices who appear to be apolitical guardians of the Constitution emphasize cultural narratives of the equal protection of the laws and due process as eternally valid promises. Imagining justices as impartial actors who merely act on the Constitution's instructions blends out forms of contemporary prejudice these justices may have adopted as a result of their being part of the society and culture they live in. Plus, historically, this perspective shields off unwanted interferences by higher authorities reminiscent of pre-Independence British rule.

By framing them as those who are merely "applying the Constitution as written," justices are not only imagined as apolitical but also as beyond contemporary prejudice. These justices are imagined as infallible since they only carry out what the Constitution states. As doubting them would imply doubting the Constitution, the violent injustice of Supreme Court cases such as *Plessy v. Ferguson* (1896) or *Bowers v. Hardwick* (1986) even reinforces the contemporary prejudice it established. Framing originalists as particularly unbiased, originalist interpreters of cases add a historical legitimacy to decisions. What these justices find to be true is what the 'Founding Fathers' would have found true, too. Consequently, originalist approaches lend from the Constitution's authority to generate the Supreme Court's. Instrumentalized like this, decisions which affirm the unequal treatment of minorities naturalize the rightfulness of such a treatment by establishing a pseudo-ahistorical perspective. Further, if the Constitution agrees with this treatment, minority concerns may simply not be part of U.S. culture, which then again adds meaning and cultural legitimacy to those instances of unequal treatment.

What is particularly interesting with regard to textualism's and originalism's strong reference to democratic, and by extension U.S. American, values is that Amy Coney Barrett, Neil Gorsuch, and Brett Kavanaugh, all outspoken conservatives and textualists/originalists, were appointed by an undemocratically elected president. Trump was the first president to have lost the popular vote, namely by more than 2.8 million votes (Millhiser "Anti-Democratic"), and had, for instance, Coney Barrett confirmed by a majority in the Senate. However, as Ian Millhiser states,

> while pro-Barrett senators control a majority of the Senate, they represent nowhere near a majority of the entire nation. Indeed, the senators who voted against Barrett represent 13,524,906 more people than the senators

> who voted for her. ... These two numbers — 2,865,075 and 13,524,906 — should inform how we view the actions Barrett will take now that she is one of the nine most powerful judges in the country. Barrett owes her new job to two of our Constitution's anti-democratic pathologies. ("Anti-Democratic")

These justices are now serving a life-time appointment to the highest court of the U.S. But they have neither been elected by a majority nor by representatives of a majority of the U.S. American people. Arguments for textualism and originalism as in line with 'the will of the people' seem therefore all the more hypocritical.

Judicial Precedent / *Stare Decisis*

Referring to prior decisions when the circumstances of a case are similar to previous ones is known as judicial precedent or *stare decisis*. According to Murrill, this mode is particular appealing because

> following the principle of stare decisis and rendering decisions grounded in earlier cases supports the Court's role as a neutral, impartial, and consistent decisionmaker. Reliance on precedent in constitutional interpretation is said to provide more predictability, consistency, and stability in the law for judges, legislators, lawyers, and political branches, prevent the Court from overruling all but the most misguided decisions, and allow constitutional norms to evolve slowly over time. (11–12)

Stare decisis is a preferred mode of interpretation because of its perceived "predictability, consistency, and stability in the law" (Murrill 11), often conceived of as impartiality of justices.[24] Although these considerations certainly speak for following precedent in constitutional interpretation, the Supreme Court's history shows that overturning decisions, even those considered landmarks, is not uncommon. Deciding which preceding decisions are "the most misguided" (Murrill 12) again puts the justices in an (judicially) activist position, calling on their respective moral and political beliefs. For instance, while conservative Justices Clarence Thomas and Samuel A. Alito Jr. regard *Obergefell v. Hodges* as an undemocratically made decision which needs review,[25] LGBTQ+ legal schol-

---

24 See *Payne v. Tennessee* at 827 (1991); Vasquez v. Hillery at 265–6 (1986).

25 See Alito's and Thomas' statement about *Obergefell* with regard to *Davis v. Ermold* in October 2020.

ars and activists have fought for same-sex marriage for decades and would rather call for larger protections. Admittingly, Thomas and Alito argue from a textualist perspective and would cite procedural flaws in *Obergefell* without openly criticizing the sociocultural importance of this decision.

Another aspect of judicial precedents' flawed logic is that the Court "must, in order to reach sound conclusions, feel free to bring its opinions into agreement with experience and with facts newly ascertained" (*Burnet v. Coronado Oil &Gas Co.* at 412 [1932]). In the context of sexual minorities' rights, one questions why research by queer theorists such as Jonathan Katz, Eve Kosofsky Sedgwick, or William Eskridge is not part of such newly ascertained facts, which would then influence future decisions.[26] Judicial precedents imagine an objectivity in both the Supreme Court as such and in its past decisions. While there certainly are cases which made use of new facts and thus changed existing legal norms, the heteronormative gaze of the law and of those interpreting it has to acknowledge its own limitedness and bias before there can be a queering of the "straight path of *stare decisis*" (*Vasquez* at 266; emphasis in original).

Living Constitutionalism/Organic/Evolutionist Perspective

An evolutionist perspective of interpretation considers the Constitution as organic, which means that it is understood to evolve over time and to transform due to social, cultural, and political changes without needing amendments. Also known as living Constitutionalism or loose constructionism, this approach is considered the opposite of originalism, vaguer, and less methodologically strict. Instead of relying on what the Constitution's framers might have had in mind during the time of ratification, evolutionists read the text from a contemporary perspective and apply current understandings to the case at hand. Originalists criticize this method as judicially activistic because it relies on one's own perceptions of society and not on a supposedly authoritative entity like the Constitution's framers.

Organists stress that the framers had a constitution in mind which is able to adapt. This is why the 'Founding Fathers' did not define the concepts used more specifically, i.e., equality, liberty, freedom are not accompanied by explanations. This mode is typically associated with more progressive judges and

26 Admittingly, Eskridge and other queer theorists are quoted by Courts, see for instance *Lawrence v. Texas*. Interestingly, in this instance, Justice Scalia uses Eskridge's findings in his *Lawrence* dissent to depict the majority opinion as flawed see *Lawrence* at 598.

justices, while conservatives would reject this mode because of its judicial activism. As already mentioned, textualism is far from being an objective constitutional approach, yet textualists consider an organic approach as too subjective, risking a flawed application of the Constitution's cultural values. This cultural essentialism inherent in textualist readings is juxtaposed to an organic understanding of culture as socioculturally and discursively constructed and thus subject to transformations the law needs to respond to.

Modes of Interpretation and Their Relation to the Politics of the Supreme Court

While the different modes of constitutional interpretation are associated with specific political convictions, traditionally conservative modes do not always lead to conservative rulings. For instance, following the wording of the Fourteenth Amendment, i.e., that "no State shall deny the equal protection of the laws to any person within its jurisdiction," does "any person" involve *any* person (*textualist*), including women, or only those who were originally covered by this wording, i.e., African-Americans and slaves (*original intent*)?[27][28] Using this example, the closeness of the different approaches becomes apparent. While in the twenty-first century the legal personhood of women is part of Western societies' legal systems, textualism makes this assumption based on the wording and not on account of sociocultural transformations. Although including women in the interpretation of 'any' person may seem progressive in this particular instance, it is simply a formalist understanding of the written text.

Following these logics of constitutional interpretation, namely that conservative modes of interpretation may disguise themselves as (reliable) producers of sometimes also progressive interpretations, the dangers of conceiving of justices and their legal theories in binary pairs becomes apparent. Strictly adhering to a conservative mode of constitutional interpretation may over time result in some progressive opinions. Likewise, progressive modes may also produce conservative outcomes. However, the U.S.'s specific medial focus

27 The Fourteenth Amendment was passed in 1868 as part of the so-called Reconstruction Amendments. These amendments to the Constitution were part of legally anchoring and culturally negotiating the role of freed persons, who were no longer enslaved after the Civil War ended in 1865 and the North abolished slavery in all states.

28 The 1971 Supreme Court decision *Reed v. Reed* ruled that discrimination based on sex violates the Equal Protection Clause and is thus unconstitutional. In 1976, the Court's *Craig v. Borden* decision elevated gender-based discrimination to the status of quasi-suspect classification by using intermediate (or heightened) scrutiny.

on the justices and the politico-cultural status of the Supreme Court is prone to evaluate these instances as 'judicial turns' which change the Court's ideological leanings substantially, or as evidence that the Court is not politically motivated but impartial.

The different outcomes of modes of constitutional interpretation cannot be accessed by only judging the progressiveness of one opinion. This could evoke the impression that conservative justices have had progressive epiphanies and are now joining the ranks of social justice warriors. A recent example of this trend, discussed in detail in Chapter III.3, includes Chief Justice John Roberts whose vote in *Bostock* was publicly labeled as proof of the Court's independence from the Trump administration and mirror of his consciousness about social justice (Lithwick). Interestingly, those conservative actors who disagreed with the progressive decision condemned its judicial activism, which let the Court's justices "invoke 'textualism' and 'originalism' in order to reach their preferred outcome" (Hawley). Here, conservative commentators condemned textualism and originalism as too progressive, simply because they were discontent with the decision's outcome.

In a more critical reading, the framing of this decision was also a political strategy to convince the U.S. American public of the objectivity of a Supreme Court during highly polarized political times. Indeed, landmark decisions such as *Bostock* receive heightened media coverage and its outcomes contribute to the public discourse about the Court and the legal system. As discussed in Chapter II.4, the cultural-constitutional imaginary of a SCOTUS which is beyond prejudice is fed by such framings, and the Court continues to be added with cultural authority.

However, the logics of constitutional interpretation go beyond a simple equation that identifies certain modes as more harmful for sexual minorities as others; they illustrate that the politization of the Court and its justices puts the lives of minorities in the hands of people who are as entangled in sociocultural and political processes as any other person within the legal system, yet way more privileged and powerful. Higher constitutional protections which are not dependent on who sits on the bench are needed for LGBTQ+ in order to become independent of judges' and justices' understanding of legal philosophy and constitutional and cultural values. Using legal scholar Peter Nicolas' words, "the closest substitute [to having a permanent, pro-queer rights deciding vote on the Supreme Court; lb] would be a clear, class-based equal protection decision declaring sexual orientation a suspect or quasi-suspect classification" ("Squandered" 138).

The next chapter goes further than dogmatically historicizing Supreme Court decisions, examining their implementation and effect on a cultural level, and analyzing five landmark decisions' lines of argumentation. It argues that the Supreme Court's decisions concerning sexual orientation in the twenty-first century may not be consistently conservative with regard to their specific ruling, yet their legal and cultural consequences are. Apparently liberal decisions are only opposing the political character of the Roberts Court, – considered even more conservative than the preceding Rehnquist Court, – on the surface while narcotizing and silencing the overall movement of sexual orientation's constitutional protection. The tool of suspect classification would effectively resolve the question of higher protection on both a cultural and legal level.

III.3. Case Studies

Trying to pin down the political and legal alignment of the Supreme Court would assume an *a priori* political will of the judiciary in general, or at least of the Court as an entity. This view would ignore the changing personnel of the Court as well as the unpredictability of decisions based on the justices' respective legal philosophies. However, it is exactly this dogmatic adherence to legal theory which separates justices from each other, and allows a historization of decisions along the lines of modes of interpretation. Since justices base their reasoning on their respective legal-theoretical beliefs, and are outspoken about what these are, their written opinions are mostly consistent with regard to their underlying theory of interpretation. As the following part shows, this does not result in similar rulings but in similar argumentations.

This section analyzes the Supreme Court's most important decisions for sexual orientation's constitutional protection in the twenty-first century. By doing so, I establish a connection between legal philosophy and political beliefs, examine the political character of legal theories, and lay down how U.S. landmark decisions about sexual orientation have developed along these legally dogmatic lines. As only the most prominent opinions are close read, this historization is by necessity only a small segment of the Court's *modus operandi* and stance on sexual minorities. However, by uncovering and analyzing the most important concepts employed in these cases, i.e., privacy and equality, this chapter's findings may be applied to other case studies as well.

As the Supreme Court's set-up changes over time, it is not possible to refer to 'the' Court but rather to different forms of this highest arm of the judiciary depending on its personnel. In the twenty-first century, William H. Rehnquist served as Chief Justice from 1986 until 2005, and John G. Roberts Jr. from 2005 until today. Their respective Courts, i.e., the Rehnquist Court and the Roberts Court, had each five retirements and five appointments during their time as well as two deaths for the Roberts Court.[29] Since Supreme Court justices are not elected by the American people but nominated by the president who is in office when one of the permanent nine seats becomes vacant,[30] the choice of personnel becomes a political one.

Although judges and justices must officially be impartial, which also includes not supporting a political party, the way they decide their cases and the arguments they use while doing so makes it impossible for them to be apolitical. For instance, it is unlikely that a conservative Republican president appoints a judge which is known for their liberal stance on trans individuals' access to health care or adoption rights for LGBTQ+ parents, or that a justice known for their pro-choice views will write an opinion which celebrates anti-abortion laws.

Even if justices can be characterized as being conservative or progressive in terms of their opinions on a case's circumstances, their decisions are not always in line with these labels. For instance, Chief Justice Roberts dissented in *Obergefell v. Hodges*, repeatedly evoking Western-centric, biologistic ideas of

---

29 For the Rehnquist Court, these were: William J. Brennan Jr. retired in 1990 and was followed by David Souter; Byron White retired in 1993 and was followed by Ruth Bader Ginsburg; Thurgood Marshall retired in 1991 and was followed by Clarence Thomas; Harry A. Blackmun retired in 1994 and was followed by Stephen Breyer; Lewis F. Powell retired in 1994 and was followed by Anthony Kennedy. For the Roberts Court, these were: John Paul Stevens retired in 2010 and was followed by Elena Kagan; Sandra Day O'Connor retired in 2006 and was followed by Samuel Alito; Antonin Scalia died in 2016 and was followed by Neil Gorsuch; Anthony Kennedy retired in 2018 and was followed by Brett Kavanaugh; David Souter retired in 2009 and was followed by Sonia Sotomayor; Ruth Bader Ginsburg died in 2020 and was followed by Amy Coney Barrett; Stephen Breyer retired in 2022 and was followed by Kentanji Brown Jackson.

30 During the process of nominating a candidate for the Supreme Court, the president needs to consult the U.S. Senate according to Article II Section 2 of the Constitution. The Senate Judiciary Committee is then responsible for vetting and questioning the candidate with, among other intelligence sources, the help of the FBI. After a vote by the Judiciary Committee, the nomination will go through a Senate debate, after which the U.S. Senate then votes on the candidate.

universal cultural concepts such as family, reproduction, and marriage,[31] but joined the majority opinion in *Bostock v. Clayton County*, which argued that sexual orientation and gender identity are protected by existing employment laws, more specifically by Title VIII of the Civil Rights Act 1964. Roberts, generally considered a conservative justice based on his views, is also an outspoken originalist and thus his decisions may appear paradox (with regard to his personal opinion) but are indeed very consistent (with his legal philosophy).

In the following, the Supreme Court's most important decisions with regard to sexual orientation are analyzed. While the Court has decided on various cases of gender identity discrimination in the past,[32] these cases are not part of the analyses as this chapter's focus is on sexual orientation decisions regardless of one's gender identity.

The arguably most important Supreme Court decisions concerning sexual orientation and politics in the twenty-first century are *Lawrence v. Texas* (2003), *U.S. v. Windsor* (2013), *Obergefell v. Hodges* (2015), *Masterpiece Cakeshop v. Colorado Civil Rights Commission* (2018), and *Bostock v. Clayton County* (2020). While debates about the repeal of the *Affordable Care Act* would also possibly result in life-changing conditions for LGBTQ+ individuals, this aspect is not part of the analysis as it is not distinctly about sexual politics or sexual orientation.

Human rights scholar Robert Wintemute identifies three major arguments "that a constitution of treaty contains a prima facie prohibition of sexual orientation discrimination" (17). According to Wintemute (16–20), these arguments differ in their approach to sexual orientation as one makes assumptions about its causality/origin (1), one considers its position with regard to other, potentially conflicting fundamental rights (2), and one focusses on the position of the person whose sexual orientation is looked at (3):

---

31 See for instance *Obergefell* 4: "For all those millennia, across all those civilizations, 'marriage' referred to only one relationship: the union of a man and a woman;" or *Obergefell* 5: "for the good of children and society, sexual relations that can lead to procreation should occur only between a man and a woman committed to a lasting bond."

32 See, for instance, *Karnoski v. Trump*. Following the 2016 elections, President Trump announced via X (formerly *Twitter*) that trans people should no longer be able to serve in the military. *Karnoski v. Trump*, along with similar law suits, aimed at preventing this ban from going into effect. The Supreme Court decided in January 2019 to lift the stay on the order; trans people were thus no longer allowed to serve openly on the military (Jackson and Kube; Barnes and Lamothe). This ban was lifted on January 2021 by President Biden in an executive order (Biden "Enabling").

> 1. an *immutable status argument*: because many gay men and lesbian women believe that their sexual orientation (as direction of attraction) is unchosen, sexual orientation may be an 'immutable status' like race or sex.
> 2. a *fundamental choice argument*: because every person's sexual orientation (as direction of conduct) is chosen and is extremely important to their happiness, it may be a 'fundamental choice (or right or freedom)', like religion or political opinion, and come wholly or partly within a specific 'fundamental right' such as freedom of expression, association or religion, or a residual and more general 'right of privacy' or 'right to respect for private life'.
> 3. a *sex discrimination argument*: because of the acceptability of the direction of a person's emotional-sexual attraction or conduct depends on their own sex, sexual orientation discrimination may be a kind of sex discrimination, like sexual harassment or pregnancy discrimination. (Wintemute 17)

The following case studies link the modes of constitutional interpretation discussed earlier to these three arguments, and characterize most cases as using a fundamental choice argument (*Lawrence*, *Windsor*, *Masterpiece*, *Obergefell*),[33] one as using a sex discrimination argument (*Bostock*), and none of them an immutable status argument. This chapter situates these approaches according to their usefulness for today's queer rights projects and uncovers the wobbly sociocultural grounds upon which they stand. Ultimately, these case studies serve to underline the need for an anti-discrimination protection via suspect classification.

Throughout the previous chapters, the decisions in *Obergefell* and in *Bostock*, their legal dogmatic reasonings, and their importance for the LGBTQ+ community have been commented on and used as examples for why more thorough protections for queers are needed. These decisions are particularly important because they are the most recent ones and because they have resulted in fierce political and legal backlash on the state level. The following subchapters illustrate the arguments made in favor and against the respective issues at hand by offering a qualitative analysis of these decisions. By doing so, the method of analyzing the cultural frame in which these decisions are made is employed and developed further. Consequently, these analyses require and hope to strengthen its reader's cultural-legal thinking, which is considered a handy tool in every activist's tool box.

---

33 *Bowers* would also fit into this pattern, yet is not part of the analyses as it has been decided in 1986.

Lawrence v. Texas (2003): Reforming Understandings of Sex and Privacy

In *Lawrence v. Texas* (2003), SCOTUS ruled that consensual homosexual acts, including anal and oral sex, are constitutional. This landmark decision overruled *Bowers v. Hardwick*, a decision from 1986 which found that consensual homosexual 'sodomy' is not protected by the Constitution. Both cases deal with two men who engaged in sexual activity in their private homes, and following the logics of *stare decisis*, *Lawrence* would have followed in *Bower*'s footsteps. However, as legal scholar Ronald Kahn argues, the Court's practice of social constructionalism made it possible to refer back to a series of decisions prior to *Lawrence* that made the reasoning in *Bowers* obsolete. Previous Supreme Court decisions such as *Griswold v. Connecticut* (1965) and *Roe* (1973) established the importance of the right of privacy, which *Lawrence* picked up upon (Kahn "Polarized" 182).[34]

Since John Lawrence and Tyron Garner had consensual sex in Lawrence's apartment, the right of one's privacy in their home protected them. In *Lawrence*, it becomes obvious that the Court followed an organic understanding of the Constitution:

> Had those who drew and ratified the Due Process Clauses of the Fifth Amendment or the Fourteenth Amendment known the components of liberty in its manifold possibilities, they might have been more specific. They did not presume to have this insight. They knew times can blind us to certain truths and later generations can see that laws once thought necessary and proper in fact serve only to oppress. As the Constitution endures, persons in every generation can invoke its principles in their own search for greater freedom. (*Lawrence* at 578–9)

Justice Kennedy, who delivered this majority opinion, explicitly refers to possible criticism from an originalist's standpoint, namely that the Constitution's framers were silent on the matter at hand and thus, justices today should restrain from imposing their own interpretation and judicial activism. By defending that the opinion follows an organic reasoning, Kennedy also stresses

34 See *Lawrence v. Texas* at 565: "After Griswold it was established that the right to make certain decisions regarding sexual conduct extends beyond the marital relationship. … Roe recognized the right of a woman to make certain fundamental decisions affecting her destiny and confirmed once more that the protection of liberty under the Due Process Clause has a substantive dimension of fundamental significance in defining the rights of the person."

that a living Constitution may be better equipped to respond to social, cultural, and political transformations. Justice Scalia's understanding of the opinion as "result-oriented" (*Lawrence* at 592) criticizes that organists do not refer to the Constitution's wordings or intentions of the framers as starting point for deciding cases – as would originalists – but take their envisaged outcome as starting point for their argumentation. Justices Rehnquist, Scalia, and Thomas, who are all outspoken originalists, dissented on the basis of the majority opinion's reasoning that criminalizing homosexual activity in one's home violates the Fourteenth Amendment's Due Process Clause. To Scalia, who wrote the dissent, overruling the precedent in *Bowers* is not the issue here but the judicial activism of the argument.[35] Since the Due Process Clause does not originally grant the fundamental right to liberty, they consider this reasoning flawed. Scalia even used his dissent to comment on *Roe*. Claiming that if the Court decides to overrule *Bowers* in *Lawrence*, it also needs to overrule *Roe*, Scalia uses constitutional arguments to bring across his dissatisfaction with granting minorities rights, and to refer to a particular, heterosexist, patriarchal condescending legal-cultural order:

> What a massive disruption of the current social order, therefore, the overruling of Bowers entails. Not so the overruling of Roe, which would simply have restored the regime that existed for centuries before 1973, in which the permissibility of and restrictions upon abortion were determined legislatively State-by-State. (*Lawrence* at 591)

While *Lawrence* disrupts the, one might add 'natural,' social order in Scalia's perception, curling back abortion rights on a federal level would re-establish a "regime that existed for centuries," which Scalia seems to perceive as legitimate. Arguing from a legal dogmatic standpoint, Scalia frames his dissent as a matter of an objective constitutional interpretation, leaving aside his positionality as a conservative, male, cis, heterosexual, educated, able-bodied, privileged justice in the highest court of the U.S., who is not primarily affected by such regulations.

While the rich judicial and moral argumentation on both sides is certainly worth close reading, the most pivotal feature of the *Lawrence* decision is nei-

---

35 See *Lawrence* at 587: "I do not myself believe in rigid adherence to stare decisis in constitutional cases; but I do believe that we should be consistent rather than manipulative in invoking the doctrine."

ther its distinction between organic and originalist reasoning nor its pro-LGBTQ+ outcome as such, which certainly deserves landmark status. *Lawrence* illustrates that a progressive outcome of a Supreme Court case does not equal progressive legal and cultural consequences. The implications of *Lawrence* show that SCOTUS did neither rule discrimination based on homosexual activity nor the state's intrusive regulation of one's sexual orientation in other contexts unconstitutional. It merely protected the right to liberty, mirroring neoliberal tendencies to protect one's space instead of stating that sexual orientation is constitutionally protected. Fundamental choice decisions like this operate from the socioculturally constructed ideal of 'freedom,' which is predominantly linked to one's private sphere to which the state is supposed to have no access. State intrusion into one's home and by extension one's bedroom is considered unconstitutional and thus *Lawrence* was decided in favor of its gay plaintiff. However, other legal regulations concerning one's private sphere were not considered in an extension of the logic of the privacy argument. For instance, being fired because of the gender of one's partner was only federally protected in 2020's *Bostock* as discussed below.

Following this fundamental choice argument and perceiving of *Lawrence* as progressive, – which it undoubtably was with regard to its outcome and consequences for queer (sex) lives, – a cultural deconstruction of the ideals of liberty and freedom is prevented. *Lawrence* does not include questioning whom 'freedom' still excludes in twenty-first century U.S. America, it does engage in questions of who is perceived as legally worthy of rights, or even right-able in the sense of having legal agency, nor does it extend the implications of preventing the state from intruding in its citizens' lives to other realms in which LGBTQ+ persons are prone to discrimination. In this sense, *Lawrence* may be considered a (consciously) wasted opportunity to protect queer lives further.

U.S. v. Windsor (2013): Ending DOMA, Continuing an Organic Approach

U.S. v. Windsor (2013) dealt with the case of a widow, Edith Windsor, who inherited the estate from her deceased spouse Thea Clara Spyer. Windsor and Spyer married in Canada in 2007 and had their marriage recognized in the U.S. by New York state law, which was one of the states that already recognized same-sex marriage. Yet federal law, in the form of the then still valid *Defense of Mar-*

riage Act (DOMA),[36] understood marriage as "a legal union between one man and one woman as husband and wife" (DOMA, sec. 3) and it defined a spouse as "a person of the opposite sex who is a husband or a wife" (DOMA, sec. 3). As a consequence, Windsor had to pay taxes after Spyer's death on the inheritance – spousal exemption was denied by DOMA's understanding of marriage and spouse. Edith Windsor saw this a violation of her rights and sued the federal government for a refund of her money.

The Court ruled in favor of Windsor by finding the third section of DOMA unconstitutional and in violation of legally married same-sex couples' right to equal protection under the Fifth Amendment. Justices Scalia, Roberts, Thomas and Alito dissented and raised important issues connected to the Supreme Court's authority and power in U.S. America.

> This case is about power in several respects. It is about the power of our people to govern themselves, and the power of this Court to pronounce the law. Today's opinion aggrandizes the latter, with the predictable consequence of diminishing the former. We have no power to decide this case. And even if we did, we have no power under the Constitution to invalidate this democratically adopted legislation. The Court's errors on both points spring forth from the same diseased root: an exalted conception of the role of this institution in America. (Scalia 1)

Scalia criticizes that the *Windsor* Court overturned an Act passed by the legislative (DOMA), and the Court's judicial activism in doing so. To him, applying an organic approach to constitutional interpretation is misusing the Supreme Court's power. As an originalist, he is convinced that looking at what the framers of the Constitution had in mind is the better mode of interpretation as this method prevents contemporary courts from applying their own understanding and from becoming legislatively active. Taking into account sociocultural developments as the majority opinion by Justice Anthony M. Kennedy did in *Windsor* stands in contrast to how originalists like Scalia envision the Court's role, the political system in the U.S., and the Con-

36 'Valid' refers to DOMA still being enforced in 2013. While *Windsor* struck down the third section of the Act, thus making it unenforceable, *Obergefell* did so for the second section in 2015. Sec. 3 defines the terms 'marriage' and 'spouse,' while Sec. 2 lays down the states' sovereignty in deciding whether to legally recognize same-sex marriages within their jurisdiction.

stitution. Scalia's dissent also addresses the question of suspect classification by referring to the different levels of scrutiny:

> The majority opinion need not get into the strict-vs.-rational-basis scrutiny question, and need not justify its holding under either, because it says that DOMA is unconstitutional as "a deprivation of the liberty of the person protected by the Fifth Amendment of the Constitution," ante, at 25; that it violates "basic due process" principles, ante, at 20; and that it inflicts an "injury and indignity" of a kind that denies "an essential part of the liberty protected by the Fifth Amendment," ante, at 19. (Scalia 25)

It seems to be no coincidence that justices who follow originalist legal philosophies see no tradition in same-sex marriage being part of U.S. American culture. Scalia's dissent vividly illustrates how political conservativeness, methodological preferences, and cultural essentialism draw on each other. Scalia criticizes the majority's opinion both because of its judicial activism, which in his opinion "envisions a Supreme Court standing (or rather enthroned) at the apex of government, empowered to decide all constitutional questions, always and everywhere 'primary' in its role" (Scalia 2), and for its erroneous framing of those in support of DOMA as homophobic.

Scalia's argumentation rests on the general cultural sentiment when DOMA was introduced. In 1996, as his argument goes, the members of Congress and President Bill Clinton enacted and signed this law without any discriminatory motivation – they simply wanted to provide a definitional provision which "avoids difficult choice-of-law issues that will now arise absent a uniform federal definition of marriage" (Scalia 19). This historical revisionist view acquits lawmakers from the accusation of bias: They merely wanted to find a common definition and codify it. This view erases the validity of LGBTQ+ discriminatory experiences and negates queer visibilities amidst the AIDS epidemic by claiming that Congress did not want to discriminate queer people – it rather wanted to protect everyone by establishing a legal regulation. After all, "the legislation is called the *Defense* of Marriage Act" (Scalia 21; emphasis added) and "to defend traditional marriage is not to condemn, demean, or humiliate those who would prefer other arrangements" (21).

This view leaves aside the privileged position of those being legally allowed to get married, which is connected to different insurance options, better tax models, and cultural appreciation of one's relationship. Labeling the need of *having* to pick other relationship forms, e.g., domestic partnerships, as "preferred" arrangements is as inaccurate as it is vicious. It also clouds the dynamics of gatekeeping by political and legal actors.

Scalia's inability – or unwillingness – to acknowledge the discriminatory nature such a heteronormatively privileged stance entails reveals his conservative adherence to an outdated worldview that considers cis, heterosexual, possibly White couples as center of the cultural concept of kinship and family. While one may argue that Scalia's dissent speaks more to his preference for an originalist mode of constitutional interpretation and less to his personal beliefs, the link between these two can be found in the associated view on American culture an originalist understanding of the Constitution brings.

In framing the issue of a marriage's and a spouse's definition as crystal-clear, Scalia offers insights into his conception of American culture as static. Further, he refuses the majority's opinion's supposedly moral judgements about opponents of DOMA's being struck down:

> All that, simply for supporting an Act that did no more than codify an aspect of marriage that had been unquestioned in our society for most of its existence—indeed, had been unquestioned in virtually all societies for virtually all of human history. It is one thing for a society to elect change; it is another for a court of law to impose change by adjudging those who oppose it *hostes humani generis*, enemies of the human race. (Scalia 21; emphasis in original)

In Scalia's view, condemning those who believe in the naturalness of heterosexual marriage is illegitimate and morally condescending. At the same time, rejecting a definition of marriage and spouses which takes into account socially and culturally progressed notions of family is in line with the U.S.'s cultural values. Or, in other words, there is no discrimination in doing so because a heteronormative understanding of family is essential to U.S. American culture and society. Using originalism as moral credential, Scalia's culturalism, i.e., the belief in a static U.S. American culture with inherent and unchangeable values, functions as translator for his conservative political views into constitutional decision-making.

The legal starting point of *Windsor* illustrates how state and federal laws may clash and that deciding on unified regulations is also about strengthening or cutting back the political relevance of federalism. According to legal scholar Dawn Johnsen, *Windsor* mirrors

> not only constitutional change in the direction of more expansive judicial protection of equal protection and due process, but also fidelity to a mainstream approach to interpreting the Constitution that considers a range of sources and methods and allows for the consideration of evolving social norms and constitutional understandings. (2)

Reinforcing the Court's pro-organic direction in *Windsor* places yet another landmark decision for LGBTQ+ rights dogmatically in an anti-originalist position.[37] Despite the case's progressive outcome, namely finding that DOMA "impose[s] a disadvantage, a separate status, and so a stigma upon all who enter into same-sex marriages made lawful by the ... States" (majority opinion by Kennedy, *U.S. v. Windsor* at 3–4), the focus remains on the state's authority as well as general conceptions of the federal system and the concept of equality.

Windsor is all the more important for discourses about sexual orientation's legal protection as the Court decided *not* to rule on its suspect classification although the Obama administration, in favor of striking down DOMA, argued for doing so in a letter by Attorney General Eric Holder (Holder). As in *Lawrence*, the Court missed the chance to tackle the question of whether discrimination based on sexual orientation is unconstitutional.

Obergefell v. Hodges (2015): Climax of Organic Mode of Interpretation

Obergefell v. Hodges (2015) is probably the most well-known pro-LGBTQ+ rights decision in the 2010s. After striking down DOMA in *Windsor*, the Court paved the way for the federal recognition of same-sex marriage in *Obergefell* and fostered the public's opinion about the U.S.'s progressiveness in terms of acknowledging and protecting queer rights.

This perception, however, is flawed in multiple ways. Without the landmark cases *Romer v. Evans* (1996) and *Lawrence* (2003), *Windsor* and subsequently

37 These binaries are simplified characterizations of the methodological divides between justices, and the understandings of what originalism means depends on one's legal philosophy. As Johnsen points out, justices who are typically considered non-originalists such as Bader Ginsburg and Kagan have called for a pluralistic understanding of "originalisms" (4) with Kagan famously stating that "we [judges and justices; lb] are all originalists" (Kagan qtd. in "Nomination"). However, legal scholarship typically places textualist readings at a more conservative position on the originalism spectrum.

Obergefell would not have been thinkable. *Obergefell* thus may pose as progressive decision, yet it is merely the argumentatively logical and methodologically dogmatic consequence of past decisions. Thus, this decision is indicative of the dominance of modes of interpretation (organic vs. originalist and judicial precedent) and the constitutional implications of the cultural concept of liberty. It is, however, not a decidedly concession to queer demands and acknowledgement of discriminatory realities for sexual minorities.

These decisions preceding *Obergefell* – *Romer, Lawrence, Windsor* – are each dealing with discrimination based on sexual orientation, each of them has been decided with a living Constitution in mind, and each of them was authored by Justice Kennedy, who, according to legal scholar Peter Nicolas, "leave[s] behind one of the most important gay rights legacies in U.S. legal history" ("Squandered" 137). This series of Supreme Court decisions dealing with sexual minorities would have made it possible for the Court to declare sexual orientation a suspect classification. However, in Nicolas' words, the Court "squandered" this opportunity and instead left behind the nonviable promise of constitutional progressiveness for LGBTQ+ people.

Obergefell's progressive understanding of marriage equality is always only one conservative vote away from being reviewed and possibly overturned.[38] In this sense, *Obergefell* established a false constitutional protection for queer people in that it increased their visibilities, yet did not cover their vulnerabilities in areas unrelated to the fundamental right to marry. While being able to get married made same-sex partnerships legally more privileged in that they had access to more rights, and culturally more recognized by granting them equal treatment in the sphere of marriage, getting married increased queers' visibility profoundly, be it through the acknowledgement of their partnership on official documents accessible for employers, or through contact with wedding planers, register offices, or insurance companies.

From a political perspective, *Obergefell* seems confusing. The Court acted consistently in its line of argumentation, i.e., by continuing its application of the level of scrutiny and its mode of interpreting the Constitution. One could argue that slowly expanding gay rights and advancing the political queer project is a strategic way of circumventing political tensions. After all, declaring sexual orientation a suspect classification would without doubt

38 For evidence for this claim, see the statement by Alito and Thomas with regard to *Davis v. Ermold*. Justices Alito and Thomas have repeatedly voiced their disapproval of how the Court argued in *Obergefell*, and called for a review of the case.

create backlash from both within the Court and from conservative politicians. The fear of "diluting the meaning of heightened scrutiny" (Yoshino 797) has led justices to avoid expanding the list of classifications to include gender, sexual orientation, or other categories that from a queer feminist perspective warrant a stricter form of judicial review.

While these strategic considerations would arguably also be political in themselves, it is more likely that they were not intended. Reading *Obergefell* through Peter Nicolas' lens, it is unclear why the Court relied on structural arguments about the fundamentality of the right to marry when procedurally, the opportunity to make a class-based equal protection decision had been given ("Squandered" 141–2). Nicolas finds this "all the more surprising" ("Squandered" 141) when comparing the situation to other classifications' history:

> When the Court held that laws targeting African Americans were subject to strict scrutiny in *McLaughlin*, it effectively decided the constitutionality of interracial marriage, one of the most highly contested social matters of the time. *Obergefell* itself directly decided same- sex marriage, the most socially sensitive gay rights issue of this time. While other laws, such as parentage rights, targeting gays and lesbians have yet to be adjudicated by the Court, such laws do not raise issues nearly as socially sensitive as marriage—the lightning rod that generated constitutional amendments banning the practice in a supermajority of states. Accordingly, announcing heightened scrutiny in *Obergefell* would not have come close to the strong medicine that it would have been had the Court announced it earlier in *Romer* or *Lawrence*, for example. ("Squandered" 141–142)

While Nicolas's convincingly disseminates the judicial-historical and methodological levels *Obergefell* has, he fails to acknowledge the possible lack of intent for protecting sexual orientation. This is of course a rather controversial reading based on an assumed ideological or political will of the justices, which, as stated in the previous chapters, is to some scholars still a controversial claim in itself. Yet the constitutional history of minoritarian equal protection suggests that the deciding factors were not considerations about judicial activism or procedural challenges.

It is more likely that the Court hesitated to use the "strong judicial medicine" (Nicolas "Squandered" 140) of applying a class-based equal protection for sexual orientation because such an expansion of the list of suspect classifications was, and still is, politically too charged. Even without assuming anti-queer bias of the individual justices, – a benevolent reading, – the Court as a whole acted as a protector of its own interests by not tackling sexual orientation's heightened scrutiny. Doing so would undoubtably have put the Court even more in political spotlight. In trying to circumvent such sensitive issues, however, *Obergefell* opens up political debates about cultural values.

By declaring marriage a fundamental right, the Court stressed the cultural relevance of an institution which has historically oppressed women under the cloak of heteropatriarchal care. It has not acknowledged the cultural equality of marriages between non-heterosexual persons but only queers' equal right to get married. This distinction is important to keep in mind as anyone arguing for queer rights should work towards cultural equity and legal equality, using the latter as means to achieve the former but not as an end in itself.

Justice Kennedy bases the Court's decision on three key American cultural values: individual autonomy (12),[39] freedom (7),[40] and social order (16).[41] Considering marriage a fundamental right stems from the cultural importance

39 "A first premise of the Court's relevant precedents is that the right to personal choice regarding marriage is inherent in the concept of individual autonomy. ... Like choices concerning contraception, family relationships, procreation, and childrearing, all of which are protected by the Constitution, decisions concerning marriage are among the most intimate that an individual can make. ... Choices about marriage shape an individual's destiny" (*Obergefell* at 12–3).

40 "Indeed, changed understandings of marriage are characteristic of a Nation where new dimensions of freedom become apparent to new generations, often through perspectives that begin in pleas or protests and then are considered in the political sphere and the judicial process" (*Obergefell* at 7).

41 "Fourth and finally, this Court's cases and the Nation's traditions make clear that marriage is a keystone of our social order. Alexis de Tocqueville recognized this truth on his travels through the United States almost two centuries ago: 'There is certainly no country in the world where the tie of marriage is so much respected as in America . . . [W]hen the American retires from the turmoil of public life to the bosom of his family, he finds in it the image of order and of peace . . .. [H]e afterwards carries [that image] with him into public affairs.' ... In *Maynard* v. *Hill* (1888), the Court echoed de Tocqueville, explaining that marriage is 'the foundation of the family and of society, without which there would be neither civilization nor progress.' Marriage, the *Maynard* Court said, has long been "'a great public institution, giving character to our whole civil polity'" (*Obergefell* at 16).

American society puts on one's right to privacy, which the Court already used in its *Lawrence* argumentation and which now finds continuation in *Obergefell*.[42]

Privacy arguments reproduce the ideas connected to individualism, namely that the issues at hand are within one's ability and responsibility to shape and possibly to change. More explicitly, by dressing privacy as fundamental right, the Court stresses individual responsibility as fundamental duty in a society that outsources unpleasant tasks from the public to the private sphere. For instance, unpaid care work such as child-rearing or taking care of sick family members becomes delegated to private realms so as not to expect responsibility from governmental actors. At the same time, these private spaces are demarcated as sometimes the only possibility to live out one's identity without social, political, or legal restraints, e.g., post-*Lawrence* same-sex sexual conduct.

The private sphere is the locus of a freedom which ultimately is none. It is a mere spatial and also timely restriction of what an individual is allowed or supposed to do when they are not in the public:

> Relegating sexuality to the private sphere revives an element of the old "separate but equal" doctrine – the belief that the separation of one group from the world of more general social interaction is neither unequal nor stigmatizing. Withholding social recognition from the public aspects of gay personhood while "[h]eterosexual society revolves around its sexual orientation" is inherently unequal not only in its substantive restriction of gay liberties, but also in its imputation of stigma: homosexuality, like obscenity, may be tolerated only if quarantined. ("Constitutional Status" 1290–1)

This reading of the private sphere becomes all the more apparent in a post-Covid-19 society in which images of lockdowns are all too readily evoked. Doing things in the privacy of one's home is more than often a restriction than a liberty, and how you do things in your private sphere is decisive of how you are treated in public. Social control about how one lives, behaves, and loves does

42 Privacy is what Justice Kennedy subsumes under autonomy and freedom as indicated by his reference to *Griswold* (*Obergefell* at 10). *Griswold* states that "We deal with a right of privacy older than the Bill of Rights -- older than our political parties, older than our school system. Marriage is a coming together for better or for worse, hopefully enduring, and intimate to the degree of being sacred" (at 486).

not stop right before your doorstep and may find its way in through the permeable borders of one's space which are constantly penetrated by one's own normativized socialization, legal regulations, social media feeds, neighboring gazes or actual people. In this context, it is important to note that while sexual *conduct* and sexual *orientation* are different issues, with the former indicating sexual activity and the latter romantic and/or sexual desire; *conduct based on sexual orientation* seems to constitute yet another meaningful category of cultural-legal consideration. While the law has already dealt with the right to engage in same-sex intercourse and with the right to same-sex marriage, it does not seem to have fully digested the cultural-legal implications of feeling entitled to openly live out one's sexual orientation in ways approaching cisgender heterosexual norms.

Having '[h]eterosexual society revolv[ing] around its sexual orientation' emphasizes that there is no organic distinction between the public and the private sphere to which law merely responds to. Quite the contrary, it stresses that sexuality is more complex than sheer conduct, and engrained in one's identity. Thus, when "privacy analysis assumes a dual structure – a division between the home and the outside world – that does not adequately capture the complexity of social life" ("Constitutional Status" 1289), basing the fundamental right to marry on these grounds may seem irritating, but basing the foundation of a queer rights project on these grounds seems more than shaky. While the argument of privacy has had considerable impact on gay rights, taking it as starting point for re-thinking other aspects of queer inequalities, or for stressing its importance as fundamental right, poses the danger of giving power to a cultural ideal which is void of inherent equality.

Needing a Piece but Still Not Having it: *Masterpiece Cakeshop v. Colorado Civil Rights Commission* (2018)

The SCOTUS 2018 decision *Masterpiece Cakeshop v. Colorado Civil Rights Commission* further illustrates this unreliability of privacy arguments. In *Masterpiece*, a Colorado bakery was sued by a gay, married couple, Charlie Craig and David Mullins, because the owner refused to bake a wedding cake for them in 2012. Arguing that his religious beliefs prevent him from creating such a cake, and that his cakes are pieces of art, the baker Jack Phillips offered the couple to buy anything else in his shop. While Colorado did not recognize same-sex marriage in 2012, the state law provided that

> [i]t is a discriminatory practice and unlawful for a person, directly or indirectly, to refuse, withhold from, or deny to an individual or a group, because of disability, race, creed, color, sex, sexual orientation, marital status, national origin, or ancestry, the full and equal enjoyment of the goods, services, facilities, privileges, advantages, or accommodations of a place of public accommodation … . (Colorado State)

The explicit inclusion of sexual orientation in Colorado's Anti-Discrimination Act resulted in the winning of the case for Craig and Mullins. This outcome forced the bakery to provide their wedding cakes for same-sex weddings. However, the cake shop asked the Supreme Court to review the case, which then had to decide "[w]hether applying Colorado's public accommodations law to compel Phillips to create expression that violates his sincerely held religious beliefs about marriage violates the Free Speech or Free Exercise Clauses of the First Amendment" (*Masterpiece* Petition for a Writ of Certiorari). In other words, the Court had to decide whether religious beliefs are protected by the First Amendment, which would outplay state regulations.

The importance of this case cannot be underestimated. In *Masterpiece*, the simmering conflict between religious and queer rights is reignited in the arena of private businesses. *Masterpiece* uses what Robert Wintemute refers to as 'fundamental choice argument' only to find religious beliefs to be more worthy of protection than sexual orientation. Culturally, this view does not surprise. After all, the right to privacy, which is often evoked in the discourse about sexual orientation, now enters the public sphere when private businesses are to serve same-sex clients. This rupture, one may argue, is especially controversial when it is done within the context of same-sex marriage – the Judeo-Christian ideal of marriage between a (cis) man and a (cis) woman has already been legally defeated by *Obergefell* but forcing individuals to serve those they disapprove of brings this conflict even closer to their lives. This difference in tolerating, – or having to, – queer emancipation in the realm of queer private lives and accepting queer legal emancipation meandering into the public sphere and ultimately affecting one own's realm evokes separate-but-equal notions and a perverted understanding of equality which limits itself at the threshold of others' liberty. The cultural overemphasis of marriage not only mars people's understanding of the status of equal rights for queers as discussed earlier, – same-sex marriage is still considered a huge victory and leads to perceiving queer rights demands as already accomplished, – but it also uncovers how the legal right to get married does not translate into the cultural right to celebrate queer marriages equally.

Masterpiece therefore illustrates how a separate-but-equal logic finds their way into cultural and legal discourses, how religious beliefs are fundamental to U.S. American (legal) culture and arguably the U.S. public space, and which areas still suffer from legal lag in terms of protection. *Obergefell*'s heightened visibility of queer couples is still contributing to unprotected discrimination in areas of life other than marriage and adoption. Moreover, the legal right to marry seems still to be accompanied by the cultural imaginary of a married couple as heterosexual and cis.[43] Violations of this imaginary such as in the case of *Masterpiece* stress that these cultural imaginaries at work are not only descriptive but also prescriptive ones. The cultural and constitutional narrative of equality before the law and the equal protection of the laws are upheld by granting minorities certain rights while simultaneously, the cultural imaginary polices these rights' *de facto* implementation into lived equal realities for queers.

A New Era? *Bostock v. Clayton County* (2020)

Bostock v. Clayton County combined several similar law suits in one. *Bostock* dealt with the case of cis man Gerald Bostock, who was fired by his employer after he told people at work about his participation in a gay recreational softball league. *Bostock* also featured the case of skydiving instructor Donald Zarda, a cis man who was fired by his employer after he told a client about his husband, and funeral director Aimee Stephens, a trans woman who got fired after informing her employer that she will "live and work full-time as a woman" (*Bostock* at 1). Each case dealt with someone being fired because of their sexual orientation or gender identity, and each of these employees sued their employer for sex discrimination under Title VII of the Civil Rights Act of 1964. Title VII, which "makes it unlawful to discriminate against someone on the basis of race, color, national origin, sex ... or religion" ("Laws Enforced"), protects individuals against employment discrimination, including, among others, "hiring and firing; compensation, assignment, or classification of employees; transfer, promotion, layoff, or recall" ("Laws Enforced").

43 This cultural imaginary and possibly idealtype of marriage would presumably also include White, able-bodied, middle-class, normatively attractive as marriage is closely connected to fantasies about proper procreation and national survival.

Bostock is remarkable in many respects. First, it is the most recent pro-LGBTQ+ decision by a growingly conservative Roberts Court, and more than that – it has been decided during the Trump presidency with two Trump-nominated, conservative justices on the bench. Given the numerous anti-queer attacks by the government from 2016–2020 and beyond, *Bostock* stands out as unexpected and celebrated victory for queer rights advocates, activists, and allies.

Second, the decision established a constitutional foundation for LGBTQ+ protections in a wide array of areas. With its implementation by the Biden administration, it also enjoys governmental support and is unlikely to be challenged by the Department of Justice.

Third, *Bostock* is the first Supreme Court decision that followed what Wintemute labels a 'sex discrimination argument.' This argument does not look at sexual orientation as such, thus refraining from any inquiries into its biological or social origins, as would an immutable status argument. It also does not consider the violation of any fundamental right(s) which may intersect with others' rights; it approaches discrimination on basis of sexual orientation from the perspective of the person whose sexual orientation is addressed, as would a fundamental choice argument. This means that the sex discrimination argument "does not require the recognition of any new fundamental right or suspect classification, but rather attempts to use, in sexual orientation discrimination cases, an existing quasi-suspect classification (i.e. sex)" (Wintemute 83–4).

While the new employment protections for sexual minorities this outcome brought are progressive and worth applauding, the mode of interpretation applied was a textualist one. As Justice Gorsuch, who delivered the majority opinion, states:

> From the ordinary public meaning of the statute's language at the time of the law's adoption, a straightforward rule emerges: An employer violates Title VII when it intentionally fires an individual employee based in part on sex. It doesn't matter if other factors besides the plaintiff's sex contributed to the decision. And it doesn't matter if the employer treated women as a group the same when compared to men as a group. If the employer intentionally relies in part on an individual employee's sex when deciding to dis- charge the employee—put differently, if changing the employee's sex would have yielded a different choice by the employer—a statutory violation has occurred. (at 9)

Referring back to how the statute would have been understood at the time of its adoption (*original intent*), Gorsuch finds the cases at hand to be in clear violation of Title VII. Originalism, traditionally associated with judicial restraint, is here favored as a mode of interpretation and implies that the Supreme Court has merely applied the law instead of enlarging, bending, or re-inventing it.

Justices Thomas, Alito, and Kavanaugh dissented to this opinion. The dissent by Alito, which Thomas joined, criticizes Gorsuch's majority opinion exactly because of its judicial activism. Stating that "[t]here is only one word for what the Court has done today: legislation. The document that the Court releases is in the form of a judicial opinion interpreting a statute, but that is deceptive" (dissent at 1), Alito accuses the Court to be "[u]surping the constitutional authority of the other branches" (dissent at 3). This view seems surprising because Gorsuch, as well as Alito, place their argumentation on originalist reasoning: "[O]ur duty is to interpret statutory terms to 'mean what they conveyed to reasonable people *at the time they were written*'" (dissent at 3; emphasis in original). Alito then goes on to label Gorsuch's opinion as "a pirate ship … [which] sails under a textualist flag" (dissent at 3), denying Gorsuch's majority opinion its 'proper' textualist methodology.

Both the majority opinion and the dissent then take on textualist interpretations but conceive of them inherently oppositional based on the reading's respective outcome. Citing homosexuality's legal criminalization and the medico-biologistic pathologization of homosexuality as mental disorder according to the 1964's *DSM*-I[44] (28–9) as well as gender dysphoria's pathologization as laid out in *DSM*-III (35), Alito emphasizes that Gorsuch's textualist reading is flawed. For Alito, it is "clear as clear could be that [sex discrimination; lb] meant discrimination because of the genetic and anatomical characteristics that men and women have at the time of birth" (dissent at 4). Because not "a single dictionary from that time … defined 'sex' to mean sexual orientation, gender identity, or 'transgender status'" (at 4), Gorsuch's argument follows that 'sex' in 1964 only encompassed "reproductive biology" (at 5, majority opinion) to lay out a more sophisticated reading.

Gorsuch argues that Title VII "prohibits employers from taking certain actions 'because of' sex" (at 5, majority opinion), which means something hap-

---

44 The *Diagnostic and Statistical Manual of Mental Disorders* (*DSM*) is a publication series by the American Psychiatric Association (APA). The manual offers a standard catalogue for classifying mental disorders. First published in 1952, the DSM has been updated several times with its most recent publication in March 2022, DSM-5TR.

pens "'by reason of' or 'on account of'" (at 5, majority opinion) sex. This 'but-for causation' lays out that each employee would not have been fired but for their respective sex. If, for instance, Donald Zarda talked about his husband as a cis woman, he would not have been fired. Thus, his sex was the cause of his notice:

> So, taken together, an employer who intentionally treats a person worse because of sex—such as by firing the person for actions or attributes it would tolerate in an individual of another sex—discriminates against that person in violation of Title VII. … That's because it is impossible to discriminate against a person for being homosexual or transgender without discriminating against that individual based on sex. Consider, for example, an employer with two employees, both of whom are attracted to men. The two individuals are, to the employer's mind, materially identical in all respects, except that one is a man and the other a woman. If the employer fires the male employee for no reason other than the fact he is attracted to men, the employer discriminates against him for traits or actions it tolerates in his female colleague. Put differently, the employer intentionally singles out an employee to fire based in part on the employee's sex, and the affected employee's sex is a but-for cause of his discharge. (at 7; 10, majority opinion)[45]

As both the majority opinion by Gorsuch and the dissent by Alito refer to a textualist interpretation of Title VII, yet come up with different readings based on textualism, the subjectivity of textualist approaches becomes obvious. Claiming to use an apolitical approach which shies away from enforcing a justice's subjective view to constitutional law, namely one which leaves aside justices' moral and political convictions, Alito's and Gorsuch's differing opinions show that textualism does not offer unambiguous, judicially restrained interpretations. *Bostock* illustrates that sticking to certain modes of interpretation is indeed not objective but can be used as a strategic tool to invisibilize and hide conservative justices' political motivations and anti-queer bias.

Further, *Bostock* shows how justices' positionality influences their reading of a case. Although both Gorsuch and Alito are regarded as conservative jus-

45 Gorsuch continues to extend this argument to gender identity: "Or take an employer who fires a transgender person who was identified as a male at birth but who now identifies as a female. If the employer retains an otherwise identical employee who was identified as female at birth, the employer intentionally penalizes a person identified as male at birth for traits or actions that it tolerates in an employee identified as female at birth. Again, the individual employee's sex plays an unmistakable and impermissible role in the discharge decision" (at 10, majority opinion).

tices and both are outspoken textualists, their differing interpretations show that neither commonality of legal philosophy, shared political sides nor a combination of both result in a similar understanding of a case. Following Donna Haraway's understanding of situated knowledge (1988), *Bostock* sheds light on how the idea of 'objective' knowledge is even in a highly dogmatic and rule-driven system an imaginary which can be (mis)used for political maneuvering. Pro-queer and anti-queer readings of a legal case are therefore a matter of perspective and political will. Again, the necessity to conduct cultural analysis of law to foster queer lives is emphasized.

***

As these wide readings show, the Supreme Court's approach towards protecting sexual orientation has not changed over the last three decades. While important protections for queers have been won, the underlying arguments have been decidedly neutral and at times hostile towards the LGBTQ+ community. Both the fundamental choice argument and the sex discrimination argument have proven to further cement neoliberal notions of liberty and heteronormative notions of sexuality into law. Despite the evident tremendous *de jure* improvements for queers, the Supreme Court emerges as even bigger beneficiary from these decisions. Strategically placing pro-queer outcomes amidst increasingly fierce politico-cultural tensions while sticking to *de facto* stereotypical and queer-hostile arguments, the Court validates itself in front of allies, opponents, and proponents of queer rights.

It is not surprising that of all these important LGBTQ+ decisions none is using what Wintemute refers to as 'immutable status argument.' Using this argument would mean the Court recognizes sexual orientation as an immutable criterion, affirming one of the more controversial criteria for suspect classification. Despite the danger of essentializing an individual's sexuality, it would also acknowledge that a person's sexual orientation is fundamental to their identity and experiences. This decision by the highest court in the United States would already be a concession to those fighting to have their struggles legally recognized.

Having passed on the opportunity to review sexual orientation with heightened scrutiny on multiple occasions in the course of the twenty-first century may have several reasons: One may argue that not expanding its list of suspect classifications indicates the Court's anxiety in diluting the Equal Protection Clause's impact as suggested by Kenji Yoshino and his perspective on pluralism anxiety. Similarly, one may argue that the Court could be wanting to protect its political authority and legitimacy in increasingly politicized and polarized times, mirroring its current conservative supermajority and its justices' originalist tendencies of restraint. However, given the strong entanglements of law, culture, sexuality, and morality in the decisions analyzed here, it seems more likely that the Court above all fears losing its moral mandate and cultural authority. As seen by the analyses, the rights granted to sexual minorities in the twenty-first century always come with ideological freight and serve to ultimately strengthen the positions of those granting them and the dominant systems in which they are being negotiated. Declaring sexual orientation a suspect classification would undermine this endeavor of regulating queer rights one at a time; the Supreme Court's practice of taking case after case illustrates how legal queer liberation is still dependent on political sentiments, and that sociocultural equity is far from being accomplished. It is rather a controlled process of manipulating public sentiments and cultural imaginaries about the Court, the legal system, and U.S. moral superiority and the progressiveness of its sexual order. This gradual development allows conservative justices with anti-queer sentiment to slowly advance conservative movements' legal aims, perfect the constitutional reasoning behind curling back minority rights, and maintaining cultural authority while doing so.

The Court's unwillingness to review sexual orientation cases with heightened scrutiny serves yet another function. Granting rights to queers establishes the Court's authority and cultural legitimacy as it responds to sociocultural developments, yet refraining from making such a crucial constitutional reading of the Equal Protection Clause maintains the Constitution's and, by extension in the public imaginary, the Court's moral purity. Equal Protection jurisprudence is therefore not 'stained' by queer rights while the Court gets to keep its moral credentials by having granted the LGBTQ+ community the right to sexual freedom, the fundamental right to marry, and employment discrimination protection.

Further, these close readings stress the need for a critical cultural legal literacy in research and education. As shown, an analysis of both legal and cultural factors is needed to understand the implications of judicial decisions. Instead, what is most prominently discussed in public through media coverage of important decisions is *what* has been decided and not *why* it has been decided that way, which would include analyses of the respective argumentations and the connection to justices' modes of interpretation as well as a zooming in on cultural value systems and imaginaries. Without such an informed analysis, the legal strategies of conservative actors remain opaque and their implications impenetrable, limiting the response options to counter and challenge such decisions.

IV. Judging More Queerly

IV.1. Zooming in On Different Sources of Legal Orders and Attempts of Maintaining Them

The previous chapters have paid particular attention to the Supreme Court and the Constitution, thereby putting an emphasis on judicial approaches to law and the narratives and imaginaries associated with the legal system. While cultural narratives and imaginaries also do legal work in the form of challenging or legitimizing legal norms as argued in Chapter II.4, other legal and extra-legal dynamics of meaning-making are equally important for tactical queer rights activism and for establishing a queer hermeneutics of law. These dynamics this chapter sets out to examine, however, are not only important for developing actionable strategies. They are also foundational for understanding anti-discrimination projects as neither solely situated within sociocultural nor legal frameworks but entangled within diverse settings and thus need to be approached from an intersectional and interdisciplinary perspective.

The point that law is embedded in other sociocultural processes has been made, among others, by important scholars in queer studies,[1] sociology,[2] cultural studies,[3] law,[4] and psychology.[5] While the latter discipline has con-

1 For instance, see Valdes; Kepros; Katz *Invention*.

2 For instance, see Cotterrell; Schaefer.

3 For instance, see Coombe "Contingent;" Olson and Schillings.

4 For instance, see Hart; Rosen; Häberle *Verfassungslehre*.

5 See Kite and Whitley 35 for an overview of the sociocultural theory of stereotyping and prejudice. They argue that "most individuals internalize their culture's stereotypes along with other cultural norms and attitudes" (35), and link changing research findings in psychology and medicine to changing attitudes towards gay rights (8). See also Allport 461–78 for an overview on the entanglements of legal norms and group relations.

tributed meaningful insights into the sociocultural and neuronal origins of discrimination, challenging these mechanisms is still considered to be a legal issue with legal manifestation of stereotypes and prejudice often being conceived of and depicted as in need of a court room. Relegating queer rights to this battlefield, however, invisibilizes and silences the multidimensional entanglements of law and culture, i.e., how law codifies sociocultural norms and stereotypes, and how sociocultural norms and stereotypes reenter the legal realm when not challenged. Zooming in on different origins of legal meaning-making thus needs to take into account processes of normativization as well as codification, it needs to examine the interplay between legal and sociocultural change, and it needs to thoroughly question and deconstruct the very foundations on which legal reasoning takes place.

To do so, Queer Theory provides the necessary analytical perspectives to question seemingly 'natural' distinctions and binaries, deconstruct terminologies and concepts, and look at sexualities as fluid and dynamic. Additionally, Critical Legal Studies approaches law with an interest in its social implications and consequences. Both subdisciplines are critical towards traditional hegemonies and examine how processes of normativization are (mis-)used to maintain existing hierarchies. This chapter uses Queer Theory and Critical Legal Studies as lenses through which to analyze cultural knowledge about law, and to queer the social constructions of legal categorizations.

'Different sources of law' are understood as various ordering principles that are directly or indirectly connected to the legal system. While some are quite obvious, for instance legislation, others are not as readily associated with law, for instance, one own's biographical background. However, all of these examples, although varying in their form and closeness to the legal system, contribute to our understanding of law. They all share their function as establishing, maintaining, or challenging existing orders of power. Legal scholar Lawrence Rosen describes this perspective on entangled cultural-legal processes succinctly:

> Features that may not seem to be linked are, therefore, crucially related to one another: Our ideas of time inform our understanding of kinship and contract, our concepts of causation are entwined with the categories of persons we encounter, the ways we image our bodies and our interior states affect the powers we ascribe to the state and to our gods. In short, we create our experience, knit together disparate ideas and actions, and in the process fabricate a world of meaning that appears to us as real. (Rosen 4)

Regarding legal and sociocultural processes as intertwined blurs the allegedly static lines between these realms and illustrates how seemingly unrelated societal, cultural, and individual aspects feed back on each other. Growing out of and giving back to sociocultural conditions, laws are thus never neutral rules for ordering everyday life. They are equally indicative of and entangled in inequalities as the conditions they want to overcome or maintain.

Discriminatory laws may be changed by choosing one of various routes, i.e., the legislation, the judiciary, protesting. Yet changing discriminatory realities necessarily has to acknowledge all of these entanglements, examine all of the strategies available, and chose the one(s) that work best to prevent a legal domino effect in which bills and court decisions pop up and challenge laws, thus creating a federal legal patchwork. Patchwork systems bear the risk of tipping from mirroring democratic polyphony to undermining democracy's legitimacy when not able to communicate the reasonableness of their decisions to those being affected by them. Recent examples of this mechanism involve struggles between the state and federal level for or against minority rights in the U.S., most prominently the re-established power of states to decide whether to criminalize or allow abortions following the overturn of *Roe* in the Supreme Court's 2022 *Dobbs* decision.

But how could an approach that takes into account different sources of law be part of an activistic practice? Is the best way to achieve lasting sociocultural change the legal route? And if so, what would be the best way to go about it? There is disagreement on whether the legal system is really able to become an ally in queer rights activism, whether it would be best to abolish it entirely (see also Chapter V.3), whether it needs to be reformed before being of use for sexual minorities (see Chapter V.2), or whether it is crucial to challenge other oppressing mechanisms simultaneously, for instance neoliberal capitalist, patriarchal, colonial structures, as claimed by material feminism. I argue that laws take on various shapes and that what is referred to as the legal system expands way beyond codified or common law to include sociocultural norms. Law-like norms also have an inherently legal character and need to be considered for tactical activism. The imaginaries surrounding the sociocultural construct of marriage work to illustrate this point. If, for instance, one continues to support and (re-)produce notions of the family as only proper when involving two married people, yet denies the legal possibility to get married to certain groups (non-heterosexual, non-cis individuals), the legal system operates unequally. Even if these excluded groups now gain the right to get married through legislation or the judiciary, such as in *Obergefell*, the norm of being married has not been challenged, only its legal implementation for a specific group. The consequences of such an unchallenged cultural norm can then be seen by looking at *Masterpiece*. Exclusions for other groups to this normatized status are not addressed and continue to pose barriers for marginalized and invisibilized groups.

For establishing a more just and equal system of justice it is not sufficient to challenge the existing legal system; actively enabling conditions that allow for imagining and working towards alternatives to this system is equally important and goes beyond a mere abolishment of what is (the legal system as a whole) or a relocation of where to establish alternatives. This latter argument falsely considers economic, capitalist, political, neoliberal, colonial, or gender/sex political, patriarchal conditions as more important battlefields for activism while they need to be simultaneously tackled. Zooming in on other oppressive systems, away from the legal sphere, ignores the entanglements of these areas and their inherently legal character. Focusing on achieving more rights and establishing anti-discrimination laws for minorities is not about merely getting more say in an unequal system, it is about transforming said unequal system from within.

Certain conditions have explicitly or implicitly been inscribed into Western legal and moral cultures and continue their influence on legal communities even after they have been legally or socioculturally challenged. For instance, the existence of anti-abortion laws after *Roe* now enables states to re-establish pre-1973 conditions in their territory. States such as Oklahoma, Arkansas, Mississippi, and Alabama banned abortions before the Supreme Court de-criminalized it federally in 1973, and these states are very likely to re-install this legal stance now that the Court decided in *Dobbs* that it is up to the states whether to allow or prohibit abortions if they have not done so already (Messerly; Sneed). The continuing existence of anti-abortion laws even during the time of *Roe* has established an anti-abortion stance as moral, cultural, and legal standard in these states. The continuing existence in law enabled imagining anti-abortion as culturally and morally codified in these states, necessitating legal measures to prohibit it.

Schulzke and Caroll argue that those aiming to change existing policies need to take into account that "governmental support is often necessary for reform, ... even when they are successful in acting outside of government" (2), for example, when using extra-institutional ways of putting legal norms under pressure. These extra-institutional means may range from organizing and taking part in protests and signing petitions to publicly criticizing the norms in question and imagining, discussing, and sharing alternative, utopian forms of living and being.[6] When confronted with choosing between governmental forms of challenging policies, the most crucial question is whether to aim for legislative measures or to turn to the judiciary as these two strategies

> represent two fundamentally different ways of thinking about basic rights. Common law, which is the law created through judicial decisions, can have similar practical effects as new legislation, but the symbolism is much different. Courts cannot establish a new right, but they can interpret existing laws as affirming a right that has not been widely recognized. Judicial decisions may also explicitly reject previous legislation. When laws affecting culture are passed through legislative mechanisms, they create new rights and responsibilities. Unlike judicial decisions, legislative actions imply that the rights and responsibilities did not exist previously. This difference can have long-term consequences. (Schulzke and Caroll 2–3)

While legally, both legislative and judicial means promise similar results, culturally, these approaches have distinct effects. Although some scholars remark on the undemocratic process of judicially established legal norms,[7] the symbolic power of judicial decisions, especially when handed down by the Supreme Court, demands closer attention as the general political climate in the U.S. continues to become more polarized.

The previous chapters have commented on the affective relation between feelings of Americanness, of belonging to the U.S., and the Constitution and its narratives of equality, liberty, and autonomy. In its function as the custodian of this founding document, the Supreme Court is readily imagined as a higher authority in interpreting those ideals that are at the core of Americanness. These American ideals need to be defended in the cultural-legal imagination, yet have never been successfully implemented into the socio-legal reality. SCOTUS therefore enjoys an imaginatively increased moral power while it is *de jure* not more powerfully situated within the *trias politica* model than the legislature.

Further, looking back on past legislative decisions, one wonders whether these attempts are in fact more democratic than judicial interventions in the

6 However, in its most successful and arguably most consequent form, imagining alternative legal and sociocultural orders may ultimately abolish the need for governmental support, as discussed in Chapter V.4.

7 See Schulzke and Caroll 2; Bickel.

law. As seen with Obamacare, the COVID-19 relief fund, and the *Equality Act*, the political maneuvering around and filibustering of these bills puts pressure on the idea that public opinion and the electorate's votes evidently influence processes of lawmaking – even though the election of lawmakers is a more democratic process than the appointment of judges and justices. As for the U.S., this imaginary of public participation in lawmaking is even more challenged by systematic voter suppression in forms of gerrymandering, inhibited access to polling stations, and identification laws (Newkirk).

The instances discussed in this chapter, from Supreme Court decisions and categorizations to models of equality and essentialism, constitute different sources of law-like norms because they share regulatory and ordering functions for the social groups they are employed in. These legal and quasi-legal norms feed back into Western moral and legal cultures, i.e., they shape one's understanding of what is right and wrong, legal and illegal, and allowed and to be sanctioned.

In establishing the need to link activist efforts to legal reform, Chapter IV stresses the importance of thinking strategically about the relationship(s) between law and culture, and to work in dialogue with activists on various levels to achieve lasting anti-discriminatory realities for marginalized and oppressed social groups. The following parts illustrate how this utopian idea needs to expand from legal endeavors to active collaboration and dialogue between social groups, a questioning of allegedly fixed cultural frameworks and concepts, and the acknowledgement and challenging of one's own biased situatedness, privileges, and position.

IV.2. Cultural Transformations through Supreme Court Decisions

While the 2016 U.S. election marks a turning point in the public's affective reaction towards political decisions and an intensified notion of the so-called 'culture wars,' Supreme Court decisions have caused political and sociocultural responses throughout history. In 1896, *Plessy v. Ferguson* decided that racial segregation is constitutional, laying the foundation for decades of various forms of discrimination, including unequal access to resources, and invisibilization of BIPoC voices in sociocultural discourses. In 1973, *Roe v. Wade* decriminalized abortion on a federal level, thus supporting female emancipation and fostering the notion of having agency over one's body. In 2003's *Lawrence v. Texas*, the Court struck down sodomy laws on a federal level and laid the foundation for extending the fundamental right to marry to same-sex couples in *Obergefell v. Hodges* (2015). These examples illustrate how powerful Supreme Court decisions can be and the major sociocultural, economic, and political consequences they can have.

This chapter sets out to analyze how legal orders are influenced by cultural concepts, how legal and cultural categorizations of sexual orientation feed on and influence each other, and how sexual hierarchies are maintained in twenty-first century U.S. America. Taking legal norms and those who interpret them as its case studies, the chapter looks at the relation between legal and cultural-legal norms and power, and thereby establishes a queer hermeneutics within law.

The sociocultural transformations enabled by Supreme Court decisions can be observed by looking at *Plessy*, *Roe*, and *Lawrence*.[8] However, the more interesting question is whether such transformations are caused or merely intensified by these decisions. In other words, do Supreme Court decisions inhabit a jurisgenerative[9] nature, meaning that they have the power to establish a new "nomos", that is a new "normative universe" (Cover "Nomos" 4)? And if so, would this new normative universe hold the power to initiate cultural transformations within mainstream society and culture simply by the act of deciding a legal case? Does a Supreme Court's issued opinion serve as a performative utterance of cultural change? Or, does a decision merely reflect on the social movements' claims that preceded the decision?

Critical Legal Studies often approach legal processes in terms of power formations and social hierarchies following a Marxist understanding of law (West 147–50), rendering the cultural arch which frames legal systems invisible. When law and power are analyzed from a sociological or political perspective, power hierarchies within cultural notions of what is 'normal' are often left underdiscussed. The cultural frames which inform legal conditions function as a given, and more than often remain invisible in legal analysis. For instance, the discourse about adoption regulations for non-heterosexual and trans individuals is often approached from the call for equal treatment, while the broader issues of the cultural constructs of family, kinship, and gender are left underdiscussed. This way, law works to regulate around unquestioned,

8 See Chapter IV.1.

9 Robert Cover uses the term "jurisgenesis" to refer to "the creation of legal meaning" ("Nomos" 11).

naturalized and already flawed cultural notions of what is 'normal' and what should be policed.

Legal Norms and Cultural Frames in *Pavan v. Smith*

The 2017 Supreme Court decision *Pavan v. Smith* works well to illustrate this point. In *Pavan v. Smith*, two lesbian couples sued the director of the Arkansas Department of Health, Dr. Nate Smith, because the Department issued a birth certificate for their children which only had the name of the biological mother on it. From a legal perspective, the case seemed rather clear as Arkansas state law violated the ruling in *Obergefell* that same-sex couples have the constitutional right to marry, which is the "basis for an expanding list of governmental rights, benefits, and responsibilities" (17), including "birth and death certificates" (17). Consequently, the Supreme Court decided in favor of the plaintiff, and the Department of Health had to issue a birth certificate with both mothers on it.

From a cultural perspective, however, both the Arkansas supreme court and the U.S. Supreme Court in the form of Justice Gorsuch's dissent, joined by Justices Thomas and Alito, took issue with the addition of a same-sex, non-biological partner to the child's birth certificate. For them, a birth registration system based on biology is legitimate because only then are states able to collect "reliable and comprehensive statistics of all vital events for purposes of public health research and identification of public health trends" (2016 Arkansas 437 S.Ct. at 14).[10] This argumentation seems spurious, yet appealing because it speaks to our cultural desire of feeling protected and evading considerations of mortality through medical and biological certainty.

Interestingly, this medico-biologistic perspective on bodies is also reflected in an overemphasis on biological sex in legal discourse. When looking at the increasingly fierce way of regulating trans and non-binary bodies in states such as Mississippi with its 2021 "Mississippi Fairness Act,"[11] a pattern

---

10 This line of argumentation which focusses on vital records and public health concerns can also be observed in multiple state bills aiming to prohibit changing trans individuals' gender markers on their birth certificates. See South Dakota's HB 1076 from 2021; see also *Ray v. McCloud* (2020) in which a federal court struck down an Ohio state policy.

11 Mississippi Senate Bill 2536, also known as the "Mississippi Fairness Act" prevents trans and non-binary youth to compete or even join athletic teams according to their gender identity. The Act mandates youth to join teams according to their biological sex.

of using biological sex as "supposed shelter of reliability even when existing understandings of gender, identity, and social equality are being actively challenged elsewhere" (Olson and Borchert 391) emerges. Operating similar to the tracking of genetic information for the purpose of 'public health,' biological sex is then naturalized as essential and scientific relevant category of ordering social life – from issuing birth certificates to regulating youth's sports activities to collecting information about potentially terminal illnesses.

It is doubtful whether a culture that has a different view on death and sickness, one that does not displace mourning and loss to its margins, would lay an equal emphasis on tracking health records to genetic lineage. It is equally questionable whether a cultural understanding of non-binary sexualities would continue to use a heteronormative lens for these considerations. However, this and similar arguments against equal treatment of minorities function as moral credentials which allow people to consciously and unconsciously mask their discriminatory stance towards LGBTQ+ people under the disguise of other cultural anxieties.

Additionally, the issues surrounding birth certification mirror other cultural anxieties about the loss of family cohesion and the endangerment of the heteronormative core family. One could also argue that a fear of non-heteronormative family models and an increasing fluidity in sex and gender relations is the original cultural anxiety which only stains the others. However, from a psychoanalytical perspective, fearing a dissolution of one's presumably clear-cut identity and the omnipresent fear of dying may be equally threatening. As analyzed by queer theorist Gayle Rubin in her seminal 1984 essay "Thinking Sex," Western conceptualizations of sexuality follow a certain hierarchy which values "heterosexual, marital, monogamous, reproductive, and noncommercial" (151) sexuality while condemning sexualities that are "homosexual, unmarried, promiscuous, nonprocreative, or commercial" (151). The cultural prioritization of these forms of sexuality mirror what Butler referred to as the "heterosexual matrix" (*Gender* 208). The binary understanding of stable biological sexes translates into a cultural expectation to behave a certain way (gender) and to feel attracted to the opposite sex (compulsory heterosexuality) (Butler *Gender* 101; 208).

Cultural and Legal Notions of Kinship and Family

Transgressing any of these borders, crossing any of those lines or violating any of the socioculturally mandated expectations Rubin and Butler mention, sets into motion "a domino theory of sexual peril" (Rubin 151) in which, if not acting according to these heavily policed sexual norms, "something unspeakable will skitter across" (151). Here, the quasi-legal character of non-legal, sociocultural norms and the dawning punishment when neglecting them proves to be equally threatening and coercive as codified or common law. This cultural understanding of family as consisting of a cis man, functioning as husband, patriarch, breadwinner, and a cis woman, functioning as wife, mother, and care worker, has historically been enforced through legal and social norms, making it a dominant narrative of what is normatively perceived as 'normal.' These notions are also influenced and reinforced by legal-economic regulations which tied marriage, — until the Court's 2015 *Obergefell* decision in many states only applying to heterosexual couples, — to certain financial benefits such as tax deductions (such as inheritance taxes, as seen in *Windsor*) or insurance rates.

Interestingly, while we are socialized to accept and, in some cases, unquestioningly follow this notion of what 'family' consists of, the religious, economic and cultural inkings of this concept go unnoticed. Becoming a husband or a wife respectively is inherent to what a 'real,' i.e. (morally) good and happy, family looks like. The historic development of this institution is not part of the sociocultural imaginaries about it. Marriage's patriarchal-capitalist logic of a husband's ownership of his wife are today at best incidentally remembered when choosing wedding rings or taking off one's maiden name. [12] While weddings rings originate in the tradition of marking one's property (Case "Feminists" 1210), taking on the husband's name as legal name was not merely a tradition but state-level patriarchal force. The decision which name to use was not up to the wife but mandated and expected by society and law; if a woman would not comply with this expectation, she risked not being granted citizenship, getting a mortgage on property, or having troubles in voter registration (Case "Marriage" 1768; Kohout 105). Further, bourgeois promises of happiness, which include classed notions of property and privateness in one's own four walls, evolve around the marriage contract as rite of passage into familyness. In this sense, the religious symbolism of marriage as a threshold to valid and meaningful relationships, and bureaucratic state procedures of becoming married qualify gender relations and knight them culturally.

The entanglements between cultural, religions, and legal conceptualizations of the family reinforce the impression of this heteronormative family structure as universally valid because they all support and build on each other.

12 For more on marriage as a patriarchal institution see Boucai 4; Case "Feminists" 1213–5; *Frontiero* at 685.

Consequently, religious understandings of normativity have become part of ordering human relations and continue to exercise this privileged status onto others by establishing quasi-legal norms and forms of sociocultural control – be it through adhering to religious ceremonial procedures, introducing moral orders, or enforcing traditional belief systems.

As a consequence of this normalization of heteronormative family structures, conceptualizations of models that deviate from this norm are more difficult and possibly taboo for us to imagine. Following a determinist understanding culture, these cultural frames and the organization of cultural realms, e.g., how do we perceive of gender relations, limit and determine our abilities to produce knowledge about our world.

Non-heteronormative family models, especially queer understandings of family cause cultural anxieties of blurring those structures a majority of people were socialized to believe are natural. While the sources of these anxieties remain unclear, – may they stem from discriminatory beliefs, the inability to understand these conceptualizations which are so 'foreign,' or discriminatory beliefs which result from the inability to understand these conceptualizations which are so 'foreign,' – they focus on adjusting the legal norms instead of the cultural understandings pertaining to the concept of family. 'Family' today more than often includes non-biological family members instead of biological ones, and trans or non-binary parents who gave birth to children qua their biological set-up while or before their decision to let others in on their identity, i.e., before their 'coming-out.'

While *Pavan v. Smith* was straight forward with regard to the legal questions about whether to add the biological mother's female spouse to the birth certificate, it may need more cultural inquiries into legal norms before these official documents are framed along the lines of parentage, regardless of biological kinship and gender. For instance, in Canada, the Ontario "All Families Are Equal Act" from 2016 recognizes more than two parents of a child.[13] This

13 Another more recent example is the German government's *Koalitionsvertrag* (coalition contract) from 2021. In this document, the parties *SPD*, *Bündnis 90/Die Grünen*, and *FDP* announce that they want to establish a new legal institution next to adoption called "small custody" (SPD 101; "kleines Sorgerecht"). This form of custody is directed at social parents and may include up to two adults next to the legal parents. This is all the more progressive as they claim that they want to introduce an "institution of collective responsibility" (101; "Institut der Verantwortungsgemeinschaft") to provide security beyond and next to marriage or romantic relationships.

model still includes medico-biological considerations about lineage, – possibly even more so as those who contribute sperm and ovum are listed as parents plus their respective partners, – yet it is a progressive step towards a queering of cultural kinship concepts and the legal recognition thereof. Such progressive regulations not only queer the cultural concept of the family but they also circumvent legal discrimination of queer family models.

In order to initiate cultural transformations, it seems necessary to understand law not as a corrective of culture but as an ally in de-masking cultural conditions which enable social inequalities. This view presupposes that cultural control works unconsciously to maintain social stratification and acts as a legal order in itself this way. In this understanding, law may be utilized to understand cultural values and ways of upholding hierarchies implicitly instead of seeing legal norms or lawmakers as explicit, unique, and most important enforcers of legal orders.

What *Pavan v. Smith* also teaches is that discriminatory legal norms, or the failure or unwillingness to apply norms correctly in this case, make queer lives harder. Coming back to the introductory questions, namely whether sociocultural transformations are caused by Supreme Court decisions, one can safely say: Yes, they do. Following social psychologist Gordon Allport, if "we can be entirely sure that discriminative laws *increase* prejudice – why, then, should not legislation of the reverse order *diminish* prejudice?" (467; emphasis in original). Even if social movements have paved the way for legislative or judicial measures to strengthen minority rights, the implementation of those demands through institutional powers brings queer right claims into the public consciousness and opens up debates about their sociocultural implications. This heightened awareness fosters an active engagement with minority groups and naturalized cultural concepts, and makes intergroup contact more likely. Thus, learning about other people's realities reflects on how one perceives their claims and helps contextualizing, or even empathizing with those claims through taking the other's perspective.

The role of the Supreme Court in this endeavor is powerful. The strong authoritative force of the Constitution and the Court's role as its interpreter or even guardian make constitutional decisions arguably more affectively binding than legislative ones. It is again Allport who succinctly lays down this connection:

> While it is true that unless a fairly large percentage of the people are in favor of a law it will not work, yet it is false to say that folkways must al-

> ways take precedence over stateways. ... It is often said that the way must be paved for remedial legislation through education. ... But when the initial work has been done, then the legislation in turn becomes educative. The masses of people do not become converts in advance; rather they are converted by the *fait accompli*. ... Actually, in the United States, stateways – at least as expressed in the Constitution – are in advance of folkways. The Constitution is clear in its intentions that total democracy shall prevail. Thus the "official" morality of this country is high ... . (470–1)

I quote Allport here at length because of his argument's importance for queer rights discourse. Although Allport refers to legislative means, judicial decisions by the highest court are arguably even more educative. They continue to exert affective force because of their reference and closeness to the Constitution, even in times of an increasing politization and polarization of the Court. Similar to the Constitution's ideals of equality and liberty, which have arguably not been implemented into U.S. American legal or cultural praxis, emancipatory Supreme Court decisions may equally exert affective and imaginary power. Such decisions then become true landmarks in that they guide the way for fostering equity throughout legal and cultural realms. Following this understanding, stateways or rather federal legal land gains for minority groups may not necessarily be in advance of folkways, for instance, in the form of social movements that advocate for queer rights. Rather, they advance folkways, meaning stateways influence the majority's prejudices and stereotypes about LGBTQ+ people. This view supports the claim that queer rights activists should aim for constitutional protections.

As in the example of *Pavan v. Smith*, one needs to zoom in on the respective parties' lines of legal argumentation, and then zoom out to analyze which cultural purposes the arguments made seem to fulfill. Utilized this way, law may work to uncover inequalizing conditions. The following part expands on the method of queering law in the sense of troubling, questioning, and deconstructing it. Strengthening sensibilities for queer realities and cultural-legal education again serves as an essential tool for improving legal conditions and aiming for overcoming discriminatory conditions. The subsequent parts establish legal norms' and judges' inadequacy in ruling on queer realities without challenging cultural-legal orders, and examine the possibility of responding to identity political demands and calls for legal protections via a rejection of generalizations and a favoring of specific classifications.

IV.3. Processes of Categorization

Categorization is defined by social psychologists as "the process of simplifying the environment by creating categories on the basis of characteristics (such as hair color or athletic ability) that a particular set of people appear to have in common" (Kite and Whitley 87). While simplification may prove useful in situations that may seem overwhelming, such as when being overexposed to information or forced to make a decision quickly, it reduces complexity in favor of a (over-)generalization, which social scientists have identified as one of the bases for developing stereotypes and prejudice.[14] Cultural approaches to law have similarly recognized that the "limited ability of legal categories to acknowledge multiple forms of social subordination was one of the early insights from identity-based scholarship" (Coombe "Cultural Studies" 40); with scholars noting that "[t]he normative distinctions that are reproduced by law systematize our experience of the world" (Olson and Schillings 3), and that "the particular value of studying the law from the perspectives of literary and cultural studies lies in explicating these legal categories' specific cultural valences" (Olson and Schillings 3). In other words, critical cultural approaches towards law aim to deconstruct and de-naturalize the authority of legal categories and assumptions by questioning the process(es) of categorization.

The critique inherent in these approaches does not seem surprising, and similar critiques of categorical thinking can be found in other disciplines as well. Queer theorist Eve Kosofsky Sedgwick's famous axioms start with claiming that "people are different from each other" (22), which "prove[s] that even people who share all or most of our own positionings along these crude axes [i.e., gender, race, class, nationality, sexual orientation; lb] may still be different enough from us, from each other, to seem like all but different species" (22). While these perspectives signal the need for more conceptual tools for dealing with pluralisms in general, they also emphasize concerns about the usefulness/harmfulness of legal and sexual classifications in particular.

Feminist legal scholar Kimberlé Crenshaw's intersectionality theory, as well as activists' educational work and fights against multi-layered forms of oppression, has contributed to an advanced understanding of intertwined axes of multiple discrimination. As Coombe puts it, "[t]he concept of intersectionality developed from the understanding that persons rarely occupy just one legal category of identity and that the law fails to recognize the complexity

14 See Tajfel 84–6; Tajfel et. al. 154–7; Kite and Whitley 331.

of their situations as a consequence" ("Cultural Studies" 40).[15] One, if not the, most important analytical tool for examining oppression based on multiple identities, intersectionality exceeds law as a discipline by acknowledging the uniqueness of one's being and thus providing a site for negotiating and experiencing pluralistic identities.

In legal practice, however, this theory is not only difficult to apply given that "[l]egislating rigid distinctions between categories of human populations is a necessary condition of contemporary Western law and statehood" (Olson and Schillings 3). But it also clashes with a lack of consciousness about what these identities entail. In these instances, stereotypical perceptions and judgments based on ignorance are prone to fill in. Prominent examples of this can be found in Richard Posner's controversial *Sex and Reason* which he introduces with the

> belated discovery that judges know next to nothing about the subject [sex] beyond their own personal experience, which is limited, perhaps more so than average, because people with irregular sex lives are pretty much (not entirely, of course) screened out of the judiciary—especially the federal judiciary, with its elaborate preappointment investigations by the FBI and other bodies. (1)

Posner, an important figure for the Law and Literature project,[16] has been heavily criticized by other scholars[17] for adopting an essentialist and reductionist perspective on sexual orientation,[18] contributing to an ongoing invisibilization of lesbian experience,[19] and reproducing heterosexist assumptions about gays, lesbians, and bisexuals as Other[20] in his book. While *Sex and Reason* draws attention to the project of queer rights by benefitting from Posner's status as

---

15 While Coombe rightly attributes Crenshaw with the advent of intersectionality, the underlying logics of multiple oppression can be traced back to the Combahee River Collective Statement in 1977.

16 See his seminal 1988 book *Law and Literature: A Misunderstood Relation*.

17 Posner responded to some of this criticism by Gillian K. Hadfield, Martha Fineman, Katharine T. Bartlett, and Ruthann Robson in "The Radical Feminist Critique of *Sex and Reason*." His response summarizes *Sex and Reason*'s main arguments and sheds light on how Posner tries to legitimize his heteronormative position by discrediting feminist views as radical and continuing to ignore the need to engage with his own biases that a male-centered socialization inevitably creates.

18 Kepros 293; Eskridge "Critique" 365–8.

19 Robson 201; Eskridge "Critique" 334.

20 Eskridge "Critique" 359–60.

"a celebrated mainstream legal academic and judge" (Eskridge "Critique" 335), it also illustrates how judges and legal academics are affected by stereotypical thinking and continue to reproduce these simplifications in their works. Images of gay men as "effeminate" (Posner *Sex* 304) and "somewhat more neurotic" (*Sex* 304) than straight people feed back into modern Western moral and ultimately legal cultures.

Another instance is former SCOTUS Justice Lewis F. Powell Jr.'s statement "I don't believe I've ever met a homosexual" (Greenhouse). By now, this statement has a tragicomical ring to it because the law clerk he talked to was gay, and Powell's vote was the decisive one for the continuing criminalization of (particularly gay) oral and anal sex in *Bowers v. Hardwick* (1986) (Lazarus). In both of these instances, judicial power over queer lives was in the hands of people who admittedly had no concept of how queer lives (could) look like. Lack of knowledge paired with the inability, or sometimes unwillingness, to imagine the forms of exclusion and discrimination that deviating from heterosexual norms brings with results in a judicial representation without cultural legitimation. Judges like Posner and Powell may enjoy the legal authority to decide on queer lives, yet their heteronormative situatedness and unfamiliarity with queer culture(s) deprives them from the competence to shape queer realities.

In this book's understanding, queer culture consists of a shared set of values and discriminatory experiences, however heterogeneous within the non-homogeneous group one often refers to as 'the' queer community. While acknowledging the individual, intersectional, lived experience and processes of knowledge production, facing discrimination on basis of one's non-normative ways of identifying oneself in terms of gender, sexuality or performance, still constitutes a shared set of experience. Non-normativity thus functions as a complex to which experiences of discrimination, non-acceptance, violence, and economic struggles are attached to for queers. The various ways of attachments to this complex then constitute a common denominator.

Even in settings which see assimilation by queer people and also possibly queers who identify with conservative values, it is queers who assimilate to a heterosexual, cis norm and not the other way around. The power of these norms is mirrored in considerations of law's authority and legitimacy. Following Habermas that law "can preserve its socially integrating force only insofar as the addressees of legal norms can understand themselves, taken as a whole, as the rational *authors* of those norms" (33; emphasis in original), the question arises of how legal norms can remain accepted in a diversified, pluralistic sociocultural setting which still inhabits rather homogeneous power relations that benefit mostly White, male, cis, heterosexual, able-bodied, propertied persons with citizenship rights. This perspective is also reflected in Hart's view on the relationship between law and those it governs: "[I]f a system of rules is to be imposed by force on any, there must be a sufficient number of who accept it voluntarily" (201). Agreeing with Hart's assertion that "the coercive power of law presupposes its accepted authority" (203), which, again mirrors the sociocultural constructed nature of law since it is only as powerful as it is constructed to be, one wonders if legal authority necessarily corresponds to a moral one. Hart contests this view and argues that following legal rules may have various reasons, only a few of which require conceiving of law as morally binding or universally 'right' (201–3). In this sense, legal authority does not equal moral validity, and it also does not translate into cultural competence or legitimacy.

In the U.S., this relationship is more tense than in other legal cultures. Tracing back the development of the U.S.'s legal system and specifically the U.S. Constitution's perception as the 'law of the land,' considerations of moral validity, legal authority, and cultural legitimacy were always closely entangled. Without perceiving of British rule as unjust and cruel, and without perceiving of the American colonies as distinct communities culturally different from those who governed them, the legal system of the U.S. as laid down in the Constitution would not have been thinkable. Federalism, checks-and-balances, and the separation of powers doctrine speak to this moral, political, cultural, and legal understanding of a legal system's validity, which "incorporate[s] principles of justice or substantive moral values" (Hart 204).

Connected to the questions of legal authorship or law's authorship is the issue of interpretative authority. The increasing reliance on the judiciary's intervention in legal questions, an instance of and catalyst for the growing politization of this governmental branch, necessitates, following Habermas, inquiring into the interpreters of those norms. By extension, of course, this also means examining the structures which still benefit those already in power and those likely to fill in positions which come with the power to shape sociocultural conditions by interpreting laws.

This view may appear controversial because it risks being misunderstood as reproducing contested identity political demands that only those are granted permission to speak who are directly affected and part of a community. This is not what the critique of heteronormative and privileged positions entails, here exemplified by looking at Posner and Powell. Their competence to rule is not lacking because they are not queer but because they have failed to look through the heterosexist matrix they are part of, and because they have failed to take the perspectives of those being ruled on, thus strengthening exactly those structures anti-discrimination laws aim to overcome. Moreover, given Posner's and Powell's status as important and powerful figures in their respective fields, their statements indicate at least a touch of saturated ignorance; they might not have met a queer person or are knowledgeable on the subject of sex, yet they neither need to be nor do they have to show a particular interest in these matters to remain in their powerful positions. This close reading of these instances is, of course, symptomatic of a wider logic of heteronormative, cis entitlement.

Denying Posner's and Powell's competence to rule does not equal denying their right, or their (legal) authority, to do so. Picking up the argument made by Habermas, Roger Cotterrell is however right to point out that in terms of law's legitimacy "questions about its *moral authority* remain" (28; emphasis in original) even when its prescriptive force is made clear. In the context of the Posner/Powell discussion above, questions about law's moral authority are inevitably linked to questions about judges' and justices' cultural competence. In Cotterrell's words, this is because "as the nature of the social changes, sociolegal [and cultural-legal; lb] research is challenged to consider these questions [of authority and competence; lb] anew, perhaps long before they become dilemmas disrupting law's everyday practice of the method of detail" (28).

It is true that today's cultural landscape is quite different from 1992 when Posner published his book and from 1986 when Powell decided in *Bowers*. Complex medial representations[21] of, among others, homo-, a-, bisexual, queer, and trans characters onscreen, for instance in seminal shows such as *Pose* (2018–2021), *Sense8* (2015–2018), or *Orange Is the New Black* (2013–2019) as well as activistic work done by those being part of the #MeToo movements, Women's March, #BlackLivesMatter and less medially present movements have strengthened public sensibilities for identities and experiences beyond the normative mainstream. These growing visibilities, both in terms of creators of and characters in media products, advance and multiply possibilities

21 These representations have not increased quantitatively but most of all qualitatively, reducing tokenism in favor of more nuanced representations of queer characters. This way, the pressures put on one character to represent a whole community have been reduced and the notion of queers as homogenous group has been challenged. I thank Rahel Sixta Schmitz for this insight and the vivid discussion about representational politics.

of perspective-taking and contribute to the development of pluralistic gazes on others' lives. While one can only guess whether today's judges and justices watch *Netflix* or to what extent they are familiar with activists' demands, it remains true "that on a court composed of human beings, biography matters" (Greenhouse).

One's biography, however, does not exist in a vacuum untouched by sociocultural conditions. Even queer judges may be impeded to rule in favor of queer demands based on their fear of being publicly condemned –, especially if not being 'out,' –, anxiety to become accused of uncritically pursuing identity political activism, or internalized self-hatred due to the still valid fact that "modern American culture is unusually antihomosexual" (Eskridge "Critique" 340).[22] One may therefore argue that not only in courts but in a legal system dependent on human actors in general, sociocultural conditions matter as legal and cultural realms affect each other and the people within them constantly.

These consideration about the interplay of individuals within the legal system and those realities which are affected by this system tie into what is perceived to be one of the key issues within jurisprudence, the relationship between legal norms and facts. Similar to the dogmatic differences in textual and organic modes of constitutional interpretation, one's understanding of how norms shape realities or vice versa influences one's openness to inter- and transdisciplinary perspectives.[23] Pointing to the indeterminate character of legal norms, i.e., those parts within the law which lack precision and leave room for interpretation,[24] legal scholar Hermann Kantorowicz emphasizes the importance of judges who are familiar with the social realities they decide on:

---

22 A claim which may easily be expanded by including unusually anti-transgender or unusually hostile towards other identity categories defying medical-biologist notions or binary concepts of sexuality.

23 For a succinct introduction to different directions in the sociology of law, see Baer *Rechtssoziologie* 25–27: While Puchta's *conceptual jurisprudence* considers legal norms to be self-sufficient for resolving conflicts, Ehrlich's *living law* stresses the simultaneous existence of pluralistic legal cultures within society, and the *free law school*, advocated by Kantorowicz, Fuchs, and Sinzheimer, calls for filling in the gaps in legal norms by looking at social realities.

24 For Kantorowicz, these imprecise parts make up much of what we consider law: "It is not the case that there are some gaps here and there within the law, no, one may confidently say that there are as many gaps as there are words" (15), (dt.: "Denn nicht so liegt der Sachverhalt, daß Lücken im Gesetz sich hier und da wohl vorfinden, nein, getrost darf man behaupten, daß nicht weniger Lücken als Worte da sind."). My translation.

> We want judges who, drawing from them [living conditions; lb] and their own experience, know how to rule with full awareness of the social functions of every legal norm and the social consequences of their decisions. To comprehend everything means ruling on everything justly. … For partiality which – it must not be denied – is found in so many decisions, especially those in criminal law, is not rooted in ill will, but in naked unawareness of social facts and views, and in those biases in naive class prejudices which find their root and excuse precisely in this unawareness.[25] (Kantorowicz 46)

Certainly, when Kantorowicz wrote these words in 1906, ignorance to other people's realities was circumstantial and not intentional – at least more so than today. However, this in *dubio pro reo* view on an unawareness of lives peripheral to privileged sociocultural sites can today, at best, be considered as a form of reverse victimization: *Barbarus hic ergo sum, quia non intellegor ulli*;[26] judges claiming to be unaware of queer living conditions and thus impaired in their rulings reject their position's responsibility to educate themselves and take other perspectives in order to represent not only their respective peer groups. Resorting to lack of knowledge means putting oneself in a victim position and redirecting the responsibility for changing sociocultural conditions back to those who suffer from them, in this case LGBTQ+ individuals without judicial representation.[27] Given these indeterminate legal categorizations and the difficulties in relying on judges to fill them out adequately, approaching legal norms with more specificness and perspective-taking may be useful.

---

25 The German original reads: "Und Richter wollen wir, die, auf sie und die eigne Erfahrung gestützt, in voller Kenntnis der sozialen Funktionen jedes Rechtssatzes und der sozialen Wirkung ihrer Entscheidung, zu urteilen wissen. Alles verstehen, heißt alles gerecht bewerten. … Denn die Parteilichkeit, welche – es darf nicht geleugnet werden – aus so vielen besonders strafrechtlichen Urteilen spricht, stammt nicht aus bösem Willen, sondern aus nackter Unkenntnis der sozialen Tatsachen und Anschauungen und aus jener Befangenheit in naiven Klassenvorurteilen, welche eben in jener Unkenntnis ihre Wurzel und Entschuldigung finden." My translation.

26 The English translation is: I am a barbarian here (only) because nobody here understands me. This Latin aphorism is attributed to Ovid.

27 While one may argue that this judicial representation is growingly diverse, this cannot, at least until 2024, be said for the set-up of the Supreme Court.

IV.4. Legal Generalizations vs. Legal Specificness

The positive correlation between complex queer representations on and off screen, public discourses about LGBTQ+ rights, and the growing visibilities of queers increase public and individual awareness of sexual minorities. Being and constantly becoming aware of others' realities is crucial for assessing socio-legal conditions, and it is certainly an idealtypical democratic necessity to allow for pluralism within a society. Yet these developments suggest that most LGBTQ+ struggles have been won, and that sexual orientation is not a political, least legal, issue anymore. From this perspective, strengthening universal rights seems more important than establishing particular rights for queers or other minorities. Even for those arguing in favor of greater protections for queers, the idea of post-class-based legal protection seems the ultimate remedy for discriminatory legal classifications. Claiming that "there is no such thing as 'gay rights'; there is only the question of which rights, such as sexual privacy, qualification to volunteer for military service, marriage, and so forth, must be equally enforced," (Gerstmann *Underclass* viii), scholars imagine a legal system which is rather dedicated to protecting substantive rights of all instead of expanding the rights of some to more groups.

This impression has also found its way into legal scholarship and into the cultural imaginary that minority rights are discriminatory because they favor one group over others. Thinking back of Kenji Yoshino's generalizing approach to civil rights (792), one may feel inclined to follow his argumentation that gaining and maintaining equality works best when "newly visible kinds people" (747), in this case queers, are at least reminded of "the ideals of assimilation and integration" (751) into U.S. American legal culture rather than annexed via 'special' protections:

> The liberty claim is more persuasive because it performs the empathy it seeks. It frames the right at a high enough level of generality that opposite-sex couples are urged to imagine a world in which they were denied the right. In contrast, *equal protection claims tend to stress distinctions among us*, even as they ask us to overcome those distinctions. That exhortation is a performative contradiction. It asks us to transcend a distinction that the entity urging transcendence is unable itself to achieve. (Yoshino 794; emphasis added)

According to this view, "[l]iberty-based dignity claims" (Yoshino 792) seek to be more effective in uniting U.S. Americans than equality-based ones because the former takes being human as criterion which warrants protection while the latter draws attention to distinction and thus stresses difference. Yoshino is right to question the potentially divisive character equal protection brings with it, – and has historically been criticized for,[28] – but neglects the equally divisive notion of legal understandings of liberty. In Western legal cultures, this fundamental right is culturally framed and constructed around an imagined White, cisgendered, heterosexual, able-bodied, propertied man as the prototypical, and idealtypical receiver, and rightfully bearer, of such liberty.

Yoshino fittingly criticizes the divisive power of categorizations in general, yet fails to acknowledge their cultural embeddedness. While scientists[29] are still out on the question about whether sexual orientation is socially constructed or an essential part of one's being (caused either through biology or socialization), the importance Western cultures attach to this category most certainly is constructed. When ordering categories of sexuality shifted from focusing on certain behaviors to certain identities during the early twentieth century,[30] new forms of group memberships became available. Following the queer theoretical observation that from all possible combinations of sexuality it is interesting that we place so much emphasis on object-choice, categories which subsume people into homo-, hetero-, bi-, a-sexual or other appear both arbitrary and inevitable. It is difficult to imagine that the decision to view sexuality through the lens of object-choice will change anytime soon because these categories have become and continue to be meaningful in Western moral and legal cultures. Identity political discourses add to this development and cement these socially constructed categories into cultural-legal norms. Whether someone identifies as gay or straight then may have legal consequences such as being denied certain rights or being persecuted. It may also result in being treated differently by one's neighbors or family members. Within this cultural frame, however, sexual preference in terms of coital positions, forms of intimacy, what one enjoys listening to while having sex, or other individual likes are not nearly

---

28 The Court's 1898 decision *Plessy v. Ferguson* speaks to this perverted understanding of equality in equal protection jurisprudence and how equal protection claims have been politicized in the past.

29 'Scientists' refers to both scholars in the natural and social sciences, incorporating Wilton's critique of the academic hegemony of natural science, see Wilton 18.

30 See Foucault *History* 192; Jagose 11; Katz "Questioning" 45.

as relevant for discrimination. These preferences are also less likely to wield such identity-formating power over individuals compared to questions of object-choice.

Coming from a queer theoretical perspective, overcoming categories of sexual orientation seems promising for smashing sexual moral hierarchies and finally arriving at what Yoshino imagines as a "Supreme Court jurisprudence that focuses on universal liberties guaranteed to all persons or citizens under the Constitution" (Yoshino 796). It is the same queer theoretical perspective, however, which maintains that this road to more liberty, or equity as I would argue, needs to take a detour via heightened, group-specific equal protections. Without critically analyzing and deconstructing the sociocultural mechanisms which enable discriminatory realities, legal protections cannot offer sufficient authority for shielding minorities off biases and violence; without drawing attention to and visibilizing group-specific realities and discrimination, universal legal regulations remain void of understanding for and acknowledgement of LGBTQ+-specific experiences and thus empty of promises for queers.

The current legal-political tendency to subsume discrimination based on sex, gender, sexual orientation or gender identity under one generalized umbrella speaks to this misinformed understanding of the relationship between legal and cultural mechanisms. What we can learn from the 2020 Supreme Court landmark decision *Bostock v. Clayton County*, and its implementation in the Biden administration's Executive Order 13988 on "Preventing and Combating Discrimination on the Basis of Gender Identity or Sexual Orientation" is that sexual minorities are certainly better protected legally but their discrimination's cultural foundations are not being challenged. Distinctions between concepts relating to sexuality are already blurred and growing sensibilities for identities make it even more difficult for people within and outside of the LGBTQ+ community to keep track of the various ways in which people make sense of their being. Throwing the big blanket of one general protection for gender identity and sexual orientation makes the legal situation of sexual minorities more predictable and their lives safer. Yet it also inhibits a distinct engagement with gay, lesbian, trans, bisexual and other demands. To protect everyone then means not having to distinctively engage with the particular claims of anyone. Plus, it prevents a thorough analysis of why these categories have become added with meaning rather than meaningful categories of group membership in the first place.

Some queer people may criticize that their respective and specific demands are not heard. As a consequence, they might reject legal reforms because they do not feel represented by them. This is particularly true for controversial legal land gains such as same-sex marriage, which is by some considered as an inherently heteronormative, patriarchal-capitalist and oppressive institution. Further, demands for an intersectional and individual approach to considering people's realities by scholars such as Sedgwick and Crenshaw are ignored. Considering sexual minorities' rights from a universal rights standpoint impedes the analysis of the biases and discriminatory foundational beliefs about queers that contribute to their sociocultural marginalization. Without this tracking of sociocultural foundations of discrimination, this marginalization will continue to find its way into legal norms and judicial reasoning via biased or ignorant law-makers, politicians, and judges. This marginalization will continue to be displayed in cultural-legal orders which may not be as formal as statutes but maybe even more effective in excluding and violating queer bodies.

The results of this approach can already be witnessed. In 2021, the number of state-level anti-LBTQ+ bills which have been proposed and introduced has increased drastically,[31] marking 2021 as "record-breaking year" (Krishnakumar) of anti-trans legislation – a trend that goes on ever since (ACLU "Mapping"). Admittedly, the state-level backlash to progressive minority emancipation is not a unique consequence of *Bostock* or Biden's presidency. However, the increasing fierceness to implement such anti-minority laws, as evidenced by their growing numbers, speaks to the claim that legal developments need to be accompanied by cultural re-negotiations.

Another explanation for the increase in these legal responses may be the growing inability to culturally regulate queerness; with heightened on and off-screen visibilities of LGBTQ+ people and only a few, yet medially bloated federal law victories, resorting to state law promises a closer-to-home tool for counteracting queer emancipation. Imagining states as resources for support of one's political beliefs, introducing bills which defy federal regulations becomes

31 Wyatt Ronan states that "(m)ore than 250 anti-LGBTQ bills have been introduced in state legislatures in 2021," while Krishnakumar lists "more than 100 bills that aim to curb the rights of transgender people across the country" as of April 2021. For instance, May 2021's Texan "Heartbeat Bill" (SB 8) serves as a significant land gain for those aiming to curl back the right to determine one's bodily autonomy.

more and more important in times of declining trust in institutions such as the Supreme Court.[32]

Sociocultural Constructions of Sexual Orientation

The staticness of perceptions of queerness is already inscribed in today's legal understandings, which is by no means different for other legal categories. When scholar John Boswell asks, "do categories exist because humans recognize real distinctions in the world around them, or are categories arbitrary conventions, simply names for things that have categorical force because humans agree to use them in certain ways?," (36) he succinctly frames the issue at hand: the epistemological question about whether categories relating to identity, for instance sexual orientation, are 'real' or 'constructed' concepts.

What Boswell labels as a controversy between "'realists'" and "'nominalists'" (37) is more aptly known as the essentialism vs. social constructionalism debate in queer theory (among others, see Stein 325–27). In both instances, the discourse evolves around the issue whether sexual orientation is a universal category, reflecting a 'real' biological and natural order that is temporally and spatially the same, or whether sexual orientation is established by the society it emerges in with culture-specific implications that vary historically. Those who understand sexual orientation in the latter sense

> aver that categories of sexual preference and behavior are created by humans and human societies. Whatever reality they have is the consequence of the power they exert in those societies and the socialization processes that make them seem real to persons influenced by them. ... The category "heterosexuality," in other words, does not so much describe a pattern of behavior inherent in human beings as it creates and establishes it. (Boswell 37)

Important queer scholars and activists have analyzed and de-constructed the connection between categorizing sexual orientations according to object-choice and attributing meaning to these categories, taking a rather social constructionist perspective on sexuality, gender, gender identity and sexual orientation. Most famously, Henry Havelock Ellis and later Jonathan Ned

32 This is all the more relevant at a time when only 40% of the U.S. American public approves of the Supreme Court, marking a historical low in the twenty-first century (Jones). These numbers affirm the Court's pressure to legitimate its actions.

Katz claimed that hetero- and homosexuality are not essential categories of human sexuality but that they have merely been 'invented' during the course of the nineteenth century (Havelock Ellis 19; Katz *Invention* 10).[33] Once these categories have been established, it was possible to police, regulate, and add meaning to them. For instance, while the concept of a homosexual would not have been something people were able to relate to before 1868, in 1948, gay men were already imagined, portrayed, and persecuted as "sexual psychopaths" (sec. 201, *Miller Act*) and "'degenerate sex offenders'" (FBI Director Hoover qtd. in Eskridge *Gaylaw* 60).[34] Given this rather swift progression in meaning, one questions the functions of this development of sexual orientation's cultural and legal perception. Moreover, one wonders whether this concept carries inherent meaning or might simply have been added with such; in other words, one is interested in whether sexual orientation is a meaningful distinction between living beings or whether it is merely a product of our societal and culture-specific perspective on sexuality.

This "social constructionist controversy" (Stein 325) is at the core of political, medical, social, and legal forms of control and sociocultural processes of normatization. As essentialism assumes an inherent nature of, for instance, one's gender, it works to parcel different issues into controllable units. Framing a woman's love for her newborn child as her inherent, natural capability of experiencing empathy and providing care for another being is essentializing her and simultaneously assuming and expecting that these characteristics are shared by all women.[35] These essentialisms provide the basis for (lack of) legal regulations and cultural expectations of work. As child-rearing and care

33 As they have noted, the term 'homosexual' was firstly used in 1868 (Havelock Ellis 19; Katz *Invention* 10), and picked up alongside the term 'heterosexual' for the U.S. American context firstly in 1892 in Dr. James D. Kiernan's article "Responsibility in Sexual Perversion" (Katz *Invention* 10; 19). Back then, both concepts had an entirely different meaning than they do today, with heterosexuality signifying a sexual perversion, namely unreproductive sex (Katz "Questioning" 44).

34 The years indicated in this example have been chosen because Katz and Havelock Ellis refer to 1868 as the first instance when the term 'homosexual' has been used in a publication (Katz *Invention* 10; Havelock Ellis 19); 1948 refers to the year in which the District of Columbia introduced the *Miller Act*, which punished sodomy particularly harshly when conducted between two gay men and laid the legal foundation for conversion 'therapies' (Francis and Felts 2–5; Eskridge *Gaylaw* 61–5).

35 Since these essentialisms usually work with a normative understanding of gender roles in mind, and those establishing these power relations are predominantly hetero and cis, this example would typically only work for biological cis mothers.

are traditionally associated with female responsibilities in Western cultures, parental leave most of the time aims to support mothers who stay at home and is at least partially included in economic logics of paying men more. In return, this serves as further legitimization of having mothers stay at home – economically, it would simply make more sense for men to continue work. In turn, the hypervisibility of women doing unpaid care work and their underrepresentation in jobs where empathy and qualities associated with traditional care work are not valued, for instance leading management positions,[36] blurs the lines of how these mechanisms are intertwined and perpetuates the belief that essentialisms are objectively true. As Grosz succinctly put it, "[e]ssentialism thus refers to the existence of fixed characteristics, given attributes, and ahistorical functions which limit the possibilities of change and thus of social reorganization" (334).[37]

As for the medical and political forms of control, conversion 'therapies' operate from the premise that sexual orientation is changeable and thus take on a rather social constructionalist perspective. Conservative politicians, on the other hand, are more likely to reject progressive attempts at challenging sexual hierarchies. A reason for this is that they stress the naturalness and importance of heterosexuality, following an essentialist notion of sexual orientation (see also Boswell 38). Both examples, although juxtaposed, show how the discourse about sexual orientation's core is instrumentalized for one's own agenda. In this sense, sexual orientation is always socially constructed and culturally added with meaning in political discourses, regardless of whether it is indeed a universal or a relative category of human relations.

The power of categories is also mirrored when looking at strategies to circumvent, tackle or adjust to them. In this context, assimilation may serve as another way of upholding hierarchies and defying social change. By "becoming a part, or making someone become a part" ("Assimilation") of societal or cultural norms and standards, differences may be smoothed and demands silenced. This mechanism usually affects those who need to assimilate, i.e., those in the minority, and it works two-fold. On the one hand, assimilating comes

36 Arguably, since so-called 'soft skills' continue to become economicalized, empathy and emotional intelligence have already been appropriated by neoliberal capitalist logics and thus are higher valued in such positions of power.

37 For an overview about the relationship between essentialism, biologism, naturalism, and universalism, see Grosz 333–6.

with more privileges – a minority adjusts to the mainstream and thereby inhabits a more powerful position. On the other hand, assimilationist strategies risk depoliticizing a group's demands. The example of same-sex marriage illustrates this point well. *Obergefell* can be read as an assimilation of gay couples to the heteronormative understanding of family relations, and as a concession to privatized notions of liberty inherent in granting same-sex couples equal rights within the private sphere, yet leaving them vulnerable in public domains such as employment, housing, credit regulations.[38] As a consequence of *Obergefell*, demands for further rights of queers have been silenced as this seemingly victory of being included in the fundamental right to marry is now being utilized as proof of a post-homophobic society. Feeding on this narrative of being beyond 'homophobia,'[39] queer rights' demands risk being framed as insatiable. Even more, wanting too much also stands to lose those privileges that have already been won. Assimilation is therefore to be treated with caution. While some regard it as step-by-step way of gaining more thorough rights, it most prominently serves to promote the illusion that there is neither further need nor the wish for more rights. After all, being granted access to the mainstream is perceived as good enough by the mainstream.

These considerations show how sexual orientation is constructed, also in legal discourse. There is no unambiguous or neutral definition of this category, which makes it more difficult to apply judicial reasoning without taking into account sexual orientation's epistemology.

IV.5. Legal Sexual Orientationism

Given the inflexibility of categorizations, the questionable sociocultural mandate of those making and interpreting laws, and the uncertainties surrounding the concept of sexual orientation itself, the question remains whether a specified legal understanding of sexual orientation is able to perform anti-discrimi-

38 On the homonormativity inherent in Supreme Court decisions, see Huffer 101–5 and Franke.

39 The term 'homophobia' is put in quotation marks as it is my understanding that referring to hostility towards queers as a phobia invisibilizes actively adverse behavior towards LGBTQ+ by implying that anxiety is a reason for anti-queer animus. Such implications negate both individual responsibilities and harmful sociocultural discourses about queer persons by perpetuating insecurities and ambiguities about sexual Otherized groups.

nation work. As this section argues, not only is the current legal understanding of sexual orientation as an inflexible as other categories, but it also reinforces and reproduces existing biases outside of the law. Thus, an updated definition of sexual orientation in law is necessary to reflect pluralistic and intersectional conceptions of sexuality, to strengthen the possibility of perspective-taking, and to do legal-cultural educational work.

The monolithic perception of LGBTQ+ people in law is here being referred to as 'legal sexual orientationism.' This chapter uses legal sexual orientationism as an analytical lens to illustrate how heteronormative cultural orders and heterosexist bias permeate legal norms. My claim is that sexual orientation, as it is currently constructed in U.S. American law, is indeed not a neutral ordering category but already marred by sociocultural implications of 'proper' sexuality, and a subsequent victimization, pathologization, and criminalization of those being constructed as deviant from the norm.

Legal sexual orientationism refers to the generalizing treatment of sexual orientation as an umbrella term for a variety of diverse sexual identities including, but not limited to homo-, bi-, and a-sexuality. It typically does not include heterosexuality for several reason, which all illustrate the essentializing power of legal sexual orientationism: Heterosexuality functions as the meta-norm of Western sexual cultures. Heterosexuality is in no need of legal protections because laws are already tailored to fit the needs of those who adhere to this sociocultural standard of sexual orientation. This mechanism will be explained in more detail below and constitutes what I call the heteronormative gaze of the law.

Accepting heterosexuality as the default mode, this dominant form of sexual orientation becomes invisible in discourses about legal protections. Legal scholar Laura Adamietz explains this succinctly with regard to the legal category of *Geschlecht*, here referring to biological sex, in the German legal context:

> Historically and currently relevant as societal ordering category, "sex" has, comparable to skin color, the quality of being invisible especially when being unproblematic, meaning adhering to the ideas about what is considered the "normal subject" in societal and legal terms. (15)[40]

40 The German original reads: "Die historisch wie aktuell relevante gesellschaftliche Ordnungskategorie 'Geschlecht' hat – vergleichbar mit der Hautfarbe – die Eigenschaft, insbesondere dann unsichtbar zu sein, wenn sie unproblematisch ist, das heißt der Vorstellung des gesellschaftlich (und rechtlich) gesetzten 'Normal-Subjekts' entspricht." My translation.

Adamietz' observation is particularly important for legal sexual orientationism as it refers to how societal expectations and legal orders reinforce each other. The "normal subject," the one who adheres to the sociocultural norm of being heterosexual, White, middle-class, educated, able-bodied, is imagined to be the idealtypical rights-bearer and default addressee of legal norms. From a legal perspective, this idealtypical subject is conceived of as worthy of protection since it is imagined to cover the majority of people in a society. However, law's operating with defaults, in this context heterosexuality, forces the non-heterosexual subject to become (hyper)visible when claiming rights, and thereby instantly posing a threat to existing, queer-non-inclusive legal orders. The violence of having to 'come out' to the law is therefore experienced by both parties: by the one claiming their rights and by the legal system and its different branches which have to respond to this claim.

Further, demands for (extra) protections of sexual orientation as a legal category only cover all non-heterosexual identities, risking a victimization and Othering of those outside the sociocultural and legal norm while perpetuating the normalization and normativization of heterosexuality. Heterosexuality then appears as unproblematic and adaptable norm while orientations apart from it continue to cause trouble by disrupting law's workings.

Legal sexual orientationism claims that an exotization and Othering of non-heterosexual orientations is established by and through law. Closely resembling Edward Said's concept of Orientalism orthographically, legal sexual orientationism shares its logic of Othering with Said's concept,[41] yet lacks a distinct intersectional focus with regard to the entanglement of race, ethnicity, and sexual orientation, which is found in research on homonationalism (Puar), and discourses about (sexual) citizenship (see for instance Altman; Sabsay; Richardson). Legal sexual orientationism approaches legal norms and discourses about queer rights with an interest in disentangling the notion of sexual orientation as a merely descriptive, neutral category. It constitutes a specific way of thinking which separates the concept of sexual orientation, meaning non-heterosexual orientations, from heterosexuality, implicitly presuming that these concepts are inherently different. Taking legal sexual orientationism as a lens, legal norms and legal systems are analyzed to uncover their underlying cis, heterosexist and -normative logic.

---

41 However, these findings primarily cover the Western legal hemisphere; any analyses for non-Western legal cultures would have to be conducted by scholars and activists whose knowledge and experience is not limited to U.S. and German contexts.

Discourses about the legal protection of sexual orientation inevitably illustrate heteronormativity's hegemony. Conceiving of non-heterosexual orientations as in need of (more) protection, not only are these orientations victimized but they are also depicted as inferior and unable to protect themselves. While this paradox between wanting to protect, and stressing and thus reinforcing existing vulnerabilities has been elaborated on in feminist discourses as detailed below, legal sexual orientationism explicitly criticizes the heternormative and -sexist gaze of the law. Whether one examines taxes, reproductive rights, inheritance or adoption laws, heterosexual, oftentimes married couples are advantaged and taken as default for considerations of legal regulations. *De facto*, these couples are even more privileged when being (read as) cis, White, and monied. Queer people are then included or annexed to an existing legal system evolving around heterosexual subjects. For instance, being able to inherit from your same-sex partner has only been decided by the Supreme Court in *U.S. v. Windsor* in 2013.[42] This rather late decision underlines how a heteronormative legal logic refuses to acknowledge and include, and thereby continues to disadvantage, people who live outside the preferred sexual norm on various levels. Before 2013, same-sex partners were not able to make use of the same legal provisions as heterosexual partners, showing how law was designed to assume heterosexual individuals as its primary, and oftentimes only, right-bearing and legally agentic subjects.

Beyond the psychological and mental distress these conditions pose for the individual, i.e., knowing one is never the default but always has to fight to become included, the material disadvantages reinforce the impression that legal norms want to punish queers economically. In these instances, legal sexual orientationism functions as a gate-keeping mechanism for maintaining sociocultural orders and neoliberal capitalist power structures; property and opportunities to accumulate wealth are then sites where deprivation is felt more affectively than elsewhere.[43]

---

42 Examples of these heteronormative regulations can be found throughout U.S. and German legal contexts. In Germany, many insurance companies or banks only offer packages and shared accounts to married couples, which again emphasizes the cultural importance of marriage and oftentimes excludes queer couples, who consciously refuse to support this historically patriarchal and oppressive social institution and are thus economically disadvantaged.

43 Admittedly, neoliberal capitalist power structures are already part of the sociocultural orders analyzed here. Yet, to stress this particular aspect of legal sexual orientationism, both are mentioned next to each other.

The interplay between maintaining sociocultural and legal norms has been analyzed throughout this chapter. However, legal sexual orientationism goes further than that. The concept conceives of legal norms as working *a priori* with a biased understanding of sexual orientation which, even when trying to increase protection for sexual minorities, always does so from a heteronormative and -sexist outlook. This way, law is understood to be heterosexualized, a claim which resembles claims that law is cultured (Rosen 4), gendered (Olson "Turgid" 65), or cised (Olson and Borchert 2022).

Subsuming these diverse concepts of sexuality, and those identifying with them, under the term sexual orientation is believed to be necessary and useful for establishing a working definition for legal considerations. As stated above, law needs categorizations in order to be effective.[44] Legal sexual orientationism, however, includes more than the mere legal treatment of sexual orientation. The legal praxis of subsuming so much under one term, yet excluding heterosexuality, mirrors the most problematic tendencies in anti-discrimination law. Working with sexual orientation as a legal category, legal norms perpetuate the importance of this socioculturally constructed phenomenon and thus stress its vulnerability and visibility while originally aiming to increase the level of protection. Further, the act of categorizing blurs the lines between distinct parts within the category and contributes to an essentialization of sexual orientation as deviant, possibly harmful, and in need of containment and policing.

The inability to move beyond the classifications given within a legal system illuminates the subaltern position of the legal subject and raises questions about the degree of agency one's legal citizenship entails. This issue is what (legal) feminist theory calls "dilemma of difference,"[45] as introduced by feminist legal scholar Martha Minow:

> [W]hen does treating people differently emphasize their differences and stigmatize or hinder them on that basis? ... I call this question "the dilemma of difference." The stigma of difference may be recreated both by ignoring

44 This claim holds for now, yet will be critically questioned in Chapter V's section on post-categorical anti-discrimination law. Current legal discourses in anti-discrimination law and asylum laws discuss the possibility to establish 'post-categorical' approaches to law. See Liebscher et al.; Foljanty 89–91.

45 As stated by Berger and Purth, the dilemma of difference, also being referred to as feminist dilemma, has been picked up by many feminist scholars, see, for instance, Baer "Dilemmata" 242; Cornell 1–20.

> and by focusing on it. Decisions about education, employment, benefits, and other opportunities in society should not turn on an individual's ethnicity, disability, race, gender, religion, or membership in any other group about which some have deprecating or hostile attitudes. Yet refusing to acknowledge these differences may make them continue to matter in a world constructed with some groups, but not others, in mind. The problems of inequality can be exacerbated both by treating members of minority groups the same as members of the majority and by treating the two groups differently. (20)

Minow points out the dual character of difference succinctly. While people with different abilities or different experiences have distinct needs and may need special treatment, treating people differently because of their abilities or experiences may (further) contribute to their stigmatization and discrimination. The dilemma of difference, however, exceeds the legal realm, and its entanglements can be found in a variety of sociocultural conditions, which are all variations of legal orders. These legal orders, and cultural hierarchies, are constructed around a certain (legal) subject which stands in as default, unquestioned norm, and preferred standard for cultural and legal considerations. In the context of sexual orientation, this legal subject is imagined to be heterosexual; in the context of gender identity, it would be cisgendered. For instance, critiques of family laws which discriminate against same-sex couples when it comes to adoption regulations, marriage, inheritance, or birth certificates – as analyzed in *Pavan v. Smith* in Chapter IV.1, – illustrate how these legal norms have been "constructed with some groups, but not others, in mind," in this case heterosexual, oftentimes married, probably White, propertied, educated, able-bodied couples. In an extended argument for this consideration, one may also look at why romantically partnered couples who involve two persons remain the unquestioned cultural and legal norm of familyness while single people, friend groups or chosen families continue to be marginalized, not legally recognized, and possibly stigmatized in a multitude of social, cultural and legal contexts.[46]

Minow's findings are as vital for queer rights discourses as they are for a critique of legal categories. Suggesting that it "grows from the ways in which this society assigns individuals to categories and, on that basis, determines

46 See the German *Koalitionsvertrag* as instance of a countermodel to this norm in sociocultural and legal discourse (SPD) as discussed in IV.2. See also Ontario's "All Families Are Equal Act."

whom to include in and whom to exclude from political, social, and economic activities" (21), Minow frames the dilemma of difference as resulting of and contributing to processes of essentialization and exclusion within society:

> Because the activities are designed, in turn, with only the included participants in mind, the excluded seem not to fit because of something in their own nature. Thus, people have used categories based on age, race, gender, ethnicity, religion, and disability to decide formally and informally who is eligible to enroll in a given school, who is excluded from a particular sports activity, who may join a particular club, who may adopt a given child, and a variety of other questions. (21–22)

In this understanding, categories employ similar functions to legal norms, even without being read and applied in the context of law. For instance, taking Minow's considerations as starting point, the gendered division of sports teams has taken on such a strong quasi-legal force that legal endeavors to de-binarize and de-cisgender the system and include trans and non-binary athletes are met with heavy political backlash. This backlash includes attempts to proactively protect and police the gendered participation in sports teams.[47] (Cis) Female and male are thus classifications which bear orders out of themselves and warrant normative perpetuation of stereotypes and hierarchies. Lauren Sudeall Lucas is similarly critical of classifications in U.S. law in an assessment of equal protection claims as "identity-based jurisprudence:"

> [E]qual protection relies on identity as a proxy, standing in to signify the types of discrimination we find most troubling. Equal protection's current use of identity as proxy leads to a number of problems, including difficulties in defining identity categories; the tendency to privilege a dominant-identity narrative; failure to distinguish among the experiences of subgroups within larger identity categories; and psychological and emotional harm that can result from being forced to identify in a particular way to lay claim to legal protection. Moreover, because the Court's identity-as-proxy jurisprudence relies on superficial notions of identity to fulfill

47 As discussed earlier, starting in 2021, an increasing number of states have passed legislation targeting trans and non-binary children and youth, mostly in the realm of sports. For instance, Mississippi's governor Tate Reeves has signed SB 2536, known as the "Mississippi Fairness Act" in March 2021. The bill assigns sport teams according to athletes' biological sex.

> a substantive commitment to equality, it is susceptible to co-option by majority groups. (1605)

Sexual orientation's deviance is indicated by its use in distinction to the norm of heterosexuality. Legal cases and publications which analyze sexual orientation primarily deal with homosexuality, bisexuality or other forms of sexual identity which are not heterosexuality. The use of the term 'sexual orientation' in legal texts is mostly used as heterosexuality's Other, reinforcing notions of heterosexuality as 'natural' default while sexual orientations, meaning non-heterosexual identities, are the exception.

Legal sexual orientationism thus disparately impacts non-heterosexual orientations, while the heterosexual norm remains the golden standard against which other orientations have to legitimate themselves. This sociocultural bias directly affects legal decision-making. If sexual orientation would be understood as including heterosexuality, it most probably would have already been regarded as a suspect classification. This argument finds proof in the way *Charles E. Moritz v. Commissioner of Internal Revenue* (1972) was decided. Arguing that excluding an unmarried man from the same tax deduction benefits as a woman is in violation of the Equal Protection Clause, Ruth Bader Ginsburg successfully represented the plaintiff and helped establish that discrimination on the basis of sex is unconstitutional. In this case, fostering equal rights for women by making sex a protected legal category was only successful through arguing how a (cis) man was discriminated against because of his sex. Similarly, the Supreme Court's 2020 landmark employment law decision *Bostock* was based on the "because-of-sex"-argument by the Court's majority (see Chapter III.3). This argument made clear that none of the queer and trans plaintiffs would have been fired if they had been of a different sex assigned at birth. While *Bostock* decidedly draws on biological sex as a legal category, its implicitly heteronormative (and cised) gaze becomes obvious. *Bostock*'s queer and trans plaintiffs have been granted rights only because the Court used the default scenario of a heterosexual (and cis, respectively) person as the foundation for its reasoning. Applying this test by imagining how a heterosexual person would be treated (and feel) in the same situation, the Court's justices perpetuate the heteronormative gaze of the law in their majority opinion. Their reasoning underlines how legal norms are constructed with an idealtypically heterosexual (and cis) legal subject as rights-receiver in mind and how sexual orientation is defined in negative distinction to what is perceived to be the invisibilized norm.

Legal sexual orientationism thus invisibilizes heterosexuality's belonging to the category of sexual orientation(s) because sociocultural notions of its 'naturalness' and desirability place heterosexuality not only high in the sexual orientation hierarchy but outside of it; heterosexuality is not a sexual orientation, it is an essential part of being human. This claim is emphasized by Evan Gerstmann's analysis of the suspect classification/class 'switch:'

> When gays seek to move up in the equal protection hierarchy, the courts tell them they are not a *suspect class* because they are not politically powerless. But when whites seek protection against affirmative action programs, courts do not ask them to prove that they are politically powerless (obviously they are not). Instead, courts subtly switch terminology; they hold that race is a *suspect classification* and thereby protect whites from racial preferences. Similarly, the courts protect men from discrimination by holding that gender is a quasi-suspect classification. By switching between the terms *suspect class* and *suspect classification*, the Supreme Court can require some groups to show they are politically powerless but allow other, far more politically powerful groups to benefit from strong constitutional protection. The Court has never explicitly recognized that it does this, and it has never attempted to justify it. (*Underclass* 9; emphasis in original)

Gerstman illustrates how judicial decision-making picks up upon biased perceptions of sexual orientations. Supreme Court justices have added to the "protection" of the dominant norm of heterosexuality even in cases primarily concerned with minorities. Both the direct and the disparate impact of judicial decision-making are therefore often positive for the heterosexual norm and those seeking to guard it.

Legal sexual orientationism supports the essentialist assumption that sexual orientations are fixed and static by taking heterosexuality out of the sphere of protection. Implying that those who *are* heterosexual are safe, the possibility, and appeal, of questioning what one *identifies* with over the course of one's life becomes limited. (Note that heterosexuality is seldomly referred to as identity category but as a given.) In this context, it is important to acknowledge what needs no protection legally because it already is untouchable socioculturally. Here, sociocultural orders and legal orders intertwine. The emphasis on and biologization of heterosexuality as dominant sociocultural norm establishes a sexual hierarchy which inferiorizes and Others those orientations that differ from this norm. Only this social-culturally constructed hierarchy translates into the need to protect sexual minorities legally.

Perceptions of sexual orientation's deviance and cultural anxieties about its possible harmfulness culminate in cases that deal with non-procreational sex. As *Bowers* and *Lawrence* show, negotiating legal norms that regulate sexual practices also put in relation cultural fears about vulnerabilities of the corporeal and political body. Linking non-procreational sex to immorality and disease, queer sex is both dangerous for those partaking in it and society as a whole. Assuming that "good citizenship relies on appropriate sexual behavior and proper gender performance" (Nagel 30), and that "[s]exuality and gender, thus, are important building blocks of the nation" (30),[48] violating these conditions of sexual citizenship threatens the collective's cohesion. Even more so, queering the cultural assumptions about proper object-choice, sexual moderation, and socioculturally shared knowledge about 'natural' forms of desire incites existential cultural fears about the dissolution of fixed and reliable categories of knowledge. This anxiety of having to constantly negotiate and question processes of knowledge production, exposed vulnerabilities of the nation-state and mortal corporality, and possibly shifting sexual and gender hierarchies results in a politics of containment and policing of sexual orientation. While these figurations of sexual orientation's essence take place through and in legal praxis, they are influenced by socially transmitted stereotypes and feed back into social processes of knowledge production.

To effectively challenge stereotypical thinking, resulting biases, and discrimination, anti-discrimination laws need to better depict pluralism within legal classifications. This demand is bold, given the constructiveness of Western legal and cultural systems as based on categories. However, as judicial decisions concerning sexual orientation rely on judges' and justices' ability to disentangle their own sexual orientationized knowledge, specifying living conditions of queers in legal norms may challenge the judicial praxis of making recourse to simplified notions of LGBTQ+ lives. Especially those judges and justices whose knowledge is situated in hetero-patriarchal, White, middle to upper class, cis, able-bodied, and otherwise privileged settings[49] are prone to

48 Turner goes even further by suggesting a "'reproductive citizenship'" (qtd. in Richardson 212) instead of one based on sexuality. In this view, "the reason for the historical exclusion of lesbians and gay men from full citizenship" (Richardson 212) is "the non-reproductivity of same sex unions and, therefore, their failure to contribute fully to society" (212).

49 See also Mazukatow and Binder 460–61; Haraway 592: "Situated knowledges require that the object of knowledge be pictured as an actor and agent, not as a screen or a

introduce these stereotypical templates and thereby continue to inscribe sexual orientationized knowledge into legal norms.

The explicit inclusion and repeated naming of heterosexuality as part of sexual orientation is necessary for crashing the underlying heterosexist matrix. It is this matrix which denaturalizes non-normative orientations while simultaneously negating the need to address its own hegemonic position. Being aware of these reasons for including heterosexuality, Wintemute uses the term "'sexual orientation discrimination'" (12) rather than "'gay, lesbian, and bisexual rights' ... to suggest that prohibitions of such discrimination should be symmetrical, protecting not only gay, lesbian and bisexual persons, but also heterosexual persons" (12). While one may be skeptical about why heterosexual persons may need such a protection, Wintemute's further points are important:

> It is also intended to emphasize the importance of thinking of sexual orientation as neutral, universal characteristic, with several different manifestations, rather than a phenomenon unique to gay, lesbian, and bisexual persons. Heterosexual persons need to be reminded that they too have a sexual orientation, and that theirs is not the only possibility. (13)

Stressing that sexual orientations exist on a spectrum and in flux, a legal-cultural education that takes into account the importance compulsory heterosexuality plays for legal-cultural orders needs to replace legal sexual orientationism. Where legal sexual orientationism tends to argue from a subaltern perspective of non-normativity, a possibly more effective legal-cultural education equips its audience with an understanding of how processes of sociocultural knowledge production work. This includes becoming or making more aware of what compulsory heterosexuality entails and how it feeds back into perceptions of what/who is in need and worthy of protection. Approaching legal protections for sexual minorities in this way is thus decidedly aiming for anti-discrimination laws instead of merely establishing non-discriminatory ones. In an ideal world, anti-discrimination laws may work to *prevent* discrimination not merely police it. It is again Wintemute who calls for a more holistic perspective on anti-discrimination laws by advocating for what I repeatedly refer to as legal-cultural education, i.e., the need to consider discrimination not as

---

ground or a resource, never finally as slave to the master that closes off the dialectic in his unique agency and his authorship of 'objective' knowledge."

a self-contained concept occurring in the vacuum of legal regulations but as connected to other sociocultural realities:

> Such protections [which cover both private and public spheres; lb] could perhaps help break the vicious circle whereby fear of discrimination on the part of gay, lesbian, and bisexual persons prevents their being open with heterosexual persons, and thereby precludes the educative process that would increase understanding and reduce prejudice and discrimination. (Wintemute 15)

This approach, although dependent on the sociocultural climate and legal conditions, would allow for more dialogue between social groups. Maybe it would have even enabled Justice Powell to learn about his law clerk's reality. Advocating intergroup contact, perspective-taking, and empathy, Wintemute's take on legal protections is decidedly humanistic and democratic. Plus, it is taking into account sociocultural orders that inhibit legal regulations from being useful. Without keeping in mind extra-legal sources of discrimination, intra-legal solutions are ultimately ineffective. Additionally, by reinforcing neoliberal notions of individual responsibility, collective endeavors are limited to social group membership. Thus, promoting discussions that extend one's carefully parceled units of interests invites pluralisms, strengthens democratic structures, and hopefully underlines the necessity for collective activism.

V. Approaches Towards a Queer Legal Future

V.1. Queering Constitutional Cultures

Speaking of a 'queer legal future' is already a bold statement in itself. It supposes that there will be a futurity in and for queerness and that it is also reflected in law. Thinking back a few decades and even in many states and countries today, being or being read as queer, especially when intersecting with other categories of difference such as being Black, brown, trans, non-binary, dis/abled, poor, and/or having no access to education, meant and still means fearing for one's life. For people facing such situations, making and having made these experiences, the promise of a queer legal future may sound shallow and deceiving – how can law, as a state-centered mechanism, achieve justice for those the state has oppressed, violated, murdered, and persecuted for years? This skepticism about what law is, whom it benefits, and which subjects it constitutes is mirrored in the various responses throughout academic disciplines and activist practices. Two of the most recent strands in thinking about law are found in feminist jurisprudence's approaches towards a post-categorical law (see Liebscher et al.) and activist endeavors to fundamentally transform law by eventually abolishing the current legal system (see Abolition Collective). These two perspectives will be examined in this chapter, and add to establishing a queer hermeneutics of law, between those making law and those being affected by law, beyond what is and towards what could be. In addition to this analysis of recent discourses about law's future(s), this chapter proposes its own practical perspectives on anti-discrimination protections. By applying a queer legal theoretical lens, the Supreme Court's way of deciding on suspect classifications is troubled and queer(ed) alternatives to existing constitutional practice are proposed. Queer and queering in this context not only refer to the importance of establishing a queer legal hermeneutics of constitutional law and equal protection but they also serve to reclaim cis-ed, heteronormativized legal territory. Suspect classifications, as this chapter argues, need to include sexual orientation for both legal-protective purposes and sociocultural space holding.

So far, this book has analyzed how law holds the possibility to be utilized as an emancipatory instrument, yet has historically rather been (ab)used as a tool for maintaining and legitimizing power hierarchies. Aiming to strengthen the queer legal hermeneutics this book constructs, this chapter examines different approaches towards a reformation of the entanglements of queer lives and law. As argued throughout, law is not to be approached as a secluded domain within a system of meaning-making; law is rather a vital part of culture's set-up and something we need to (learn to) navigate. Thus, even if our understandings of what a 'legal order' constitutes differ, – codified legal norms, judicial interpretation, sociocultural norms that order and regulate behavior just as well as legal ones, a state-made instrument of oppression, – our conceptualizations of legality and justice are in parts shaped by the legal and moral cultures surrounding us (Ewick and Shelby; Legrand "Comparative;" Olson *Legality*). Even in discourses about abolishing the legal system in its current form (see Chapter V.3), Western understandings of the concept of 'law' lead to finding other, community-based approaches that one may nevertheless regard as law because they fulfill an ordering and regulatory function.[1] An important distinction is that such alternatives promise less discrimination and more intersectionality.

My analyses of constitutional law and sexual orientation's suspect classification are situated within the belief that changing legal and sociocultural norms need to go together to proactively challenge backlash. While this is but one approach to thinking about queer rights, this chapter also takes into account the affective power of feelings of justice in its discussion of abolitionist ideas and utopian configurations in order to (re-)imagine what law means and whether it is necessarily an instrument of power or of those in power. While these approaches reject a state-based solution to justice, these movements do foundational work for changing sociocultural norms and learning from them

1 This understanding of law and hierarchies is also mirrored in Danielle Allen's assessment that "[b]ut not least, the world without rule is not a world without hierarchy, nor a world without constraints, it is rather that hierarchy and constraints, such as laws, must be legitimate" ("Nicht zuletzt ist die Welt ohne Herrschaft keine Welt ohne Hierarchie und auch keine Welt ohne Zwänge, vielmehr müssen Hierarchie und Zwänge, wie zum Beispiel Gesetze, legititm sein") (71 qtd. in Thiele 398).

is necessary for building a queer legal future which acknowledges its own communities' heterogeneity and endures differences within.

The approaches introduced here start from different political-activist assumptions, propose more or less radical transformations, and offer views of sociocultural processes from functional, conflicting and/or feminist angles. What they all share, however, is their understanding that norms challenging discrimination need to be reformed – because, and in order to guarantee that, there is a (legal) futurity in and for queerness.

V.2. The Cultural and Legal Significance of Sexual Orientation's Constitutional Protection

This book has commented on the history of equal protection, the politicization and polarization of the Supreme Court, and cultural imaginaries surrounding constitutional processes. While the previous chapters have established *how* sexual orientation is treated legally, it remains yet to uncover *why* this treatment should be reformed via considering it a suspect classification. After all, anti-discrimination laws could simply be introduced by the legislative. Starting from the premise that anti-discrimination is more affectively, symbolically, and legally powerful when emerging out of a constitutional reading, this subchapter analyzes why a class-based protection for sexual orientation is relevant from both a cultural and legal standpoint.

From a legal perspective, this question has already been approached through close readings of cases which had discrimination based on sexual orientation as their foundation (see Chapter III). It is important to stress again that any project aiming at legal protection of sexual minorities needs to carefully consider which tools are the most efficient in establishing long-lasting change. As we have seen by looking at statues, bills, but also landmark cases such as *Bowers* and *Roe*, legal conditions bear the risk, and possibility respectively, of being overturned in the future with some being more resistant to change than others. The analyses of important landmark decisions such as *Lawrence* or *Windsor* showed the fragility of Acts and stressed the need to find reliable legal protections for sexual minorities.

Foreshadowing the Trump administration's attacks on queer rights, Evan Gerstmann already anticipated in 2003 the vulnerability of merely reforming government policies and federal laws without challenging "the position of gays and lesbians at the bottom of the equal protection hierarchy [which] denies them constitutional protection against the reinstatement of any of these policies should the political climate change" (*Underclass* 7). To Gerstmann, this position at the 'bottom of the equal protection hierarchy' has been established by the number of equal protection cases gays, lesbians and bisexuals have lost (*Underclass* 5–6) as well as by the lack of "any *legal* standard to protect them from discrimination" (*Underclass* 8; emphasis in original), leaving them at the hands of "judicial sympathy and intuitions about fairness" (8).[2] As the concept of legal sexual orientationism makes explicit (Chapter IV.4), Gerstmann's assessment is not surprising given that law assumes its default subjects to be heterosexual and cisgendered, and thereby continues to constitute this legally idealtypical, rights-holding individual. Rather than standing at the bottom of the equal protection hierarchy, these subjects seem to be annexed in hindsight because those dominating the U.S. constitutional interpretive community simply did not consider sexual minorities a part of equal protection's promise.

Current demands to review progressive Supreme Court landmark decisions illustrate this point, with justices seeking to reopen the debate about the validity of *Obergefell*'s constitutional reading[3] and land gains for opponents of abortion rights. From January 2021's finding that restrictions of access to abortion medication are constitutional in FDA v. American College of Obstetricians and Gynecologists to September 2021's "Texas Heartbeat Act" (HB 1515 / SB8), in which Texas banned abortions after six weeks of pregnancy except in cases of medical emergency (see TX SB 8 Sec. 171.205 a), the Supreme Court has granted anti-abortion actors more space and authority. In May 2022, a leaked Supreme Court draft majority opinion written by conservative Justice Samuel Alito confirmed these anxieties of an overturning of Roe v. Wade. In Alito's draft, which is the opinion for *Dobbs v. Jackson Women's Health Organization*, the Court is set

2 This view on sexual minorities is also found in William Eskridge Jr.'s work, see *Gaylaw* 2: "Although it is not illegal to be gay in the United States, the law continues to treat gay people as second-class citizens." While Eskridge and Gerstmann have conducted their analyses before landmark decisions such as *Obergefell* and *Bostock*, it remains true that queers have to legitimate themselves and their desires before being granted equal rights compared to cis-heterosexuals. As (cis-)heterosexuality continues to be the sociocultural norm in U.S. America, queers are subjected to a comparison to this norm and an implicit, and sometimes even explicit, social, political and legal expectation to assimilate to this norm, see also Chapter IV.6 on legal sexual orientationism.

3 See the statement by Justices Thomas and Alito in *Kim Davis v. David Ermold* (2020), as well as Thomas' opinion in *Dobbs* (2022).

to find that since "[t]he Constitution makes no reference to abortion" (5, draft majority opinion by Alito) and "Roe was egregiously wrong from the start" (6, draft majority opinion by Alito), "Roe and Casey must be overruled" (6). With June 2022's Dobbs decision, the Supreme Court finalized its gradual work towards gutting abortions rights and strengthening both state authority and religious conservatives. These increasingly successful attempts of changing existing progressive legal conditions are direct and coordinated attacks on minority rights and overregulate sexuality through means of law.

In order to counteract such developments, legal projects need to ask themselves which route is most promising for achieving their aims without being curled back anytime soon. Admittedly, activists and legal scholars are no clairvoyants and as the previous chapters have made clear, legal norms are as fluid as sociocultural ones. However, aiming to accommodate groups' needs and working towards a pluralistic future need to evolve around changing people's perceptions in addition to tackling legal regulations.

One preferred route is change via legal acts. Proposals such as the *Equality Act* are important for drawing attention to LGBTQ+ realities and they foster public discourse about legal protections of minorities. The *Equality Act*, which has been introduced several times in Congress by Democrats but always failed to gain a majority vote, aims to tackle "the patchwork nature of state non-discrimination laws and the lack of permanent, comprehensive federal non-discrimination laws leaves millions of people subject to uncertainty and potential discrimination that impacts their safety, their families, and their day-to-day lives" (*Equality Act*).

The enactment of the *Equality Act* would legally achieve the same protections as sexual orientation's suspect classification: prohibiting discrimination on the basis of sexual orientation in the areas of public accommodation (sec. 3), public facilities (sec. 4), public education (sec. 5), employment (sec. 7), housing (sec. 10), credit (sec. 11), and juries (sec. 12) on a federal level. Even more, this Act would apply to discrimination based on sexual orientation *and* sex *and* gender identity, making it even more sweeping than a mere protection of one of those categories.

Yet, acts are introduced by politicians and have to go through both chambers in Congress to become law. This means that acts in general and the *Equality Act* in particular depend on the ruling government's political stance towards queers. In addition, as analyzed in the context of the *Defense of Marriage Act* (DOMA) in Chapter III.3, acts may be superseded by the Supreme Court or, as with the *Equality Act* itself, are stalled by the respective political majority opposing it.[4] As both of these instances illustrate, acts prove to be rather vulnerable to political volatilities, making them wobbly foundations for minority protections. This is even more concerning at a time of (il)legal moves of self-empowerment by extremist political groups and politicians. The rise of far-right politicians and those who sympathize with organizations supporting conspiracy myths such as QAnon[5] have made it more difficult to reach compromises in Congress. The power play between the U.S.'s two major political parties has become more polarized and violent over the last years as seen in the capitol attack by a mob of Trump supporters in January 2021, the peak of an ongoing struggle for political hegemony. Moreover, attempts to legally investigate and culturally process the violence against democratically elected officials have been filibustered and stalled by Republicans.[6] As these instances show, legal-political compromises continue to become more contested, making the option of achieving long-lasting change for queer demands via legal acts less likely.

Of course, constitutional protections of sexual minorities are no less dependent on democratic structures which preserve their validity and frame the social order than acts are dependent on politicians. Thus, one may argue that law, regardless of whether it is established through state made bills, constitutional amendments or executive orders, is only as authoritative as the institutions that issue it. But while trust in politicians and lawmakers seems to plummet since the 2010s, (re)turning to supposedly eternal ingredients of Americanness seems to increase. The Constitution, as important pillar of U.S. American identity, still evokes more positive feelings and adherence than legislatively enacted acts. This affective relation to the Constitution is (closely) connected to the narratives and imaginaries described in Chapter II.4, and the understanding of one's fundamental rights as inalienable, natural and potentially universal. For instance, one is more familiar with hearing someone else invoke their

4 Democratic Congressman David Cicilline (RI) introduced the *Equality Act* in 2019 in the House of Representatives but, after passing, it remains for consideration at the Republican-controlled senate as of January 2021.

5 Among them are Representatives Marjorie Taylor Greene from Georgia and Colorado's Lauren Boebert (Kirkpatrick). QAnon followers believe in the existence of a 'deep state' in the U.S. which is controlled by Democratic satanists. The network of QAnon supporters is believed to be involved in a number of coordinated attacks, most prominently the attack on the U.S. Capitol on 6 January 2021(Kirkpatrick).

6 In May 2021, Senate Republicans under minority leader Mitch McConnell tried to prevent the creation of a bipartisan commission to investigate the events of January 6, see Smith.

freedom of speech than claiming their rights laid down by a state bill with equal fierce and determination. Constitutionally protected rights are not only more readily available in one's legal imagination but also more affectively charged than are state ordinances, local regulations, or city statutes.

The differences in affective and symbolic weight of legal texts are not only dependent on the governmental branch that decides on them but also on their socioculturally created meaning. Although a state bill and a fundamental right both allow or prohibit certain conducts, the former has certainly a less prominent place in how people imagine their legal systems, i.e., how they perceive of what is legal or illegal in their respective state. This fuzziness of compartmentalized legal norms, the 'big' ones stated in the Bill of Rights and found under Due Process and the 'small' ones consisting of state bills, local regulations, city policies, influences U.S. moral cultures as well. While fundamental rights are ingrained into one's understanding of what is allowed, or even prescribed, and (a) right from birth onwards due to popular cultural invocations in television series, films, and novels, state and local laws play a significantly less important role in one's legal knowledge and moral understandings. This claim requires more elaboration. By stating that constitutional rights are imagined as more fundamental or more readily available as such, I am not referring to the general relationship between federal and state law. States have historically tried to enact laws which reflect the sentiment of their citizens, and federal regulations have had the tendency to divide the federal and states' governments along ideological lines. A prominent example can be found in different states' different legal regulations about religious liberty or toleration in the seventeenth and eighteenth century.

Today, these ideological divides ultimately refer back to how one interprets the words and ideals laid out in the Constitution and how much autonomy it grants to the states. Yet, it is still conspicuous that constitutionally protected rights such as the right to bear arms are more readily invoked than are specific state regulations. One's affective relationship and feelings of belonging to one's state may thus influence one's *Rechtsgefühle* without having knowledge about state-specific legal norms. In these instances, one can again observe how legal-cultural education, or lack thereof, bears legal-cultural imaginaries: Imagining Texas, for example, as more liberal than California may hold affective truth for those conceiving of "woke" laws such as the right to bodily autonomy as paternalistic and constraining. It does however not indicate which of these states indeed has more liberal laws than the other.

This cultural argument for a constitutional instead of a legislative solution for queer legal vulnerabilities is packed by the Supreme Court's ability to shape cultural sentiments and thus works to de-escalate legal stalemates between fundamental rights, in particular when it comes to religion and freedom of speech. As the 2018 landmark decision *Masterpiece Cakeshop v. Colorado Civil Rights Commission* shows, the threat of striking down LGBTQ+ and women's protections is particularly imminent in questions of religious belief and moral convictions and continues to raise questions about the relationship between liberty and equality (see Chapter III.3).

Another option to induce legal change is via Executive Orders such as President Biden's Executive Order 13988 on "Preventing and Combating Discrimination on the Basis of Gender Identity or Sexual Orientation." This order has been celebrated by mainstream media as a progressive pro-LGBTQ+ measure that forcefully heralded the start of a post-Trumpist political era. In fact, from a sociocultural perspective, this order was successful in conveying the impression that better times are coming and it therefore did affective legal work. The Biden administration managed to evoke the impression of being decidedly in favor of queer and trans issues and ready to fight for them, too. The emotional first section of the order speaks to this:

> Every person should be treated with respect and dignity and should be able to live without fear, no matter who they are or whom they love. Children should be able to learn without worrying about whether they will be denied access to the restroom, the locker room, or school sports. Adults should be able to earn a living and pursue a vocation knowing that they will not be fired, demoted, or mistreated because of whom they go home to or because how they dress does not conform to sex-based stereotypes. People should be able to access healthcare and secure a roof over their heads without being subjected to sex discrimination. All persons should receive equal treatment under the law, no matter their gender identity or sexual orientation. ("Preventing" sec. 1)

This romanticized description of what an America under Biden/Harris should look like with regard to LGBTQ+ protections resembles the narrativization of public personae found in presidential candidates' biographies. In both instances, a person-centered version of events is insinuated to obtain a political benefit. Issuing the order was certainly important for the public acknowledgement and the continuation of discourses on queer rights, and it sent the message to the queer community that the Biden/Harris administration aims at making LGBTQ+ individuals feel safer. Moreover, the Order serves as powerful demarcation to what the new government refers to as "four years of relentless attacks on LGBTIQ* rights" under the Trump administration (White House "Fact Sheet"), using a narrative of progress and condemning the past as uncivilized, thereby establishing a founding myth of queer protection.

Aiming to protect anyone, regardless of 'who they are or whom they love' frames the political and legal question of equal protections for sexual minorities in an easily digestible manner: Using the cultural ideal of romantic love as means to assimilate LGBTQ+ to cis hetero norms, queer rights more made more appealing – after all, they are people like you and me, just wanting to love someone. Next to using the almost fundamental cultural right of romantic love as social glue, the Executive Order makes recourse to the trope of the imperiled child for affective back-up. Not denying the importance of the protections laid out in the Biden/Harris Order, this reading illustrates how legal demands by sexual minorities need to go through a process of sociocultural legitimation before appearing valid in the eyes of the cis hetero majority.

However, the political advantage of this Order outweighs its legal importance as it did not do any factual, progressive legal work. The Supreme Court's *Bostock* decision laid the foundation for the Order, and the new Biden/Harris government merely implemented what the Court said is constitutional. As ACLU's Deputy Director for Transgender Justice Chase Strangio stated, "[b]y stating the administration's intention to follow Supreme Court precedent and federal law, at core all the newly-elected president did was lay out what the law is and agree, unlike his predecessor, to follow it" ("President Biden's"). It is thus true that "[t]hose who claim to be victims of Biden's affirmation of these legal protections are really angry about legal rules that were drafted by Congress decades ago and affirmed by the Supreme Court in June" (Strangio "President Biden's"), but the same goes for those celebrating this Order as a legal victory, though a sociocultural land gain it may be.

Culturally, it is important to stress the entanglements of law and culture, examine whether a constitutional protection is able to change cultural perceptions of sexual orientation or vice versa or not at all, and recognize the transformative power of the Supreme Court's decisions. By passing on the opportunity to declare sexual orientation a suspect classification, the *Windsor* and *Obergefell* Courts have judicially failed to establish this status and politically circumvented debates about expanding the classifications which warrant heightened or strict scrutiny. More importantly, however, SCOTUS's decisions communicated that the explicit and heightened protection of sexual orientation is neither culturally nor legally relevant. By deciding cases about sexual orientation, the Court establishes legal precedents future decisions have to consider, and how these precedents influence the prevalence, and possibly preference, of certain modes of interpretation as seen in the case studies of Chapter III. By not deciding on the vulnerabilities and questions of equality of sexual orientation, for instance by opting for an 'all marriages equality' instead of same-sex marriage equality, the Court is prioritizing fundamental rights over minority rights. By doing so, the Court forms frames of legal reference, in the form of precedents and (dis-)continued lines of modes of interpretations, and cultural reference, in the form of evaluating what and who needs protection.

A constitutionally anchored anti-discrimination protection for sexual minorities is all the more relevant in twenty-first century U.S. America. While acts and legislative decisions may aim for the same outcome, and are possibly equally able to achieve it, a reading of the Constitution which sees sexual orientation as in need of strict scrutiny reverberates culturally.

Feeding on U.S. American civil religion and its quasi-sainting of the Constitution as well as the imagined identicalness of the Supreme Court and the Constitution, a group-based equal protection would position sexual orientation in the Court's aegis and into the Constitution's canon of categories that make up U.S. American cultural identity.[7] This way, a constitutional protection of sexual orientation may have the same or similar legal implications as one based on legislature, for example the *Equality Act*, but a different and arguably stronger cultural backing. In this instance, cultural implications add legitimacy to the current legal order, and thus may work to establish similar or even more meaningful orders, and maintain or construct cultural norms which again feed into processes of legal knowledge production and development of legal norms. Another advantage of the push for suspect classification is its sweeping impact:

> Unlike the seemingly limited protection offered by the right of privacy or the First Amendment, the suspect classification argument is seen as capable of protecting both public and private same-sex emotional-sexual con-

---

7 This view sees the already protected categories race, religion, national origin, and alienage as indicative of what the Court found to be parts of the U.S.'s cultural identity, namely U.S. America as immigrant culture, culturally diversity, place of equal opportunity, moral role model, and rooted in Judeo-Christian traditions.

> duct, and potentially encompassing all aspects of public sector discrimination against gay, lesbian, and bisexual persons, especially in employment, housing, and services, and with respect to the right of couples and parents. (Wintemute 61)

Wintemute compares what he labels 'fundamental choice argument,' discussed in more detail in Chapter III, to the 'immutable status argument.' In comparison, the latter seems more promising for enabling thorough legal protection and sociocultural change: "A Supreme Court decision that sexual orientation constitutes a suspect classification might thus serve as the *Brown v. Board of Education* that gay, lesbian, and bisexual persons in the U.S. have been seeking" (Wintemute 61). Referencing *Brown*, Wintemute invokes the powerful cultural memory of a Supreme Court decision that substantially changed U.S. America. By doing so, he draws attention to law's transformative power and alluding to a supposedly post-queerphobic society – a utopian idea because post-racist sociocultural conditions have also been merely imaginary after *Brown*.

Further, Wintemute calls upon the common analogy between race and sexual orientation in terms of their discriminatory potential and legal treatment. Legal discourses about sexual orientation's suspect classification have in the past picked up the argument that "gay is the new black" (Gross) as both race and sexual orientation are approached similarly in law. Although their histories of discrimination are not comparable, both categories are important sites of civil rights movements, both are socioculturally constructed phenomena, and both are subject to discrimination based on stereotypes. The next chapter examines how sexual orientation fulfills or does not fulfill the four major criteria required by suspect classification, and focusses in particular on the question of immutability as constitutional criterion and sociocultural (moral) construct. This way, suspect classification's four criteria are being questioned, deconstructed, and, as is the constant goal of this book's approach to law, queered.

V.3. Queering Suspect Classification's Four Criteria

An important instance of the interplay between cultural and legal norms is the legal reasoning behind suspect classification. As laid out in more detail in Chapter II.3, in order for a characteristic to be considered a suspect basis for classification in U.S. American Constitutional Law, the Supreme Court has come to identify four main requirements over time: immutability, a history of incorrect stereotypes, political powerlessness, and a history of discrimination.[8] However, this list is neither an official nor exhaustive one. As Wintemute states, "the Supreme Court has referred to different combinations of these requirements, but has never provided a coherent theory explaining their purpose and relative importance" (63).[9] Even more, as laid out by Gerstmann, "all the criteria the courts use to decide where different groups belong in the equal protection hierarchy are so loaded with contradictions, double standards, and unresolvable ambiguities that principled decision making in this area is virtually impossible" (*Underclass* 9–10).

Acknowledging the difficulties a system which is not consistent in its reasoning poses, this chapter aims to propose changes to the most important hurdles to sexual orientation's suspect classification. Despite the inconsistencies in finding a classification suspect, there is an underlying structure of the dominant factors which are most picked up upon. Suspect classification evolves around the central questions of whether the respective group has been treated unequally over a long period of time (historical dimension), whether the group has to suffer from particular types of stereotypes (moral dimension), whether the group is considered a minority and not able to represent its interests (political dimension), and whether the classification is unchangeable and constituted by birth (essentialist dimension).

Qualifying these criteria as historical, moral, political, and essentialist poses an arbitrary attempt at classifying them according to their respective

---

8 See, e.g., Wintemute 61–4 for dissenting views on the number of criteria. While Wintemute identifies seven criteria, he asserts that "[s]ome of the criteria, such as history of unequal treatment and prejudice or stigma, prejudice and stereotypes, or immutability and irrelevance, are frequently lumped together" (63, footnote 24).

9 This observation has also been made by other scholars; see for instance Simon 141: "The various cases in which the Court has considered whether or not a class qualifies as suspect leave the Court's analysis in disarray. The Court uses a mixture of criteria to determine suspectness, creating an analytical muddle, and the boundary line between suspect classes and non-suspect classes is drawn in a haphazard way. Thus, the process model fails to provide a coherent and viable framework for the Court's suspect class analysis;" see Strauss 138: "The Supreme Court has not provided a coherent explanation for precisely what factors trigger heightened scrutiny;" see Wilkinson 983: "The criteria of suspectness have not been thoughtfully defined or consistently applied."

foci; while the essentialist dimension might as well be labeled 'natural,' the political dimension 'historical,' and all of them have a 'discriminatory' quality, basically all dimensions are inherently politically instrumentalized, if not weaponized, and socioculturally constructed as I argue. This means that each of these factors functions as a gatekeeping device for furthering legal protections of minorities. Employing a queer theoretical perspective, these factors' heteronormative logic is visibilized and subverted. In a first step, I lay down the covert political functions and sociocultural origins of these four criteria before proposing alternatives to traditional approaches to suspect classification's requirements, thereby offering an updated, queered understanding of the politics of constitutional protection.

The cultural relevance of these legal terms emerges when questioning their meaning. As mentioned in Chapter IV.1, legal norms are characterized by their indeterminate, even gappy character, which legal scholars, judges and justices are filling with interpretations. However, when trying to interpret legal terms, it becomes obvious that their meaning is connected to other cultural realms. Therefore, legal interpretation feeds on culturally relevant programming, i.e., on those processes of meaning-making relied upon for navigating one's social and cultural world. Assessing the legal meaning of suspect classification's criteria therefore necessarily involves looking at those criteria's sociocultural constructed meaning: What does immutability mean? When are stereotypes incorrect and who decides on that? Does increasing visibility equal increasing political power? Who writes the history the judiciary looks at? Which version of it will matter at which occasion? While these questions are by no means new inquiries into this particular part of constitutional law,[10] they illustrate that legal terms do neither evolve out of thin air nor out of themselves but always use existing cultural notions and understandings as their points of reference.

By now, several lower court judges and state supreme court justices have found that sexual orientation qualifies for a group-based equal protection because it fulfills these four dimensions. Among them is the Supreme Court of California, which held that sexual orientation is a suspect classification in 2008.[11] In this instance, the court compared sexual orientation to other already

10 See Strauss 139 about other questions concerning the "significant uncertainty about the precise definition and measure of each factor."

11 See also the following cases holding that sexual orientation is a quasi-suspect classification: Iowa's *Varnum v. Brien* (2009); Connecticut's *Kerrigan v. Commissioner of Public Health* (2008). See also Eskridge "Political" 9.

recognized suspect classifications such as religion and alienage. Arguing that "one's religion, of course, is not immutable but is a matter over which an individual has control" (*In Re Marriage Cases* 842) and quoting the 1972 decision *Raffaelli v. Committee of Bar Examiners* in which "alienage [was] treated as a suspect classification notwithstanding circumstance that [an] alien can become a citizen" (842), the Californian Supreme Court based their decision which level of review to use not on solving the issues surrounding sexual orientation's immutability. Instead, the court questioned the implications of these requirements with regard to other classifications which are considered suspect. This understanding of a less formalist application of the four criteria may also be influenced by a changing relation to the concepts of religion and alienage as both have become highly politicized during the twenty-first century.

What can be gained from the Californian Supreme Court's approach to suspect classification is that there is both a willingness and a possibility to re-think these seemingly static requirements and thus challenge traditional notions of class-based jurisprudence. The following investigations, de- and re-constructions of legal classifications are thus in good judicial company.

'Political Powerlessness'

Measuring the need for a group's constitutional protection has its origins in the question of political representation. In 1938, Justice Harlan Fiske Stone laid the foundation for SCOTUS's different levels of review by directly addressing "prejudice against discrete and insular minorities ..., which tends seriously to curtail the operation of those political processes ordinarily to be relied upon to protect minorities, and which may call for a correspondingly more searching judicial inquiry."[12] While Stone's footnote remains highly abstract with regard to what constitutes "those political processes ordinarily to be relied upon" or how prejudice effectively translates into serious curtailments, today's understanding of his words is that the judiciary, mostly in the form of the Supreme Court, "must protect groups that are vulnerable to legislative bias" (Strauss 153). This vulnerability is predominantly measured quantitively by looking at voting rights or the lack thereof, the size of a group (sheer number of members), laws that benefit the group, and political representation (number of held political offices).[13]

12 Footnote four, *U.S. v. Carolene Products Co.* (1938); see also Chapter II.3.

13 See also Strauss 154: "Judges and scholars have suggested four possible approaches, used either separately or in combination, to assess power. These approaches consider (1) the group's ability to vote; (2) the pure numbers of the group; (3) the existence

The reasoning behind this approach is that minorities are perceived to be unable to represent their interests or propose statues when they are left out of majoritarian political processes. This view is interesting for several reasons. First, it suggests that political powerlessness is necessarily connected to political participation. In the case of sexual orientation, it seems to suggest that those who are not openly queer, whether they are closeted or not identifying as queer, cannot represent queer demands. The power to shape legal norms from within the legislative branch is here understood to be decisive; influencing legal norms from an external position, for example by imagining alternatives to existing legal realities and putting pressure on the legal status quo,[14] is not considered. Neither is approaching elected officials and proposing bills to them. Additionally, it leaves out the political power of social movements which work towards legal recognition without being (yet) able to participate politically. However, allyship plays an important role in gaining rights and strengthening public sensibilities for the need of those rights. Labeling these influences unpolitical would betray their power to shape law, politics, and sociocultural understandings for minority concerns.

Admittedly, the view on political power(lessness) as best measured by political representation corresponds to an identity political understanding of who is qualified to speak for whose interests. This objection to consider sexual minorities powerful in the understanding of suspect classifications' logic is vital for tackling existing sociocultural hierarchies. Questioning the legitimacy of advocating for queer rights as a cis-hetero person in power is thus not meant to denounce efforts at allyship but to stress the need to acknowledge one's own privileges and to work towards dismantling inequalities beside the legal ones at hand. This way, unequal legal and sociocultural orders are simultaneously addressed and visibilized. However, arguing that sexual minorities are politically powerless because they are still underrepresented in political offices also shifts responsibility away from those in power while simultaneously putting extra pressure on queer politicians. While cis-hetero politicians are perceived as only able to represent their respective interests, thereby negating the possibility of common ones, queer politicians have to represent an entirely het-

of favorable legislative enactments that might demonstrate political power; and (4) whether members of the group have achieved positions of power and authority."

14 See also Mazukatow and Binder who state that "the process of imagining does not only contribute to the stabilization of knowledge about society but it also belongs to the repertoire of critical practices aiming for change" (460).

erogenous community accurately or else they risk losing support and credibility.

Second, linking political powerlessness to a lack of political representation establishes illusory scientific evidence for political power and naturalizes a political system that works hierarchically. The logic that representation, mostly in the form of who is part of Congress and state legislatures, equals power denies any engagement with the reasons for exclusion and their extended influence on the Supreme Court. The Court as well as state supreme courts, which are responsible for deciding on whether the criterion of political powerlessness is met, have to interpret what constitutes powerlessness. Is one in a hundred a minority and thus powerless? Probably. But what about forty in a hundred? The scale is completely arbitrary and up for debate. As the power to decide on such questions is in the hand of a few, unelected justices, who are already highly biased as I argue in Chapter III, the interpretation of what constitutes power remains with those who already got it. In addition to the issue of interpreting statistics and adding them with meaning, setting up statistics is already entangled in biased economies of knowledge production. In the U.S., polls and surveys play an important role in elections, yet the money politicians spent on campaigns, including paying companies to conduct surveys, make statistics never an *a priori* innocent instrument but one that is already situated within power relations and likely to reproduce them (Kennedy "Key Things").

Understanding political powerlessness as connected to "a group's inability to rely on the legislative process to protect its interests" (Strauss 153) inevitably raises the question how a supposedly democratic system is able to create such a group. The paradox of using this criterion for considering how thoroughly a court reviews cases in which a group is discriminated without addressing the urgent question how this political exclusion came into being in the first place and thus tackling one's own (and one's group's) responsibility in supporting this system seem to stem from a dissociative national identity disorder. Undoubtably, equal protection acknowledges the need to protect vulnerable minorities, yet it does not address the inherent discrepancy between democratic equalitarian ideals and the definition of political powerlessness. This criterion is based on the very assumption that the U.S. American legal system is based on inequal options of representation which can only be balanced out when in office. Thus, the reasoning behind political powerlessness works with two juxtaposed, yet simultaneously maintained understandings of suspect classification and the role of the U.S. American legal system in general.

The access to political participation is important and there certainly are less visible and less politically powerful groups than the LGBTQ+ community, and also less visible and less politically powerful groups than the White, able-bodied, cis, propertied, gay members within the LGBTQ+ community. Yet, approaching the issue of political power from the question of congressional or state legislature's representation assumes that laws are merely made within these parameters, betraying any analysis of the multiple entanglements of law(makers), culture, and society. As the number of openly gay, lesbian, bisexual, asexual, and other non-heterosexual politicians increases,[15] considerations of political powerlessness may become obsolete despite heavy legal backlash against queers. Lack of political powerlessness, i.e., political power in the form of political representation and participation, may thus work as a disadvantage of being granted a higher form of constitutional protection. Gerstmann commented on this scenario as early as 2003 when he claimed that

> Gays and lesbians are told that they must remain at the bottom of the constitutional hierarchy because they are too politically powerful to require heightened scrutiny. In order for this assertion to make sense, we would have to believe that gays and lesbians are more powerful than are women, or, even more implausibly, than are the white students who were recently given the protection of heightened scrutiny in their challenges to the University of Michigan's affirmative action policies. (*Underclass* viii-ix)

In 1996's *Romer v. Evans*, Justice Scalia's dissenting opinion followed this argumentation by stating that "[i]t is also nothing short of preposterous to call 'politically unpopular' a group which enjoys enormous influence in American media and politics, and which, as the trial court here noted, though composing no more than 4% of the population had the support of 46% of the voters on Amendment 2" (652). Interestingly, understanding politically unpopular as synonymous with politically powerless smoothens the negation of this criterion; while popularity may indicate a sociocultural climate which is not entirely hostile to queers, – a claim which would also be challenged by many within

15 See Goldmacher: "The number of gay, lesbian, bisexual and transgender elected officials has continued to surge, growing by about 17 percent in the last year to nearly 1,000 nationwide — more than double the number just four years ago, according to a new annual report." According to the "Out for America 2021" census, 0.19% of elected officials in the U.S. are queer, necessitating that "28,116 more LGBTQ people must be elected to achieve equitable representation" ("Out").

the LGBTQ+ community today –, winning votes, being elected to positions of power, and ultimately passing laws is not a causality or logical consequence of being popular.

The criterion of political powerlessness is connected to what I label 'legal sexual orientationism' (see Chapter IV.2) and to what Gerstmann considers the "class/classification switch" (*Underclass* 9). Approaching questions of political power with the aim to protect gays, lesbians, asexuals, bisexuals and other non-heterosexual individuals, i.e., thinking about these persons as potential *suspect classes*, the Court would most probably negate the lack of political power. However, considering sexual orientation as *suspect classification* would involve potential protections also for those who identify as heterosexual, making the call to protect the category instead of specific groups a strategic one. Yet, given the logic inconsistencies and political uneasiness about only being able to fulfill this criterion when appropriating heterosexist reasoning, a thorough reform of this criterion may be the cleaner option – and one which may prove more promising for future struggles for a group's rights.

Abolishing questions of political power(lessness) entirely in the context of suspect classification would pose the threat of ultimately benefitting those already in power – which the current legal situation more than often does. Working with power structures is thus necessary to capture existing socio-cultural inequalities and to compensate for them legally. Instead of taking political powerlessness or lack of political representation as criterion, a reversal of the burden of proof may work better to suit the demands of queer right projects. Comparing the number of discriminatory bills that are issued, the number of anti-discrimination bills and laws that have successfully been implemented in contrast with those which are being stalled, and the court cases which deal with LGBTQ+ discrimination and have been decided in favor of queers may work better to represent actual legal realities instead of the potential political opportunity to influence them. This approach would also satisfy this criterion's affinity for quantitative measurements.

'History of Discrimination'

The history of a group's discrimination examines whether a group has been treated unequally and been denied the same treatment as other groups over a long period of time. This criterion is connected to political powerlessness as legal scholar Bruce Ackerman explains:

> [A]lthough each of us cannot always expect to convince our legislators, we can at least insist that they treat our claims with respect. At the very least, they should thoughtfully consider our moral and empirical arguments, rejecting them only after conscientiously deciding that they are inconsistent with the public interest. If a group fails to receive this treatment, it suffers a special wrong, one quite distinct from its substantive treatment on the merits. (738)

This closeness to the question of political powerlessness and lack of legislative protection has led commentators to consider a group's history of discrimination "to be a subset of the political powerlessness criteria rather than its own separate and distinct criterion" (Strauss 150). Both criteria start from the premise that there is a historical and/or structural inequality which warrants legislative interference.

Similar to the aspect of political powerlessness, a group's history of discrimination lacks a coherent definition,[16] making considerations about whether a group meets this criterion or not again highly subjective to a court's interpretation. The respective political set-up of the Court and its justices' biographies and philosophies therefore play an important part in deciding upon the way of interpreting this criterion – this finding of course also applies to the other criteria.

Despite these differences in modes of interpretation, the legal legacy of *Brown*, "the Court's most famous equal protection decision" (Eskridge "Powerlessness" 5) as well as the origin of the Equal Protection Clause, namely serving to protect the formerly enslaved after the Civil War, still influences the discourse on suspect classification. After the Court decided in 1954 that racial segregation in public schools is unconstitutional, the 1967 landmark decision *Loving v. Virginia* picked up on the Court's reasoning and established race as a suspect classification (see also Eskridge "Powerlessness" 5). Taking *Loving* as a blueprint, different minorities tried to demand strict(er) scrutiny by comparing their situation to racial minorities.[17] Race then again appears as

16 See Strauss 151; Wilkinson 981.

17 See Eskridge "Powerlessness" 5: "The form of the argument was usually this: like people of color, our group has suffered from pervasive state discrimination founded on prejudice and unfair stereotypes; like race, our stigmatizing trait is not one whose deployment usually contributes to the public good; and like racial minorities, our group is not politically powerful enough to resist or repeal these unjust discriminatory laws. This represented a concept that focused on harm, irrationality, and lack of

continuing reference point for considerations about suspect classification and its criteria.

The first pertinent issue when it comes to a group's history of discrimination is the period of time one choses to look at. Legal scholars have commented on this aspect multiple times and even courts have exhibited a surprisingly high degree of self-reflective sociocultural analysis as in respect to the history of discrimination of women in U.S. American society:

> There can be no doubt that our Nation has had a long and unfortunate history of sex discrimination. ... Traditionally, such discrimination was rationalized by an attitude of "romantic paternalism" which, in practical effect, put women not on a pedestal, but in a cage. ... As a result of notions such as these, our statute books gradually became laden with gross, stereotyped distinctions between the sexes, and, indeed, throughout much of the 19th century, the position of women in our society was, in many respects, comparable to that of blacks under the pre-Civil War slave codes. Neither slaves nor women could hold office, serve on juries, or bring suit in their own names, and married women traditionally were denied the legal capacity to hold or convey property or to serve as legal guardians of their own children. (*Frontiero* 684–85; majority opinion by Justice Brennan)

If the Court is able to acknowledge and historically trace back such inequalities to systematic pattern of sexism, one wonders why dismantling these structures has not been a consistent red thread in SCOTUS' decisions ever since. Equally important, the question arises why the comparison to formerly enslaved persons and Blacks is necessary to perceive of sex discrimination's unconstitutionality as legitimate. In fact, the reasoning in *Frontiero* mirrors a general practice when trying to determine a group's history of discrimination:

> Because of the lack of precise guidance in determining whether a group has the requisite history of discrimination, courts often decide discriminatory history by comparing the experience of the group to that of African-Americans or women. Presumably, if a history is not analogous to that of either African-Americans or women—the former a suspect class and the latter a quasi-suspect class—the group is probably nonsuspect. (Strauss 151–2)

---

a political remedy as the classic instance when equal protection analysis by judges ought to be particularly scrutinizing."

Although there are common interests and comparable parameters of women, people of color/Blacks, and the LGBTQ+ community, – most importantly experiences of discrimination in an oppressive, structurally and institutionally discriminatory system, – the distinct history of each group makes a comparison impossible. When non-heterosexual orientations, and arguably also heterosexuality itself, became increasingly important and added with cultural meaning during the nineteenth century, colonialism, slavery and racism have had already violated and killed Blacks and people of color for centuries, while women had to navigate patriarchal structures of sexism, economic exploitation, and legal subordination. As Eskridge states, "[t]he sexual orientation concept barely existed at the turn of the century but is charged with normative meaning at the turn of the millennium" (*Gaylaw* 9). Moreover, sexism and racism and the conditions they enable have not disappeared after declaring sex a quasi-suspect classification and race a suspect classification. In addition, this focus on racial and sex inequalities ignores any intersectional experiences and thus invisibilizes the experience of those who have to face multiple oppression such as queer Black women. For them, their 'history of discrimination' entails a plurality of experiences and is more adequately captured as *histories* of discrimination.

So, why would the Supreme Court work with such a flawed analogy that is neither able to adequately reflect differences between groups nor mirror the still prevalent forms of discrimination Blacks, people of color, and women face? In his brilliant article "The Id, the Ego, and Equal Protection. Reckoning with Unconscious Racism,"[18] law professor Charles R. Lawrence III analyzes the unconscious racial bias permeating U.S. American culture. Perceiving racially discriminatory laws as not always intentional but as a result of "a common historical and cultural heritage in which racism has played and still plays a dominant role" (322), Lawrence proposes to include a more thorough cultural analysis in legal doctrine; the "'cultural' meaning test" (328), which

18 Lawrence's article deals with the disparate impact test the Supreme Court has established in its 1976 *Washington v. Davis* decision, yet offers important findings applicable for considerations about suspect classification. In *Davis*, the Court decided that laws which have a discriminatory effect on racial minorities are only unconstitutional when there is a provable discriminatory intention, meaning that "the invidious quality of a law claimed to be racially discriminatory must ultimately be traced to a racially discriminatory purpose" (*Davis* at 240).

"posits a connection between unconscious racism and the existence of cultural symbols that have racial meaning" (324).[19] Aiming at detecting racialist motivated governmental action, a court would then

> analyze governmental behavior much like a cultural anthropologist might: by considering evidence regarding the historical and social context in which the decision was made and effectuated. If the court determined by a preponderance of the evidence that a significant portion of the population thinks of the governmental action in racial terms, then it would presume that socially shared, unconscious racial attitudes made evident by the action's meaning had influenced the decisionmakers. As a result, it would apply heightened scrutiny. (356)

While it remains unclear how a court should determine the objectivity and neutrality of evidence, historical or social context, and which part of the population is being asked in the first place, Lawrence offers important suggestions for re-thinking suspect classification. Examining the cultural meaning of a legal norm de-emphasizes historical context by trying to visibilize covert discriminatory attitudes which have not yet entered into public, meaning majoritarian, consciousness but already showed their cultural significance and presence in public discourse. For instance, at the time of *Bowers v. Hardwick*, the 1986 U.S. Supreme Court decision which criminalized consensual homosexual activity, public opinion about sex between consenting adults of the same-sex may not have been as progressive as it is nowadays,[20] yet the perception of sex was heavily loaded with cultural meaning. As indicated by the opinion of Chief Justice Warren E. Burger, who joined the majority's opinion in *Bowers*,

> the proscriptions against sodomy have very "ancient roots." Decisions of individuals relating to homosexual conduct have been subject to state inter-

19 Lawrence defines his test further: "It suggests that the 'cultural meaning' of an allegedly racially discriminatory act is the best available analogue for, and evidence of, a collective unconscious that we cannot observe directly. This test would thus evaluate governmental conduct to determine whether it conveys a symbolic message to which the culture attaches racial significance" (324).

20 This view takes into account the medial and cultural visibility of homosexual, bisexual, pansexual and other persons, and pro-LGBTQ+ landmark decisions such as *Obergefell* and *Bostock*. The argument considers these examples as evidence for a majoritarian public opinion which, if not welcomes, at least condones homosexual persons as part of society.

> vention throughout the history of Western civilization. Condemnation of those practices is firmly rooted in Judeo-Christian moral and ethical standards. Homosexual sodomy was a capital crime under Roman law. (196, footnote 8)

Making an undoubtably culturalistic and religious argument for criminalizing homosexual sex, – and its moral and legal rightfulness, – Burger unwillingly argues for an acknowledgement of homosexuals' history of discrimination. However, while his perspective on history is subjective and influenced by a Western, heteronormative gaze which fails to acknowledge the development of cultural perceptions of sexuality and sexual orientation, the strong emphasis and recourse to moral cultures and power hierarchies reveals the degree of cultural and affective loadedness of the topic.

Thus, a useful cultural meaning test would not take into account how society thought about a particular topic at a certain time, it would refer to the degree of tabooization and affective responses to a topic. Analyzing these aspects then takes into account how much a topic is loaded with cultural meaning, including anxieties, moral panics, and/or scapegoating. Utilizing Lawrence' proposed test for sexual minorities, one would have to examine the cultural meaning of legal decisions discriminating against queers.

Similar to questions about political powerlessness, the importance placed on a group's history of discrimination should suffice as evidence for affirming that this criterion is fulfilled. As seen by looking at *Bowers*, there is a cultural, legal, and moral distinction between homosexual and heterosexual sex, making sexual orientation an important marker of social stratification in the U.S. By distinguishing between different sexual orientations when criminalizing consensual behavior between adults, not only can we observe a hierarchization of homo- and heterosexuality, but we can also extract the cultural meaning of this ordering category. Following Lawrence's idea of a cultural meaning test, in U.S. American culture, sexual orientation matters as a legal category warranting heightened or strict scrutiny because law and culture treat people differently based on their respective sexual orientation. Thus, this category is loaded with cultural meaning.

'Immutability'

The criterion of immutability is possibly one of the most difficult ones to prove, and the most controversial to interpret. In suspect classification cases, immutability evolves around the question whether a trait is integral to one's identity or, in other words, whether it is "determined solely by the accident of birth" (*Frontiero* 686). With regard to sex, ethnicity and race, the Court has already established these characteristics' immutability by affirming their innateness and connecting the protection of these characteristics to "the basic concept of our system that legal burdens should bear some relationship to individual responsibility" (Weber v. Aetna Casualty & Surety Co. 175). This means that if someone is not responsible because they did not choose to be, look, or feel a certain way, they are excused by the legal system. According to this logic, if laws would discriminate against any trait over which the individual has no control and is not responsible for, they would be inherently unfair. As for race, it is argued that one's racial or ethnical lineage are beyond one's control, therefore the individual holds no responsibility for the respective trait. This approach is problematic for several reasons.

First, stressing individual responsibility as an important factor, suspect classification's immutability criterion affirms that the classification, be it race, ethnicity, or sex, does matter and is a meaningful category for law. By doing so, judges and justices risk perpetuating existing stigmata and contribute to further loading these categories with sociocultural meaning and stressing the need for legal interference. This emphasis on individualism ties into U.S. American cultural narratives that the individual is solely responsible for their material, bodily, and sociocultural standing. Second, this approach negates and blends out the sociocultural constructedness of such identity categories, thereby shying away from a thorough analysis of power structures and existing legal-cultural orders. This contributes to a further essentialization of race, ethnicity, sex, and other categories as it conceives their degree of staticness to be decisive for legal protections. If they are found to be changeable or reversable, they would not be considered immutable. Arguing that a trait is not immutable, meaning not integral to one's identity or changeable respectively, works to control its place in the cultural imaginary as inferior, negligible, or potentially unimportant.

This approach poses similar pitfalls and problematic consequences for queers as found in essentialist and constructionist controversies about sexuality (see Chapter III). As elaborated on by Elizabeth Grosz and John Boswell, essentialist and constructionist perspectives on sexuality are switched for political purposes as needed; in order to legitimate the ongoing pathologization of sexual orientation, medical professionals have taken on constructionist views and advocated for conversion 'therapies' based on the notion that sexual orientation is not immutable and thus possible to change. Simultaneously, the naturalness of heterosexuality is emphasized as an essentialist norm to which those with other sexual orientations need to return to.

Scholars, judges, and justices have rightfully deconstructed the paradox of considering religion an immutable characteristic, such as the Californian Supreme Court in its 2008's *In Re Marriage Cases*: "one's religion, of course, is not immutable but is a matter over which an individual has control" (842). As Eskridge states, "it is not clear that sexual orientation is a matter of choice-and in any event, sexual orientation is less mutable than religion and alienage, both of which are suspect classifications" (*Gaylaw* 9). Given the still not extinct discourse around this criterion reveals its appeal as a power tool. Arguing for a trait's immutability approaches legal uncertainties through lending legitimacy from supposedly more objective sciences, most importantly biology. The notion that there is a clear-cut answer to what is 'natural,' meaning biologically given, and what is added later on by society and culture speaks for a longing for what I have elsewhere called a "supposed shelter of reliability" (Olson and Borchert 391). Immutability is perceived as a criterion which offers guidance in increasingly complex questions of identity and legal personhood while simultaneously being an instrument for gatekeeping more thorough legal protections and rights.

Considering immutability a decisive criterion perverts and weaponizes scientific evidence about the sociocultural constructedness of sexual orientation. Acknowledging the fluidity of sexual orientation equals denying this legal category the status of immutability and thus negating the worthiness of its stricter legal protection. Sexual orientation remains associated with non-heterosexual orientation, stressing legal sexual orientationist perspectives, and non-normative, deviant even, by choice. Those not willing to change their (non-hetero-) sexual orientation are considered rule-breakers and troublemakers when this trait is considered changeable. In this sense, immutability serves to maintain a cisnormative, heterosexist, patriarchal power structure whether it is considered as applying to sexual orientation or not.

From a legal perspective, immutability establishes a dichotomy of 'good' and 'bad' traits, reminiscent of Gayle Rubin's findings about sociocultural perspectives on and hierarchization of sexuality. Innateness functions as a moral carte blanche, making its holder free from judgement because of a characteristic they cannot control. Culturally, innateness makes recourse to genetic and biologistic notions of one's 'true' or core identity, neglecting any argument for fluidity. This understanding is reinforced by immutability's second aspect, a trait's irreversibility. As immutability is understood to combine that a trait is both unable to change by the individual and part of them from birth onwards, the question arises which trait would be able to fulfill this definition.

Focusing on a trait's immutability reproduces existing sociocultural hierarchies and biases. Considering race an immutable criterion naturalizes race as ordering category by presuming it is not a socially constructed phenomenon but a genetic or biological given. The same logic applies to considerations for sexual orientation and gender identity. For instance, if the Court finds that gender is not immutable because it acknowledges the right of determining one own's gender identity and neglects medical-biologistic notions of gender, it ultimately reinforces medical-biologistic notions of having to refer to 'natural,' meaning biological circumstances to evaluate a legal situation. Then, gender would not qualify as suspect classification. However, if the Court finds that gender is immutable, it ignores sociocultural realities of those who consider their trans, non-binary, or gender queer identity as fluid – but gender would qualify for suspect classification. In both cases, immutability as a legal criterion fails because it operates with sociocultural paradoxes. Or, as Martha Nussbaum states, "the legal notion of immutability is confused" (122).

Further, having to prove that a trait is immutable stigmatizes the group asking for suspect class status or their trait's suspect classification when the law already privileges their majoritarian Other. When queers demand suspect classification for sexual orientation, having to prove immutability again illustrates legal sexual orientationism. Law, in its normative power, operates with heteronormative categories and privileges those who adhere to this norm. As these categories and their protections are considered natural, other, non-heteronormative orientations have to legitimate themselves and prove their worthiness of protection. While the immutability of heterosexuality is not questioned when establishing legal norms that prioritize and thus protect it 'naturally' more, non-heterosexual orientations have to bring on the impossible task for proving themselves to those unable or unwilling to grasp their realities.

In addition to being 'confused,' the need for closure immutability demands also yields violence over queer bodies beyond the legal realm. Over the last decades, researchers have tried to determine the source of homosexual orientation by, inter alia, conducting twin studies, analyzing possible genetic predispositions within one's family, examining the mixture of certain hormones within one's body post- and prenatally and by observing one's brain morphology (Green 539–54). Additionally, therapies such as psychoanalysis, religious faith healing and chemical and electrical aversion treatment have been tried to eradicate (non-hetero-) sexual preference. Most of these treatments were not successful, "psychologically wrenching" and "sometimes physically painful" (Green 569). Attempts at finding the cause of sexual orientation and trying to reverse it proved to be ultimately inconclusive or short-lived.[21] The persistent search for more (natural-) scientific evidence about sexual orientation not only serves legal endeavors to regulate sexuality, it also feeds into nationalist imaginaries:

> Homosexuality does not fit easily into ideologies stressing traditional family life as the cornerstone of ethnic community. Thus, homophobia is a common feature of racial, ethnic, and nationalist ideologies and programs of social control. Unlike racism and prejudice that "seek targets *outside* ethnic boundaries, homophobia can be directed *inside* ethnic communities as well, and used to create an internal sexual boundary that excludes or 'disqualifies' a group's own members (Nagel 26; emphasis in original).

Homosexual orientation violates the implicit societal assumption of having to procreate to guarantee national survival (see Nagel 30). In this context, scientific evidence about the causalities and implications of sexual orientation risks being misused for attempts at 'curing' such a genetic predisposition by prenatal genetic testing, medication, or, as predicted by Katrin C. Rose, even by societal planning in the form of eugenics.[22] This notion is also what Waites refers to when stating that

> research has shown how medical and psychological perspectives on sexuality inform and structure political debates ... together with work demonstrating the international power of health and medicine discourses ... suggests the value of examining the extent to which biomedical and psychological expertise concerning 'sexual orientation' is implicated in global configurations of power" (145).

---

21 See Green 539: "However, the hope of finding a single gene or set of genes to explain fully the development of any syndrome has met with failure except in the case of some chromosomal disorders (such as Down's syndrome). With other behaviors ... , research has found that while there may be some contribution from genetics, this is far from being the entire story. Much of the contribution appears to be either environmental or some complex interaction between nurture and nature."

22 See Rose 57–8: "History has provided too many examples of questionable governmental practices based on notions of better living through 'genetic cleansing.' ... Would a gay gene be something that society accepts and protects? Or would society mark this gene as an item to be cured or eradicated?"

Approaching anti-discrimination laws from this stance of ruling on a trait's immutability makes it easier to put traits into binary pairs of what is worthy of special protection and what is not by using a biologistic, or respectively essentialist, understanding of identity. Immutability, in this context, illuminates thus how different areas of knowledge/research function as legal gate-keepers and thus become part of legal orders themselves, and how these different legal orders intertwine to uphold cultural narratives of equality. Biologistic-essentialist findings are being utilized to prove what law failed to do, namely that a trait should not receive heightened protection. Debating the immutability of a trait thus may suggest analyzing its significance for an individual's identity, yet it ultimately proves this trait's impact in sociocultural value systems and negotiations of power and identity. This logic, however, only holds true in cultures which put emphasis on biologistic, medical evidence which still qualifies over sociocultural self-analysis.

To avoid these unsolvable nature-nurture-controversies, suspect classification's argumentation needs to be based not on how a characteristic is constituted, i.e., its immutability, history, neutrality, but what it constitutes, i.e., a discriminatory legal pluralism in which some holders of the characteristic are treated differently than others. Historic instances of these discriminatory legal pluralisms are most prominently found in separate-but-equal logics of the Jim Crow era, which saw race as a criterion that demanded special treatment. Interestingly, all of these biases only work in comparison to a norm, which is imagined as, among others, White, cis, heteronormative, able-bodied, non-immigrant.

Immutability proves a dangerous criterion for queer bodies because of its problematic implications. If sexual orientation is considered immutable, it essentializes the individual and pathologizes them; if sexual orientation is considered not immutable, it allows for measures to change the respective orientation to adjust to the heteronorm. The continuing emphasis on this criterion, however, offers an opportunity to de-essentialize it. As Nussbaum states,

> the case for heightened scrutiny for sexual orientation is very strong. Sexual orientation, like being female, is irrelevant to many things for which society confusedly holds it to be relevant. It is also deep and central in people's lives, like religion, in a way that makes us think asking people to give up acting on their orientation is a kind of cruelty. (122)

This "idea of relevance and the idea of depth or centrality" (122) might then replace the biologistic emphasis on innateness. Moving towards an understanding of core importance also smoothens the logical inconstancies regarding other classifications such as alienage, religion or illegitimacy of birth. Although determined by one's birth, the status of each of these classes can be changed, i.e., by naturalizing citizens, legitimizing illegitimates and by converting to another religion, which makes them something over which the individual has control, can be held responsible for, and that is no longer immutable. In this sense, the Supreme Court's definition of the criterion of immutability should be adjusted accordingly, if not abolished altogether. This way, sexual orientation's status as immutable part of one's identity would satisfy suspect classification's criterion of immutability, leaving the proof of moral neutrality as only remaining factor to be satisfied.

'Moral Neutrality'

Established together with immutability in the Court's 1973 *Frontiero* decision, this criterion deals with historically evolved stereotypes, which are considered incorrect. Such stereotypes can be used to justify statutes and institutional discrimination and thus contribute to the political and social powerlessness and disadvantages of certain social groups. For instance, the hostile stereotype of perceiving of gay men as pedophiles and as potentially molesting children has "been used to justify sodomy statutes, employment discrimination and housing discrimination" according to Culverhouse and Lewis (243).

The concept of historic and incorrect stereotypes has also been used to prove whether a characteristic is 'morally neutral,' meaning in line with religious and sociocultural values of a majoritarian legal collective. Linking minority protection to questions of morality already anticipates the highly problematic application of this criterion. In a diversifying pluralistic society, referring to (Christian) religious values, linking them to inherently cultural ones and applying them to legal issues naturalizes cultural and legal orders. Conceiving of Christianity as default authority for moral questions, the Court establishes a hierarchy of state-sanctioned religions and inevitably inferiorizes others. Additionally, working with the concept of morality in legal discourse makes recourse to an essentialist understanding of justice in which there is indeed an unbiased, objectively 'right' and just *teleos*.

The criterion of moral neutrality thus means that the trait in question has to be in accordance with religious and sociocultural principles which constitute a legal collective's cultural and legal value system. Proving that a characteristic is not immoral and thus makes up one criterion which warrants extraordinary legal protection to the highest court of the society that discriminates exactly against this trait is one of the main issues in the context of suspect classification since existing biases have to be reversed. The difficulty of this task is reinforced by the political powerlessness of the minorities involved.

The criterion of moral neutrality can be seen as the reversed definition of a classification which reflects historic and incorrect stereotypes with no basis in fact. In this context, the aspect of incorrectness refers to traits which are wrongfully perceived as being harmful, morally bad or which are wrongfully said to influence a person's ability to perform in or contribute to society negatively. Thus, moral neutrality has alternatively been described as a characteristic which is "relevant to [a group's; lb] ability to perform or contribute to society" (Strauss 145).

Finding a coherent definition for moral neutrality to make this criterion legally applicable without reference to Christian religion seems at best highly difficult given the Supreme Court's shift to the religious right in its recent decisions (*Dobbs*; *Kennedy*). Having to legitimize heightened scrutiny for sexual orientation through religious understandings of morality undermines the separation of church and state and thereby perverts the claim that SCOTUS is apolitical, and by extension secular, even further. In addition, determining what is morally neutral can change over time with formerly immoral conducts becoming morally neutral and vice versa. An example for such a reversal is the Supreme Court's 1967 decision in *Loving v. Virginia* which ruled that a Virginia statute banning interracial marriages was unconstitutional. Here, the State of Virginia argued that its objectives for prohibiting interracial marriages were "'to preserve the racial integrity of its citizens,' and to prevent 'the corruption of blood,' 'a mongrel breed of citizens,' and 'the obliteration of racial pride'" (7), which were reversed by the Supreme Court's ruling that there is "no legitimate overriding purpose independent of invidious racial discrimination" (11).

This constellation illustrates that even in a society which shares the same legal and sociocultural heritage, the definition of moral and immoral conduct seems to differ, with the recognition of race as morally neutral trait as prime example in U.S. American cultural-legal history. Stating that the Supreme Court has broadened the reach of equal protection by "distilling from the principle of the moral irrelevance of race the more general principle of the moral irrelevance of any trait that reveals nothing about the moral worth or desert of a person" (Perry 1065), Perry proposes how one can identify such a morally neutral criterion. Each characteristic which "indicates nothing about the person's physical or mental capacity – in the form of native talent, acquired skills, temperament, or the like – to make particular choices or engage in particular activities" (1066) should be regarded as morally neutral since it is neither relevant to one's ability to perform in society nor does it influence the morality of one's character.

This definition, however, again presupposes an element of neutrality towards a trait, which is not always given. Whether one takes the incorrect stereotype of race as an indicator of low intelligence,[23] or the bias that gay men are always effeminate,[24] the establishment and persistence of incorrect stereotypes attributed to a classification influence how members of these social groups are perceived. Consequently, legal recognition of a characteristic's moral neutrality proves difficult for a class facing such prejudices.

For sexual orientation, this is especially true when considering the bias that anything besides or beyond the heteronorm is "antisocial behavior" (Altman qtd. in Duncan 398). Using a reference to Martin Luther King to add authority to his claims, outspoken Christian and law professor Richard F. Duncan states that "people should be judged by the content of their character, not by the color of their skin" (402) but that (non-hetero-) sexual orientation is an indicator of one's character:

> Race tells us nothing about a person's character. Sexual behavior and orientation, however, tell us much about a person's character because they tell us what a person does (or what he is inclined to do). Sexual conduct and preferences are fraught with moral and religious significance. To be sure, not everyone agrees that homosexual behaviors and inclinations are immoral. But the point is that, unlike race, sexuality is morally controversial. (403–5)

Duncan seems to believe that race is not an immoral trait because the individual cannot in some way behave racially but that sexual orientation always goes together with at least questionable sexual behaviors. According to his essentialist perspective, same-sex sexual practices are deemed immoral by "our society's three major religions" (404) and triggers infections and diseases such

23 During World War I, the U.S. army conducted demeaning IQ tests which aimed at showing an alleged "[B]lack inferiority" (Schuman et al. 11).

24 See Chauncey 13: "The abnormality (or 'queerness') of the 'fairy,' that is, was defined as much by his 'woman-like' character or 'effeminacy' as his solicitation of male sexual partners."

as AIDS (404). This view presupposes that any non-heterosexual orientation, in particular homosexuality, is a sin which also endangers others and that this sexual behavior reflects on a person's identity and thus gives insight into their somewhat 'flawed' character. This essentialization of sexual orientation only applies to deviant ones whereas heterosexuality is regarded by Duncan as the normative, morally pure sexual status quo. The logic of legal sexual orientationism takes on Christian religious claims to moral superiority and nationalistic notions of protecting the people from diseased sexual Others.

Duncan's argument, which is based on the implicit assumption that homosexual conduct should be criminalized, disregards its own historicity. Non-heterosexual orientations may only be deemed morally controversial because of their histories of discrimination and the persistence of incorrect stereotypes through time. Consequently, arguing that some characteristic is immoral because it has been historically regarded as such seems to recycle established stereotyped notions without examining their plausibility.

Unfortunately, Duncan is right when he claims that "sexuality is morally controversial" (405). Today still, the lines between gender, sexuality, sexual orientation, and sexual conduct are blurred and one would have to spread awareness about each terms' implications before promoting equal protection. However, it is especially the invisibilization of heterosexuality as one of many sexual orientations which others sexuality, and feeds the belief that discourse about sexuality is always stickily perverse and abnormal.

Granting sexual orientation heightened scrutiny would elevate this category to the same level as race and religious affiliation. As indicated by Duncan's views, stereotyped preconceptions and flawed prior knowledge about queer realities indicate that the criterion of moral neutrality is the most difficult to satisfy since it evolves around biased perceptions of sexual orientation in general and non-heterosexual ones in particular. These stereotypes and the subsequent unequal social treatment, the very reason for demanding extraordinary legal protection, prove to be difficult to reverse because they intertwine with other fundamental rights such as religion and have been established over a long period of time. Consequently, overcoming the bias that sexual orientation is not morally neutral is the most problematic task for the proponents for sexual orientation's suspect classification, and increasingly so in times of the Supreme Court's positive stance towards religious conservatism. To re-establish the separation of church and state, and to de-hierarchize the cultural order of acceptable and privileged religions, the criterion of moral neutrality needs to be abolished.

V.4. Queer Legal Imaginaries

Landmark Supreme Court decisions such as *Bostock* or *Lawrence* have sustainably influenced both the U.S. American constitutional landscape and queer lives. However, as the chapters in this book make clear, legal changes may take time and are subject to ongoing negotiations, (re-)transformations, and outright attacks. Most recently, infamously coined 'Don't Say Gay' bills show how contested queer rights still are today and that states increasingly target LGBTQ+ youth. Individual or group relations to one's surrounding legal environment are not only impacted by actual legal developments but also, and arguably even more so, by cultural narratives and cultural-constitutional imaginaries. Chapter II.4 already introduced the notion of cultural-constitutional imaginaries as a certain form of legal affects which are cognitively and affectively appealing. This subchapter supplements the concept of cultural-constitutional imaginaries by commenting on the affective power of configuring alternatives to the legal status quo, and their relevance for queer activism.

The understanding of imaginaries as "encounters with alternative imagined configurations which can be recognized as making both cognitive *and* affective sense" (Lennon 107; emphasis in original) is central here. Law and rights discourses are not conducted from objectively true and neutral positions but always subjectively and affectively experienced. Configurations of power and affect are therefore entwined in how legal cultures imagine themselves and their subjects. Following Mazukatow's and Binder's understanding of imaginaries, I claim that the social praxis of imagining alternatives to the established legal system and existing legal norms reconfigures, subverts, and ultimately queers cultural-legal orders. This subchapter uses the term 'configurations' because these constructs differ from the imaginaries introduced in Chapter II.4 as they have been narrativized, shared, and altered within a legal collective. Drawing on Wolfgang Iser's theory of the real, the fictive, and the imaginary as triad (1), configurations as introduced here are closest to his category of "fictionalizing acts," which he understands as "a crossing of boundaries" (3):

> This transgression function of the fictionalizing act links it to the imaginary. ... The act of fictionalizing is therefore not identical to the imaginary with its protean potential. *For the fictionalizing act is a guided act.* It aims at something that in *turn endows the imaginary with an articulate gestalt* – a gestalt that differs from the fantasies, projections, daydreams, and other

> reveries that ordinarily give the imaginary expression in our day-to-day-experience. Here, too, we have an overstepping of limits, as we pass from the diffuse to the precise. Just as the fictionalizing act outstrips the determinacy of the real, so it provides the imaginary with the determinacy that it would not otherwise possess. (3; emphases added)

The act of becoming articulated and guided is what I refer to as higher degree of narrativization of configurations compared to imaginaries as introduced earlier. This transgression from affectively and cognitively experienced imaginaries to affectively shared, altered, and narrativized configurations is what Iser coins as endowing the "imaginary with an articulate gestalt" (3). Thus, the act of imagining reoccurs in the configurations presented and stands out as giving rise to their establishment. Referring to configurations instead of fictionalizing acts as suggested by Iser is due to the formers' cultural-political relevance. While Iser's theory may also be read as having a political impact on how one approaches literary texts, the cultural-legal texts analyzed here have an immediate impact on queer lives. Configurations are thus highly charged with affective and political meaning. They are not only observations of ongoing negotiations with the legal-cultural status quo, they are also queer utopian horizons towards which to work. In this sense, they all work with an envisioned reality after what is now, something that is post the current situation. At their core, these configurations imagine cultural-legal realities which underlie their logic.

A system of law that is in a temporal sense *post* its current form, either post-discriminatory, post-categorical, or post the current status quo implies that law is able to overcome its current form and to evolve into something new, something post current experience. This necessarily involves an abolitionist element of deconstructing, or queering, the status quo to make room for something else. This assumption operates from the premise that a) there is something a legal collective agrees on that *needs* changing, and b) that this status *is able* to be reformed. While this book has elaborated on the aspects that indeed need a reconceptualization and the suspectness of discrimination against sexual minorities, it has yet to comment on the larger question of whether there is something inherently suspect about the legal system as such.

So far, the argument has been made that suspect classification, an already existing tool in constitutional law's box, should and could be adjusted to serve queers' legal protection. While this may be regarded as an important step towards approaching what is oftentimes socioculturally imagined as 'equality' but would rather be labeled equity for queer purposes, the analyses and insights into legal and sociocultural processes prompt the question: If law and culture are so closely connected, would it not make more sense to re-conceptualize existing notions of law as a whole instead of fixing only certain parts of it? Attempts at answering this question have been made by a number of jurists, scholars, and activists, whose voices this subchapter amplifies. Further, these views' compatibility to what this book has established in terms of sexual orientation's relation to law, sociocultural notions of equality, and political power relations will be elaborated on.

All of these perspectives share their innovative, queered, sometimes even rebellious outlook towards the law. They all envision a law which is contrary to, questioning, or deconstructing what we understand to be part of a 'proper' legal system.[25] In this sense, these alternatives to the status quo imagine a queered version of the law, one that challenges established notions and works against inflexible categorizations and attributions. Simultaneously, the perspectives examined here often share their background in Critical Theory, Queer Theory, and Postcolonial Studies, and/or have in common that their activism is rooted in, has been influenced by, or has helped to establish these academic concepts. In this sense, this subchapter introduces configurations about what constitutes a possible legal future (co-)created by and welcoming for queers.

The argument for strengthening legal protections by using already existing concepts of law may be rejected by those who feel and think law in its current form cannot provide the necessary tools for queer emancipation given its discriminatory and oppressive effects on queer realities. Acknowledging these voices, this subchapter sets out to outline some of the most vocal calls for such a law-exherent, or extralegal, solution. Indeed, this outlook is meant to provide space for possible further research on queer rights and it acknowledges the importance of these claims while continuing to argue that law-inherent, and even more importantly sociocultural solutions, must step in first – because without challenging cultural knowledge about queer lives, both law-inherent and law-exherent solutions will ultimately fail.

25 Of course, this overgeneralization mostly refers to those familiar with what constitutes a (Western) legal system. Those with no experience with (state-centered) legal orders may not perceive of these alternatives to the existing system as innovative or even particularly rebellious.

Disentangling Cultural Knowledge about Rights

Similar to what has been claimed in the presiding chapters, queering takes place on the premise of questioning, de-constructing and re-constructing. As illustrated by the analysis of law's and culture's entanglements (see Chapter IV), one needs to break through established pattern of thinking and to question socioculturally and legally naturalized concepts in order to succeed at a holistic analysis.

One of the most naturalized assumptions in this context is that 'rights' hold an emancipatory and transformative power, and are thus important tools for establishing and maintaining formal, if not substantive, equality. The sociocultural understanding of rights found in the U.S. American legal context is therefore a positively connotated one based on an implicit cultural knowledge about rights as enabling tools. 'Rights' are one vital concept this book has been dealing with and that a large part of the queer community are demanding. Comparable to sociocultural imaginaries about law, namely that is it an unemotional, scientific and allegedly neutral sphere,[26] rights are readily associated with ability, agency, and power. In this sense, rights are connotated as something generally positive and to long for, although the living conditions for those who do not currently have them may be more than often at least precarious. Additionally, this culturally embedded notion of rights mirrors a tendency to conceive of this legal construct as gendered mirror of masculinistic expectations about hegemonies (Olson "Turgid;" Olson and Borchert).

These imbalances caused by rights may already be indicative of their bias towards power, yet one has to define what exactly rights are before analyzing their sociocultural meaning. While it is necessary to work with legal concepts that are universally graspable, i.e., they need to share a (culture-)specific meaning to become addressable and nameable in legal discourses, the implication of these concepts may not be entirely obvious and thus contributing to a marred understanding of fundamental cultural values such as equality, liberty, and privacy.

In Western legal cultures, rights are commonly understood as indicative of a privileged status. Either one needs to fight to gain this status or one is, for instance qua birth, holder of this status, indicating belonging to a certain entitled group. In both cases, rights are fundamentally important because they demarcate the borders of one's radius of movement – figuratively, yet often also literally. Whether they lay out which countries one is allowed to travel, which places

---

26 For an analysis of this claim, see Siegrist and Sugarman 15.

one is allowed to occupy, which person one is allowed to marry, or which bathroom one is allowed to use, rights dictate the boundaries of one's being. Since rights come with this implicit notion of demarcation, it does not surprise that scholars increasingly focus on what is being referred to as a "propertization" of rights. While property rights are a part of the law, the propertization of rights refers to what historian Hannes Siegrist calls the "expansion, distension, and dissolution of property" ("Propertisierung" 14):

> "Public goods" such as information, knowledge, symbols, and forms of expression are protected under property law with the help of patent law, copyright, and trademark law in order to make them marketable in the interests of private providers. Critics warn against the "proliferation" of intellectual property protection for technical production processes, computer programs, texts, images, forms and artistic products because this would restrict cultural access and slow down cultural creativity and economic dynamics. ("Propertisierung"13)[27]

The concept of property includes more than merely one's house, car, or clothes. It transgresses traditional notions of which objects belong to a person to more immeasurable things such as ideas, art, or services. This tendency to consider more and more aspects through a lens of private property, and to appeal to legal means to gain ownership over these goods is connected to the changing sociocultural role of property, which is, similar to other cultural realms such as law and culture, subject to temporal and spatial developments (see also Siegrist and Sugarman 12). This tendency towards a propertization of rights thereby reproduces the logic behind private property regulations into rights of all sorts:

> If we consider that property represents and regulates the handling of social relations in relation to material as well as immaterial objects, and bundles of rights, propertization means that the guiding idea of private property

27 The German original reads: "'Öffentliche Güter' wie Information, Wissen, Symbole und Ausdrucksformen werden mit Hilfe des Patentrechts, Urheberrechts und Markenrechts eigentumsrechtlich geschützt, um sie im Interesse privater Anbieter marktfähig zu machen. Kritiker warnen vor dem 'Ausufern' des geistigen Eigentumsschutzes für technische Herstellungsverfahren, Computerprogramme, Texte, Bildzeichen, Formen und künstlerische Leistungen, weil dadurch kulturelle Zugangsrechte eingeschränkt und die kulturelle Kreativität und wirtschaftliche Dynamik gebremst werden." My translation.

> prevails and becomes the central institution for governing and regulating action. (Löhr)[28]

The concept of property reveals itself to be a vital guiding principle and force behind considerations about rights and those who hold them, and one of the "key themes of modern social and cultural history" (Siegrist and Sugarman 9). Understanding rights not only as an indicator of what one is allowed (or denied) to do but also as a reflection of how Western cultures value the concepts of property (what or who can be owned) and ownership (who can own), one comes to question whether current U.S. American cultural understandings of legal rights contribute to the maintaining of unequal sociocultural orders.

As rights continue to demarcate cultural space and serve as important allies in what is discursively being referred to as 'cultural wars,' holding rights has been supplemented with an element of legitimacy. As legal scholar Duncan Kennedy states, "rights are mediators between the domain of pure value judgments and the domain of factual judgments" ("Critique" 184), thus stressing the authority rights grant to its recipients' position in sociocultural hierarchies. Within this logic, the absence of rights for queers in areas such as housing, credit services, or public accommodation may erroneously be taken as evidence for queers' punishable, socioculturally contestable, or pathological sexual orientation. This mechanism not only emphasizes legal sexual orientationism by othering non-heterosexual orientations, but it also legitimizes the overruling or curtailment of existing queer rights. Notions of property which feed into legal discourse are thus directly connected to establishing, maintaining, or subverting legal and cultural orders.

Beyond Law's Discriminatory Potential

I argue that law is not *a priori* proprietarian in essence but rather that these implications are socioculturally constructed and based on the cultural knowledge of what law is and what rights are supposed to do. Since there is no intrinsic character of what law is, much as there is no intrinsic character of what culture is, understandings of these categories of meaning-making may differ

28 The German original reads: "Geht man davon aus, dass Eigentum den Umgang mit sozialen Beziehungen in Bezug auf materielle wie immaterielle Gegenstände und Bündel von Rechten repräsentiert und regelt, meint Propertization, dass die Leitidee des privaten Eigentums vorherrschend und zur zentralen, handlungsleitenden und –regelnden Institution wird." My translation.

across time, locations, and groups. Trying to adjust laws with a gold standard in mind, e.g., proprietarian or consumptive conceptualizations of rights, degrades law to a static and inflexible tool which re-produces power hierarchies but fails to respond to changing notions of emergency. Even if, for instance, LGBTQ+ persons reject turning to the courts to get their relationships formally recognized, – which was a controversy within different strands of the LGBTQ+ community during the time of arguing for same-sex marriage with some demanding the right to get married and others refusing to be included in this heteronormative, patriarchal institution, – *Obergefell* has resulted in positive changes for the material equality of queers. While the concept of rights, in this example the highly controversial fundamental right to get married, needs to be put under strict scrutiny from a sociocultural perspective, including examining its oppressive, binary, heteronormative history and efficacy, the material and cultural situation of queer couples who are discriminated by, e.g., their insurance companies, adoption agencies, or bank for not being in a married relationship (may) necessitate the claim for such a right while being critical of the concept of such.

Responding to these crises is ultimately prevented not by existing legal norms but by cultural anxieties of deprival. According to social psychology's relative deprivation theory,[29] when people feel deprived of what they had in the past or what others have, they are more likely to turn to scapegoating people with a high visibility but low social status. Following this logic, the pressing fear of losing one's ability to own or consume results in a seemingly inextricable conflict. While the idea of resolving these emergencies leads to angst about losing resources, this angst bears more blaming, possible exclusion, and discrimination of minority groups.

Gunnar Myrdal's seminal study on race relations in the U.S., *An American Dilemma*,[30] examines the cultural foundations of this "ever-raging conflict" (xlvii) between "moral valuations on various levels of consciousness and

---

29 See Whitley and Kite 312–15 on William Sumner's 1906 theory which was in 1966 picked up and expanded on by Muzafer Sherif in his Robbers Cave Study, and in 1994 analyzed with regard to groups with different social status by John Duckitt.

30 This analysis of Myrdal explicitly ignores his warning that using his findings "for wider conclusions concerning the United States and its civilization than are warranted by is direction of interest is misusing them" (lix) as the issues of racism, social inequality, and discrimination still dominate twenty-first century U.S. American society and culture and have come to be regarded not only as "a corner – although a fairly big one-of American civilization" (lviii) but at least a whole floor.

generality" (xlvii): To Myrdal, the "American Dilemma" exists between two fundamentally opposing value systems, the

> American Creed, where the American thinks, talks, and acts under the influence of high national and Christian precepts, and, on the other hand, the valuations on specific planes of individual and group living, where personal and local interests; economic, social, and sexual jealousies; considerations of community prestige and conformity; group prejudice against particular persons or types of people; and all sorts of miscellaneous wants, impulses, and habits dominate his outlook. (xlvii)

Arguably, Christianity has been replaced in its impact on U.S. American cultural identity by quasi-sacred civil religious symbols and texts, and, for instance, *Identitätsangebote* by online communities, political groups, and grassroots activists. Today, these "high national precepts" would still include the ideal of equality among all U.S. Americans, both conceptually and socio-economically, and personal liberty but also expand to mean ecological sustainability and awareness of the climate crises, and political struggles against inequalities such as #BlackLivesMatters, Women's March, and #MeToo. Stressing that especially these 'newer' values which include ecological and minoritarian considerations clash not only with regard to the American Creed but also with other "valuations on specific planes of individual and group living," namely socio-economic protectionism, sexual hegemonies, and political scapegoating, the American Dilemma becomes a trilemma for those involved but ultimately able to be resolved collectively. By adjusting the values inscribed in the American Creed to include the fundamental right to live for all species while acknowledging individual jealousies not as obstacles but as sites which warrant more sensitive ways of negotiating, the American Dilemma may become the new version of American Exceptionalism.

However, up to today, this ideal remains unattainable. While the concepts that influence the individual may have changed over time, Myrdal's analysis remains highly accurate in its assessment that

> Trying to defend their behavior to others, and primarily to themselves, people will attempt to conceal the conflict between their different valuations of what is desirable and undesirable, right or wrong, by keeping away some valuations from awareness and by focussing attention to others. For the same opportune purposes, *people will twist and mutilate their beliefs of how social reality actually is.* (xlix; emphasis in original)

This reminder of people's intrinsic tendency to shape their social realities may also be read in a positive light. It is this ability to shape, imagine, and create which makes up an individual's and group's power to establish new realities and give meaning to them. This view also opposes culturalisms and legalisms which conceive of realities as indicative of 'natural' orders or merely mirrors of God-given, biological or 'normal' circumstances that warrant no questioning as they are given and unchangeable.

Aiming to change law has to evolve challenging other power regimes, too. This includes neoliberal capitalism and its (sociocultural) interpretations of individualism, liberty, property, and consumerism, gender belief systems, cultural-legal constructions and emphases on sexuality and sexual orientation, processes of knowledge production, transfer, and validation.

Not law or the law is discriminatory, but specific legal norms, decisions, and regulations may be if they are utilized for upholding inequalizing hierarchies. Although this distinction may seem peripheral at first sight, its implications are vital. As voiced by various German legal scholars, most prominently Rudolf von Jhering in his seminal *Der Kampf ums Recht* (*The Struggle for Law*), law is an arena which constantly invites and requires fights, affective, methodological, and even violent social ones in order to be able to adequately respond to and mirror sociocultural transformations. Considering law as *a priori* repressive and/or discriminatory is deciding to see law's transformative and corrective potential only in its abusive/negative implementation, and as a domain which needs revision. This view ignores that law, as culture, is in constant revision and malleable to changing circumstances. Put differently, law's "pluralistic character" (Olson "Mapping" 234) is often perceived of in terms of its function as instrument of power with an emphasis on its oppressive forces, thereby underrating its usefulness for queer activism, and reifying its binary, masculinistic gendering.

Seeing law in terms of power seems increasingly problematic. The ongoing politization and polarization of U.S. American society does not only respond to (ab)uses of power, but it also reproduces demands for more. This *perpetuum mobile* of power drags law into its dynamics by utilizing it to produce outcomes which in themselves again bear the very forces that divide people along the lines of identity, social group memberships, and ideologies. Whenever groups of people within society decide on legal norms for the collective, there will be groups who benefit and groups who are harmed.

However, law exceeds these realms of conflicts of power. Beyond these emancipatory or oppressive properties, law may also serve as an agent of uncovering inequalizing conditions. In this function, law works as a magnifier of those areas in which lived equality is unachievable due to pre-existing conditions. By shedding light on these preconditions, law is able to guide discourses to the origins of inequalities, which are mostly so engrained in cultural and social imaginaries and sustained through narratives that discovering them proves highly difficult. In this idealistic understanding, law manages to stay agentic and able to bring about change without being harmful.

Configuration 1: Towards a Post-Categorical and Anti-Identitarian Law

The first queer configuration is picking up on proposals to replace existing legal categories and de-emphasizing identity-based classifications in law. It is thus closest to leaving the current U.S. legal system as it is. While this book has argued for considering sexual orientation a suspect classification throughout, this configuration rejects the very idea of protecting singular categories such as sexual orientation but instead argues for the need to include the multitude of complex identity sections which produce distinct discrimination experiences (Foljanty 91). Calling for an intersectional approach to discriminatory legal norms and realities, a post-categorical law envisions a legal system which is not beyond categories but beyond essentializing ones. Liebscher et al. describe this mechanism as follows:

> In academia and everyday life, widespread notions of "the (two) sexes," "the lesbians," "the foreigners" or "the disabled" shape the practice of legal argumentation. Similar stereotypes also reside in the minds of those who establish and apply anti-discrimination laws. Conversely, law shapes and legitimizes social ideas about the comprehensiveness of discrimination categories *qua* its normative authority and narrative power. Beyond its legitimatory function, law also has a productive effect in the field of categorial classifications and perpetuates them. (206)[31]

31 The German original reads: "In Wissenschaft und Alltag verbreitete Vorstellungen von 'den (zwei) Geschlechtern', 'den Lesben', den 'Fremden' oder 'den Behinderten' prägen die juristische Argumentationspraxis. Derartige Stereotype sitzen auch in den Köpfen der Personen, die Antidiskriminierungsrecht setzen und anwenden. Umgekehrt prägt und legitimiert das Recht qua normativer Autorität und narrativer Kraft gesellschaftliche Vorstellungen über die Verfasstheit von Diskriminierungskategorien. Über die Legitimation hinaus wirkt Recht zudem produktiv im Feld kategorialer Zuordnungen und verstetigt diese." My translation.

Similar to my argument in Chapter IV about the situatedness of cis, heterosexual judges and justices, Liebscher et al. draw attention to the persistence of stereotypes which enter the legal system through sociocultural discourses and persist through repetition in and invocation by law. This entanglement then results in the legal-cultural imaginary that the person being at the center of a case, for instance a widowed lesbian cis woman as in *Windsor*, becomes endowed with all the essentializing notions of what a lesbian constitutes according to the justices' precedential, discursively established knowledge, made up, among others, of sociocultural representations and medially established templates. The lesbian is imagined by the Court as a certain type of person and accordingly judged; a distinct and intersectional analysis is, while not necessarily prevented at all times, at least complicated by the force of established categories law offers. An increasingly persistent *stare decisis* then applies to both the justices' mode of interpretation and their essentializing knowledge about queer lives.

Legal categories are thus not objective and innocent but already charged with meaning. Quoting Susanne Baer, Liebscher et al. contest that "because group rights are essentializing difference and inequality, and solidify collective identity concepts, they are – according to Susanne Baer – 'no solutions but a central problem of anti-discrimination rights'" (204).[32] Baer therefore advocates for a post-categorical anti-discrimination law (*postkategoriales Antidiskriminierungsrecht*). But how could such a law look like in practice?

One proposed solution to undermine categories would be to establish broader universal rights for everyone in society (Liebscher et al. 212). Agreeing with taking such a human rights stance, legal scholar Kenji Yoshino claims that a group-based civil rights approach to protecting fundamental rights of all humans will be easier to achieve politically than protecting individual group's rights more thoroughly (792–95). To Yoshino, such a universal approach would also help reducing distinctions between social groups as neither would feel left out, disadvantaged, or deprived of their rights (792–95).[33] This view can also be

32 The German original reads: "Da Gruppenrechte Differenz und Ungleichheiten essentialisieren und kol- lektive Identitätskonzepte verfestigen, sind sie – so Susanne Baer – 'keine Lösung, sondern ein zentrales Problem von Recht gegen Diskriminierung.'" My translation.

33 See also Chapter III.3 on the *Bostock* case, which features the appealing, yet dangerous argument that discrimination based on sexual orientation should be treated akin to discrimination based on sex.

found in lesbian demands of the 1970s in which the collective Radicallesbians state that "[i]n a society in which men do not oppress women, and sexual expression is allowed to follow feelings, the categories of homosexuality and heterosexuality would disappear" (17–18, qtd. in Wilton 14). While it is true that "lesbianism, like male homosexuality, is a category of behaviour possible only in a sexist society characterised by rigid sex roles and dominated by male supremacy [and that] [h]omosexuality is a by-product of a particular way of setting up roles (or approved patterns of behaviour) on the basis of sex" (17–18, qtd. in Wilton 14), the current situation demands working with the already heterosexist conditions the legal system provides.

The underlying premise to these approaches, namely that social tensions would be reduced if everyone got the same rights, neglects already existing inequalities, which necessitate positive discriminatory measures to arrive on a level playing field. Further, intersectional forms of discrimination are ignored because distinct approaches to tackle interlocking forms of oppression are replaced by inflexible one-fits-all legal templates.

Legal scholars have come to consider anti-discrimination laws in general, and the equal protection doctrine in particular, as problematic contributors to essentializing and victimizing perceptions of certain social groups. Liebscher et al. describe how "discrimination features" (*Diskriminierungsmerkmale*; 204) such as ethnicity, race, able-bodiedness or gender force those who are being discriminated against to classify themselves according to these features in order to be granted legal protections. This argumentation illustrates both the inherent violence in categorizations and processes of categorizing (see Chapter IV.1), and the legal necessity of relying on already established and shared understandings of group membership.

Approaching minority rights form such a universal rights perspective thus invisibilizes and also inferioritizes minority concerns. Thinking about specific, intersectional anti-discrimination measures, however, takes the distinct experiences of groups and individuals seriously and legally negotiates what being, for instance, a Black, lesbian, disabled, cis woman socioculturally means and how existing inequalities attached to this identity may be balanced out by the legal system.

While a focus on identity in law is needed given these sociocultural entanglements of discrimination, identity-based laws and policies are also contested from a postmodern, anti-foundational queer theoretical standpoint (Fineman 6). As queer scholar Janet Halley attests, "queer work will be more interested, descriptively and normatively, in practices than identities, in performativity than essences, and in mobility than stabilities" (28). Moving away from affirmations of identity and towards a focus on the dynamics of challenging, adhering to, trying to fixate or responding to identity, recent proposals to adjust anti-discriminatory legal norms include protecting individuals not because of their respective identity but because of the discriminatory experiences based on their identity. For sexual orientation, this would for instance mean protecting individuals against heterosexism instead of protecting their gay, lesbian, or other identity. This approach prevents perpetuating stigmatized identity categories and making recourse to essentialized, biologistic, or culturalistic notions of personhood, while drawing attention to the practices involved in setting up sociocultural hierarchies and inequalities (Liebscher et al. 217). Post-identitarian, post-categorical law is thus a law that does not protect groups or classifications, i.e., traits that are socioculturally constructed to group people, but one that focuses on and thereby magnifies areas of unequal treatment. This way, disparate impact, that is indirect forms of discrimination, may be easier to spot and challenge. Plus, it challenges legal categories and thus contributes to a legal and cultural deconstruction of stereotypes, allowing for considering intersectional perspectives. Identity political demands are therefore important for refiguring law's normative force. Yet in order to allow for the legal development of more pluralistic structures, identity needs to be used as an analytical tool for identifying and deconstructing oppressive norms, and not as an inflexible category of protection.

Configuration 2: Towards an Anti-Proprietary and Anti-Consumptive Understanding of Law and Fundamental Rights

By upholding the high status of property in legal areas of life, transplanting the underlying logic of property into sociocultural realms, and conceiving of rights as something one owns, sociocultural validations, the economic order of private property, and legal norms reinforce each other. Rights reflect on those (not) having them and vice versa. Even more, laws that reproduce this proprietarian logic beget a sociocultural imagination which is fueled by the desire to become or remain owners; (im)material objects as well as ideas and rights then necessarily belong to someone who is legally able to be granted ownership based on – depending on time and context – citizenship status, gender, age, race/ethnicity, sexual orientation, gender identity, or dis/ability. These decisions over the agency and legal maturity of potential rights-owners make recourse to existing sociocultural hierarchies and established means of categorization. In these cases, law assumes agency over questions of reliability and degrees of own-ability.[34]

Stressing the central place proprietary structures takes on in cultural-legal orders by preferring certain values and rights, Siegrist and Sugarman claim that those structures directly affect the individual:

> those who own property, or those who are at least not principally excluded from accessing it, are ascribed specific qualities, such as diligence, eagerness to work, and the agency over their own life. Throughout history, certain groups have been excluded from property, personal, and civil rights: slaves, natives in the colonies, servants, and laborers, members of religious minorities, and women (especially when married) were considered incapable of owning property because they did not determine their own work and manage their own affairs. The poor were denied the right to own property because this would only tempt them to become idle. The assumption that married women were incapable of managing property independently, responsibly, and efficiently justified a paternalistic society, while the wealthy simultaneously and repeatedly circumvented and increasingly disputed this assumption. (Siegrist and Sugarman 17).[35]

Linking Siegrist's and Sugarman's observations to queer rights discourses, current state attempts to paternalistically 'protect,' 'safe' or 'enable' youth

34 This claim is similar to the legal treatment and non-consentability of trans and non-binary persons, see Olson and Borchert. On the relation between social groups and their historically changing perception as not "eigentumsfähig" see Siegrist and Sugarman 17.

35 The German original reads: "Denjenigen, die Eigentum haben, oder wenigstens prinzipiell vom Zugang dazu nicht ausgeschlossen sind, werden spezifische Eigenschaften zugeschrieben, wie Fleiß, Arbeitseifer und die Fähigkeit, das eigene Leben zu meistern. Im Laufe der Geschichte wurden immer wieder bestimmte Gruppen von den Eigentums-, Persönlichkeits- und Bürgerrechten ausgeschlossen: Sklaven, Eingeborene in den Kolonien, Knechte, Dienstboten und Arbeiter, Angehörige religiöser Minderheiten sowie Frauen (insbesondere verheiratete) galten aufgrund der Behauptung, daß sie ihre Arbeit nicht selber bestimmten und ihre Angelegenheiten nicht selbst verwalten könnten, als eigentumsunfähig. Den Armen sprach man das Recht auf Eigentum ab, da sie dadurch nur zu verschwenderischem Nichtstun verführt würden. Die Annahme, daß die verheiratete Frau unfähig sei, Eigentum selbstständig, verantwortlich und effizient zu verwalten, rechtfertigte die paternalistische Gesellschaft, wurde allerdings von den Vermögenden immer wieder umgangen und zunehmend bestritten" (Siegrist and Sugarman 17). My translation.

and (cis) women mirror the same logic of codifying legal-cultural orders by stigmatizing those who already lack rights. Trans, non-binary, and gender-nonconforming individuals are legally Othered and labeled as non-rights-hold-able by, for instance, framing them as potentially dangerous or unreliable (Olson and Borchert), while using the inherent cis-heteronormativity of the law as precedent for their continued exclusion from rights. Understanding the need to protect the supposedly innocent and defenseless as democratic and civilized value means culturalizing sexist notions of who is in need of (paternal) protections. While minority protections are important, the explicit exclusion of certain groups, for instance trans women or immigrant children, speaks for the hypocrisy and bias of calls for protecting those who are cis and hold citizenship rights. Additionally, such demands legitimize legal endeavors to codify or judicially establish these culturalist misconceptions, thereby perpetuating the imaginary that cis women and young children are indeed 'weaker' or less able to stand in for themselves. This, in turn, necessitates more paternalistic laws and law's duty to become the guardian of those perceived to be unagentic and possibly unreliable (see also Olson and Borchert).

If one recognizes that property and ownership are culturally cherished values which are not established by legal norms but more fundamentally have found their way into our culture and thus are enacted through law and are merely reflected in norms, one has to question how law's proprietarian character influences how we imagine legal realities and forms of justice in times which see violent contestations of minority rights. This observation departs from the understanding that "[a] 'right' does not directly nourish us without the systems in place to ensure that people can demand, enforce and realize the fruits of that right," as ACLU's Deputy Director for Transgender Justice Chase Strangio states ("The Court"). The upcoming configurations shed light on some queer strategies, which move away from a focus of rights as ultimate goal of emancipation and towards law-exherent, or extralegal, possibilities.

Configuration 3: Towards an Extralegal Network of Care

The unrelenting attacks on LGBTQ+ rights, queer-hostile statements by politicians such as Abbott or DeSantis, and the Supreme Court's dooming overruling of *Roe v. Wade* in its *Dobbs v. Jackson Women's Health* decision shackle queer trust in governmental actors and courts. Strangio succinctly describes the current moment of queer legal issues as follows:

> Dobbs [sic] is not a turning point. Rather, it's a reflection of where we currently are ... The current precarity of queer and trans life might be best understood as an over-reliance on legal system wins and an under investment in material redistribution. ... Narrowly focusing our attention on a hypothetical future problem while so many people are under constant, immediate attack betrays the current problem: Our movement is too focused on formal legal equality and blockbuster Supreme Court victories. ("The Court")

Strangio, one of the most active and outspoken litigators for LGBTQ+ rights in the U.S., advocates for a queer legal future which is not dependent on the legal system. This apparent paradox, a successful lawyer arguing for extralegal ways to organize as a community, mirrors how the ongoing politization of the U.S. judiciary makes configurations for a more thorough queer protection by the judiciary rather hopeless. As Strangio states,

> [u]ltimately, we cannot trust the Supreme Court, or any court, to honor the capaciousness and complexity of our bodies and lives. If we are to ensure that transgender youth are not criminalized, that our community members are not over-policed and incarcerated, that our lives are not reduced to reductive and sensationalized headlines about "What Makes a Woman?", then we need to do more than just ask the state for our rights ("The Court").

Strangio critiques the lacking queer hermeneutics within the current U.S. American legal system. His perspective mirrors the distrust in the Supreme Court's justices which have demonstrated their inability to make sense of queer realities in past decisions and are unwilling to tackle the heterosexist matrix underlying their reasoning (see Chapter III). However, there are already configurations how a queer (extra)legal form of organization could look like. These 'alternative configurations,' in Kathleen Lennon's sense, try to appropriate and regain power from governmental institutions, which have failed to offer sustainable protection to queer, trans, non-binary, gender-nonconforming and other(ed) bodies. Speaking of an extralegal network of care, the act of caring is understood as a social practice situated between queer legal, social, financial, medical, and affective needs, all of which are understood to be interconnected. For instance, as current state bills restrict trans youth access to health care (AR HB 1570, which was blocked from enforcement but also OH HB 4, SC S1259, and AL SB 184), and states increasingly move from youth to targeting adults (Abbott "February"), trans people will face forced de-transition if not getting access to puberty blockers or hormones (Walker). These challenges to circumvent discriminatory bills result in higher emotional, financial, and organizational efforts for trans people to have their needs met.

One proposed concept for such an extralegal network of care would be the expansion of material aid projects to a larger number of queer people. Taking the Covid-19 pandemic as starting point, legal scholar and activist Dean Spade explains the concept of mutual aid as a "collective coordination to meet each other's needs, usually from an awareness that the systems we have in place are not going to meet them" (*Mutual Aid* 7). Giving concrete examples of how such an organized, collective care works in practice, Spade refers to "every single social movement" (*Mutual Aid* 7) of the past decades,

> whether it's people raising money for workers on strike, setting up a ride-sharing system during the Montgomery Bus Boycott, putting drinking water in the desert for migrants crossing the border, training each other in emergency medicine because ambulance response time in poor neighborhoods is too slow, raising money to pay abortions for those who can't afford them, or coordinating letter-writing to prisoners. (*Mutual Aid* 7)

At the time of this writing, with *Roe*'s demise and the attacks on trans people on multiple levels, the need to organize is particularly visible for those lacking the material resources to access life-saving procedures and supplies such as abortions or hormones.[36] According to Spade, such envisioned alternatives to the current system acknowledge the interdependence of legal and sociocultural realms by identifying "the systems, not the people suffering in them, as the problem [, which] can help people move from shame to anger and defiance" (*Mutual Aid* 13). The configuration of establishing an extralegal network of care is this closely connected to legal realities, yet conceives of lived equality as in need of extralegal, material solutions and less reliance on courts and the legislature.

36 Being aware of the apparent paradox of this statement for those unfamiliar with LGBTQ+ issues, I argue that it is vital to address these consequences as life-threatening. For those unable to get abortions or hormones, these decisions directly impact one's options for education, economic status, social and geographic mobility, and they increase visibility which may lead to more violence for trans people.

Configuration 4: Abolitionism

While jurists approach anti-discrimination laws with an interest in improving legal norms' ability to protect an increasingly differentiated set of people,[37] Black, PoC (people of color), queer, and trans activists call for more radical transformations. For instance, a central claim of #BlackLivesMatter activists has been to defund the police[38] as a consequence of the murder of George Floyd, the abuse of power by police officers. While this demand already seems radical for many, the police abolition movement calls not only for a defunding but also for an abolishment of the police because it is perceived to be an inherently discriminatory institution.[39]

Abolitionism, originally referring to the movements calling for the abolition of slavery before the U.S. Civil War, finds a revitalization in contemporary activist movements. Today's movements understand abolitionism in W.E.B. Du Bois' and Angela Davis' sense, namely that the abolition of slavery has not ended Black Americans' oppression but only relocated it to other state-made institutions such as the police, the industrial prison complex, and capitalism:

> We can trace a direct lineage from those penal practices to today's policing and punishing. In fact, sometimes, we can even trace the legal precedent directly back to the law of slavery. ... Our abolitionist efforts today—whether they target the police, prisons, capital punishment, or more broadly our punitive society—have to be understood through this perspective: the dark legacy and long history of the still uncompleted abolition of slavery. (Harcourt)

The entanglement of oppressive systems and the diverse forms of discrimination inherent to them has been one of the major points of intersectionality the-

37 See also Cotterrell 100: "Law's interpretive communities now reflect the patterned differentiation of the social."

38 See for instance the #BlackLivesMatter petition following George Floyd's death (BlackLivesMatter).

39 In fact, the movement(s) differ in their understanding of what abolishing and defunding police means, yet they all agree that the current police system needs to be challenged. See Illing, quoting Christy Lopez: "'Police abolition' and 'defund the police' are not terms I came up with, and different people mean different things when they use those terms. But a shared objective among most defund proponents, which I also share, is that we need to reset public safety in order to eliminate our overreliance on law enforcement, discrimination, and avoidable harm in public safety, including unnecessary police killings."

ory and can be found throughout other disciplines as well. It is especially a class perspective which finds way into discourses about power relations, mirroring configuration 1's anti- proprietary and anti-consumptive stance. According to Du Bois, slavery was abolished at the expense of those who lacked education, property, and money to actively make use of their new freedom. Without these requirements to make it in a capitalist society, newly freed people were forced to become dependent on Whites again:

> DuBois argued that the abolition of slavery was accomplished only in the negative sense. In order to achieve the comprehensive abolition of slavery—after the institution was rendered illegal and black people were released from their chains—new institutions should have been created to incorporate black people into the social order. … Slavery could not be truly abolished until people were provided with the economic means for their subsistence. They also needed access to educational institutions and needed to claim voting and other political rights, a process that had begun, but remained incomplete during the short period of radical reconstruction that ended in 1877. DuBois thus argued that a host of democratic institutions are needed to dully achieve abolition—thus abolition democracy. (Davis *Abolition* 8; emphasis in original)

This understanding of abolition as a project of the elites that benefitted more from the new conditions than those who were *de jure* freed, thus an uncompleted endeavor, too often accompanied by the establishment of oppressive and discriminatory proxies is mirrored in current discourses about queer rights. As discussed in Chapter IV, top-down legislation and decisions concerning queer lives are similarly problematic as forms of queer activism which only focus on White, propertied, educated, able-bodied gay men or the demands of the gay (monied) mainstream. In these cases, already privileged and over-represented individuals are imagined to stand in for a diverse group of people, falsely essentializing both the demands, needs, and experiences of the queer community and reproducing unequal power hierarchies in which rights are "granted" from above.

Further, the fight for queer rights seems to have lost impetus after *Obergefell* and risks becoming perceived to be obsolete after *Bostock*. While these decisions have had enormous consequences for the lives of many queers, a society and culture which still operates under the assumption of a heteronormative standard, moral values derived from an arguably anti-queer quasi-state religion, and a neoliberal capitalist logic of exploitation and utilization will inevitably reproduce anti-queer orders. This observation is supplemented by the narcotizing function of pro-queer landmark decisions which mobilize and bind resources of the LGBTQ+ community only to find them lacking in other areas. As Chase Strangio points out, this was already the case when in 2013 the *Defense of Marriage Act* (DOMA) was struck down and continues until today:

> While the mainstream LGBTQ movement celebrated the end of DOMA, there was a lack of movement focus on the breathtaking implications of the *Shelby County v. Holder* decision [Voting Rights Act; lb], which led to immediate voter suppression measures being implemented across the country. Our reductive celebration ultimately diverted focus away from the post-Shelby County world in which state legislatures shifted further and further to the political right and legal protections for everyone became increasingly precarious. Landmark wins at the Supreme Court almost always come with significant cost. In order to reform our legal system, we must examine the consequences and limitations of both our victories and defeats. ("The Court")

Strangio, who was part of the litigation team for *Obergefell* and worked on one of the cases which were combined in *Bostock*, claims that Supreme Court decisions, even pro-queer ones, are only able to cover the demands of some while leaving others (more) vulnerable, visible, and prone to backlash from conservative, right-wing actors. Interestingly, these observations mirror Angela Davis' finding that after the abolition of slavery, other discriminatory institutions and practices were in place which contributed to an ongoing subordination of the newly freed while *de jure* slavery was abolished. Similarly, the continuing hyper visible Supreme Court gains by queers are accompanied by the gutting of rights in other areas and in seemingly unrelated ones such as deciding on states' rights to determine their rules for elections. Decisions such as in *Shelby* prey on the general public's inability to grasp the enormous consequences for even those legal questions which are not directly connected to queer demands, making a strong case for a more thorough legal-cultural education. In the case of *Shelby*, the now legalized practice of altering election rules enables states and local governments to gerrymander, i.e., establish burdens which are particularly hard or impossible to overcome for some social groups which are more likely to vote for the undesired party.[40] Thus, a queer rights project cannot be but uncompleted and in constant progress.

However, what is new in recent discourses about abolitionism is their focus on actively working towards alternatives to what activist Mariame Kaba refers to as "death-making institutions, which are policing, imprisonment, sentencing, and surveillance" (qtd. in Taylor). This claim, which may sound extreme and also threatening to those fearing a disruption of established social orders and a rise in crimes, finds its equivalent in queer activism. Referring back to the historical roots of queer resistance in the Stonewall riots, queer activists have connected the call to abolish the police to their own emancipatory endeavors and the police's and government's roles in oppressing these.[41] As trans rights activist and scholar Dean Spade explains:

> Queer and trans liberation is inextricable from other leftist liberation movements — feminism, migrant justice, Black liberation, disability justice, and more. All marginalized and targeted groups face not only poverty and housing insecurity, but also police violence and targeted criminalization and deportation. All these movements imagine another world where all people have what they need, no one is exploited to enrich others, and we don't live with a violent standing army of police endangering our lives and using resources that could be better put toward housing, health care, and childcare. ... We are abolitionists because we know it is not a broken system that needs to be fixed — it is a system operating exactly as it was designed to operate and hurting the people it has always hurt, and it needs to be dismantled. ("The Queer and Trans Fight")

Spade's argumentation is important on several grounds. First, he conceives of queer activism as embedded in a collective approach to justice. This form of allyship is decisive for advocating for a pluralistic, intersectional, diverse, and culture-sensible cultural-legal education which challenges discriminatory

40 Following *Shelby*, states such as Georgia and North Dakota have introduced new voting bills. In Georgia, the "exact match" bill requires voters to present a form of identification which is issued by the government and matches their voter registration exactly, without "a missing hyphen, an extra space, or a typo" (Nilsen). In North Dakota, a new law requires voters to show an identification with a residential address on it, making "this ... the most controversial because much of the state's Native American population and other rural voters don't have fixed street addresses; they use PO boxes instead" (Nilsen).

41 See Bassichis, Lee, Spade; Spade "The Queer and Trans Fight."

thinking at its roots before these stereotypes and prejudices are full-grown and might find their ways into legal, social, cultural, physical, mental, or economic violence. This is especially important when looking back at abolitionism's history and how discriminatory and oppressive systems such as Black codes filled in where the abolishment of slavery left off. Today, one can also observe how state-made bills find ways to discriminate against queer and trans youth in areas which are not yet covered by federal protections. These instances show how forms of violence and oppression are relocated and constantly adapted because the abolishment of one discriminatory system or practice has not been able to supply alternatives to people's behavior and thinking.

Second, Spade refers to the power of envisioning alternatives to the status quo. Imagining an ideal world, a utopia serves both as fuel for activism and as a force that puts existing discriminatory realities under legitimatory pressure. Third, he proposes concrete alternatives to existing inequalities and offers practical solutions to current issues, thus suggesting an activism that is realistic and non-threatening to those fearing a disruption of social life as we know it. Fourth, Spade extracts the very idea of abolitionist movements: A system that was meant to trigger discriminatory outcomes cannot be trans- or reformed but only abolished and replaced.

Spade voices the need to treat the U.S. American legal system similar to the police, thus challenging a system that was designed to discriminate. But is abolishing the legal system as it is currently constructed really the *ultima ratio* for queer rights projects? Indeed, queer abolitionists are right to criticize the smarmy approaches by homonormative queers whose demands become depolitized when having been legally included into neoliberal, class-based agendas, including the right to form a core family, consume, and serve in the military. As history shows, however, these gains are by no means socioculturally irrelevant, although their value for the individual may be disputed.

Looking back to the development of the Fourteenth Amendment and the Civil War, i.e., the beginnings of the original abolitionist movement, the decision to allow African-Americans to serve in the military (see also the Militia Act of 1862) had not only strategic consequences for outmanning the South but also enabled African-Americans to imagine themselves, and let others imagine them, as citizens of the U.S. While we today know that emancipation and equality have to be perceived as two distinct goals of any oppressed group, the possibility to imagine alternative realities is vital for gaining both. Within an oppressed community, imagining emancipation sometimes bears out of the need to endure inequalities and one's will to survive, thus making the act of imagining both a political and existential issue. In order to enable those outside of the community to imagine equality, however, they must be confronted with the possibility to imagine those realities, and in the context of sexual orientations, challenge and question the heterosexist matrix they are socialized in. While it is too much to ask of those fighting for those rights to educate those against them on the way, both tasks need to be accomplished in order to initiate change.

Without this legal-cultural education, the faulty legal system may be abolished, yet only to allow equally discriminatory and hierarchizing cultural orders to step in the newly created gap and (re-)establish the abolished legal orders in a different form. As abolitionism calls for an abolishment of inherently discriminatory institutions such as the legal system, it fails to consider what happens to those who believe in, sustain, and profit from them. My claim is that abolishing these systems without educating about their inequal implications on the way, without engaging in dialogues about future alternatives inevitably represses negative affects, which then find their expression elsewhere. As Ferguson states with regard to trauma in law:

> [A] story wrongly refused by the law will return in the republic of laws as cultural narrative and, often enough, as renewed legal event. The law does not get beyond what it has not worked through. The pendulum swings back because the culture has made an ideological commitment to social justice and because the expectation of justice causes injustice to loom large. (Ferguson 97)

Ferguson makes clear that reforming legal norms needs to include sociocultural reconsiderations, too. This is also supported by historical developments in the U.S. In a historically comparative perspective, Black codes are examples of how the abolishment of one violently unjust system, slavery, translates into the establishment of further inequalities and injustices when not targeted in a holistic manner, taking into account all implicit and explicit legal and quasi-legal, i.e., legal-cultural, norms connected to the system, and the underlying prejudice and stereotypes which give birth to these norms.

Of course, queer abolitionists do not claim that abolishing is enough; any restructuring needs to be accompanied by a re-thinking, re-conceptualizing, and re-creating. But one wonders why this latter part, the re-imagining of alternative realities cannot be the starting point. Imagining queer(er) laws, queering laws, constituting queer realities and queering constitutional cultures may then become the activistic and academic tools for engaging in re-shaping the legal system. Ultimately, this conversation inevitably translates into a new system by renovating its foundation instead of demolishing it. So, while it may be true that the master's tool will never dismantle the master's house following Audre Lorde's understanding, disowning the masters, who lack the cultural mandate to rule over queer lives, knowledge about queer realities, and empathy for queer concerns, will make these tools useable again. And ready to dismantle.

VI. Conclusion

The starting point of this book was an interest in the mismatch of hypervisible pro-LGBTQ+ Supreme Court victories such as *Obergefell v. Hodges* (2015) and *Bostock v. Clayton County* (2020), and the increasing targeting of queers on a state level and areas unrelated to marriage and employment. Analyzing the compartmentalized U.S. American legal system and influential actors in it, I have laid out how legal considerations are always connected to political processes, which leaves laws ultimately in the hands of those in positions of power. The aim of this book was to draw attention to law's potential not only as an instrument of power but also as an agent of change, to deconstruct processes of establishing legal norms and the cultural conditions connected to them, and to establish Law and Culture's relevance for queer rights projects. To do so, I set out to argue for a heightened constitutional protection of sexual orientation in the form of a class-based equal protection, to stress the importance of Law and Culture approaches to analyzing legal-cultural entanglements, and to examine legal categorizations from a Cultural and Queer Studies perspective.

To engage with these research questions, Chapter I introduced the most important theories, concepts, and perspectives this book works with. Going beyond a mere theoretical and methodological introduction, this chapter is also a positioning among various former and current queer scholars whose voices I aim to amplify in my research. Further, it is meant as an invitation and call to action for other queer cultural-legal interlocuters who wish to engage in the shift from a cultural studies of law to a queer legal hermeneutics.

Chapter II introduced the fundamentals of the U.S. Constitution's Equal Protection Clause and commented on its cultural and legal histories, those culturally emphasized with equality as cherished U.S. American value, and those invisibilized with the Supreme Court's continuous attempts at circumventing equality for all. Revisiting the history of suspect classification served to understand the logic of using categories for equal protection and as illustration how the cultural narrative of equality does not fit cultural-legal realities of minority groups from the 1860s to now. The last part turned to current cultural-legal developments by focusing on constitutional imaginaries and how they feed into sociocultural discourse and thus affect queer realities. This last subchapter demonstrated how cultural imaginaries and cultural narratives surrounding the Constitution, the Supreme Court, and the U.S. American (cultural-)legal system are picked up by political actors and are thus constantly being (re-)shaped and (mis-)used. The efficacy of American Constitutionalism affects people on a both legal and cultural level, arguing for a heightened constitutional protection of sexual orientation therefore ties into this logic and draws on the entanglements of quasi-sacred cultural notions of constitutional law to gain legitimacy.

Chapter III conducted a heightened review of the Supreme Court as an institution and of its justices. By looking at historic developments of the Court and dissecting contemporary dynamics of its polarization and politization, the claim that SCOTUS is an apolitical institution has been exposed as flawed and political in itself. Conducting a wide, critical legal reading of the most influential Supreme Court cases involving sexual orientation in the twenty-first century, this chapter established the biases in justices' modes of interpretation and their personae as such, making a strong argument for a form of anti-discrimination law that is not dependent on a fifth vote and trust in the egalitarian socialization of those on the bench. This chapter also illustrates how closely tied cultural and legal norms are and that deconstructing them may involve trying to rearrange systems which resist reorganization. The frustration and limited capacity to change legal and cultural norms while being still informed and ordered by them leaves this book's second aim in a state that is never accomplished but always in the process of becoming. Evading the finalization of deconstruction by reconstructing themselves constantly, legal and cultural norms continue to evolve, however (un)desired this development may seem. Thus, it requires endless efforts, patience, and discipline from everyone involved, academics and activists, to tackle these issues on a regular basis without losing faith in one day seeing the change one fights for.

Chapter IV set out to examine the various entanglements of law and culture within the realm of sexuality, particularly sexual orientation, and the connections between cultural and legal orders. Having shown in its first part that legally progressive decisions may not (always) contribute to cultural change or even encourage a distinct analysis of cultural, often naturalized concepts, part two established how processes of (legal) categorization make law an inflexible tool for responding to queer demands and for reflecting queer realities adequately. Picking up on this notion of representing queer lives, part three analyzed why class-based protections are necessary as a first step towards an equitable queer legal future. This form of protection ties into identity political demands which see struggles as specific to certain groups, yet supplements this view with the claim that distinct legal analysis and treatment of minority demands strengthens cultural-legal sensibilities and may thus be able to foster cultural transformations through law. Parts four and five completed this analysis by offering a more general critique of law's essentialist and essentializing qualities. Introducing the concept of legal sexual orientationism, this chapter supplied a tool for tackling cis, heterosexist and -normative regimes which are already inscribed in and often invisibilized by law.

Chapter V shed light on some queer configurations of the U.S. legal system and introduced proposals for how to achieve them. Calling for a queering of constitutional cultures, the need to protect sexual orientation more thoroughly has been illustrated from both a cultural and legal perspective. I claim that revising legal and sociocultural norms needs to be conducted simultaneously to prevent repressing legal affects, which may (re-)enter legal and cultural spheres when not challenged. To support his claim, this part contextualized the call for sexual orientation's suspect classification by commenting on contemporary attacks on LGBTQ+ and women's rights. Having conducted a queer cultural-legal analysis of suspect classification's four criteria, I queered the notion that there needs to be solid proof for non-heterosexual orientation's imagined essentialisms of immutability or moral neutrality. Plus, I established that the Court's reluctance to review cases involving sexual minorities with strict scrutiny crystallizes as politically motivated instead of legally valid. The last part introduced configurations to the current legal system as voiced by queer scholars and activists. To do so, the interconnectedness between cultural and legal understandings of rights has been analyzed and deconstructed.

Findings

This book has illustrated the suspectness of categories and processes of categorization, and the sociocultural and legal imaginaries which continue to marginalize LGBTQ+ people. By uncovering inequalizing conditions, law is able to initiate discourses about these conditions, which means relegating discriminatory issues back to the cultural realms that give birth to them. In this function, Law and Culture invites questioning the cultural conditions which seem 'natural' or 'given.' This fragility and volatileness of law may temporally be overcome by aiming for constitutional protections and solutions connected to polarizing contemporary legal issues. This logic feeds on the quasi-sacred place the Constitution inhabits in U.S. American culture and the Supreme Court's legitimacy in the U.S. American imagination. The authority the Constitution and other civil religious texts and symbols still hold speaks for the power and appeal of cultural texts that aim to build and maintain collective belonging and cohesion.

All of these findings support a human rights approach which stresses equality, a problematic concept in itself as this book laid out, on the expense of class-based protections. While sexuality and gender are legally overregulated in U.S. and one should consider erasing sex, possibly even identity-based categories, from legal considerations all together, this route is currently not the one queers should be arguing for, let alone possible to cement socioculturally. As William Eskridge claims, one "cannot go that far, for the feminist reason that sex remains a potent weapon of patriarchy, a way in which women are subordinated in relationships, the workplace, and society" (*Gaylaw* 11). Likewise, when it comes to queer rights and the question whether it would not make more sense to remove class-based protections altogether, an argument made by, for instance, legal scholar Kenji Yoshino, one has to acknowledge that such a transformative change ultimately has to fail in the current sociocultural climate. If one approaches anti-discrimination projects from this perspective, framing group-based protections as minoritarian endeavors and cultural considerations as identity politics merely serves to keep demands in check. The sexualized, racialized, gendered, ethnicized, and culturalized Other remains othered by stressing individualism, arguments about privacy, and thinking about rights in terms of social group membership. This claim is highly controversial as universal rights are in fact not universal but specific. As I have shown, law's universality is illusionary as long as *de jure* law continues to produce *de facto* discriminatory realities.

Thinking about the queer rights project in terms of universal rights, independent of social group membership and identity politics, may thus not be instrumental in creating equal social realities. But what else is there? Intersectional perspectives, universal right claims, and identity politics are vital for sensibilizing others for a group's or individual's concerns, needs, and realities. Yet, basing rights' claims on universal rights grounds will fail as long as rights have to be granted in order to become valid in our Western cultural understanding, and as long as having rights requires someone to give them to us. This call for rethinking rights, not with regard to specific ones but with regard to the concept of rights as such, needs to evolve around cultural notions of law and more explicitly around our understanding of what rights do and how they are conceived of. These findings emphasize the need for "new texts" of minority protections in Robert Cover's sense. Such texts are equally important in the form of new constitutional protections and cultural configurations of how queer subjects in and outside the law are imagined and constructed. These new texts are all the more important at a time in which the affective force of constitutional-cultural imaginaries adds to processes of judicial politization and political polarization.

In her presentation at the November 2021 workshop for the research group *Global Contestations of Women's and Gender Rights* at the *Zentrum für interdisziplinäre Forschung* at Bielefeld University (Germany), Mishuana Goeman quite impressively linked considerations about rights to ecological and political issues by claiming that "if we all got the equal right to destroy the environment, it doesn't matter." A cultural revision of what law and rights entail, particularly in regard to notions of liberty, privacy, and equality, would need a frame to think about these issues and one which allows deconstructionist endeavors to be planted on democratic and pluralist soil. Law and Culture may provide such a locus when it is rediscovered as a hub of practical and theoretical approaches to how communal life should be organized. However, this discipline needs to be bold enough to alienate its academic co-disciplines by opening up and inviting non-academic voices, bodies, and experiences. This way, Law and Culture can enable anti-discriminatory projects to make use of its resources and emerge as the locus of mediating between legal pluralist understandings.

What Is Next

The most recent developments with regard to the Court, namely the overturn of *Roe* in *Dobbs* and increasingly Christian conservative decisions such as *Kennedy v. Bremerton School District*[1] make an acknowledgement of sexual minorities' unequal position in constitutional protection highly unlikely. They also show that queer rights efforts are always in progress and that even finally accomplished rights are not secure forever. Even more, referring to *Lawrence v. Texas* and *Obergefell v. Hodges* in *Dobbs v. Jackson Women's Health Organization* as "errors" the Court has "a duty to 'correct,'" Justice Clarence Thomas' opinion

1 In *Kennedy*, the Supreme Court held 6–3 that a (public) high school football coach's engagement in Christian prayers during and after games is protected by the Free Exercise and Free Speech Clause of the First Amendment.

foreshadows that queer and trans bodies are expected to be even more policed, pathologized, and violated in the near future. The force of the *Dobbs* decision and the public backlash against it also bear questions about the harmfulness of strong judicial review and the power it grants to the Supreme Court justices.

Further, *Dobbs* and state-level anti-queer laws stress the need to engage in cultural-legal analyses of conservative actors' narrative strategies. This will prove increasingly important to understand how LGBTQ+ bodies are constructed as not only non-normative but also harmful, contagious, and unnatural. Such attempts at de-humanizing sexual minorities growingly take on human rights semantics to add more authority to them.

While these developments oppose this book's aim, i.e., to argue for sexual orientation's suspect classification, they add emphasis to the claim that queer, cultural analyses of law deserve a more prominent place in academic and activist discourses. *Dobbs* as well as state-level anti-LGBTQ+ bills and laws crystalize conservative anger and backlash against queer and trans possibilities and thereby directly comment on sociocultural transformations. Having to turn to law as the source of authority in times of diversifying sociocultural pluralism stresses the need for LGBTQ+ scholars to engage with this field, too, and to work towards queering and transing the legal system.

Remembering Fransisco Valdes' call to "introduce[] Queer cultural consciousness into jurisprudence—which has not yet recognized meaningful legal identities for sexual minorities" (Kepros 294), my analyses reiterated and strengthened some of Valdes' points from 1995:

> [W]e have gone from being "queers" and "homosexuals" to being "gay" and "lesbian" and "bisexual" and, most recently, to being 'Queer' ... This progression also has included the construction of a culture, the cultivation of a history, the organization of communities, and the study of the tribe. ... This progression, in turn, now can provide a point of transition from Queer cultural politics and studies to Queer legal theory and, ultimately, to Queering legal culture and doctrine. (350–1)

Law and Culture needs to queer cultural and legal consciousness(es) which are yet too concerned with recognizing only heteronormative identities, whether in cultural or legal terms. Strengthening sensibilities and understanding for sexual hierarchies and implicit and explicit legal orders cannot only be accomplished by establishing *de jure* equality. As my findings show, *de facto* equality needs to evolve out of legal regulations and cultural conditions which secure and back legal orders.

Just as legal and cultural realms are entangled, queering cultural and legal consciousness(es) cannot take place within one discipline or on one platform alone. Legal and cultural literacy can only be gained through various media and research fields with different forms of visibilities of identities, diverse forms of narrativization of events, different forms of discourses, and different forms of imagined and experienced, collective and individual realities. Fostering a legal-cultural, bias-sensitive education has to acknowledge and keep in mind pluralistic positions in order to evade illiberal and undemocratic instrumentalization.

Defining political work then exceeds party politics and expands to include forms of fostering pluralism and strengthening democratic processes in our respective realms. This way, reading, talking, writing, thinking, and loving become the most important tools in fights against oppression. Changing existing laws thus may be possible via proposing bills as a politician, interpreting existing legal norms as a judge or justice, protesting against inequalities as an activist, educating students about legal systems and cultural processes as an academic, questioning one own's role in maintaining oppressive structures as a member of society, or doing a mixture of all of the above during the course of one's intersectional life time. In my understanding, not only are all of these measures beneficial for strengthening an equitable sociocultural reality but they are also mutually supporting each other.

This book has illustrated the strict scrutiny sexual orientation minorities have to face everyday while simultaneously being denied more thorough legal protections. The ongoing politization and polarization of democratic institutions, most prominently the Supreme Court, reinforce the volatility of legal norms and constitutional land gains for minorities. Whether it is female bodily autonomy as seen in the 2022 Supreme Court *Dobbs* decision which re-delegated abortion rights to the states, or same-sex marriage as seen in Justice Alito's and Thomas' 2020 statement about the faultiness of *Obergefell* – formerly gained fundamental rights are not secure. The currency of having to fear for the loss of one's rights is arguably connected to the thinning out of political moderatism and the growth of religious conservativism in the U.S. Thus, fearing for a complete paradigm shift in terms of rights is an affective part of each election.

***

I wished to draw attention to the entanglements of law and culture, and the need for incorporating analyses of these connections into academic and activist practice. The intersections of law and culture are today arguably still underresearched, and in terms of academic disciplines oftentimes perceived of in binary pairs; law is then the rather rational, clear, instrumental part, and cultural studies stands in for the more emotional, fluid, almost erratic field. Here, gendered stereotypes of academic disciplines apply and again mirror how much sexual hierarchies are culturally embedded. However, to both law and culture these qualities are not essential but rather have been essentialized. In this sense, law is not *a priori* discriminatory and cultural concepts not per se natural. It is up to us as academics, and activists, to deconstruct these false assumptions and thus to contribute to encouraging queers to make use of the legal resources available to us while also working to expose cultural imaginaries and narratives which wield essentializing power. Only this way will queers be able to tackle discriminatory cultural and legal orders simultaneously.

Bibliography

"All Families Are Equal Act (Parentage and Related Registrations Statute Law Amendment)." S.O. 2016, c. 23 – Bill 28. 2016. *Government of Ontario*. Queen's Printer of Ontario, www.ontario.ca/laws/statute/S16023.

"Assimilation." *Cambridge Dictionary*. Cambridge UP, 2021, dictionary.cambridge.org/dictionary/english/assimilation.

"Cicilline Introduces Equality Act to Prohibit Discrimination Against LGBT Community." *Congressman David Cicilline*, 23 July 2015, cicilline.house.gov/press-release/cicilline-introduces-equality-act-prohibit-discrimination-against-lgbt-community.

"Equal Protection Violation." *Wiggins Law Group*, www.wigginslawgroup.com/equal-protection-violation.html.

"Equal Protection" ["Equal"]. *Legal Information Institute*, Cornell U Law School, www.law.cornell.edu/wex/equal_protection.

"Equality Maps. Conversion 'Therapy' Laws." *Movement Advancement Project*, 31 Mar. 2022, www.lgbtmap.org/equality-maps/conversion_therapy.

"Equality Maps. Gay/Trans Panic Defense Bans." *Movement Advancement Project*, 31 Mar. 2022, www.lgbtmap.org/equality-maps/panic_defense_bans.

"Equality Maps. Nondiscrimination Law. Credit." *Movement Advancement Project*, 31 Mar. 2022, www.lgbtmap.org/equality-maps/non_discrimination_laws/credit.

"Equality Maps. Nondiscrimination Law. Housing." *Movement Advancement Project*, 31 Mar. 2022, www.lgbtmap.org/equality-maps/non_discrimination_laws/housing.

"Equality Maps. Nondiscrimination Law. Public Accommodation." *Movement Advancement Project*, 31 Mar. 2022, www.lgbtmap.org/equality-maps/non_discrimination_laws/public-accommodations.

"Equality Maps. Religious Exemption Laws." *Movement Advancement Project*, 31 Mar. 2022, www.lgbtmap.org/equality-maps/religious_exemption_laws.

"Facts and Case Summary – *Korematsu v. U.S.*" *United States Courts*, n.d., www.uscourts.gov/educational-resources/educational-activities/facts-and-case-summary-korematsu-v-us.

"In Photos: Protestors Rally Against Supreme Court Nominee Brett Kavanaugh." *CNN*, 7 Oct. 2018, edition.cnn.com/2018/10/05/us/gallery/anti-kavanaugh-protests/index.html.

"Laws Enforced by the Employment Litigation Section." *U.S. Department of Justice*, 10 Mar. 2021, www.justice.gov/crt/laws-enforced-employment-litigation-section.

"Mapping LGBTQ Equality: 2010 to 2020." *Movement Advancement Project*, Feb. 2020, www.lgbtmap.org/2020-tally-report.

"Nomination of Brett Kavanaugh to the U.S. Supreme Court." *Ballotpedia*, ballotpedia.org/Nomination_of_Brett_Kavanaugh_to_the_U.S._Supreme_Court.

"Out for America 2021." *Victory Institute*, July 2021, victoryinstitute.org/out-for-america-2021/.

"Remarks by President Trump Announcing Judge Brett M. Kavanaugh as the Nominee for Associate Justice of the Supreme Court of the United States." *The Trump White House Archives*, 9 July 2018, https://trumpwhitehouse.archives.gov/briefings-statements/remarks-president-trump-announcing-judge-brett-m-kavanaugh-nominee-associate-justice-supreme-court-united-states/.

"Textualism's Mistake." *Harvard Law Review*, vol. 135, 2022, pp. 890–911. *Harvard Law Review*, harvardlawreview.org/2022/01/textualisms-mistake/.

"The Constitutional Status of Sexual Orientation: Homosexuality as a Suspect Classification" ["Constitutional Status"]. *Harvard Law Review*, vol. 98, no. 6, April 1985, pp. 1285–309. *JSTOR*, www.jstor.org/stable/1340944.

"The Nomination of Elena Kagan to Be an Associate Justice of the Supreme Court of the United States." *United States Congress*, Committee on the Judiciary and Unites States Senate, 111th Congress, Second Session, Serial No. J-111-98, June 28–30/July 1, 2010, www.congress.gov/111/chrg/shrg67622/CHRG-111shrg67622.htm.

"Usage Notes. 'Equity' and 'Equality.' How They Differ and Overlap." *Merriam-webster.com*. *Merriam Webster*, www.merriam-webster.com/words-at-play/equality-vs-equity-difference.

Abbott, Greg. "22 February 22." *Office of the Texas Governor*, 22 Feb. 2022, gov.texas.gov/uploads/files/press/O-MastersJaime202202221358.pdf.

Abbott, Greg. "6 August 2021." *Office of the Texas Governor*, 6 Aug. 2021, gov.texas.gov/uploads/files/press/O-MastersJaime202108060890.pdf.

Abolition Collective. *Making Abolitionist Worlds. Proposals For a World on Fire*. Common Notions, 2020.

Ackerman, Bruce A. "Beyond *Carolene Products*." *Harvard Law Review*, vol. 98, no. 4, Feb. 1985, pp. 713- 46. *Yale Law School*, digitalcommons.law.yale.edu/fss_papers/148.

Adamietz, Laura. "Geschlechtsidentität im deutschen Recht." *Aus Politik und Zeitgeschichte*, vol. 62, issue 20–21, 2012, pp. 15–21.

Alabama State, Legislature. Senate Bill 184. *Legiscan*, Regular Session, 7 Apr. 2022, legiscan.com/AL/text/SB184/id/2566425.

Allman, Dan. "The Sociology of Social Inclusion." *SAGE Open*, 8 Jan. 2013, https://doi.org/10.1177/2158244012471957.

Allport, Gordon W. *The Nature of Prejudice*. 25th anniversary ed., Basic Books, 1979 [1954].

Altman, Dennis. *Global Sex*. U of Chicago P, 2001.

American Bar Association. "Resolution 113A. Adopted by the House of Delegates." *American Bar Association*, 12–13 Aug. 2013, lgbtbar.org/wp-content/uploads/2014/02/Gay-and-Trans-Panic-Defenses-Resolution.pdf.

American Civil Liberties Union [ACLU]. "Mapping Attacks on LGBTQ Rights in U.S. State Legislatures in 2024." *ACLU*, 19 Jan. 2024, https://www.aclu.org/legislative-attacks-on-lgbtq-rights.

American Civil Liberties Union [ACLU]. "The Coordinated Attack on Trans Student Athletes." *ACLU*, 26 Feb. 2021, www.aclu.org/news/lgbtq-rights/the-coordinated-attack-on-trans-student-athletes/.

Anderson, Benedict. *Imagined Communities: Reflections on the Origin and Spread of Nationalism*. Verso, 1983.

Arkansas State, Legislature. House Bill 1570. *Arkansas State Legislature*, 93rd General Assembly, Regular Session, 6 Apr. 2021, www.arkleg.state.ar.us/Bills/Detail?id=HB1570&ddBienniumSession=2021%2F2021R.

Arkansas State, Supreme Court. *Pavan v. Smith*. 437 (2016). *Legal Information Institute*, Cornell U Law School, law.justia.com/cases/arkansas/supreme-court/2016/cv-15-988.html.

Ashley, Florence. "Genderfucking Non-Disclosure: Sexual Fraud, Transgender Bodies, and Messy Identities." *The Dalhousie Law Journal*, vol. 41, no. 2, art. 3, 2018, pp. 339–77. *Digital Commons*, digitalcommons.schulich-law.dal.ca/cgi/viewcontent.cgi?article=2103&context=dlj.

Baer, Susanne, and Ute Sacksofsky, editors. *Autonomie im Recht – Geschlechtertheoretisch vermessen.* Schriften zur Gleichstellung, vol. 47, Nomos, 2018.

Baer, Susanne. "Chancen und Risiken Positiver Maßnahmen: Grundprobleme des Antidiskriminierungsrechts." *Positive Maßnahmen. Von Antidiskriminierung zu Diversity,* edited by Heinrich-Böll-Stiftung, Aug. 2010, pp. 11–20. *Heinrich Böll Stiftung Heimatkunde,* heimatkunde.boell.de/sites/default/files/dossier_positive_massnahmen.pdf.

Baer, Susanne. "Dilemmata im Recht und Gleichheit als Hierarchisierungsverbot – Der Abschied von Thelma und Louise." Kriminologisches Journal, vol. 28, no. 4, 1996, pp. 242–260.

Baer, Susanne. "Speaking Law: Towards a Nuanced Analysis of 'Cases.'" *German Law Journal*, vol. 18, no. 2, 2017, pp. 271–92. *Cambridge UP*, https://doi.org/10.1017/S2071832200021957.

Baer, Susanne. *Rechtssoziologie. Eine Einführung in die interdisziplinäre Rechtsforschung*. 4rd ed., Nomos, 2021.

Bancroft, George. *History of the United States. From the Discovery of the American Continent.* Little, Brown, and Company/D. Appleton and Company, 1855.

Barnes, Robert, and Dan Lamothe, "Supreme Court allows Trump restrictions on transgender troops in military to go into effect as legal battle continues." *The Washington Post,* 22 Jan. 2019, www.washingtonpost.com/politics/courts_law/supreme-court-allows-trump-restrictions-on-transgender-troops-in-military-to-go-into-effect-as-legal-battle-continues/2019/01/22/e68a7284-1763-11e9-88fe-f9f77a3bcb6c_story.html.

Bassichis, Morgan, Alexander Lee and Dean Spade. "Building an Abolitionist Trans and Queer Movement with Everything We've Got." *Captive Genders. Trans Embodiment and the Prison Industrial Complex*, edited by Eric A. Stanley and Nat Smith, AK Press, 2011, pp. 15–40.

Baxi, Upendra. "Towards An Aesthetics of Human Rights." *Rechtsanalyse als Kulturforschung II*, edited by Werner Gephart and Jan Christoph Suntrup, Vittorio Klostermann, 2015, pp. 163–79.

Bellah, Robert. "Civil Religion in America." *Dædalus, Journal of the American Academy of Arts and Sciences*, "Religion in America," vol. 96, no. 1, Winter 1967, pp. 1–21. *Robert Bellah*, www.robertbellah.com/articles_5.htm.

Berger, Christian, and Purth, Valerie. "Feministische Rechtswissenschaft." Gender Glossar, 2017, www.gender-glossar.de/post/feministische-rechtswissenschaft.

Berman, Paul Schiff. "Jurisgenerative Constitutionalism: Procedural Principles for Managing Global Legal Pluralism." *Indiana Journal of Global Legal Studies*, vol. 20, issue 2, 2013, pp. 665–95. *Indiana U*, www.repository.law.indiana.edu/cgi/viewcontent.cgi?article=1517&context=ijgls.

Bernstein, Matt [@mattxiv]. "and this is why gays love english teachers." *Instagram*, 5 Apr. 2022, instagram.com/p/Cb8yX4psNFt/?hl=de.

Bettcher, Talia Mae. "Evil Deceivers and Make-Believers: Transphobic Violence and the Politics of Illusion." Hypatia: A Journal of Feminist Philosophy, vol. 22, no. 2, Summer 2007, pp. 43–65. *Project Muse*, muse-jhu-edu.ezproxy.uni-giessen.de/article/218001/pdf.

Bickel, Alexander M. *The Least Dangerous Branch*. Yale UP, 1986.

BlackLivesMatter. "#DefundThePolice." *BlackLivesMatter*, 30 May 2020, blacklivesmatter.com/defundthepolice/.

Blankenburg, Erhard. "Zum Begriff 'Rechtskultur.'" *Kultur und Gesellschaft: gemeinsamer Kongreß der Deutschen, der Österreichischen und der Schweizerischen Gesellschaft für Soziologie, Zürich 1988; Beiträge der Forschungskomitees, Sektionen und Ad-hoc-Gruppen*, edited by Hans-Joachim Hoffmann-Nowotny, Seismo, 1989, pp. 292–97. *Social Science Open Access Repository*, nbn-resolving.org/urn:nbn:de:0168-ssoar-147482.

Boswell, John. "Revolutions, Universals, and Sexual Categories." *Cases and Materials on Sexual Orientation and the Law*, edited by William B. Rubenstein, Carlos A. Ball, Jane S. Schacter, 3rd ed., Thomson/West, 2008, pp. 36–42.

Boucai, Michael. "Glorious Precedents: When Gay Marriage Was Radical." *Yale Journal of Law & the Humanities*, vol. 27, issue 1, 2015, pp. 1–82.

Branco, Patrícia, and Valerio Nitrato Izzo. "Intersections in Law, Culture and the Humanities." *Revista Crítica de Ciências Sociais*, vol. 112, 2017. *Centro de Estudos Sociais da Universidade de Coimbra*, journals.openedition.org/rccs/6574; https://doi.org/10.4000/rccs.6574.

Breuninger, Kevin. "AG Garland Directs U.S. Marshals to Help 'Ensure the Justices' Safety' After Leaked Supreme Court Abortion Draft." *CNBC*, 11 May 2022, www.cnbc.com/2022/05/11/garland-directs-us-marshals-to-ensure-supreme-court-justices-safety-after-abortion-draft.html.

Breuninger, Kevin. "U.S. Marshals Providing 'Around-the-Clock Security' at Supreme Court Justices' Homes, DOJ Says." *CNBC*, 18 May 2022, www.cnbc.com/2022/05/18/doj-us-marshals-providing-security-at-supreme-court-justices-homes.html.

Bump, Philip. "Chief Justice Roberts Laments Having to Do Congress's Job." *Washington Post*, 25 Sept. 2019, www.washingtonpost.com/politics/2019/09/25/chief-justice-roberts-laments-having-do-congresss-job/.

Butler, Judith. Gender Trouble. Routledge, 1990.

Butler, Paul. "The Court Should Focus on Justice Rather Than Rights." *The New York Times*, 19 July 2013, www.nytimes.com/roomfordebate/2013/06/26/is-the-civil-rights-era-over/the-court-should-focus-on-justice-rather-than-rights.

Cahn, Albert Fox. "The Supreme Court Is Building Its Own Surveillance State." *Wired*, 3 June 2022, www.wired.com/story/the-supreme-court-is-building-its-own-surveillance-state/.

California State, Supreme Court. *In Re Marriage Cases*. 43 Cal. 4Th 757. 15 May 2008. *Casetext*, casetext.com/case/in-re-marriage-cases.

California State, Supreme Court. *Sail'er Inn, Inc. v. Kirby*. 5 Cal. 3d 1. 27 May 1971. *Justia U.S. Supreme Court Center*, Justia, law.justia.com/cases/california/supreme-court/3d/5/1.html.

Carpenter, Leonore F. "The Next Phase: Positioning the Post-*Obergefell* LGBT Rights Movement to Bridge the Gap Between Formal and Lived Equality." *Stanford Journal of Civil Rights and Civil Liberties*, vol. 13, issue 2, June 2017, pp. 255–92. *Stanford Law School*, law.stanford.edu/publications/the-next-phase-positioning-the-post-obergefell-lgbt-rights-movement-to-bridge-the-gap-between-formal-and-lived-equality/.

Case, Mary Anne. "Marriage Licenses." *Minnesota Law Review*, vol. 89, 2004, pp. 1758–97. *U of Chicago*, chicagounbound.uchicago.edu/cgi/viewcontent.cgi?article=2096&context=journal_articles.

Case, Mary Anne. "What Feminists Have to Lose in Same-Sex Marriage Litigation." *U of California Los Angeles Law Review*, vol. 57, 2010, pp. 1199–236. *U of Chicago*, chicagounbound.uchicago.edu/cgi/viewcontent.cgi?article=2102&context=journal_articles.

Chauncey, George. *Gay New York: Gender, Urban Culture, and the Makings of the Gay Male World, 1890–1940*. Basic Books, 1994.

Colorado State, Congress, House. Revised Statutes. Title 24, Art. 34, Part 6, § 24–34-601, 2016. *Justia U.S. Supreme Court Center*, Justia, law.justia.com/codes/colorado/2016/title-24/principal-departments/article-34/part-6/section-24-34-601.

Combahee River Collective. "The Combahee River Collective Statement" [1977]. *How We Get Free. Black Feminism and the Combahee River Collective*, edited by Keenga-Yamahtta Taylor, Haymarket Books, 2017, pp. 15–27.

Connecticut State, Supreme Court. *Kerrigan v. Commissioner of Public Health*. 289 Conn. 135. 28 Oct. 2008. *Casetext*, casetext.com/case/kerrigan-v-commissioner-of-public-health.

Contorno, Steve. "DeSantis vs. Disney Showdown Bolsters Florida Governor's Standing in GOP." *CNN*, 20 Mar. 2022, edition.cnn.com/2022/03/20/politics/desantis-disney-florida-lgbtq-dont-say-gay-bill/index.html.

Coombe, Rosemary J. "Is There a Cultural Studies of Law?" *A Companion to Cultural Studies*, edited by Toby Miller, Blackwell, 2005, pp. 36–62.

Coombe, Rosemary J. "Contingent Articulations: A Critical Cultural Studies of Law" *Law in the Domains of Culture*, edited by Austen Sarat and T. Kearns, U of Michigan P, 1998, pp. 21–64.

Copeland, Chris R. "Personae Non Suspect: Sexual Orientation Discrimination under the Supreme Court's New Anticlassification Regime." *Georgetown Journal of Law & Modern Critical Race Perspectives*, vol. 3, issue 2, Fall 2011, pp. 279–302. *HeinOnline*, heinonline-org.ezproxy.uni-giessen.de/HOL/P?h=hein.journals/gjmodco3&i=311.

Cornell, Drucilla. *Beyond Accommodation. Ethical Feminism, Deconstruction, and the Law*. Rowman & Littlefield, 1991.

Cotterrell, Roger, *Law, Culture and Society. Legal Ideas in the Mirror of Social Theory.* Farnham, 2008.

Cover, Robert M. "The Supreme Court, 1982 Term – Foreword: Nomos and Narrative." *Harvard Law Review*, vol. 97, no. 4, 1983–84, pp. 1–68. *Yale Law School*, digitalcommons.law.yale.edu/fss_papers/2705.

Cover, Robert M. "Violence and the Word." *The Yale Law Journal*, vol. 95, no. 8, special issue Charles L. Black Jr. 1986, pp. 1601–29. *JSTOR*, https://doi.org/10.2307/796468.

Coyle, Marcia. "The Supreme Court and the 'Climate of the Era.'" *National Constitution Center*, 29 June 2020, constitutioncenter.org/blog/the-supreme-court-and-the-climate-of-the-era.

Crenshaw, Kimberlé. "Demarginalizing the Intersection of Race and Sex: A Black Feminist Critique of Antidiscrimination Doctrine, Feminist Theory and Antiracist Politics." *U of Chicago Legal Forum*, issue 1, art. 8, 1989, pp. 139–67. *U of Chicago*, chicagounbound.uchicago.edu/uclf/vol1989/iss1/8.

Culverhouse, Renee, and Christine Lewis. "Homosexuality As a Suspect Class." *South Texas Law Review*, vol. 34 August 1993, pp. 205–50. *HeinOnline*, heinonline-org.ezproxy.uni-giessen.de/HOL/P?h=hein.journals/stexlr34&i=214.

Curtis, George Williams. "A Warning from Tennessee." 10 June 1865, p. 355, c.1-2. https://quod.lib.umich.edu/h/harpersweekly/0061498.0009.441/3.

Daniels, Eric. "A Brief History of Individualism in American Thought." *For the Greater Good of All. Perspectives on Individualism, Society, and Leadership*, edited by Donelson R. Forsyth, and Crystal L. Hoyt, Palgrave Macmillan, 2011, pp. 69–84. *Springer*, https://doi.org/10.1057/9780230116269.

Angela. *Abolition Democracy. Beyond Empire, Prisons, and Torture*. Seven Stories P, 2011.

Davis, Kenneth C. "America's True History of Religious Tolerance." *Smithsonian*, Oct. 2010, www.smithsonianmag.com/history/americas-true-history-of-religious-tolerance-61312684/.

Declaration of Independence: A Transcription. *National Archives*, U.S. National Archives and Records Administration, 24 July 2020, www.archives.gov/founding-docs/declaration-transcript.

Declaration of Sentiments and Resolutions. National Women's History Museum, n.d., www.womenshistory.org/resources/primary-source/declaration-sentiments-and-resolution.

Derrida, Jacques. "Deconstruction: A Trialogue in Jerusalem." Mishkenot Sha'ananim Newsletter 7, Dec. 1986, pp. 1–7.

De Tocqueville, Alexis. *Democracy in America. In Two Volumes*. Translated by Henry Reeve. Saunders and Otley, 1835.

Diaz, Daniella. "Bill That Would Increase Security for Families of Supreme Court Justices Is Stalled in House." CNN, 8 June 2022, edition.cnn.com/2022/06/08/politics/supreme-court-security-justices-house-legislation/index.html.

Dietze, Gabriele. *Sexueller Exzeptionalismus*. transcript, 2019.

Disclosure: Trans Lives on Screen. Directed by Sam Feder, *Field of Vision/Bow and Arrow Entertainment/Level Forward*, 2020. *Netflix*, www.netflix.com.

Dregger, Sebastian. "Die Verfassungsinterpretation am US-Supreme Court. Begründungen und politische Ausrichtung zwischen 'Originalism' und 'Living Constitution.'" *Politik und Recht*, edited by Roland Lhotta, Christoph Möllers, and Rüdiger Vogt, 2019, pp. 1–506.

Dunai, Marton and Anita Komuves. "Hungary Amends Constitution to Redefine Family, Limits Gay Adoption." *Reuters*, 15 Dec. 2020, www.reuters.com/article/hungary-lgbt/hungary-amends-constitution-to-redefine-family-limits-gay-adoption-idUSKBN28P1N8.

Duncan, Richard F. "Who Wants to Stop the Church: Homosexual Rights Legislation, Public Policy, and Religious Freedom." *Notre Dame Law Review*, vol. 69, issue 3, 1994, pp. 393–446. *U of Notre Dame*, scholarship.law.nd.edu/cgi/viewcontent.cgi?article=1964&context=ndlr.

El-Tayeb, Fatima. *European Others: Queering Ethnicity in Postnational Europe*. U of Minnesota P, 2011. *ProQuest Ebook Central*, ebookcentral.proquest.com/lib/unigiessen/detail.action?docID=765495.

Eskridge, William N. Jr. "A Social Constructionist Critique of Posner's *Sex and Reason*: Steps Toward a Gaylegal Agenda." *The Yale Law Journal*, vol. 102, 1992, pp. 333–86. *JSTOR*, https://doi.org/10.2307/796779.

Eskridge, William N. Jr. "Is Political Powerlessness a Requirement for Heightened Equal Protection Scrutiny?" *Washburn Law Journal*, vol. 50, no. 1 2010–2011, pp. 1–31. *Washburn U*, contentdm.washburnlaw.edu/digital/collection/wlj/id/5772.

Eskridge, William N. Jr. *Gaylaw. Challenging the Apartheid of the Closet*. Harvard UP, 1999.

Esseks, James. "A Federal Appeals Court Will Decide if Trans Students Can Continue to Play School Sports." *ACLU*, 4 May 2021, www.aclu.org/news/lgbtq-rights/a-federal-appeals-court-will-decide-if-trans-students-can-continue-to-play-school-sports/.

Evans, David. *Sexual Citizenship: The Material Construction of Sexualities*. Routledge, 1993.

Ewick, Patricia, and Susan S. Silbey. *The Common Place of Law: Stories from Everyday Life*. U of Chicago P, 1998.

Fajans, Elizabeth, and Mary R. Falk. "Against the Tyranny of Paraphrase: Talking Back to Texts." *Cornell Law Review*, vol. 78, no. 163, issue 2, art. 1, Jan. 1993, pp. 163–205. *Cornell U Law*, scholarship.law.cornell.edu/clr/vol78/iss2/1.

Fausto-Sterling, Anne. *Sexing the Body. Gender Politics and the Construction of Sexuality*. Basic Books, 2000.

Ferguson, Robert A. "Untold Stories in the Law." *Law's Stories. Narrative and Rhetoric in the Law*, edited by Peter Brooks and Paul Gerwitz, Yale UP, 1996, pp. 84–98.

Fineman, Martha Albertson. "Introduction: Feminist and Queer Legal Theory." *Feminist and Queer Legal Theory: Intimate Encounters, Uncomfortable Conversations*, edited by Martha A. Fineman, Jack E. Jackson, and Adam P. Romero, Ashgate, 2009, pp. 1–6. *SSRN*, papers.ssrn.com/sol3/papers.cfm?abstract_id=1516647.

Fischer-Lescano, Andreas. *Rechtskraft*. August Verlag, 2013.

Fitzgerald, David Scott. "The History of Racialized Citizenship." *The Oxford Handbook of Citizenship*, edited by Ayelet Shachar, Rainer Bauböck, Irene Bloemraad, and Maarten Vink, Oxford UP, 2017.

Florida State, Legislature. House Bill 1557. *Florida House of Representatives*, 2022 Legislature, 8 Mar. 2022, www.flsenate.gov/Session/Bill/2022/1557/BillText/er/PDF.

Foljanty, Lena. "Alternativ denken und leben und ein Ausgleich für die Mühen der Emanzipation." *Autonomie im Recht – Geschlechtertheoretisch vermessen*, edited by Susanne Baer and Ute Sacksofsky, Nomos, 2018, pp. 83–92.

Foucault, Michel. *The History of Sexuality. Volume 2: The Use of Pleasure*. Penguin Random House, 2020.

Foucault, Michel. "The Subject and Power." *Critical Inquiry*, vol. 8, no. 4, Summer 1982, pp. 777–95. *JSTOR*, www.jstor.org/stable/1343197.

Francis, Charles, and Pate Felts. "Diagnosis: Homosexuality. St. Elizabeths Hospital and the Federal Assault on LGBT Americans." Conference Presentation, Historical Society of Washington, D.C. 2 November 2018. *The Mattachine Society of Washington, D.C.*, mattachinesocietywashingtondc.files.wordpress.com/2020/05/59-dchistoricalsocietypaper-1.pdf.

Franke, Katherine M. "The Domesticated Liberty of *Lawrence v. Texas*." *Columbia Law Review*, vol. 104, 2004, pp. 1399–1426. *JSTOR*, https://doi.org/10.2307/4099390.

Fredrickson, George M. "The Historical Construction of Race and Citizenship in the United States." *Identities, Conflict and Cohesion Programme*, Paper Number 1, Oct. 2003. *United Nations Research Institute for Social Development*, www.files.ethz.ch/isn/45931/1.pdf.

Gadbin-George, Géraldine. "To Quote or Not to Quote: 'Literature in Law' in European Court Decisions and Legal English Teaching." ASp, vol. 64, 2013, Nov. 2013, pp. 75–93. *Open Edition Journals*, https://doi.org/10.4000/asp.3842.

Garvin, Patrick. "What's the Asterisk in 'Trans*' Mean and Why Do Some Find It Offensive?" *The LGBTQ+ Experiment*, 18 Feb. 2019, lgbtqexperiment.com/2019/02/18/is-there-a-difference-between-trans-and-trans-is-trans-offensive/.

Geertz, Clifford. *Local Knowledge. Further Essays in Interpretive Anthropology*. Basic Books, 1983.

Geertz, Clifford.. *The Interpretation of Cultures*. Basic Books, 1973.

Gephart, Werner. "Für eine geisteswissenschaftliche Erforschung von Recht im Globalisierungsprozess: das Projekt." *Rechtsanalyse als Kulturforschung*, edited by Werner Gephart, Vittorio Klostermann, 2012, pp. 19–54.

Gephart, Werner. *Recht als Kultur. Für eine geisteswissenschaftliche Erforschung von Recht im Globalisierungsprozess.* Vittorio Klostermann, 2010. Brochure.

Gerstmann, Evan. *Same-Sex Marriage and the Constitution*. Cambridge UP, 2017.

Gerstmann, Evan. *The Constitutional Underclass. Gays, Lesbians, and the Failure of Class-Based Equal Protection*. U of Chicago P, 2003 [1999].

Goldmacher, Shane. "L.G.B.T.Q. Elected Officials in U.S. Number Nearly 1,000, Rising Fast." *The New York Times*, 28 July 2021, www.nytimes.com/2021/07/28/us/politics/gay-lesbian-elected-officials.html.

Goodkind, Nicole. "New Texas Law Opens Up Abortion Bounty Hunting." *Fortune*, 10 July 2021, fortune.com/2021/07/09/texas-abortion-law-bounty-hunting/.

Green, Richard. "The Immutability of (Homo)sexual Orientation: Behavioral Science Implications for a Constitutional (Legal) Analysis." *Journal of Psychiatry and Law*, vol. 16, no. 4, Winter 1988, pp. 537–576. *SAGE*, https://doi.org/10.1177/009318538801600404.

Greenhouse, Linda. "Black Robes Don't Make the Justice, But the Rest of the Closet Just Might." *The New York Times*, 4 Dec. 2002, www.nytimes.com/2002/12/04/us/black-robes-don-t-make-the-justice-but-the-rest-of-the-closet-just-might.html.

Grimm, Jacob. *Von der Poesie im Recht*. Hermann Gentner Verlag, 1957 [1816].

Gross, Michael Joseph. "Gay Is the New Black?" *Advocate*, 16 Nov. 2008, www.advocate.com/news/2008/11/16/gay-new-black.

Grossman, David. "5 Times the Supreme Court Changed the Future of Technology." *Popular Mechanics*, 30 Dec. 2016, popularmechanics.com/technology/g2881/supreme-court-changed-tech/.

Grosz, Elizabeth. "A Note on Essentialism and Difference." Feminist Knowledge: Critique and Construct, edited by Sneja Gunew, Routledge, 1990, pp. 332–345.

Gunther, Gerald. "The Supreme Court 1971 Term. Foreword: In Search of Evolving Doctrine on a Changing Court: A Model for a Newer Equal Protection." *Harvard Law Review*, vol. 86, no. 1, November 1972, pp. 1–48+50-306. *JSTOR*, https://doi.org/10.2307/1339852.

Häberle, Peter. *Der kooperative Verfassungsstaat – aus Kultur und als Kultur. Vorstudien zu einer universalen Verfassungslehre*. Duncker & Humblot, 2013.

Häberle, Peter. *Feiertagsgarantien als kulturelle Identitätselemente des Verfassungsstaates*. Duncker & Humblot, 1987.

Häberle, Peter. *Verfassungslehre als Kulturwissenschaft*. Duncker & Humblot, 1982.

Häberle, Peter. "'Verfassungskultur' als Kategorie und Forschungsfeld der Verfassungswissenschaften." *FernUniversität Hagen*,

IEV-Online Nr. 3, 2009, pp. 1–18. Manuscript of Lecture. *FernUniversität Hagen*, ub-deposit.fernuni-hagen.de/servlets/MCRFileNodeServlet/mir_derivate_00000375/haeberle_iev-online_2009_3.pdf.

Habermas, Jürgen. *Between Facts and Norms, Contributions to a Discourse Theory of Law and Democracy*. Translated by William Rehg, MIT Press, 1998 [*Faktizität und Geltung. Beitrage zur Diskurstheorie des Rechts und des demokratischen Rechtsstaats*. Suhrkamp Verlag, 1992].

Haferkamp, Hans-Peter. *Georg Friedrich Puchta und die "Begriffsjurisprudenz."* Vittorio Klostermann, 2004.

Hall, Stuart. "The Work of Representation." *Representation: Cultural Representations and Signifying Practices*, edited by Stuart Hall, Sage, 1997, pp. 13–74.

Hallet, Wolfgang. "Methoden kulturwissenschaftlicher Ansätze: Close Reading und Wide Reading." *Methoden der literatur- und kulturwissenschaftlichen Textanalyse*, edited by Vera Nünning, Ansgar Nünning and Irina Bauder-Begerow, J.B. Metzler, 2010, pp. 293–315. *Springer*, https://doi.org/10.1007/978-3-476-00205-1_14.

Halley, Janet [Ian Halley]. "Queer Theory by Men." *Feminist and Queer Legal Theory: Intimate Encounters, Uncomfortable Conversations*, edited by Martha A. Fineman, Jack E. Jackson, and Adam P. Romero, Ashgate, 2009, pp. 9–28.

Hamilton, Alexander. "The Federalist No. 78." *The Federalist Papers*, written by Alexander Hamilton, James Madison and John Jay, 1787–1788. Bantam Classic, 2003, pp. 471–79.

Harasym, Sarah, editor. *The Post-Colonial Critic: Interviews, Strategies, Dialogues. Gayatri Chakravorty Spivak*. Routledge, 1990.

Haraway, Donna. "Situated Knowledges: The Science Question in Feminism and the Privilege of Partial Perspective." *Feminist Studies*, vol. 14, no. 3, Autumn, 1988, pp. 575–99. *JSTOR*, www.jstor.org/stable/3178066.

Harcourt, Bernard E. "Welcome to Abolition 1/13." Abolition 13/13, 19 Sept. 2020. *Columbia U*, blogs.law.columbia.edu/abolition1313/bernard-e-harcourt-welcome-to-abolition-1-13/.

Hart, H.L.A. *The Concept of Law*. 3rd ed., Oxford UP, 2012 [1961].

Havelock Ellis, Henry. *Sexual Inversion*. F.A. Davis Company, 1915. Reprinted in: Adeptio's Vintage Edition – Adeptio Editions, 12. Sept. 2018.

Hawley, Josh. "Was It All for This? The Failure of the Conservative Legal Movement." *The Public Discourse*, 16 June 2020, www.thepublicdiscourse.com/2020/06/65043/.

Heagney, Meredith. "Justice Ruth Bader Ginsburg Offers Critique of *Roe v. Wade* During Law School Visit." *U of Chicago*, 15 May 2013. *U of Chicago*, www.law.uchicago.edu/news/justice-ruth-bader-ginsburg-offers-critique-roe-v-wade-during-law-school-visit, accessed 22 April 2022.

Hentze, Iris, and Rebecca Tyus. "Sex and Gender Discrimination in the Workplace." *National Conference of State Legislatures*, 12 Aug. 2021, www.ncsl.org/research/labor-and-employment/-gender-and-sex-discrimination.aspx.

Herek, Gregory M., and Kevin A. McLemore. "Sexual Prejudice." *Annual Review of Psychology*, vol. 64, Jan. 2013, pp. 309–33. *Annual Reviews*, https://doi.org/10.1146/annurev-psych-113011-143826.

Herek, Gregory M. "Sexual Stigma and Sexual Prejudice in the United States: A Conceptual Framework. *Contemporary Perspectives on Lesbian, Gay, and Bisexual Identities. Nebraska Symposium on Motivation*, vol. 54, edited by Debra A. Hope, Springer, 2009, pp. 65–111. Springer, https://doi.org/10.1007/978-0-387-09556-1_4.

Hesford, Wendy S. *Spectacular Rhetorics. Human Rights Visions, Recognitions, Feminisms*. Duke UP, 2011.

Hiebaum, Christian, et al., editors. *Recht und Literatur im Zwischenraum / Law and Literature In-Between. Aktuelle inter- und transdisziplinäre Zugänge / Contemporary Inter- and Transdisciplinary Approaches*, transcript, 2015.

Holder, Eric Jr. "Letter from the Attorney General to Congress on Litigation Involving the Defense of Marriage Act." *U.S. Department of Justice*, 23 Feb. 2021, www.justice.gov/opa/pr/letter-attorney-general-congress-litigation-involving-defense-marriage-act.

Holzleithner, Elisabeth, and Viktor Mayer-Schönberger. "Das Zitat als grundloser Grund rechtlicher Legitimität." *Norm und Entscheidung*, edited by Birgit Feldner and Nikolaus Forgó, Springer, 2000, pp. 318–51.

Huffer, Lynne. *Are the Lips a Grave? A Queer Feminist on the Ethics of Sex*. Columbia UP, 2013.

Illing, Sean. "The 'Abolish the Police' Movement, Explained by 7 Scholars and Activists." *Vox*, 12 June 2020, www.vox.com/policy-and-politics/2020/6/12/21283813/george-floyd-blm-abolish-the-police-8cantwait-minneapolis.

Iowa State, Supreme Court. *Varnum v. Brien*. 763 N.W. 2d 862. 3 Apr. 2009. *Casetext*, caselaw.findlaw.com/ia-supreme-court/1374250.html.

Iser, Wolfgang. "Akte des Fingierens. Oder: Was ist das Fiktive im fiktionalen Text?" *Funktionen des Fiktiven*, edited by Dieter Henrich und Wolfgang Iser, Fink 1983, pp. 121–51.

Isger, Sonja. "Viral 'Letter' Home to Parents About Gender Isn't from Palm Beach County Teachers." *The Palm Beach Post*, n. d., eu.palmbeachpost.com/story/news/education/2022/04/04/viral-letter-parents-gender-palm-beach-county-teachers-satire/7269733001/.

Jackson, Hallie, and Courtney Kube. "Trump's Controversial Transgender Military Policy Goes into Effect." *NBC News*, 12 Apr. 2019, www.nbcnews.com/feature/nbc-out/trump-s-controversial-transgender-military-policy-goes-effect-n993826.

Jagose, Annamarie. *Queer Theory. An Introduction*. Melbourne UP/New York UP, 1996.

Johnsen, Dawn. "*Windsor, Shelby County*, and the Demise of Originalism: A Personal Account." *American Constitution Society*, Issue Brief, Oct. 2013, www.acslaw.org/wp-content/uploads/2018/04/Issue-brief-Johnsen_-_Demise_of_Originalism_0.pdf.

Jones, Jeffrey M. "Approval of U.S. Supreme Court Down to 40%, a New Low." *Gallup Inc.*, 23 Sept. 2021, news.gallup.com/poll/354908/approval-supreme-court-down-new-low.aspx.

Kahn, Paul W. "Freedom, Autonomy, and the Cultural Study of Law." vol. 13, *The Yale Journal of Law and the Humanities*, issue 1, 2001, pp. 141–72. *The Yale Journal of Law and the Humanities*, hdl.handle.net/20.500.13051/7307.

Kahn, Ronald. "Supreme Court Decision-Making and the Social Construction Process: Continuity in a Polarized Age." *Constitutional Studies*, vol. 4, 2019, pp. 155–189. *Constitutional Studies*, constitutionalstudies.wisc.edu/index.php/cs/article/view/45/36.

Kantorowicz, Hermann (Gnaeus Flavius). *Der Kampf um die Rechtswissenschaft*. Carl Winters Universitätsbuchhandlung, 1906.

Katz, Jonathan Ned. "'Homosexual' and 'Heterosexual.' Questioning the Terms." *Sexualities. Identities, Behaviors, and Society*, edited by Michael S. Kimmel & Rebecca F. Plante, Oxford UP, 2004 [1997], pp. 44–51.

Katz, Jonathan Ned. *The Invention of Heterosexuality*. Penguin Group/Dutton, 1995.

Kazai, Viktor Z and Ágnes Kovács. "The Last Days of the Independent Supreme Court of Hungary?" *Verfassungsblog*, 13 Oct. 2020, verfassungsblog.de/the-last-days-of-the-independent-supreme-court-of-hungary/.

Kelso, Randall R. "Styles of Constitutional Interpretation and the Four Main Approaches to Constitutional Interpretation in American Legal History." *Valparaiso University Law Review*, vol. 29, no. 1, art. 2, 1994, pp. 121–234. *Core*, core.ac.uk/download/pdf/303857964.pdf.

Kennedy, Anthony. Majority Opinion. *U.S. v. Windsor*, vol. 570, 26 June 2013, pp. 744-_. *Supreme Court of the United States*, www.supremecourt.gov/opinions/12pdf/12-307_6j37.pdf.

Kennedy, Courtney. "Key Things to Know About Election Polling in the United States." *Pew Research Center*, 5 Aug. 2020, www.pewresearch.org/fact-tank/2020/08/05/key-things-to-know-about-election-polling-in-the-united-states/.

Kennedy, Duncan. "The Critique of Rights in Critical Legal Studies." *Left Legalism/Left Critique*, edited by Wendy Brown and Janet Halley, Duke UP, 2002, pp. 178–227.

Kepros, Laurie Rose. "Queer Theory: Weed or Seed in the Garden of Legal Theory?" *Tulane Journal of Law and Sexuality*, vol. 9, 1999, pp. 279–310. *Howard Tilton Memorial Library*, journals.tulane.edu/tjls/article/view/2738.

Kirkpatrick, David D. "Who Is Behind QAnon? Linguistic Detectives Find Fingerprints." *The New York Times*, 19 Feb. 2022, www.nytimes.com/2022/02/19/technology/qanon-messages-authors.html.

Kite, Mary E., and Bernard E. Jr. Whitley. *The Psychology of Prejudice and Discrimination*. 3rd ed., Routledge, 2016.

Klarman, Michael J. "Rethinking the Civil Rights and Civil Liberties Revolutions." *Virginia Law Review*, vol 82, no. 1, Feb. 1996, pp. 1–67. *JSTOR*, www.jstor.org/stable/1073565.

Knox, Sara L., and Cristyn Davies. "The Force of Meaning." *Cultural Studies*, vol. 27, no. 1, 2013, pp. 1–10. *Tandfonline*, https://doi.org/10.1080/09502386.2012.722288.

Kohout, Joan S. "The Right of Women to Use Their Maiden Names." *Albany Law Review*, vol. 38, no. 1, 1973, pp. 105–124. HeinOnline, heinonline-org.ezproxy.uni-giessen.de/HOL/P?h=hein.journals/albany38&i=115.

Kosofsky Sedgwick, Eve. *Epistemology of the Closet*. U of California P, 2008 [1990].

Krasmann, Susanne. "Über die Kraft im Recht: On the Force of Law." *Zeitschrift für Rechtssoziologie*, vol. 35, no. 2, 2015, pp. 185–200.

Krishnakumar, Priya. "This Record-breaking Year for Anti-Transgender Legislation Would Affect Minors the Most." *CNN*, 15 Apr. 2021, edition.cnn.com/2021/04/15/politics/anti-transgender-legislation-2021/index.html.

Künzel, Christine. "Imaginierte Fakten." *Recht und Literatur im Zwischenraum / Law and Literature In-Between. Aktuelle inter- und transdisziplinäre Zugänge / Contemporary Inter- and Transdisciplinary Approache*, edited by Christian Hiebaum, Susanne Knaller, and Doris Pichler, transcript, 2015, pp. 171–88.

Lacan, Jacques. *Écrits. The First Complete Edition in English*. Translated by Bruce Fink, in collaboration with Héloïse Fink and Russel Grigg, W. W. Norton & Company, 2006 [1966].

Laqueur, Thomas. *Making Sex: Body and Gender from the Greeks to Freud*. Harvard UP, 1992 [1990].

Latour, Bruno. *The Pasteurization of France*. Translated by Alan Sheridan and John Law, Harvard UP, 1988.

Lawrence, Charles R. III. "The Id, the Ego, and Equal Protection: Reckoning with Unconscious Racism." *Standford Law Review*, vol. 39, no. 2, Jan. 1987, pp. 317–88. *JSTOR*, https://doi.org/10.2307/1228797.

Lazarus, Edward. "The Ghost of Justice Powell: How His Cautious Conservatism Still Haunts the Supreme Court." *Supreme Findlaw*, 10 July 2003, supreme.findlaw.com/legal-commentary/the-ghost-of-justice-powell.html.

Legrand, Marc. "Suspect Classes. Defining Suspect Classes." *Columbia U*, Law in Contemporary Society, 22 Jan. 2013, moglen.law.columbia.edu/twiki/bin/view/LawContempSoc/MarcLegrandFirstPaper.

Legrand, Pierre. "Comparative Legal Studies and Commitment to Theory." *The Modern Law Review*, vol. 58, no. 2, Mar. 1995, pp. 262–73. *HeinOnline*, https://doi.org/10.1111/j.1468-2230.1995.tb02009.x.

Legrand, Pierre. "European Legal Systems Are Not Converging." *International and Comparative Law Quarterly*, vol. 45, no. 1, Jan. 1996, pp. 52–81. *HeinOnline*, https://doi.org/10.1017/S0020589300058656.

Lemos, Margaret H. "The Politics of Statutory Interpretation." *Notre Dame Law Review*, vol. 89, issue 2, 2013, pp. 849–908. *U of Notre Dame*, scholarship.law.nd.edu/cgi/viewcontent.cgi?article=1717&context=ndlr.

Lennon, Kathleen. "Imaginary Bodies and Worlds." *Inquiry*, vol. 47, no. 2, 2004, pp. 107–22.

Liebscher, Doris, Tarek Naguid, Tino Plümecke, and Juana Remus. "Wege aus der Essentialismusfalle: Überlegungen zu einem postkategorialen Antidiskriminierungsrecht." *Kritische Justiz*, vol. 45, issue 2, 2012, pp. 204–218. *JSTOR*, hwww.jstor.org/stable/24240676.

Lithwick, Dahlia, and Mark Joseph Stern. "The Political Genius of John Roberts." *Slate*, 9 July 2020, slate.com/news-and-politics/2020/07/political-genius-supreme-court-john-roberts.html.

Lithwick, Dahlia. "Is John Roberts Moving to the Left? Or Is He Just Playing the Long Game?" *Slate*, 6 July 2020, slate.com/news-and-politics/2020/07/john-roberts-june-medical-abortion-moving-left.html.

Locke, John. *Two Treatises on Civil Government.* G. Routledge and sons, 1887. *York U*, www.yorku.ca/comninel/courses/3025pdf/Locke.pdf.

Löhr, Isabella. "Tagungsbericht: Eigentum und Handlungsrechte im Zeitalter der Propertization. Sozial- und kulturwissenschaftliche Perspektiven auf die Entgrenzung des Eigentums, 27.01.2006 – 28.01.2006 Leipzig." *A Journal for Historians and Area Specialists*, 5 May 2006. *Connections*, www.connections.clio-online.net/conferencereport/id/tagungsberichte-1120.

Lucas, Lauren Sudeall. "Identity as Proxy." *Columbia Law Review*, vol. 115, no.6, 2015, pp. 1605–74. *SSRN*, ssrn.com/abstract=2614470.

MacKinnon, Catharine A. "Feminism, Marxism, Method, and the State: Toward Feminist Jurisprudence." *Signs*, vol. 8, no. 4, Summer 1983, pp. 635–58. *JSTOR*, www.jstor.org/stable/3173687?seq=6.

MacKinnon, Catharine A. *Women's Lives, Men's Law.* Harvard UP, 2005.

Madison, James. *Essay on Sovereignty*. Virginia UP, n. d. [Dec. 1835], *Rotunda*, rotunda.upress.virginia.edu/founders/default.xqy?keys=FOEA-print-02-02-02-3188.

MacKinnon, Catharine A. "The Federalist No. 10." *The Federalist Papers*, written by Alexander Hamilton, James Madison and John Jay, 1787–1788. Bantam Classic, 2003, pp. 50–58.

MacKinnon, Catharine A. "The Federalist No. 49." *The Federalist Papers*, written by Alexander Hamilton, James Madison and John Jay, 1787–1788. Bantam Classic, 2003, pp. 308–10.

Mallory, Christy, and Brad Sears. "Evidence of Housing Discrimination Based on Sexual Orientation and Gender Identity: An Analysis of Complaints Filed with State Enforcement Agencies, 2008–2014." *The Williams Institute*, Feb. 2016, williamsinstitute.law.ucla.edu/wp-content/uploads/LGBT-Housing-Discrimination-US-Feb-2016.pdf.

Mazukatow, Alik, and Beate Binder. "Imagination und Recht. Rechtsbezogene Wissenspraktiken aus geschlechtertheoretischer Perspektive." *Kritische Justiz*, vol. 53, issue 4, 2020, pp. 457–67. *Nomos*, https://doi.org/10.5771/0023-4834-2020-4-457.

McIntosh, Mary. "The Homosexual Role." *Social Problems*, vol. 16, no. 2, Autumn 1968, pp. 182–192. *JSTOR*, www.jstor.org/stable/pdf/800003.pdf?refreqid=excelsior%3A958ef96a356d41900c620bc09b0611c5&ab_segments=&origin=.

Melville, Gert, and Hans Vorländer. *Geltungsgeschichten. Über die Stabilisierung und Legitimierung institutioneller Ordnungen*. Böhlau, 2002.

Merry, Sally Engle. *Legal Consciousness Among Working-Class Americans*. U of Chicago P, 1990.

Messerly, Megan. "Abortion Laws by State: Where Abortions Are Illegal After Roe v. Wade Overturned." *Politico*, 25 June 2022, www.politico.com/news/2022/06/24/abortion-laws-by-state-roe-v-wade-00037695.

Miller Act. 62 Stat. 347–350 (1948). Library of Congress, 80th Congress, Session 2, tile.loc.gov/storage-services/service/ll/llsl//llsl-c80s2/llsl-c80s2.pdf.

Miller, Mark C. "Legal Discrimination in the United States Based on Sexual Orientation and Gender Identity." *Nordic Association for American Studies (NAAS)*, vol. 49, no. 1, 2017, pp. 41–59. *Nordic Association for American Studies*, rauli.cbs.dk/index.php/assc/article/view/5462/6025.

Millhiser, Ian. "How an Anti-Democratic Constitution Gave America Amy Coney Barrett." *Vox*, 26 Oct. 2020, www.vox.com/2020/10/26/21534358/supreme-court-amy-coney-barrett-constitution-anti-democratic-electoral-college-senate.

Millhiser, Ian. "The Controversy Over Chuck Schumer's Attack on Gorsuch and Kavanaugh, Explained." *Vox*, 5 Mar. 2020, www.vox.com/2020/3/5/21165479/chuck-schumer-neil-gorsuch-brett-kavanaugh-supreme-court-whirlwind-threat.

Millhiser, Ian. "The Troubled History of the Constitution's Most Important Amendment." *Thinkprogress*, 9 July 2015, archive.thinkprogress.org/the-troubled-history-of-the-constitutions-most-important-amendment-8b5ab2241a48/.

Millhiser, Ian. "4 Things We Know, and One Big Thing We Don't, on the Draft Opinion Overruling Roe v. Wade. Justice Samuel Alito's Leaked Opinion is a Full-Bore Attack on the Right to an Abortion." *Vox*, 3 May 2022, www.vox.com/2022/5/3/23054543/supreme-court-roe-wade-abortion-samuel-alito-overruled-draft-politico.

Minow, Martha. *Making All the Difference. Inclusion, Exclusion, and American Law*. Cornell UP, 2016 [1990].

Mississippi State, Legislature. Senate Bill 2536. *Mississippi Legislature*, 2021 Regular Session, 2021, billstatus.ls.state.ms.us/documents/2021/html/SB/2500-2599/SB2536IN.htm.

Muñoz, Esteban José. *Disidentifications. Queer of Color and the Performance of Politics*. U of Minnesota P, 1999.

Murrill, Brandon J. "Modes of Constitutional Interpretation." *CRS Report*, 15 Mar. 2018, *Congressional Research Service*, crsreports.congress.gov/product/pdf/R/R45129/3.

Myrdal, Gunnar. *An American Dilemma. The Negro Problem and Modern Democracy*. Harper & Brothers Publishers, 1944.

Nagel, Joane. *Race, Ethnicity, and Sexuality: Intimate Intersections, Forbidden Frontiers*. Oxford UP, 2003.

Newkirk II, Vann R. "Voter Suppression Is Warping Democracy." *The Atlantic*, 17 July 2018, www.theatlantic.com/politics/archive/2018/07/poll-prri-voter-suppression/565355/.

Nicolas, Peter. "*Obergefell*'s Squandered Potential." *California Law Review*, vol. 6, Nov. 2015, pp. 137–44. *U of Washington*, digitalcommons.law.uw.edu/cgi/viewcontent.cgi?article=1282&context=faculty-articles.

Nicolas, Peter. *Sexual Orientation, Gender, Identity, and the Constitution*. Carolina Academic Press, 2013.

Nilsen, Ella. "Republicans Are Making It Harder for People to Vote in Key 2018 Elections. The Over Voting Rights in Key 2018 States, Briefly Explained." *Vox*, 25 Oct. 2018, www.vox.com/policy-and-politics/2018/10/25/18010928/2018-midterm-elections-voting-rights-purges.

Nussbaum, Martha. *From Disgust to Humanity. Sexual Orientation and Constitutional Law*. Oxford UP, 2010.

Ohio State, Legislature. House Bill 4. *Legiscan*, 134th General Assembly, 30 May 2022, legiscan.com/OH/bill/HB4/2021.

Olson, Greta, and Laura Borchert. "Narrative Authority, Affective Unreliability, and Transing Law." *The Research Handbook in Law and Literature*, edited by Peter Goodrich, Daniela Gandorfer, Cecilia Gebruers, Edward Elgar Publishing, 2022, pp. 378–400.

Olson, Greta, and Sarah Copland. "Towards a Politics of Form." The European Journal of the Study of English, vol 20, no. 3, special issue on "The Politics of Form," 2016, pp. 207–21. *Tanfonline*, www.tandfonline.com/eprint/gGChCZ6u6zMJrK6bZFEW/full.

Olson, Greta, and Sonja Schillings. "On Un-Doing Law." *On_Culture: The Open Journal for the Study of Culture*, edited by Greta Olson and Sonja Schillings, issue 3, Summer 2017, n. pag. *On_Culture*, https://doi.org/10.22029/oc.2017.1195.

Olson, Greta. "Futures of Law and Literature. A Preliminary Overview from a Culturalist Perspective." *Recht und Literatur im Zwischenraum / Law and Litera-*

ture In-Between. Aktuelle inter- und transdisziplinäre Zugänge / Contemporary Inter- and Transdisciplinary Approache, edited by Christian Hiebaum, Susanne Knaller, and Doris Pichler, transcript, 2015, pp. 37–69.

Olson, Greta. "Introduction. Mapping the Pluralist Character of Cultural Approaches to Law." German Law Journal, vol. 18, no. 2, 2017, pp. 233–54. German Law Journal, https://www.cambridge.org/core/journals/german-law-journal/article/introduction-mapping-the-pluralist-character-of-cultural-approaches-to-law/9F26A6A3B2BE90D8265B6477C843101F.

Olson, Greta. "Law is Not Turgid and Literature Not Soft and Fleshy: Gendering and Heteronormativity in Law and Literature Scholarship." *Australian Feminist Law Journal*, vol. 36, 2012, pp. 65–86. *SSRN*, ssrn.com/abstract=2174937.

Olson, Greta. "Narration and Narrative in Legal Discourse." *The Living Handbook of Narratology*, edited by Peter Hühn et al., Hamburg U, Jan. 2014. *Hamburg U*, www.lhn.uni-hamburg.de/node/113.html.

Olson, Greta. *From Law and Literature to Legality and Affect*. Oxford UP, 2022.

Orange Is the New Black. Created by Jenji Kohan, *Lionsgate Television*, 2013–2019. *Netflix*, www.netflix.com.

Perry, Michael J. "Modern Equal Protection: A Conceptualization and Appraisal." *Columbia Law Review*, vol. 79, no. 6, October 1979, pp. 1023–84. *JSTOR*, https://doi.org/10.2307/1121988.

Pollvogt, Susannah W. "Beyond Suspect Classifications." Journal of Constitutional Law, vol. 16, issue 3, Feb. 2017, pp. 739–804. *Legal Scholarship Repository U of Pennsylvania*, scholarship.law.upenn.edu/cgi/viewcontent.cgi?referer=&httpsredir=1&article=1519&context=jcl.

Pose. Created by Ryan Murphy, Brad Falchuk, and Steven Canals, *20th Television/Disney-ABC Domestic Television*, 2018-present. *Netflix*, www.netflix.com.

Posner, Richard. *Law and Literature: A Misunderstood Relation*. Harvard UP, 1988.

Posner, Richard. *Sex and Reason*. Harvard UP, 1992.

Posner, Richard. "The Radical Feminist Critique of *Sex and Reason*." *Connecticut Law Review*, vol. 25, 1992, pp. 515–32. *U of Chicago*, chicagounbound.uchicago.edu/cgi/viewcontent.cgi?referer=&httpsredir=1&article=6192&context=journal_articles.

Post, Robert, and Reva Siegel. "Roe Rage: Democratic Constitutionalism and Backlash." *Harvard Civil Rights-Civil Liberties Law Review*, vol. 42, no.2, 2007, pp. 373–433. *Yale*, law.yale.edu/sites/default/files/documents/pdf/Faculty/Siegel_RoeRageDemocraticConstitutionalismAndBacklash.pdf.

Puar, Jasbir K. *Terrorist Assemblages: Homonationalism in Queer Times*. Duke UP, 2007.

Reilly, Katie. "Here Are All the Times Donald Trump Insulted Mexico." *Time*, 31 Aug. 2016, time.com/4473972/donald-trump-mexico-meeting-insult/.

Richardson, Diane. "Rethinking Sexual Citizenship." *Sociology*, vol. 51, no. 2, 2017, pp. 208–24. *SAGE*, https://doi.org/10.1177/0038038515609024.

Ritchie, David T. "Organic Constitutionalism: Rousseau, Hegel and the Constitution of Society." *Journal of Law and Society*, vol. 6, no. 36, Spring 2005, pp. 1–27. *SSRN*, ssrn.com/abstract=1026437.

Robson, Ruthann. Sappho Goes to Law School. Columbia UP, 1998.

Ronan, Wyatt. "2021 Officially Becomes Worst Year in Recent History for LGBTQ State Legislative Attacks as Unprecedented Number of States Enact Record-Shattering Number of Anti-LGBTQ Measures into Law." *The Human Rights Campaign*, 7 May 2021, www.hrc.org/press-releases/2021-officially-becomes-worst-year-in-recent-history-for-lgbtq-state-legislative-attacks-as-unprecedented-number-of-states-enact-record-shattering-number-of-anti-lgbtq-measures-into-law.

Rose, Katrina C. "The Gay Gene: The Key to Dismantling Laws Which Criminalize Consensual Sexual Activity of the Precursor to a New Wave of Good Ol' All- American Eugenics?" *Journal of Law & Social Challenges*, vol. 3, Spring 1999, pp. 57–87. *HeinOnline*, https://heinonline.org/HOL/P?h=hein.journals/usanfrajls3&i=65.

Rosen, Lawrence. *Law as Culture. An Invitation*. Princeton UP, 2006.

Rosenblatt, Kalhan. "Protesters Pound the Doors of the Supreme Court Following Kavanaugh Confirmation." *NBC News*, 6 Oct. 2018, www.nbcnews.com/politics/supreme-court/protests-build-capitol-hill-ahead-brett-kavanaugh-vote-n917351.

Rothman, Adam. "Slavery, the Civil War, and Reconstruction." *American History Now*, edited by Eric Foner, Lisa McGirr, and the American Historical Association, Temple UP, 2011, pp. 75–95.

Rubin, Gayle S. "Thinking Sex: Notes for a Radical Theory of the Politics of Sexuality." *Deviations*, edited by Gayle S. Rubin, Duke UP, 2012 [1984], pp. 137–81.

Rush, Sharon E. "Whither Sexual Orientation Analysis?: The Proper Methodology When Due Process and Equal Protection Intersect." *William & Mary Bill of Rights Journal*, vol. 16, issue 3, art. 3, 2008, pp. 685–745. *William & Mary Law School*, scholarship.law.wm.edu/cgi/viewcontent.cgi?article=1062&context=wmborj.

Sabsay Leticia. "The Emergence of the Other Sexual Citizen: Orientalism and the Modernisation of Sexuality." *Citizenship Studies*, vol. 16, issue 5–6, 2012, pp. 605–62. *Tandfonline*, https://doi.org/10.1080/13621025.2012.698484.

Scalia, Antonin. Dissenting opinion. *United States v. Windsor*. *United States Reports*, vol. 570, 26 June 2013. *Supreme Court of the United States*, www.supremecourt.gov/opinions/12pdf/12-307_6j37.pdf

Schaefer, Richard T. *Sociology*. 13th ed., McGraw-Hill, 2011.

Schneiderman, Eric T. "The Sexual Orientation Non-Discrimination Act." *New York State Attorney General*, perma.cc/5QG2-5H37.

Schulzke, Marcus, and Amanda Cortney Caroll. "Culture and the Court: The Judiciary as an Arbiter of Cultural Disputes in the USA." Cultural Studies, vol. 28, issue 5–6, 2014, Cultural Studies and/of the Law, pp. 1078–1102. *Tandfonline*, https://doi.org/10.1080/09502386.2014.886481.

Schuman, Howard, Charlotte Steeh, Lawrence Bobo, and Maria Krysan. *Racial Attitudes in America: Trends and Interpretations*. Revised ed. Harvard UP, 1997.

Sense8. Created by The Wachowskis and J. Michael Straczynski, 2015–2018. *Netflix*. www.netflix.com.

Sharp, Cassandra, and Marett Leiboff, editors. *Cultural Legal Studies: Law's Popular Cultures and the Metamorphosis of Law*. Routledge, 2016.

Sharpe, Alex. "Criminalising Sexual Intimacy: Transgender Defendants and the Legal Construction of Non-Consent." *Criminal Law Review*, no. 3, 2014, pp. 207–23.

Sharpe, Alex. *Sexual Intimacy and Gender Identity 'Fraud:' Reframing the Legal and Ethical Debate*. Routledge, 2018.

Shaw, Julia J. A. *Law and the Passions: Why Emotion Matters for Justice*. Routledge, 2020.

Sherman, Amy. "In Context: Is There a 'Biden Rule' on Supreme Court Nominations in a Presidential Election Year?" *Politifact*, 21 Sept. 2020, www.politifact.com/article/2020/sep/21/context-there-biden-rule-supreme-court-nominations/.

Siegel, Reva. "Why Equal Protection No Longer Protects: The Evolving Forms of Status- Enforcing State Action." *Stanford Law Review*, vol. 49, no. 5, May 1997, pp. 1111–148. *JSTOR*, https://doi.org/10.2307/1229249.

Siegrist, Hannes, and David Sugarman. "Geschichte als historisch-vergleichende Eigentumswissenschaft. Rechts-, kultur- und gesellschaftsgeschichtliche Perspektiven." *Eigentum im internationalen Vergleich (18.-20. Jahrhundert)*, edited by Hannes Siegrist and David Sugarman. *Kritische Studien zur Geschichtswissenschaft*, Band 130, edited by Helmut Berding, Jürgen

Kocka, Hans-Peter Ullmann, and Hans-Ulrich Wehler, Vanderhoeck & Ruprecht, 1999, pp. 9–32.

Siegrist, Hannes. "Die Propertisierung von Gesellschaft und Kultur. Konstruktion und Institutionalisierung des Eigentums in der Moderne." *Comparativ*, vol. 16, no. 5/6, 2006, pp. 9–52. *Comparativ*, www.comparativ.net/v2/article/view/1147.

Silbey, Susan S. "Legal Culture and Cultures of Legality." *Handbook of Cultural Sociology*, edited by Laura Grindstaff, Ming-Cheng M. Lo, and John R. Hall, Routledge, 2010, pp. 470–79.

Silbey, Susan S. "Studying Legal Consciousness: Building Institutional Theory from Micro Data," *Droit et société*, vol. 100, no. 3, 2018, pp. 685–731.

Simon, Thomas W. "Suspect Class Democracy: A Social Theory." *University of Miami Law Review*, vol. 45, no. 1, art. 9, 1990, pp. 107–58. *U of Miami*, repository.law.miami.edu/cgi/viewcontent.cgi?article=1978&context=umlr.

Smith, David. "Republicans' Blocking of the Capitol Commission Shows How Deep the Rot Is." *The Guardian*, 28 May 2021, www.theguardian.com/us-news/2021/may/28/republicans-capitol-attack-commission-vote-analysis.

Smith, Heather J., Pettigrew, Thomas F., Pippin, Gina M., and Silvana Bialosiewicz. "Relative Deprivation: A Theoretical and Meta-Analytic Review." *Personality and Social Psychology Review*, vol. 16, no. 3, Aug. 2012, pp. 203–32. *SAGE*, http://dx.doi.org/10.1177/1088868311430825.

Sneed, Tierney. "Some States Move Quickly to Ban Abortion After Supreme Court Ruling." *CNN*, 26 June 2022, edition.cnn.com/2022/06/24/politics/abortion-ban-states-move-quickly/index.html.

South Carolina, State. Legislature. General Bill S 1259. *South Carolina State House*, General Assembly, 124th Session, 14 Apr. 2022, www.scstatehouse.gov/sess124_2021-2022/bills/1259.htm.

South Dakota State, Legislature. House Bill 1076. *Legiscan*, 96th Legislative Session South Dakota Legislature, 5 Feb. 2021, legiscan.com/SD/text/HB1076/id/2252991.

Spade, Dean. *Mutual Aid. Building Solidarity During This Crisis (And the Next)*. Verso, 2020.

Spade, Dean. "The Queer and Trans Fight for Liberation – and Abolition." *Medium*, 13 Oct. 2020, level.medium.com/the-queer-and-trans-fight-for-liberation-and-abolition-caec82374018.

SPD, Bündnis 90/Die Grünen and FDP. "Mehr Fortschritt wagen. Bündnis für Freiheit, Gerechtigkeit und Nachhaltigkeit. Koalitionsvertrag 2021–2025."

SPD, 24 November 2021, www.spd.de/fileadmin/Dokumente/Koalitionsvertrag/Koalitionsvertrag_2021-2025.pdf.

Spinoza, Baruch. *The Ethics*. Classy Publishing, 2023 [1677].

Spivak, Gayatri Chakravorty. *In Other Worlds. Essays in Cultural Politics*. Routledge, 1988.

Steel, Alex, et al. "Critical Legal Reading: The Elements, Strategies and Dispositions Needed to Master this Essential Skill." *Legal Education Review*, vol. 26, issue 1, art. 9, 2016, pp. 187–213. *Bond U E-Publications*, epublications.bond.edu.au/ler/vol26/iss1/9/.

Steel, Alex. "Intertextuality and Legal Judgements." *Macarthur Law Review*, vol. 2, 1998, pp. 87–108. *Australasian Legal Information Institute*, www5.austlii.edu.au/au/journals/MacarthurLawRw/1998/5.pdf.

Stein, Edward. Forms of Desire. Sexual Orientation and the Social Constructionist Controversy. Routledge, 1992.

Stewart, Chuck. *Homosexuality and the Law. A Dictionary*. Contemporary Legal Issues, ABC Clio, 2001.

Stone, Geoffrey R. "The Supreme Court in the 21st Century." *Daedalus* vol. 142, no. 2, Spring 2013, pp. 36–48. *American Academy of Arts & Sciences*, www.amacad.org/publication/supreme-court-21st-century.

Stone, Geoffrey R. *Sex and the Constitution. Sex, Religion, and Law from America's Origins to the Twenty-First Century*. Liveright Publishing Corporation/W.W. Norton & Company, 2017.

Strangio, Chase. "The Court Won't Free Us – Only We Can." *Them.us*, 1 June 2022, www.them.us/story/chase-strangio-supreme-court-queer-rights.

Strangio, Chase. "What President Biden's LGBTQ Executive Order Does and Doesn't Do." *American Civil Liberties Union*, 21 Jan. 2021, www.aclu.org/news/lgbt-rights/what-president-bidens-lgbtq-executive-order-does-and-doesnt-do/.

Strauss, Marcy. "Reevaluating Suspect Classifications." *Seattle University Law Review*, vol. 35, Fall 2011, pp. 135–74. *Seattle U*, digitalcommons.law.seattleu.edu/cgi/viewcontent.cgi?article=2059&context=sulr.

Stychin, Carl F. *Law's Desire. Sexuality and the Limits of Justice*. Routledge, 1995.

Sunstein, Cass R. "Sexual Orientation and the Constitution: A Note on the Relationship between Due Process and Equal Protection Essays." *U of Chicago Law Review*, vol. 55, 1988, pp. 1161–180. *U of Chicago*, chicagounbound.uchicago.edu/cgi/viewcontent.cgi?article=12451&context=journal_articles.

Tajfel, Henri, et al. "Social Categorization and Intergroup Behaviour." *European Journal of Social Psychology*, vol. 1, issue 2, 1971, pp.149-78. *Wiley Online Library*, https://doi.org/10.1002/ejsp.2420010202/epdf.

Tajfel, Henri. "Cognitive Aspects of Prejudice." *Journal of Social Issues*, vol. 25, issue 4, 1969, pp. 79–97. *APA Psyc Net*, https://doi.org/10.1111/j.1540-4560.1969.tb00620.x.

Taylor, Keeanga-Yamahtta. "The Emerging Movement for Police and Prison Abolition." *The New Yorker*, 7 May 2021, www.newyorker.com/news/our-columnists/the-emerging-movement-for-police-and-prison-abolition.

Texas State, Legislature. Senate Bill 8. *Texas Legislature Online*, 87th Legislature Third Called Session, 19 May 2021, capitol.texas.gov/tlodocs/87R/billtext/pdf/SB00008H.pdf.

Texas State, Legislature. Senate Bill 1646. *Texas Legislature Online*, 87th Legislature, 3 May 2021, capitol.texas.gov/tlodocs/87R/billtext/html/SB01646S.htm.

The Constitution of the United States: A Transcription [1788]. National Archives, U.S. National Archives and Records Administration, 7 Oct. 2021, www.archives.gov/founding-docs/constitution-transcript.

The Equality Act. *The Human Rights Campaign*, 28 Apr. 2021, www.hrc.org/resources/the-equality-act.

Thiele, Alexander. *Der konstituierte Staat. Eine Verfassungsgeschichte der Neuzeit*. Campus, 2021.

Thomas, Clarence and Samuel A. Alito. Statement. *Kim Davis v. David Ermold*, vol. 592, 5 Oct. 2020. *Supreme Court of the United States*, www.supremecourt.gov/opinions/20pdf/19-926_5hdk.pdf.

Trump, Donald. "Donald Trump Georgia Rally Transcript Before Senate Runoff Elections December 5." *Rev*, 6 Dec. 2020, www.rev.com/blog/transcripts/donald-trump-georgia-rally-transcript-before-senate-runoff-elections-december-5. Transcript.

Tussman, Joseph, and Jacobus tenBroek. "The Equal Protection of the Laws." *California Law Review*, vol. 37, issue 3, Sept. 1949, pp. 341–81. *Berkeley Law U of California*, https://doi.org/10.15779/Z38PN4S.

United States Code. 26 U.S.C.A. Sec. 214(a). An Act to Amend the Internal Revenue Code of 1954. *U.S. Government Publishing Office*, www.govinfo.gov/content/pkg/STATUTE-78/pdf/STATUTE-78-Pg19.pdf. Public Law 88–272, 78 Stat., passed 26 Feb. 1964.

United States, Congress, House. Title VII of the Civil Rights Act of 1964. *U.S. Equal Employment Opportunity Commission*, www.eeoc.gov/statutes/title-v

ii-civil-rights-act-1964. 88th Congress, Public Law 88–352, 78 Stat. 241, passed 19 June 1964.

United States, District Court, S.D. Ohio, Eastern Division. *Ray v. McCloud.* 507 F. Supp. 3d 925 (S.D. Ohio) (2020). *Casetext,* casetext.com/case/ray-v-mccloud-1.

United States, District Court Western District of Washington at Seattle. *Karnoski v. Trump.* 2:17-cv-01297-MJP (2018). *Justia U.S. Supreme Court Center,* Justia, law.justia.com/cases/federal/district-courts/washington/wawdce/2:2017cv01297/249424/299/.

United States, Executive Office of the President [Joseph R. Biden Jr.]. Executive Order on Enabling All Qualified Americans to Serve Their Country in Uniform ["Enabling"]. 25 Jan. 2021. *The White House,* 25 Jan. 2021, www.whitehouse.gov/briefing-room/presidential-actions/2021/01/25/executive-order-on-enabling-all-qualified-americans-to-serve-their-country-in-uniform/.

United States, Executive Office of the President [Joseph R. Biden Jr.]. Executive Order on Preventing and Combating Discrimination on the Basis of Gender Identity or Sexual Orientation. 25 Jan. 2021. *The White House,* 20 Jan. 2021, www.whitehouse.gov/briefing-room/presidential-actions/2021/01/20/executive-order-preventing-and-combating-discrimination-on-basis-of-gender-identity-or-sexual-orientation/.

United States, Supreme Court. *Altitude Express, Inc. v. Zarda* [decided in *Bostock v. Clayton County*]. 590 U.S. ___ (2020). *Supreme Court of the United States,* www.supremecourt.gov/opinions/19pdf/17-1618_hfci.pdf.

United States, Supreme Court. *Batson v. Kentucky.* 476 U.S. 79 (1986). *Justia U.S. Supreme Court Center,* Justia, supreme.justia.com/cases/federal/us/476/79/#tab-opinion-1956654.

United States, Supreme Court. *Bolling v. Sharpe.* 347 U.S. 497 (1954). *Justia U.S. Supreme Court Center,* Justia, supreme.justia.com/cases/federal/us/347/497/.

United States, Supreme Court. *Bostock v. Clayton County.* 590 U.S. ___ (2020). *Supreme Court of the United States,* www.supremecourt.gov/opinions/19pdf/17-1618_hfci.pdf.

United States, Supreme Court. *Bowers v. Hardwick.* 478 U.S. 186 (1986). *Legal Information Institute,* Cornell U Law School, www.law.cornell.edu/supremecourt/text/478/186.

United States, Supreme Court. *Brown v. Board of Education. 347 U.S. 483 (1954). Legal Information Institute,* Cornell U Law School, www.law.cornell.edu/supremecourt/text/347/483.

United States, Supreme Court. *Bucklew v. Precythe*. 587 U.S. ___ (2019). *Justia U.S. Supreme Court Center,* Justia, supreme.justia.com/cases/federal/us/587/17-8151/#tab-opinion-4074719.

United States, Supreme Court. *Burnet v. Coronado Oil & Gas Co.* 285 U.S. 393 (1932). *Justia U.S. Supreme Court Center,* Justia, supreme.justia.com/cases/federal/us/285/393/.

United States, Supreme Court. *Charles E. Moritz v. Commissioner of Internal Revenue*. 469 F.2d 466 (1972). *Justia U.S. Supreme Court Center,* Justia, law.justia.com/cases/federal/appellate-courts/F2/469/466/79852/.

United States, Supreme Court. *Cohen v. Trump,* No. 3:2013cv02519 – Document 93 (S.D. Cal. 2015). *Justia U.S. Supreme Court Center,* Justia, law.justia.com/cases/federal/district-courts/california/casdce/3:2013cv02519/426687/93/.

United States, Supreme Court. *Craig v. Boren*. 429 U.S. 190 (1976). *Legal Information Institute,* Cornell U Law School, www.law.cornell.edu/supremecourt/text/429/190.

United States, Supreme Court. *Dobbs v. Jackson Women's Health Organization,* docket no. 19–1392, 1st draft. *Politico,* 10 Feb. 2022, www.documentcloud.org/documents/21835435-scotus-initial-draft.

United States, Supreme Court. *Dobbs v. Jackson Women's Health Organization*. 597 U.S. ___ (2022). *Supreme Court of the United States,* www.supremecourt.gov/opinions/21pdf/19-1392_6j37.pdf.

United States, Supreme Court. *Food and Drug Administration [FDA] v. American College of Obstetricians and Gynecologists*. 592 U.S. ___ (2021). *Supreme Court of the United States,* https://www.supremecourt.gov/opinions/20pdf/20a34_3f14.pdf.

United States, Supreme Court. *Frontiero v. Richardson*. 411 U.S. 677 (1973). *Legal Information Institute,* Cornell U Law School, www.law.cornell.edu/supremecourt/text/411/677.

United States, Supreme Court. *Graham v. Richardson*. 403 U.S. 365 (1971). *Justia U.S. Supreme Court Center,* Justia, supreme.justia.com/cases/federal/us/403/365/.

United States, Supreme Court. *Griswold v. Connecticut*. 381 U.S. 479 (1965). *Justia U.S. Supreme Court Center,* Justia, https://supreme.justia.com/cases/federal/us/381/479/.

United States, Supreme Court. *Gulf, Colorado & Santa Fe Ry. Co. v. Ellis.* 165 U.S. 150 (1897). *Justia U.S. Supreme Court Center*, Justia, supreme.justia.com/cases/federal/us/165/150/.

United States, Supreme Court. *Hirabayashi v. United States*. 320 U.S. 81 (1943). *Justia U.S. Supreme Court Center*, Justia, supreme.justia.com/cases/federal/us/320/81/.

United States, Supreme Court. *Kennedy v. Bremerton School District*. 597 U.S. ___ (2022). *Supreme Court of the United States*, www.supremecourt.gov/opinions/21pdf/21-418_i425.pdf.

United States, Supreme Court. *Korematsu v. United States*. 323 U.S. 214 (1944). *Justia U.S. Supreme Court Center*, Justia, supreme.justia.com/cases/federal/us/323/214/#tab-opinion-1938224.

United States, Supreme Court. *Lawrence v. Texas*. 539 U.S. 558 (2003). *Supreme Court of the United States*, www.supremecourt.gov/opinions/boundvolumes/539bv.pdf.

United States, Supreme Court. *Lindsley v. Natural Carbonic Gas Co*. 220 U.S. 61 (1911). *Legal Information Institute*, Cornell U Law School, www.law.cornell.edu/supremecourt/text/220/61.

United States, Supreme Court. *Loving v. Virginia*. 388 U.S. 1 (1967). *Justia U.S. Supreme Court Center*, Justia, supreme.justia.com/cases/federal/us/388/1/.

United States, Supreme Court. *Makaeff v. Trump University*, LLC et al, No. 3:2010cv00940 – Document 404 (S.D. Cal. 2015). *Justia U.S. Supreme Court Center*, Justia, law.justia.com/cases/federal/district-courts/california/casdce/3:2010cv00940/322533/404/.

United States, Supreme Court. *Massachusetts Board of Retirement v. Murgia.* 427 US 307 (1976). *Justia U.S. Supreme Court Center*, Justia, supreme.justia.com/cases/federal/us/427/307/.

United States, Supreme Court. *Masterpiece Cakeshop v. Colorado.* 584 U.S. ___ (2018). *Supreme Court of the United States*, www.supremecourt.gov/opinions/17pdf/16-111_j4el.pdf.

United States, Supreme Court. *Mathews v. Lucas*. 427 U.S. 495 (1976). *Justia U.S. Supreme Court Center*, Justia, supreme.justia.com/cases/federal/us/427/495/.

United States, Supreme Court. *Maynard* v. *Hill*. 125 U.S. 190 (1888). *Justia U.S. Supreme Court Center*, Justia, supreme.justia.com/cases/federal/us/125/190/.

United States, Supreme Court. *McLaughlin v. Florida*. 379 U.S. 184 (1964). *Justia U.S. Supreme Court Center*, Justia, supreme.justia.com/cases/federal/us/379/184/.

United States, Supreme Court. *Mississippi University for Women v. Hogan*. 458 U.S. 718 (1982). *Legal Information Institute*, Cornell U Law School, www.law.cornell.edu/supremecourt/text/458/718.

United States, Supreme Court. *Obergefell v. Hodges*. *United States Reports*, vol. 458, 26 June 2015, pp. 644–743. *Supreme Court of the United States*, www.supremecourt.gov/opinions/preliminaryprint/576US2PP.pdf.

United States, Supreme Court. *Pavan v. Smith*. 582 U.S. ___ (2017). *Legal Information Institute*, Cornell U Law School, supreme.justia.com/cases/federal/us/582/16-992/#tab-opinion-3752820.

United States, Supreme Court. *Payne v. Tennessee*. 501 U.S. 808 (1991). *Justia U.S. Supreme Court Center*, Justia, supreme.justia.com/cases/federal/us/501/808/.

United States, Supreme Court. *Perry v. Schwarzenegger*. 704 F. Supp. 2d 921 (N.D. Cal. 2010). *Courtlistener.com*, Court Listener, www.courtlistener.com/opinion/1440578/perry-v-schwarzenegger/.

United States, Supreme Court. *Planned Parenthood of Southeastern Pa. v. Casey*. 505 U.S. 833 (1992). *Justia U.S. Supreme Court Center*, Justia, supreme.justia.com/cases/federal/us/505/833/.

United States, Supreme Court. *Plessy v. Ferguson*. 163 U.S. 537 (1896). *Legal Information Institute*, Cornell U Law School, www.law.cornell.edu/supremecourt/text/163/537.

United States, Supreme Court. *Plyler v. Doe*. 457 U.S. 202 (1982). *Justia U.S. Supreme Court Center*, Justia, supreme.justia.com/cases/federal/us/457/202/.

United States, Supreme Court. *Raffaelli v. Committee of Bar Examiners*. 7 Cal. 3d 288. 24 May 1972. *Justia U.S. Supreme Court Center*, Justia, law.justia.com/cases/california/supreme-court/3d/7/288.html.

United States, Supreme Court. *Railway Express Agency, Inc. v. New York*. 336 U.S. 106 (1949). *Justia U.S. Supreme Court Center*, Justia, supreme.justia.com/cases/federal/us/336/106/.

United States, Supreme Court. *Reed v. Reed*. 404 U.S. 71 (1971). *Justia U.S. Supreme Court Center*, Justia, supreme.justia.com/cases/federal/us/404/71/.

United States, Supreme Court. *Roe v. Wade*. 410 U.S. 113 (1973). *Justia U.S. Supreme Court Center*, Justia, supreme.justia.com/cases/federal/us/410/113/#tab-opinion-1950136.

United States, Supreme Court. *Romer v. Evans*. 517 U.S. 620 (1996). *Legal Information Institute*, Cornell U Law School, www.law.cornell.edu/supremecourt/text/517/620.

United States, Supreme Court. Royster Guano Co. v. Virginia. 253 U. S. 412 (1920). *Justia U.S. Supreme Court Center*, Justia, supreme.justia.com/cases/federal/us/253/412/.

United States, Supreme Court. *San Antonio Independent School District v. Rodriguez*. 411 US 1 (1973). *Justia U.S. Supreme Court Center*, Justia, supreme.justia.com/cases/federal/us/411/1/.

United States, Supreme Court. *Slaughter-House Cases*. 83 U.S. (16 Wall.) 36 (1872). *Justia U.S. Supreme Court Center*, Justia, supreme.justia.com/cases/federal/us/83/36/#tab-opinion-1967657.

United States, Supreme Court. *Sony Corp. of America v. Universal City Studios, Inc.* 464 U.S. 417 (1984). *Justia U.S. Supreme Court Center*, Justia, supreme.justia.com/cases/federal/us/464/417/.

United States, Supreme Court. *United States v. Carolene Products Co.* 304 U.S. 144 (1938). *Legal Information Institute*, Cornell U Law School, www.law.cornell.edu/supremecourt/text/304/144.

United States, Supreme Court. *United States v. Virginia et al. United States Reports*, vol. 518, 26 June 1996, pp. 515–603. *Library of Congress*, tile.loc.gov/storage-services/service/ll/usrep/usrep518/usrep518515/usrep518515.pdf.

United States, Supreme Court. *United States v. Windsor*. 570 U.S. 744 (2013). *Legal Information Institute*, Cornell U Law School, supreme.justia.com/cases/federal/us/570/744/#tab-opinion-1970765.

United States, Supreme Court. *Washington v. Davis*. 426 U.S. 229 (1976). *Justia U.S. Supreme Court Center*, Justia, supreme.justia.com/cases/federal/us/426/229/#tab-opinion-1951760.

United States, Supreme Court. *Weber v. Aetna Cas. & Sur.* Co. 406 U.S. 164 (1972). *Justia U.S. Supreme Court Center*, Justia, supreme.justia.com/cases/federal/us/406/164/.

United States, Supreme Court. *Yick Wo v. Hopkins*. *United States Reports*, vol. 118, 10 May 1886, pp. 356–374. *Library of Congress*, tile.loc.gov/storage-services/service/ll/usrep/usrep118/usrep118356/usrep118356.pdf.

United States, Supreme Court. Vasquez v. Hillery, 474 U. S. 254 (1986). *Justia U.S. Supreme Court Center*, Justia, supreme.justia.com/cases/federal/us/474/254/.

Vaihinger, Hans. *Die Philosophie des Als Ob*. VDM Verlag Dr. Müller, 2007.

Valdes, Francisco. “Queers, Sissies, Dykes, and Tomboys: Deconstructing the Conflation of ‘Sex,’ ‘Gender,’ and ‘Sexual Orientation’ in Euro-American Law and Society.” *California Law Review* vol. 83, no. 1, Jan. 1995, pp. 1–377. *JSTOR*, https://doi.org/10.2307/3480882.

von Jhering, Rudolf. *Der Kampf ums Recht*. Haufe, 1992 [1872]. Translated by John J. Lalor, *The Struggle for Law*, 5th ed., Callaghan and Company, 1915.

Waites, Matthew. “Critique of ‘Sexual Orientation’ and ‘Gender Identity’ in Human Rights Discourse: Global Queer Politics Beyond the Yogyakarta Principles.” *Contemporary Politics*, vol. 15, no. 1, 1 Mar. 2009, pp. 137–56. *Tandfonline*, https://doi.org/10.1080/13569770802709604.

Walker, Harron. “Cover Star Chase Strangio Is Our Defender.” *Advocate*, 1 June 2022, www.advocate.com/politics/2022/6/01/chase-strangio-aclu-cover-twitter-trans-rights.

Walt Disney Company, The [@WaltDisneyCo]. “Statement from The Walt Disney Company on Signing of Florida Legislation.” *Twitter*, 28 Mar. 2022, twitter.com/WaltDisneyCo/status/1508494672817123330.

Warner, Michael. “Styles of Intellectual Publics.” *Just Being Difficult? Academic Writing in the Public Arena*, edited by Jonathan Culler and Kevin Lamb. Stanford UP, 2003, pp. 106–28.

West, Robin. “The New Legal Criticism.” *Columbia Law Review Online*, vol. 117, 6 June 2017, pp. 144–164. *Georgetown U Law*, scholarship.law.georgetown.edu/cgi/viewcontent.cgi?article=3012&context=facpub.

White House, The. “Fact Sheet: The Biden-Harris Administration Champions LGBTQ+ Equality and Marks Pride Month.” *The White House*, 1 June 2021, www.whitehouse.gov/briefing-room/statements-releases/2021/06/01/fact-sheet-the-biden-harris-administration-champions-lgbtq-equality-and-marks-pride-month/.

White House, The. “The Judicial Branch.” *The White House*, n.d., www.whitehouse.gov/about-the-white-house/our-government/the-judicial-branch/.

White, James Boyd. *Heracles’ Bow. Essays on the Rhetorics and Poetics of the Law.* U of Wisconsin P, 1985.

White, James Boyd. *The Legal Imagination*. Little, Brown and Co., 1973.

White, James Boyd. *When Words Lose Their Meaning*. U of Chicago P, 1985.

Widin, Douglas R. “Suspect Classification: A Suspect Analysis.” *Dickinson Law Review*, vol. 87, Winter 1983, pp. 407–50. *HeinOnline*, heinonline-org.ezproxy.uni-giessen.de/HOL/P?h=hein.journals/dlr87&i=417.

Wilkinson, J. Harvie III. "The Supreme Court, the Equal Protection Clause, and the Three Faces of Constitutional Equality." *Virginia Law Review*, vol. 61, no. 5, June 1975, pp. 945–1018. *JSTOR*, https://doi.org/10.2307/1072429.

Wilton, Tamsin. *Sexual (Dis)Orientation. Gender, Sex, Desire and Self-Fashioning*. Palgrave Macmillan, 2004.

Wintemute, Robert. *Sexual Orientation and Human Rights. The United States Constitution, the European Convention, and the Canadian Charter*. Clarendon P/ Oxford UP, 1997 [1995].

Wodak, Ruth et al. *The Discursive Construction of National Identity*. Edinburgh UP, 2009.

WWU Münster, Collaborative Research Centre 1385, "Law and Literature." Subproject B02, Niels Petersen et al. *WWU Münster*, www.uni-muenster.de/SFB1385/en/projektbereichb/teilprojektb02/index.html.

Yoshino, Kenji. "The New Equal Protection." Harvard Law Review, vol. 124, issue 3, Jan. 2011, pp. 747–804. Harvard Law Review, cdn.harvardlawreview.org/wp- content/uploads/pdfs/vol124_yoshino.pdf.

Young, Thelathia "Nikki." "Queering 'The Human Situation.'" *Journal of Feminist Studies in Religion*, vol. 28, no. 1, Spring 2012, pp. 126–31. *Project MUSE*, muse.jhu.edu/article/48026.

Laura Borchert, born in 1989, was a research associate (postdoc) in the DFG-funded project "Human Rights Discourses in Migrant Societies" and worked as a lecturer at Justus-Liebig-Universität Gießen's English Department. Borchert was a member of the International Graduate Centre for the Study of Culture (GCSC), the International PhD Programme Literary and Cultural Studies (IPP) in Gießen as well as the Gießener Graduiertenzentrum Sozial-, Wirtschafts- und Rechtswissenschaften (GGS). Her research is situated in queer studies, queer legal theory, law and X, and American cultural studies.

GPSR Authorized Representative: Easy Access System Europe, Mustamäe tee 50, 10621 Tallinn, Estonia, gpsr.requests@easproject.com

www.ingramcontent.com/pod-product-compliance
Lightning Source LLC
LaVergne TN
LVHW020412261125
826498LV00027B/366